PRAISE FOR
THE *Quote* VERIFIER

"Ralph Keyes has made it his mission to hunt down and expose false quotations, and in *The Quote Verifier* he does that brilliantly. *The Quote Verifier* is a much-needed corrective to the countless 'quotations' that are misquoted, falsely attributed, or downright wrong. Keyes takes apart with surgical precision every dubious quotation, old and new. In the process, he tells engagingly the stories behind the quotes, stories that are often surprisingly funny and always interesting."   —Sol Steinmetz, coauthor of *The Life of Language*

"*Nice Guys Finish Seventh* established Ralph Keyes as one of our leading quote sleuthers. With *The Quote Verifier,* he's become our verifier-in-chief. If you want to know who actually said what, this book is indispensable."
                    —Rosalie Maggio, author of *The New Beacon Book of*
                    Quotations by Women

"Quotations are powerful tools. Michel de Montaigne, the father of all essayists, observed, 'I quote others only to better express myself.' Intrepid quotations detective Ralph Keyes helps us to discover the clear truth about exactly what was said and who exactly said it."
                    —Richard Lederer, coauthor of *Comma Sense*

"Quotation tracers will find this an excellent book to consult. It provides all the known details about authorship and wording of a large number of quotes, maxims, observations, slogans, comments, and catchphrases. But this is not simply a reference work. Reading it is a real pleasure. The book is easy to use. Quotes are arranged alphabetically by key word and source references are provided in meticulous detail. As a valuable new scholarly resource, *The Quote Verifier* will take its place alongside standard books of quotations."
                    —Anthony W. Shipps, author of *The Quote Sleuth*

THE *Quote* VERIFIER

ALSO BY RALPH KEYES

THE

Quote

VERIFIER

WHO SAID WHAT, WHERE, AND WHEN

Ralph Keyes

 ST. MARTIN'S GRIFFIN ✖ NEW YORK

www.stmartins.com

Library of Congress Cataloging-in-Publication Data

Keyes, Ralph.
    The quote verifier : who said what, where, and when / Ralph Keyes.—1st St. Martin's Griffin ed.
        p. cm.__
    Includes bibliographical references and index.
    ISBN-13: 978-0-312-34004-9
    ISBN-10: 0-312-34004-4
    1. Quotations, English. 2. Quotations—History and criticism. I. Title.

PN6081.K489 2006
082—dc22

                                        2005043697

10 9 8 7 6 5 4 3 2

For Muriel, my wife,
who made this book possible

CONTENTS

INTRODUCTION

On the eve of the war in Iraq, variations on this quotation were ubiquitous: "No plan survives contact with the enemy." That thought was usually attributed to Dwight Eisenhower. Or did Napoleon say it? George Patton perhaps? No one seemed sure. This observation actually originated with Helmuth von Moltke in the mid-nineteenth century. The Prussian field marshal's version was not so succinct, however. What von Moltke wrote was "Therefore no plan of operations extends with any certainty beyond the first contact with the main hostile force." In a process that's routine in the world of quotation, von Moltke's actual words were condensed into a pithier comment over time, then placed in more-familiar mouths.

Discovering who actually said what, where, and when is a challenge for anyone who wishes to quote others. Misquotation is an occupational hazard of quotation. The more we quote, the more likely we are to misquote. This practice is engaged in by the well educated and poorly educated alike, the erudite and the ignorant, those with multiple degrees or with none at all.

John Kennedy, the modern president most likely to quote others, routinely misquoted them. That is why so many contemporary misquotations can be traced back to a speech by JFK. The most notable example is "All that is necessary for the triumph of evil is that good men do nothing," which Kennedy attributed to Edmund Burke. Even though no one has ever been able to confirm this attribution, or determine who actually said those words, a survey of one hundred familiar quotations by the Oxford University Press found that this admonition, usually misattributed to Burke, is the most popular one of all.

Misquotation is at least as common as accurate quotation, and for perfectly good reasons. The primary reason is that when using quotes, the reference we're most likely to consult is our memory. This is a hazardous form of research. Our memory wants quotations to be better than they usually were, and said by the person we want to have said them. For years I thought it was Lincoln who explained that he'd written a long letter because he didn't have time to write a short one. Only after undertaking to verify quotations did I discover that this comment originated with Blaise Pascal. In a previous book I mistakenly attributed "Because it's there" to mountaineer Edmund Hillary. In fact that rationale for climbing mountains is better credited to his predecessor, George Mallory. In a speech, I quoted Einstein as saying there was no hope for an idea that did not at first seem insane, something I later learned he hadn't said. Like many, I thought that Faulkner said the past is never dead in Mississippi, it's not even past, even though the author didn't limit this observation to his home state.

When it comes to quotations, memory is too much the servant of aspirations, not enough an apostle of accuracy. That is why misremembered quotations so often improve on real ones. Memory may be a terrible librarian, but it's a great editor. Excess words are pruned in recollection, and better ones added. The essence of a good remark is preserved, but its cadence is improved. Churchill's "blood, toil, tears, and sweat" becomes "blood, sweat, and tears." Durocher's "The nice guys are all over there. In seventh place" morphs into "Nice guys finish last." Gordon Gekko's "Greed, for lack of a better word, is good" ends up as "Greed is good."

Think of this as *bumper-stickering*. Quotations that start out too long, too clumsy, and too inharmonious end up shorter, more graceful, and more melodious in the retelling. As this book illustrates repeatedly, the popular recollection of a quotation routinely improves on the original. Common usage functions like a verbal sculptor, reshaping rough material into something more esthetically pleasing. A complex thought clumsily expressed is boiled down to its essence. Rodney King is justly remembered for the simple eloquence of his plea "Can't we all just get along?" This is close to what King said after the police who beat him with nightsticks were acquitted in 1992, but not word perfect. What King actually said during a press conference that day was "People, I just want to say, you know, can we all get along? Can we get along? Can we stop making it, making it horrible for the older people and the kids? . . . It's just not right. It's not right. It's not, it's not going to change anything. We'll, we'll get our justice. . . . Please, we can get along here. We all can get along. I mean, we're all stuck here for a while. Let's try to work it out. Let's try to beat it. Let's try to beat it. Let's try to work it out."

This is how we speak. It is rare for crisp, eloquent remarks to be expressed spontaneously. More often we wander around the edges of what we're trying to say before reaching its heart. When a quotable comment does emerge from someone's mouth in polished, pithy form, we can feel confident that this person spent a long time honing those words. Disraeli, Twain, Churchill, and many others kept mental archives of well-rehearsed mots to pull out and "ad-lib" as opportunities presented themselves. Oscar Wilde was notorious among his friends for testing quips in conversation, much like a comedian perfecting routines. Will Rogers spent years tinkering with different versions of his "epitaph" before settling on "Here lies Will Rogers. He joked about every prominent man in his time, but he never met a man he didn't like." Anne Herbert considered many alternatives before scribbling on a restaurant place mat, "Practice random kindness, and senseless acts of beauty."

Of course the California writer seldom gets credit for this well-known contemporary quotation. Who's heard of Herbert? This suggests another key reason for getting quotations wrong: the need to put them in familiar mouths. Quoting Mark Twain about a lie traveling halfway around the world before the truth can get its boots on is one thing. But what good does it do a speaker, or writer, to cite the Reverend Charles Haddon Spurgeon, who in a mid-nineteenth-century sermon, launched this observation into public discourse as "an old saying"?

Since clever lines so routinely travel from obscure mouths to prominent ones, it is generally safe to assume that when two parties are thought to have said something, the lesser-known party said it first. Sociologist Robert Merton devoted an entire book to exploring the origins of the saying routinely attributed to Isaac Newton about being able to see farther because he stood on the shoulders of giants. As Merton discovered, this saying antedated the great mathematician by several centuries. How did Newton get credit for an observation that was at least five centuries old when he repeated it? This proved to be one more case of an already-familiar quotation being put in the most prominent, plausible mouth. In Merton's words, the aphorism "became Newton's own, not because he deliberately made it so but because admirers of Newton made it so."

The misattribution process is not random. Patterns can be discerned. If a comment is saintly, it must have been made by Gandhi (or Mother Teresa). If it's about honesty, Lincoln most likely said it (or Washington), about fame, Andy Warhol (or Daniel Boorstin), about courage, John Kennedy (or Ernest Hemingway). Quotations about winning had to have been made by Vince Lombardi (or Leo Durocher), malaprops by Yogi Berra (or Samuel Goldwyn). If witty, a quip must have been Twain's concoction, or Wilde's, or Shaw's, or Dorothy Parker's. "Everything I've ever said will be attributed to Dorothy Parker," playwright George S. Kaufman once moaned. Parker herself disavowed authorship of most of the witticisms that were routinely put in her mouth. At the same time, Parker once wrote in a poem, when tempted to try an epigram in literate company she never sought to take credit because "We all assume that Oscar said it."

Oscar Wilde was well aware of his status as a flypaper figure to whom all manner of quotes stuck. Wilde also noted the migration of quotes from obscure mouths to prominent ones other than his own. When he toured the United States in 1882, the Irish playwright was asked by a Rochester reporter whether it was true that when he'd complained about the lack of quaint ruins and curiosities in this country, a local lady responded, "Time will remedy the one, and as for curiosities, we import them." Wilde said this was an excellent story, but one he had already heard, featuring Charles Dickens and a local wit. "I find every community has its lady who is re-markably bright in her repartee," Wilde added, "and she is always credited with the latest *bon mot* going the rounds."

A good quip invariably works better when put in the mouth of someone whose very name inspires a grin. Introducing a knee-slapper as something said by Leno, Chappelle, or Letterman starts our smile even before we hear the punch line. As a result, the wits of the hour get far more credit for funny material than they're due, as do quotable people in general. Shake-speare, Voltaire, Pope, Franklin, Emerson, Lincoln, Wilde, Twain, Shaw, Parker, Churchill, Goldwyn, and Berra are the notable figures to whom we most often misattribute quotations. Those who are often quoted get regu-lar credit for words they never said that "sound like" them. Liberal Demo-crats like to credit Harry Truman with saying, "If you run a Republican against a Republican, the Republican will win every time." Although this certainly sounds like the feisty, fiercely partisan Democratic president, re-searchers at the Harry S. Truman Library can find no evidence that he ever said it.

Patterns of misattribution change with time and circumstances. As the prestige of another era's celebrities wanes, so does the practice of putting words in their mouths. In recent years older flypaper figures such as Goethe, Pope, and Voltaire have had to step aside to make way for more recent ones such as Einstein, Gandhi, and Mandela. A quotation often attributed to Nelson Mandela takes this form: "Our deepest fear is not that we are in-adequate. Our deepest fear is that we are powerful beyond measure. It is our Light, not our Darkness, that most frightens us." When any source is given at all, this is said to be from an inaugural speech by South Africa's two-term president. Aside from the fact that these words don't even sound like him, they do not appear in either inaugural address given by Mandela.

On the other hand, those sentences can be found in the 1992 book *A Return to Love* by pop theologian Marianne Williamson.

This raises the issue of demographic status. Who we want to have said something can depend fundamentally on whom we most admire. What sociologists call "reference groups" comes into play here. Corporate executives commonly credit motivational speaker Steven Covey with saying, "No one washes a rented car." Members of the chattering class, on the other hand, such as *New York Times* columnist Thomas Friedman, attribute a more sweeping version of that comment, "In the history of the world no one has ever washed a rented car," to former Harvard president Lawrence Summers.

Geography is another important factor when credit for quotations is assigned. Who we think said something can be a function of where we live. In America, "Winning isn't everything, it's the only thing" is routinely attributed to football coach Vince Lombardi. In England, it's credited to soccer coach Bill Shankly. "Golf is a good walk spoiled" is given to Mark Twain in the United States, author Kurt Tucholsky in Germany. Depending on one's country of residence, "Oh, to be seventy again" is thought to be the quip of American octogenarian Oliver Wendell Holmes, Jr., French Premier Georges Clemenceau, or Prussian Field Marshal Friedrich von Wrangel.

Misattribution works best if the person quoted is not around to correct the record. Famous dead people make excellent commentators on current events. During George W. Bush's first term in office, a warning supposedly made by Julius Caesar raced around the Internet. This began, "Beware the leader who bangs the drums of war in order to whip the citizenry into a patriotic fervor. . . ." Barbra Streisand quoted Caesar's warning in a speech she gave to a Democratic Congressional Campaign Committee gala. In a *Los Angeles Times* editorial cartoon, Paul Conrad attributed the advisory to William Shakespeare (presumably because Shakespeare wrote the play *Julius Caesar*). There is no evidence that Caesar ever said such a thing. Certainly Shakespeare never wrote it.

Over time one gets a feel for which quotations are authentic and which phony. Those that are too eloquent, too polished, too pithy are seldom genuine. Many familiar quotations are introduced with tip-off words and phrases indicating that a thought is secondhand ("in the old saying," "it's been said that," "as a poet once observed," etc.). In other cases quotations can be scrutinized much as an authenticator examines documents for evidence of forgery. Some are not characteristic of the person to whom they're attributed. Others are simply too neat and tidy to be plausible. Still more include words or concepts not common at the time they were supposedly said.

Quotations by Thomas Jefferson are especially susceptible to this type of verbal retrofitting. A congressional aide told me of quoting Jefferson about the ramifications of paying plumbers more than teachers, only to be informed that there were no "plumbers" as such in the third president's time. A spurious Jefferson warning about the power of banks includes the word "deflation," a term coined long after his death. Many so-called Jefferson quotations peddled on conservative talk shows support positions such as the right to bear arms, or the need to keep religion in public life, which were not Jefferson's issues. But it isn't just right-wingers who misquote Jefferson. In his bestselling biography of John Adams, historian David McCullough, without citing a source, wrote that Jefferson called Adams "the colossus of independence." As an impolite reviewer pointed out, and as McCullough later acknowledged, Jefferson said no such thing.

Quotes without citations should be treated with the utmost suspicion. When a quotation routinely shows up in compilations with no source, there probably is none. "Nice guys finish last," for example, spent so many decades associated with Leo Durocher that this attribution took on its own credibility, despite the fact that no one knew when or where Durocher had said this (because he hadn't). Despite copious searching, the origins of the quotation most associated with Margaret Mead, "Never doubt that a small group of thoughtful, committed citizens can change the world," remain a mystery. When a source is cited for that quotation, it is always secondary. This is a risky type of ascription. Such sources sometimes cite yet another source that is one or more steps removed from a quotation's point of origin.

Even when a primary source is cited in a secondary work, without examining that material one cannot be confident that the citation is accurate. Wrong chapters of books and inaccurate page numbers are routinely referenced, and wording is often garbled. Alternatively, a quotation will show up where it's said to have appeared, but prove to have no reliable citation, or none at all. In such cases it's the uninformed citing the ill informed. Phantom citations appear regularly, even routinely, and even in reputable works of reference. *The Cassell Companion to Quotations* cites a speech Mark Twain never gave as the source of a quotation by him. *Bartlett's* gives Eleanor Roosevelt's autobiography as their source for her attributed comment "No one can make you feel inferior without your consent." That remark does not appear in Roosevelt's autobiography, nor anywhere else that researchers have been able to discover. *The Oxford Dictionary of Quotations* cites a long-discredited source for their attribution of "Go west, young man, go west" to Horace Greeley. *Oxford's* attribution of "There is one thing stronger than all the armies of the world, and that is an idea whose time has come" to Victor Hugo cites a nonexistent 1943 issue of the *Nation*. Their source for a Gandhi quotation is a book that says he made the remark while visiting England in 1930. Gandhi did not visit England in 1930.

These are just a few of the reasons that accurate ascription of quotations is such a slippery slope of scholarship. If reputable works of reference can't always be depended upon for the correct wording or attribution of their contents, is it any wonder that we get our quotations wrong at least as often as we get them right? Widespread, longtime assumptions about who said what are virtually meaningless. Familiar quotations are every bit as likely to be misworded or misattributed as ones that are more obscure, if not more so. Quotations that "everyone knows" someone said (but no one knows where or when) routinely turn out to be misquotations. Nor does the fact that words appear in print or pixels make them credible. A compilation of memorable quotations in *Newsweek*'s turn-of-the-century issue included several misquotations. In one case after another, a search for the source of a popular quotation dead-ends with *Reader's Digest*. In earlier issues especially, verification of the many quotable quotes they published was not the *Digest*'s strong suit.

The press in general is a shaky source of evidence about who said what. Anyone who's ever been quoted in a newspaper knows this to be true. The words he or she actually said may bear only a vague resemblance to the ones that appear in print. This is not necessarily due to negligent reporting. The need to jot down thousands of words, then write them up quickly under deadline pressure, seldom permits word-perfect accuracy. In many cases the cruelest thing a reporter can do is quote a subject correctly, including all the "uhs, ums, you knows," digressions, run-on sentences, and examples of tortured syntax. While managing the inept New York Mets, an exasperated Casey Stengel once said, "Can't *anybody* play this here game?" After reporters gave the manager a hand with his grammar, "Can't *anybody* here play this game?" became one of Stengel's most famous lines.

Cleaning up diction while preserving meaning is a service to reader and subject alike. This can be a matter of judgment, of course. When a New Orleans reporter climbed aboard a Pullman car where Vice President Jack Garner had retired for the night, and asked through the curtains of his sleeper compartment if he'd come out for an interview, Garner responded, "Hell, no; I ain't agonna get out of bed for anybody." The reporter so quoted the vice president in his copy. The next day he discovered that his paper's managing editor changed this copy to read, "No, indeed, I am not going to get out of bed for anyone." Garner's subsequent comparison of the vice presidency to "a pitcher of warm piss" was changed to "a pitcher of warm spit" in the nation's newspapers. This prompted Cactus Jack to observe "those pantywaist writers wouldn't print it the way I said it."

In a case such as this, propriety may have been in the driver's seat. In too many others reporters alter subjects' words for their own purposes: to get a crisper comment, to illustrate a point they want made, or just to impress the guy at the next desk. (Among themselves they call this "sweetening" or "piping" quotes.) Even before an interview begins, journalists sometimes have a clear idea of what comments they're looking for, and are not above steering their subject in the desired direction. As a last resort they will even suggest words for a subject to use, then report these words as if they were spontaneous. (See "A smoke-filled room.")

Pre-Internet, the prevalence of misquotation was self-limiting. The seed of a misquote that was planted in some speech, or piece of writing, or reporter's notes, could only grow fitfully in the arid soil of print on paper. Not so online. Like a verbal virus, any error committed on one website is quickly replicated on hundreds, if not thousands, more. While conducting exhaustive research on the origins of a popular quotation that cautions against "contempt prior to investigation," writer Michael StGeorge found more than forty-two hundred misattributions of the quote to social philosopher Herbert Spencer, but only seven attributions to its actual author, theologian William Paley.

In the online era, a tsunami of resources for researching the origins of quotations has crashed on our shores. The reliability of those resources is another matter. Even though the Internet hosts thousands of websites devoted to quotations, these sites rarely concern themselves with accuracy. (Finding a quotation attributed to "Ralph Waldo Emmerson" on one such site does not inspire confidence.) Most simply cut and paste material from each other. That is why most quote sites are barely better than memory when it comes to verified quotations. At best they are good for leads. Moreover, when a source is given for a quotation, it can be less than dependable. Among other reasons, such sources are rarely ones that compilers have actually examined. More often they have simply recycled a citation found elsewhere on the Internet, just as they've recycled the quotation to which it refers.

This is one among many reasons that using a search engine to look for an accurately worded, correctly attributed quotation can be problematic. Most of what such a search turns up are variations on that quotation in different forms, attributed to various parties, but seldom with any reliable source cited (if any is cited at all). A few quotation websites do commit themselves to being as accurate as possible in the wording and attribution of their contents. When attempting to verify quotations by searching the Internet, one's challenge is to sort a small amount of such wheat from a maddening amount of chaff.

Consulting reputable works of reference is more fruitful, but, as we've seen, not without pitfalls. *The Oxford Dictionary of Quotations* still reports that Leo Durocher said, "Nice guys finish last," even though no serious quote scholar believes this any longer. The two most recent editions of *Bartlett's* include "A billion here, a billion there, pretty soon you're talking about real money," attributed to Everett McKinley Dirksen. No Dirksen expert has ever been able to confirm that the Illinois senator said this. (It's actually an old gag.) In some cases the two premier quotation collections don't agree on the wording or origins of a given quotation. *Bartlett's* has Ulysses S. Grant *proposing* to fight it out on this line if it took him all summer; *Oxford* has him *purposing* to do the same thing. As discussed in the text, there is a reason for this discrepancy, and *Bartlett's* gives the more reliable version. On the other hand, before William Safire brought the mistake to their attention, *Bartlett's* included the word "ingloriously" in a Milton quotation, *Oxford* the correct word, "injuriously."

Any compiler of quotations is bound to make mistakes, of course. Getting some things wrong goes with the quote-compiling territory. Even though I've done my best to minimize them, this book undoubtedly includes errors, as I'm sure readers will call to my attention.

The Quote Verifier gathers in one place familiar and semifamiliar quotations that are easier to cite than to verify, ones that are often seen or heard, but whose exact wording, attribution, and origins are mysterious. It is not meant to be a scold of a book ("Get it right, you ignoramus!") so much as a helpful source of information about quotes in question. Who said them first? What was actually said? Where did this happen, and when? Those are the key questions informing this book.

Where evidence exists, I've tried to trace each quotation back as close as possible to its original source and wording: in a book, article, speech text, media transcript, movie script, electronic recording, or other source. Based on such evidence, it is often possible to make a probable case about who said what, where, and when. In other cases one can nail down some evidence of provenance, but only some. The original wording or attribution of many a quotation is so lost in the mists of time that one can only consider various possibilities. Nonetheless, in each case I present what information can be found about discernible origins of the quotation in question, then render a verdict in the same sense that a judge or jury does: based on the best *available* evidence. When verifying quotes, being able to say, "Case closed" with any finality is rare.

In some cases the original expression of a quotation in question seems to be apparent, and in such cases this is noted. When definite coinage cannot be established, the etymologists' concept of "earliest use" is often invoked the first time a word, phrase, or quotation is known to have appeared in print. For example, although the origins of the catchphrase "the whole nine yards" have long confounded language detectives, its earliest known appearance in print is in an 1855 account of shirtmaking. Its earliest recorded use as slang is more recent: in a 1967 book about pilots in Vietnam.

"Earliest use" is a tentative term, of course. One can only report the best information available at the time one is writing. It also is important to focus on examples of earliest *relevant* use, not simply random uses. Undoubtedly someone, somewhere, sometime said, "War is hell" before the American Civil War, but in a book such as this, we are more concerned about whether Gen. William Tecumseh Sherman himself ever uttered those three immortal words.

Quote-verification is being revolutionized by modern research tools, most of them online. The Internet is not just a treasure trove of unverified quotations; but an extraordinary resource for determining the origins of quotations in question. Powerful online tools are emerging to help with research, particularly databases of digitized books, magazines, and newspapers dating back centuries. An elite group of websites is less concerned with compiling quotations willy-nilly than with determining who actually said what. Librarians, lexicographers, and others do yeoman work in their online note-sharing about the origins of quotations.

On and off the Internet, a small band of intrepid quote sleuths commit themselves to verifying quotations as best they can. (Since no term exists to depict the members of this band, I call them *quotographers*.) One determined group takes hold of a single quotation and pursues its true origins with the determination of a Miss Marple. Another group specializes in verifying the quotations of particular individuals: Samuel Johnson, Mark Twain, or Winston Churchill (to name just a few). Nigel Rees, longtime host of the BBC radio program *Quote . . . Unquote,* publishes a quarterly newsletter by that title and has produced a number of useful books on the origins of quotations (in which one wishes he would cite sources more consistently and reliably). Other quotographers have also reported their findings in valuable, well-referenced books: *Respectfully Quoted* by Suzy Platt of the Library of Congress, Rhoda Thomas Tripp's *The International Thesaurus of Quotations,* and, of course, *The Quote Sleuth* by Anthony Shipps.

A newcomer, *The Yale Dictionary of Quotations,* benefits from the diligent efforts of editor Fred Shapiro to trace that book's entries as far back as possible to their original source. Some older books such as *Benham's Book of Quotations, Proverbs, and Household Words; The Home Book of Quotations;* and *Magill's Quotations in Context* made a serious effort to confirm their contents, or at least consider their probable origins. These works are part of a grand tradition, one I hope *The Quote Verifier* will join.

READER'S GUIDE

Although intended primarily as a reference work, *The Quote Verifier* can also be browsed or read straight through. This book is written with all such possibilities in mind.

It is organized alphabetically according to the capitalized key word in each quotation (e.g., *"Build a better MOUSETRAP and the world will beat a path to your door."*). These quotations are the most popular versions of familiar and semifamiliar remarks. Because the wording of quotations can vary, possible key words can vary too. That is why the comprehensive index at the end of this book includes several key words for most quotations. A separate name index provides another searching tool, as does a list of sidebars.

These sidebars appear periodically within the text, organized alphabetically by heading. Some feature prominent quoted and misquoted figures such as Dorothy Parker and Winston Churchill. Others consider broad categories of quotations associated with specific events, such as the war in Vietnam, or areas of particular interest, such as show business.

Quotations discussed within sidebars that also appear in the main body of the text appear in boldface, with the key word in small capitals (e.g., **"A house DIVIDED against itself cannot stand."**). Quotations that receive substantial consideration within the sidebar but that do not appear in the text are only boldfaced. Their contents are indexed. Quotations that are merely discussed in passing within sidebars are neither boldfaced nor indexed.

Sources for all quotations are given in the "Source Notes" section at the end.

THE *Quote* VERIFIER

"ACADEMIC politics are so vicious precisely because the stakes are so small." This observation is routinely attributed to former Harvard professor Henry Kissinger. Well before Kissinger got credit for that thought in the mid-1970s, however, Harvard political scientist Richard Neustadt told a reporter, "Academic politics is much more vicious than real politics. We think it's because the stakes are so small." Others believe this quip originated with political scientist Wallace Sayre, Neustadt's onetime colleague at Columbia University. A 1973 book gave as "Sayre's Law," "In any dispute the intensity of feeling is inversely proportional to the value of the stakes at issue—that is why academic politics are so bitter." Sayre's colleague and coauthor Herbert Kaufman said his usual wording was "The politics of the university are so intense because the stakes are so low." In his 1979 book *Peter's People,* Laurence Peter wrote, "Competition in academia is so vicious because the stakes are so small." He called this "Peter's Theory of Entrepreneurial Aggressiveness in Higher Education." Variations on that thought have also been attributed to scientist-author C. P. Snow, professor-politician Daniel Patrick Moynihan, and politician Jesse Unruh (among others). According to the onetime editor of Woodrow Wilson's papers, however, long before any of them strode the academic-political scene, Wilson observed often that the intensity of academic squabbles he witnessed while president of Princeton University was a function of the "triviality" of the issues being considered.

Verdict: An old academic saw that may have originated with Woodrow Wilson but was put in modern play by Wallace Sayre.

"Half the money I spend on ADVERTISING is wasted. The trouble is I don't know which half." In the United States this business truism is

most often attributed to department store magnate John Wanamaker (1838–1922), in England to Lord Leverhulme (William H. Lever, founder of Lever Brothers, 1851–1925). The maxim has also been ascribed to chewing gum magnate William Wrigley, adman George Washington Hill, and adman David Ogilvy. In *Confessions of an Advertising Man* (1963), Ogilvy himself gave the nod to his fellow Englishman Lord Leverhulme (Lever Brothers was an Ogilvy client), adding that John Wanamaker later made the same observation. Since Wanamaker founded his first department store in 1861, when Lever was ten, this seems unlikely. *Fortune* magazine thought Wanamaker expressed the famous adage in 1885, but it gave no context. While researching *John Wanamaker, King of Merchants* (1993), biographer William Allen Zulker found the adage typed on a sheet of paper in Wanamaker's archives, but without a name or source. Wanamaker usually wrote his own material longhand.

   Verdict: A maxim of obscure origins, put in famous mouths.

"If you have to ask how much they cost, you can't AFFORD one." J. P. Morgan's alleged response to an inquiry about the cost of his yachts is considered the epitome of wealthy imperiousness. (Some attribute the thought to Cornelius Vanderbilt.) No dependable evidence exists that Morgan actually said this, however, and biographer Jean Strouse doubts that he did. Calling the mot "implausible," Strouse concluded, "Morgan was a singularly inarticulate, unreflective man, not likely to come up with a maxim worthy of Oscar Wilde." The closest analogue Strouse could find on the record was Morgan's response to oil baron Henry Clay Pierce: "You have no right to own a yacht if you ask that question."

   Verdict: Morgan's sentiments, not his words.

"AFTER us, the deluge." ("Aprés nous le déluge.") This classic remark is generally thought to have been uttered by King Louis XV of France after his forces were defeated by those of Frederick the Great at the battle of Rossbach in 1757. Biographer Olivier Bernier calls the attribution "wholly apocryphal." At least two memoirs by contemporaries attributed these words in the plural to the king's mistress, the Marquise de Pompadour. Others to whom the saying has been attributed include Prince Metternich, Marie Antoinette, and Verdi. However *"Aprés moi le déluge"* was a French proverb in common use long before Louis XV or anyone else was alleged to have said it.

   Verdict: An old proverb put in many mouths, especially that of Louis XV.

"AIN'T I a woman?" This is the phrase ex-slave Sojourner Truth used to bring an 1851 convention of feminists to its feet. Or so we like to imagine. Contemporary news accounts of her talk reported no such exclamation. After exhaustive research, biographer Carleton Mabee concluded that Truth's rallying cry was actually concocted by convention chair Frances Dana Gage, a poet and antislavery feminist who inserted the phrase "Ar'n't I a woman?" repeatedly into her subsequent account of Truth's speech. According to Mabee this account, which was published twelve years after the fact, is "folklore." Most likely Gage simply abridged an antislavery motto, "Am I not a Woman and a Sister?", and translated it into dialect for her report on Truth. Over time "Ar'n't I a woman?" mutated into "Ain't I a woman?" Far from being what Sojourner Truth actually said, concluded historian Nell Irvin Painter, these famous four words are "what we need her to have said."

Verdict: Credit Frances Dana Gage for this feminist saying, not Sojourner Truth.

"It AIN'T so much the things we don't know that get us into trouble. It's the things we know that just ain't so." In various forms this popular observation gets attributed most often to Mark Twain, as well as to his fellow humorists Artemus Ward, Kin Hubbard, and Will Rogers. Others to whom it's been credited include inventor Charles Kettering, pianist Eubie Blake, and—by Al Gore—baseball player Yogi Berra. Twain did once observe, "It isn't so astonishing the things that I can remember, as the number of things I can remember that aren't so," but biographer Albert Bigelow Paine said he was paraphrasing a remark by humorist Josh Billings. (In *Following the Equator* Twain also wrote, "Yet it was the schoolboy who said, 'Faith is believing what you know ain't so.'") Billings, whose real name was Henry Wheeler Shaw, repeated this theme often in different forms. On one occasion Billings wrote, "I honestly beleave it iz better tew know nothing than two know what ain't so." A handbill for one of his lectures included the line "It iz better to kno less than to kno so much that ain't so." Across this handbill Billings wrote longhand, "You'd better not kno so much than know so many things that ain't so." Apparently the humorist considered this his signature "affurism."

Verdict: Credit Josh Billings.

"I want to be ALONE." Greta Garbo did say this, to John Barrymore, in the 1932 movie *Grand Hotel*, whose screenplay was written by William A. Drake. That movie was based on a 1929 novel with the same title by Austrian

author Vicki Baum. In the English translation of Baum's novel, the character eventually played by Garbo says, "But I wish to be alone." In time that sentiment was attributed to the reclusive actress herself. Garbo was not happy about this at all. She once told a friend, "I never said, 'I want to be alone.' I only said, 'I want to be *let* alone!' There is all the difference."

Verdict: Credit novelist Vicki Baum and screenwriter William A. Drake for Greta Garbo's most famous line.

"AMERICA is great because America is good. If America ever ceases to be good, America will cease to be great." Like presidents Eisenhower and Reagan before him, Bill Clinton was fond of attributing these words to Alexis de Tocqueville. Many another political figure, news commentator, and patriotic orator has cited this observation, said to have been made by America's most famous tourist. (The lines are thought to be preceded by "Not until I went into the churches of America and heard her pulpits flame with righteousness did I understand the greatness and genius of America.") Library of Congress researchers call the attribution "unverified." They did find the complete quotation, attributed to de Tocqueville's *Democracy in America,* in a 1941 book called *The Kingdom of God and the American Dream* by evangelist Sherwood Eddy (1871–1963). Claremont McKenna College political scientist John Pitney has devoted two essays to the misattributed quotation and its many uses. Who actually wrote these words remains a mystery. Sherwood Eddy gave no source for his de Tocqueville attribution. According to biographer Rick L. Nutt, Eddy tended to work from memory. Perhaps he'd read the 1908 copy of *The Methodist Review* in which de Tocqueville was quoted as saying he'd searched in vain for the sources of America's distinction until he entered a church: "It was there, as I listened to the soul-equalizing and soul-elevating principles of the Gospel of Christ as they fell from Sabbath to Sabbath upon the masses of the people, that I learned why America is great and free, and why France is a slave." These uncharacteristic words are not de Tocqueville's either.

Verdict: Words put in de Tocqueville's mouth.

"AMERICA is the only nation in history which miraculously has gone directly from barbarism to degeneration without the usual interval of civilization." In a 1945 magazine article, Danish writer Hans Bendix said his aunt told him French Premier Georges Clemenceau (1841–1929) made this observation about America. Bendix's article seems to be the only source for that attribution, which now appears in many a quotation collection. (The saying has also been attributed to Oscar Wilde, Henry

James, H. L. Mencken, and John O'Hara.) Judging from France's often stormy alliance with America during and after World War I, Clemenceau might well have reached such a conclusion. It "sounds like" the irascible French politician. However, as a young man, Clemenceau spent several years in the United States. He married a local woman, and considered America his "second country." Whoever was the first to say this owed an intellectual debt to Italian philosopher Giambattista Vico (1688–1744), who concluded that societies progressed in cyclical stages from barbarism to civilization, then back again.

Verdict: Author unknown; possibly Georges Clemenceau.

"We are not AMUSED." The only evidence that Queen Victoria ever made this imperious statement consists of a 1900 diary entry in an anonymously authored 1919 book called *The Notebooks of a Spinster Lady*. This British book—now known to have been written by Caroline Holland (1878–1903)—included, as "a tale" once told to the author, the queen's "we are not amused" response to an inappropriate jest. Victoria's supposed comment was in circulation long before this book was published, however, having appeared in a magazine article as early as 1902. It did not take long for this reported remark to become synonymous with imperious gravitas. Biographer Stanley Weintraub could not verify that Victoria said any such thing, and doubted that she did. "In fact," Weintraub told a reporter, "she was often amused."

Verdict: Words put in Victoria's mouth.

"An ARMED society is a polite society." This slogan is beloved by opponents of gun control, few of whom know where it originated: Robert Heinlein's *Beyond This Horizon*. In this 1942 magazine serial, which became a 1948 novel, one character says to another, "Well, in the first place an armed society is a polite society."

Verdict: Credit Robert Heinlein.

"An ARMY travels on its stomach." This bedrock axiom of military science is generally attributed to Napoleon. No one knows where or when the French emperor made that observation, however. He may not have done so. An editor of Napoleon's many observations couldn't find this one and concluded it wasn't his. (The closest comment by Napoleon he could find was "The basic principle that we must follow in directing the armies of the Republic is this: that they must feed themselves on war at the expense of the enemy territory.") An earlier saying, "An army, like a serpent, travels on its belly," is credited to Frederick the Great, but probably was not original to him.

Verdict: Not Napoleon, possibly Frederick the Great, probably someone else.

"Be ASHAMED to die until you have won some victory for humanity." Educator Horace Mann made this stirring plea as the conclusion of his last "Baccalaureate Sermon," given to students at Antioch College in 1859, where Mann was president. It is often misquoted as "some *great* victory."

Verdict: Credit Mann, avoid "great."

"ASK not what your country can do for you, ask what you can do for your country." The most eloquent line in John Kennedy's inaugural address has a rich legacy. In 1884, Oliver Wendell Holmes, Jr., asked an audience to "recall what our country has done for each of us, and to ask ourselves what we can do for our country in return." Nearly a decade later, in 1893, a British parliamentarian named St. John Broderick told a Leeds audience, "The first duty of a citizen is to consider what he can do for the state and not what the state will do for him." A decade after that, in 1904, Harvard professor LeBaron Russell Briggs said that when it came to their college, students should always ask, "not 'What can she do for me?' but 'What can I do for her?'" Warren Harding subsequently told the 1916 Republican convention, "We must have a citizenship less concerned about what the government can do for it and more anxious about what it can do for the nation." When Kennedy was a prep school student at Choate, its longtime headmaster, Rev. George St. John, continually exhorted students to consider not what their school did for them, but what they could do for their school. While admitting that the "ask not" line had antecedents, Kennedy aide Arthur Schlesinger, Jr., argued that this thought was the president's own. The historian thought it derived from a Rousseau quotation Kennedy recorded in his notebook at the end of World War II: "As soon as any man says of the affairs of the state, What does it matter to me? the state may be given up as lost." That is a stretch. More likely the thought was a rhetorical commonplace that wended its way into Kennedy's speech (speeches, actually; he used variations on this theme many times before the inauguration). In *Ask Not,* his book about Kennedy's inaugural address, Thurston Clarke concluded that the well-read president and his speechwriter Theodore Sorensen most likely were familiar with at least some of this line's antecedents. Nonetheless, Clarke reported, the final version was written with Kennedy's own hand. When it

comes to a thought this pervasive, however, that act would be more tran-
scription than invention.

Verdict: A thought in wide circulation long before JFK adopted it.

*"My center is giving way, my right is in retreat. Situation excellent. I shall
ATTACK!"* By legend French General Ferdinand Foch sent such a message
to Gen. Joseph Joffre as his position crumbled during the first battle of the
Marne in 1914. Other versions include "My right gives way, my left yields,
everything's fine—I shall attack!" and "My right has been rolled up. My left
has been driven back. My center has been smashed. I have ordered an advance from all directions." Yet another version is mounted in a frame hung on
a column in the entryway of Indiana University's Memorial Union Building:
"My left is giving way, my right is falling back; consequently I am ordering a
general offensive, a decisive attack by the center." This is a translation of
the message General Foch wrote on a piece of paper while visiting the university in 1921. (The original French, handwritten, presumably by Foch, is
*"Ma gauche plie ma roite recule la consequence f'or donne nice appen jive
générale, attaque decivise pour le centre.* F Foch 4.11.21.") Beneath this, a
typewritten addendum reads, "Message sent by Marshal Ferdinand Foch
at the decisive moment of the first battle of the Marne, September, 1914. On
the occasion of his visit to Indiana in 1921, Marshal Foch presented this
autographed copy of his message to the undersigned for Indiana University.
William Lowe Bryan [IU's president]." Although Foch was known for his
sometimes suicidal emphasis on attacking the enemy, and apparently
thought he'd made this vow during the Battle of the Marne, historians of
the First World War consider the words more likely to be ones Foch wishes
he'd conveyed than those he actually did. By one historian's account Foch's
actual telegram read, "The situation is therefore excellent; the attack directed against the Ninth Army appears to be a means to assure the retreat
of the German right wing."

Verdict: Revisionist Foch.

"Never ATTRIBUTE to malice what can be explained by ignorance." In
Robert Heinlein's 1941 story "Logic of Empire," one character says to another, "You have attributed conditions to villainy that simply result from
stupidity."

Verdict: Revised Heinlein.

"He has no more BACKBONE than a chocolate éclair." In early 2005,
The New Yorker's drama critic wrote of a play's character, "Tom has the

backbone of a chocolate éclair." He neglected to mention (and may not even have realized) that this comparison had been made a century earlier, by Theodore Roosevelt, with reference to William McKinley. Roosevelt, in turn, may have borrowed the thought from House Speaker Thomas Reed. Spinal similes were quite popular after the Civil War. TR was especially fond of this genre of invective, saying about Supreme Court Justice Oliver Wendell Holmes, Jr., "I could carve out of a banana a justice with more backbone than that." Several decades before Roosevelt compared backbones to bananas and chocolate éclairs, Ulysses S. Grant said of his successor as president, "Garfield has shown that he is not possessed of the backbone of an angle worm."

Verdict: Longstanding fill-in-the-blank invective.

"If you've got them by the BALLS, their hearts and minds will follow." These words were inscribed on a plaque hanging in the home of Richard Nixon's counsel Charles Colson. According to Colson, a former Green Beret had that plaque made up, then gave it to him because he thought this saying applied to his work in the White House. The saying subsequently received so much attention in press coverage of Nixon's hardbitten aide that it was widely assumed to have been Colson's invention. Over the years this adage became a favorite among executives who considered themselves tough. Where did it originate? One possibility is a Vietnam-era congressional debate in which a liberal Democrat pleaded for programs designed to "win the hearts and minds of the downtrodden." Hawkish Rep. Mendel Rivers (D-S.C.) responded, "I say get 'em by the balls and their hearts and minds will follow." It's doubtful that this rejoinder began with Rivers, however. It certainly didn't begin with Charles Colson.

Verdict: Author unknown; not Charles Colson.

"I laughed all the way to the BANK." In 1954 the flamboyant musician Liberace capped a triumphal thirty-day tour with the first piano concert held at Madison Square Garden since Paderewski played there two decades earlier. His performance was a sellout. New York's music reviewers were underwhelmed by the winks, grins, and candelabra of this Gorgeous George of the keyboard. In response Liberace quipped, "I cried all the way to the bank." His cheeky retort caught the public's fancy. Over time it achieved cliché status. Liberace, who recalled first telling a San Francisco audience that bad reviews made him cry all the way the bank, said he regularly repeated this mantra to his staff. It became his signature line. As the years went by, however, Liberace's quip gradually morphed

into "I laughed all the way to the bank." Today it is rare to see the lachrymose version in print.

Verdict: Credit Liberace, crying.

"Don't let the BASTARDS grind you down." ("**Illegimati noli carborundum.**") The literal translation of this mock-Latin motto is "Let there not be carborunduming by the illegitimate." (*Carborundum* derives from the abrasive carborundum, silicon carbide, and isn't Latin at all.) Alternative versions are, "Non Bastardum Carborundum" and "Ab illegitimis non carborundum est." Like introducing silly sayings with "Confucius say," creating inane "Latin" proverbs was a popular pastime in Depression-era America. This one dates back at least to World War II, when it was associated with American General Joseph "Vinegar Joe" Stilwell. Lexicographer Eric Partridge thought it originated with British intelligence officers during that war. (Partridge liked to think it was invented by his witty friend Stanley Casson, an Oxford classics scholar who directed England's army intelligence school early in the war before being killed in Greece.) Others recall hearing this slogan before the Second World War, or seeing it on placards at that time. After the war it became T-shirt-common in the English-speaking world. In 1962 the Royal Shakespeare Company mounted a play written by Henry Living called *Nil Carborundum*.

Verdict: Popular slogan invented by some unknown wit just before or during World War II.

"BEAM me up, Scotty." What *Star Trek*'s Captain Kirk actually said to Lieutenant Commander Scott was "Beam us up, Mr. Scott." Kirk also sometimes said, *"Enterprise,* beam us up" during the 1966–1969 television series. In the fourth movie based on this series, *Star Trek IV: The Voyage Home* (1986), Captain Kirk did say, "Scotty, beam me up." In their rearranged form these words became bumper-sticker-common.

Verdict: A memory-enhanced *Star Trek* command.

"Your people, sir, is a great BEAST." Haughty Alexander Hamilton is notorious for having called the people "a great beast." Historian Barbara Tuchman thought he said this during an argument with Jefferson. The more common assumption is that Hamilton called the people beastly at a New York dinner party. This anecdote was first reported in Theophilus Parsons's 1859 memoir, fifty-five years after Alexander Hamilton was killed by Aaron Burr in a duel. According to Parsons, who was John Adams's attorney general, a friend told him that a guest at this party told him he heard

Hamilton call the people a great beast. In his *History of the United States* (1891), Henry Adams referred twice to Hamilton's portrayal of the people as a great beast. Generally fastidious about citing sources, Adams gave none for this proclamation. After extensive research, historian William Ander Smith concluded that Adams's source could only have been the memoir by Theophilus Parsons. Henry Adams must have known this source was dubious but was intent enough on using the Hamilton remark that he did so anyway. Adams had a well-known antipathy toward Hamilton dating back to this man's conflicts with his great-grandfather, John Adams. Reporting Hamilton's portrayal of the people as a great beast hung him posthumously with his own words. Despite much searching, no historian has ever been able to verify the fourth-hand dinner-party rumor that was the probable basis of Adams's account. While researching the attribution of this thought to Hamilton, William Ander Smith uncovered an 1867 letter in which Henry Adams himself wrote to his brother Charles about the pressure of public opinion on writers, "It is the public which controls us, and in the long run we must obey the beast."

Verdict: Words put in Alexander Hamilton's mouth.

"BECAUSE it's there." During George Mallory's 1923 lecture tour of the United States, a *New York Times* article reported that the British mountain climber had said this was why he persisted in trying to reach the summit of Mount Everest. The unsigned *Times* article gave no context for this remark, which became Mallory's epitaph. On other occasions the mountaineer's depiction of his motives was more elaborate, even verbose. Those who knew Mallory puzzled over this uncharacteristically pithy comment. No other reporter ever heard him say such a thing, and Mallory himself never used the phrase with colleagues. Biographers Tom Holzel and Audrey Salkeld wondered if the terse remark might have been a compression of Mallory's thoughts by a reporter who knew a memorable quotation when he crafted one. Biographers Peter and Leni Gelman disagreed, concluding that the remark was consistent with others made by Mallory. In a 1986 letter to London's *Daily Telegraph,* Mallory's niece said he'd told his sister, her mother, that this silly response of his was suited to a silly question. The remark is sometimes credited to Sir Edmund Hillary.

Verdict: Credit Mallory, gingerly.

"Where's the BEEF?" Americans of a certain age recall the classic 1984 Wendy's ad in which Clara Peller, an eighty-something, four-foot-ten

retired manicurist, asked this question at the top of her bullfrog voice while patronizing THE HOME OF THE BIG BUN. Peller's question—composed by New York copywriter Cliff Freeman—quickly became a national catch-phrase. It entered history books when Walter Mondale posed Peller's question to Gary Hart while pressing his fellow Democrat about the substance of his "new ideas" during 1984's Democratic presidential primaries. That rhetorical booster rocket made "Where's the beef?" one of America's best-remembered, most enduring advertising catchphrases.

Verdict: Credit Cliff Freeman as author, Clara Peller as spokesperson, Walter Mondale as publicist.

"I don't want to BELONG to any club that would have me as a member." According to Groucho Marx's son Arthur, this assertion was made in the comedian's letter of resignation from the Friars Club. Groucho's brother Zeppo confirmed this, as did his friend Arthur Sheekman. (Biographer Hector Arce gave a somewhat different version, also involving the Friars.) Hollywood chronicler Neal Gabler thought it was the Hillcrest Country Club Marx resigned from, with this explanation. In time it became Groucho's most famous line. In his own autobiography, Groucho said he wired a prominent theatrical group called the Delaney Club, PLEASE ACCEPT MY RESIGNATION. I DON'T WANT TO BELONG TO ANY CLUB THAT WILL ACCEPT ME AS A MEMBER. Groucho often used the name "Delaney" when referring to an apocryphal person. The voluminous Internet search engine Google has no record of an actual Delaney Club.

Verdict: Credit Groucho for concocting this line, even though he probably never used it.

YOGI BERRA

Yogi Berra is one of the most quoted, and misquoted, figures in modern America. As Berra himself once asserted, "I really didn't say everything I said." This is because the demand for Berraisms by speakers and writers far exceeds the supply. As a result, creating spurious comments by the former Yankee catcher is something of a cottage industry. According to onetime *New York Herald Tribune* sportswriter Harold Rosenthal, putting words in the mouth of Yogi—whom he called "the least communicative of the Yankees in the [Casey] Stengel era"—was a popular pastime during the catcher's years in the major leagues.

In general, it is safe to assume that most of the most popular sayings attributed to Yogi Berra are spurious. They include:

"It's déjà vu all over again." Berra first denied, then agreed that he made this observation. He probably didn't. Aside from any lack of direct evidence that Yogi ever said such a thing, "déjà vu" is not a term he'd be likely to use. On the other hand, as quotographer Fred Shapiro discovered, "It's déjà vu all over again" did appear in a 1966 *Chicago Tribune* movie review.

"Always go to other people's funerals; otherwise they won't go to yours." Berra also initially denied saying this one, and with good reason. That line appeared in slightly different form in Clarence Day's 1935 bestseller *Life with Father*.

"Nobody ever goes there anymore; it's too crowded." Yogi recalled saying this about Ruggeri's restaurant in St. Louis. His wife, Carmen, thought he said it about a restaurant in New York. According to quote compiler Phil Pepe, this Berraism referred to Charlie's in Minneapolis. Yogi's longtime friend Joe Garagiola said he'd heard it applied to restaurants in Boston, Kansas City, and Sarasota. In a 1943 *New Yorker* story, however, John McNulty wrote about a couple of characters: "They were talking about a certain hangout and Johnny said, 'Nobody goes there any more. It's too crowded.'"

"It ain't over 'til it's over." Yogi is renowned for saying this in 1973 while managing the New York Mets. While researching a profile of Berra for *Sports Illustrated,* the closest Berra remark Roy Blount, Jr., could find in news clippings was "We're not out till we're out," said about the 1974 National League pennant race. Blount traced the evolution of that remark from "You're not out of it till you're out of it," through "The game's never over till it's over," to, at last, "It ain't over 'til it's over."

Another unlikely Berraism is **"The future isn't what it used to be,"** also attributed to Paul Valéry and Arthur C. Clarke (among others). On the other hand, **"When you come to a fork in the road take it,"** is something Yogi recalls saying while giving directions to his friend Joe Garagiola.

During "Yogi Berra Night" in his hometown of St. Louis in 1947, the Yankees' catcher said, **"I'd like to thank everyone who made this night necessary."** Yogi thinks this was the original "Berraism." Another authentic example of the genre is: **"You can observe a lot by watching."** After being named manager of the New York Yankees in 1963, Yogi told reporters that this was why his previous year as a coach had prepared him to manage.

"The BEST and the brightest." The title of David Halberstam's 1972 bestseller is among the most repeated catchphrases of modern times. Although Halberstam thought it originated with him, at the time his book appeared, Episcopalians had long been singing "The Brightest and the Best," a hymn written in 1811 by Anglican Bishop Reginald Heber. Halberstam's own form had already been used by Junius (1769), Shelley (1822), Trollope (1858), Dickens (1855–1857), Henry Adams (1901), Kipling (1903), and Maxim Gorki (1921).

Verdict: David Halberstam's popularization of a phrase with a long heritage.

"The BIGGER they are, the harder they fall." This maxim is sometimes attributed to boxer John L. Sullivan, occasionally to his colleague James Corbett, but most often to Bob "Ruby Robert" Fitzsimmons. Fitzsimmons popularized the slogan at the turn of the century when, on the eve of a heavyweight title fight with big Gus Ruhlin, he said, "You know the old saying, 'The bigger they are, the further they have to fall.' " (Fitzsimmons won.) Author Albert Payson Terhune later reported seeing a version of this saying on an old English sporting print. Among various related proverbs recorded in medieval England was "Who climbeth highest most dreadful is his fall." In the fourth century A.D. the Latin poet Claudian wrote, "Men are raised on high in order that they may fall more heavily."

Verdict: An old boxing saw based on longtime proverbial wisdom.

"A BILLION here, a billion there. Pretty soon you're talking about real money." This witticism is so routinely attributed to Illinois Senator Everett McKinley Dirksen (1896–1969) that it's virtually his epitaph. No Dirksen biographer or archivist has ever found a reliable source for this quotation, however. The Dirksen Center's director has scoured the senator's writing, notes, and speeches on the Senate floor looking for the statement. He has read transcripts of Dirksen's press conferences and media interviews as well as newspaper articles about him, and even listened to recordings of the senator's observations—all to no avail. Dirksen is on record as having

said, "A billion for this, a billion for that, a billion for something else." On another occasion he said, "A billion here, a billion there . . ." but not the clever conclusion. A caller to the Dirksen Center said that while seated next to Dirksen on an airplane, he'd asked the Illinois senator about the quotation so associated with him. "Oh, I never said that," the man said Dirksen responded. "A newspaper fella misquoted me once, and I thought it sounded so good that I never bothered to deny it." So where did the quip originate? It actually evolved from a common catchphrase that predates the Depression. In 1925, a *New York Times* article included the line "A billion here and a billion there might be piled up . . ." Thirteen years later, in 1938, the *Times* ran this unsigned observation about the federal budget: "It's a billion here and a billion there, and by and by it begins to mount up into money." (*The Los Angeles Times* reprinted that item a few days later.) In 1954 a *Saturday Evening Post* cartoon by Edwin Lepper portrayed two senatorial-looking men walking past the Capitol building. One says to the other, "You save a billion here, a billion there, and the first thing you know it adds up." Two years later former president Herbert Hoover was quoted as saying that if the government saved a billion here and a billion there, it would soon add up.

Verdict: A Depression-era gag that gained currency after World War II, landing in a cartoon, in Herbert Hoover's mouth, and in Everett Dirksen's.

"From BIRTH to age 18, a girl needs good parents. From 18 to 35, she needs good looks. From 35 to 55, she needs a good personality. From 55 on, she needs good cash." Biographer Michael Freedland is one among many who have attributed this saying to Sophie Tucker (1884–1996). According to *Bartlett's* the singer said these words when she was sixty-nine. But in 1948, when Tucker was sixty-four, this saying ran without attribution in a newspaper's humor column. Other versions have been credited to novelist Kathleen Norris (1880–1966).

Verdict: Possibly Tucker, or Norris, or an author yet to be determined.

"When a dog BITES a man, that isn't news. When a man bites a dog, that's news." By legend this was the response of *New York Sun* city editor John Bogart (1845–1921) to a cub reporter who, in the early 1880s, asked him to define "news." The author of a 1918 history of the *Sun* credited Bogart with this comment. It was recalled when he died in 1921. The observation has also been attributed to *Sun* editor Charles A. Dana, to its first managing editor, Amos Cummings, and to early-twentieth-century British press baron Lord Northcliffe (Alfred Harmsworth). Whoever first defined

news as "man-bites-dog" may have got that notion from Oliver Goldsmith's "An Elegy on the Death of a Mad Dog." In this 1766 poem, a kindly man in Islington is bitten by a dog whom he'd befriended. To the consternation of all, "The man recovered of the bite, / The dog it was that died." This popular bit of doggerel was adapted in many forms, including one in which a man actually bit a dog. Lexicographer Eric Partridge believed that this might have inspired the classic definition of news.

Verdict: Someone at the *New York Sun* apparently said this in the late nineteenth century, John Bogart being the leading suspect, perhaps inspired by an Oliver Goldsmith poem.

"BLOOD and iron." (*"Blut und Eisen."*) During an 1862 debate in the Prussian Diet, Otto von Bismarck—Prussia's "Iron Chancellor"—uttered the words that became his epitaph: "Not by speeches and majorities will the great questions of the day be decided . . . but by iron and blood." As would later happen with Churchill's "blood, toil, tears, and sweat," the order of Bismarck's words was quickly revised in the popular mind, in this case to "blood and iron." Eventually Bismarck himself adopted the more popular form. Perhaps this was because in the first century Quintilian had observed, "Warfare seems to signify blood and iron."

Verdict: Credit Bismarck, and Quintilian.

"BLOOD, sweat, and tears." During his first speech as prime minister, in 1940, Winston Churchill said, "I have nothing to offer but blood, toil, tears, and sweat." In time our memory rearranged his words to "blood, sweat, and tears." This phrase had a distinguished heritage. Cicero and Livy wrote of "sweat and blood." A 1611 John Donne poem included the lines "That 'tis in vaine to dew, or mollifie / It with thy Teares, or Sweat, or Bloud." More than two centuries later, Byron wrote, "Year after year they voted cent per cent / Blood, sweat, and tear-wrung millions—why?—for rent!" In his 1888 play *Smith,* Scottish poet-playwright John Davidson wrote of "Blood-sweats and tears, and haggard, homeless lives." By 1939, a Lady Tegart reported in a magazine article that Jewish communal colonies in Palestine were "built on a foundation of blood, sweat, and tears." That same year, Churchill (who had previously used the phrases "blood and tears," and "their sweat, their tears, their blood" in his writing) himself used the "blood, sweat, and tears" version in an article on the Spanish Civil War. Since this phrase was obviously familiar when Churchill gave his memorable speech the following year, even though he rearranged the words and added "toil" for good measure, our ears and our memory quickly

returned them to the more familiar form. Churchill himself (or his publisher) called a 1941 collection of his speeches *Blood, Sweat and Tears*.

Verdict: An old phrase given new life by Winston Churchill.

"A man is known by the BOOKS he reads, by the company he keeps, by the praise he gives. . . ." In 1830, Ralph Waldo Emerson wrote in his journal, "A man is known by the books he reads, by the company he keeps, by the praise he gives, by his dress, by his tastes, by his distastes, by the stories he tells, by his gait, by the motion of his eye, by the look of his house, of his chamber; for nothing on earth is solitary but every thing hath affinities infinite." This has been long known. Digging deeper, however, a librarian discovered that an updated version of William Law's *Christian Perfection* (1726, revised 1973) included the line "We say that a man is known by the friends he keeps; but a man is known better by his books." Law's original words were "We commonly say, that a man is known by his Companions; but it is certain, that a Man is much more known by the Books that he converses with." In various forms the thought that "a man is known by his company" is longtime proverbial wisdom in many cultures. According to Euripides, "Every man is like the company he is wont to keep."

Verdict: Credit William Law, Euripides, and proverbial wisdom for the basic idea, Ralph Waldo Emerson for its most common expression.

"The man who does not read good BOOKS has no advantage over the man who can't read them." Advice columnist Abigail Van Buren once made this observation in her column. A reader said she should have credited the thought to Mark Twain. Abby apologized, explaining that she genuinely thought the idea was her own. Perhaps it was. Although this saying is often attributed to Twain, no one has ever confirmed that he wrote or said it.

Verdict: Possibly Abby Van Buren.

"He was BORN on third base and thinks he hit a triple." When Texas agriculture commissioner Jim Hightower said this about George H. W. Bush in a speech at the 1988 Democratic convention, he was hailed for his wit. After Hightower was voted out of office and made an unsuccessful attempt to host a radio show, this quip was more often attributed to Texas governor Ann Richards. When Richards lost her reelection bid to George W. Bush, it was introduced by the phrase "as Democrats say," or attributed to no one at all. It's unlikely that the quip originated with Hightower, however, let alone with Richards. This observation had appeared in print—attributed to an unnamed Texan—five years before the 1988 convention, and was credited to Oklahoma football coach Barry Switzer in 1986. The catchphrase "born on third base," signifying inherited privilege, dates back to the Depression era. In 1935 a conservative speaker charged that Franklin Roosevelt's "Brain Trust" was filled with "professors and others . . . who were born on third base . . ."

Verdict: An old American saw.

"When I was a BOY of fourteen, my father was so ignorant I could barely stand to have the old man around. But when I got to be twenty-one, I was astonished at how much the old man had learned in seven years." Reader's Digest attributed this thought to Mark Twain in 1937, without giving a source. Twain's own father died when he was eleven. When the Library of Congress asked Twain scholars whether the author had ever said this, none could confirm that he did. Its true source remains a mystery.

Verdict: Author undetermined; not Twain.

"The Pottery Barn rule: You BREAK it, you own it." In his 2004 book *Plan of Attack,* Bob Woodward credited Secretary of State Colin Powell and Deputy Secretary of State Richard Armitage with warning President George W. Bush in 2002 that if he invaded Iraq, he would own it. "Privately," wrote Woodward, "Powell and Armitage called this the Pottery Barn rule: You break it, you own it." As a result, Powell is often credited with the "Pottery Barn rule." But *New York Times* columnist Thomas Friedman has taken every opportunity to remind others that it was he who originated this concept and fed it to the secretary of state via Armitage (as Powell confirmed). As early as September 2002, Friedman told National Public Radio interviewer Scott Simon that he had a "Pottery Barn view" of invading countries such as Afghanistan or Iraq, based on the sign BREAK IT AND YOU OWN IT, which he thought was posted in those stores. When Pottery Barn pointed out that no such sign appears in any of their stores, Friedman conceded his mistake. In his February 12, 2003, *New York Times* column, Friedman wrote, "The first rule of any Iraq invasion is the pottery store rule: You break it, you own it."

Verdict: Credit Thomas Friedman; delete "Pottery Barn."

"Nobody ever went BROKE underestimating the intelligence of the American public." H. L. Mencken's most familiar quotation takes various

forms. "Taste" and "idiocy" are sometimes substituted for "intelligence," depending on what point the quoter is trying to make. Mencken citers have a lot of latitude on this quotation because it does not appear in his published works. According to quotation compiler George Seldes, Mencken's actual words—made in reference to the success of *Reader's Digest*—were "There's no underestimating the intelligence of the American public." His associate Charles Angoff wrote Seldes that Mencken had repeatedly made that observation in conversation. But the closest known Mencken comment on the record did not even mention Americans. This was recorded in the *Chicago Tribune* in 1926: "No one in this world, so far as I know,—and I have searched the records for years, and employed agents to help me—has ever lost money underestimating the intelligence of the great masses of the plain people."

Verdict: Credit Mencken for this general idea, and some version of the words.

"The BUCK stops here." This comment is so associated with Harry Truman that it's easy to conclude the words came straight from his mouth. They didn't. Early in Truman's presidency, a friend of his saw a sign on the desk of an Oklahoma prison warden that read, THE BUCK STOPS HERE. This friend had a replica made for the president and gave it to him in October 1945. Truman displayed this sign on his desk off and on for most of his presidency, and sometimes referred to it in speeches. The sign's message became central to Truman's credo. (It plays off the expression "pass the buck," which originated among poker players who passed a buck knife among themselves to indicate whose turn it was to deal.) The original sign is now on display at the Harry S. Truman Library in Independence, Missouri. According to a mid-1946 press account, the desk of Oklahoma governor Robert Kerr also sported a sign reading, THE BUCK STOPS HERE.

Verdict: Credit an anonymous sloganeer as originator, Harry Truman as primary publicist.

"We shape our BUILDINGS, then they shape us." In the fall of 1943, members of Britain's parliament debated how to rebuild the House of Commons, which had been destroyed by German bombs two years earlier. Some wanted to replace it with a roomier building that had enough seats for every member. Others, including Prime Minister Winston Churchill, wanted to re-create the original structure, which could seat only about two-thirds of all parliamentarians. Churchill thought that being a bit overcrowded lent intensity, drama, and a sense of history to parliamentary

proceedings. "We shape our buildings," said the prime minister, "and afterwards our buildings shape us. Having dwelt and served for more than forty years in the late Chamber, and having derived very great pleasure and advantage therefrom, I, naturally, would like to see it restored in all essentials to its old form, convenience and dignity." Churchill's position carried the day, and in 1950 the House of Commons was rebuilt in its traditional form. Churchill's famous words are sometimes misquoted as "We shape our dwellings and afterwards our dwellings shape us."

Verdict: Credit Churchill, for buildings.

"The BUSINESS of America is business." The remark for which Calvin Coolidge is best remembered is an unfair condensation of his actual words. During a 1925 speech to the Society of American Newspaper Editors, Calvin Coolidge said, "After all, the chief business of the American people is business." Coolidge's actual words are similar to the terser version, but their meaning is quite different.

Verdict: An unfair revision of Coolidge's actual words.

"The BUTLER did it." While investigating a famous 1835 crime case in London, detective Henry Goddard was able to prove that a butler had faked a robbery. Goddard did this by making a cast of a bullet from the butler's own gun, then comparing the imperfection revealed in this cast with an identical imperfection in a bullet that the butler said had been fired at him. That was the first known use of this type of forensic evidence, and may have inspired the phrase "the butler did it." We don't know who first used the phrase in fiction (if it was ever used at all), on stage, or in a movie. No one has ever confirmed the widespread assumption that Mary Roberts Rinehart used the line in one of her many mystery novels, although the butler *did* do it in Rinehart's 1930 novel *The Door*. A butler was also guilty in any number of other mysteries—including an 1893 Sherlock Holmes case called "The Musgrave Ritual" (in *The Memoirs of Sherlock Holmes*). Damon Runyon's 1933 story "What, No Butler?" in *Collier's* magazine, and the appearance of "The butler did it" as a throwaway line in a 1938 *Punch* cartoon, suggest how familiar this concept was by then. P. G. Wodehouse satirized the literary cliché in his 1957 novel *The Butler Did It*.

Verdict: A catchphrase of unknown origins.

"How can you BUY or sell the sky, the land?" During his fabled conversations with Bill Moyers on public television in 1988, mythologist Joseph Campbell recited a long, eloquent statement by Chief Seattle of the

Suquamish and Dwanish tribes. This began: "The President in Washington sends word that he wishes to buy our land, but how can you buy or sell the sky, the land? The idea is strange to us. If we do not own the freshness of the air and the sparkle of the water, how can you buy them? Every part of this earth is sacred to my people. Every shining pine needle, every sandy shore, every mist in the dark woods, every meadow, every humming insect. All are holy in the memory and experience of my people." Though the Indian leader to whom they're attributed had been dead for well over a century, his reverence for the earth spoke to our times. That could be because Seattle's famous words were written in 1971 by screenwriter Ted Perry for an ABC-TV documentary on the environment. Unable to find any authentic speech by a prominent Native American to illustrate his point, Perry made one up and put it in Seattle's mouth (incorporating a few of the Indian's own words). Only when he watched the program did the writer realize that "written by Ted Perry" did not appear in its credits. When Perry complained, the program's producers explained that they felt deleting his name from the credits lent authenticity to Chief Seattle's words. The film was widely distributed with the name "Chief Seattle" included in its writing credits.

Verdict: Credit Ted Perry.

"Let them eat CAKE," ("Qu'ils mangent de la brioche.") Marie Antoinette's supposed solution for the shortage of bread among peasants predated her 1770 arrival in France by quite a few years. Jean-Jacques Rousseau's *Confessions,* which was written in the late 1760s and drew on journal entries he wrote long before Antoinette's birth in 1755, included this passage: "Finally I remembered the way out suggested by a great princess when told that the peasants had no bread: 'Well let them eat cake.'" (It was not actually cake that the unnamed princess recommended, but the pastry called *brioche.*) A French book published in 1760 credited the Duchess of Tuscany with offering the same advice. In 1823, Louis XVIII fingered Marie Therese, wife of Louis XIV, who supposedly said that the poor could eat pâté. Versions of this comment have also been attributed to John Peckham, an Archbishop of Canterbury during the thirteenth century, and to an ancient Chinese emperor who said of his rice-starved subjects, "Why don't they eat meat?"

Verdict: Myths put in mouths, especially Marie Antoinette's.

"First they CAME for the communists, and I didn't speak up. . . ." In many different forms, the eloquent statement about not speaking up for groups

oppressed by the Nazis is usually attributed to Martin Niemoller. Niemoller was a German clergyman who spent eight years in two concentration camps for criticizing of Hitler and his henchmen. After the war, Reverend Niemoller was contrite about not challenging the Nazis earlier in the 1930s, when he could have had more impact. Indeed, in the early 1930s the nationalistic Niemoller sympathized with Hitler's National Socialists. In the late 1940s Niemoller led a movement among German Protestants to accept responsibility for not speaking out against the Nazis. Extensive research by journalists and academics (especially Harold Marcuse, professor of German History at the University of California/Santa Barbara) has established the following: 1. After World War II, Niemoller recited different versions of his "First they came . . ." statement during speeches and sermons. 2. Because Reverend Niemoller rarely recorded his speeches and sermons, there is no written record to confirm this. 3. No one knows where, when, or in what form the thought was first expressed. 4. For their own purposes various interest groups—Catholics, Gypsies, homosexuals, and others—routinely add themselves to the quotation. Niemoller's version apparently included communists, socialists, trade unionists, and Jews (as well as himself, of course), in that order. After studying various alternatives, in consultation with Niemoller's widow, Methodist minister Franklin H. Littell has concluded that the following version most accurately characterizes the one Niemoller used in speeches: "First they came for the communists, and I did not speak out—because I was not a communist; then they came for the socialists, and I did not speak out—because I was not a socialist; then they came for the trade unionists, and I did not speak out—because I was not a trade unionist; then they came for the Jews, and I did not speak out—because I was not a Jew; then they came for me—and there was no one left to speak out for me."

Verdict: Credit Martin Niemoller, discussing communists, socialists, trade unionists, Jews, and himself.

"You CAMPAIGN in poetry, you govern in prose." This political adage is most often attributed to former New York governor Mario Cuomo. Beginning in the early 1980s, Cuomo used it often, in speeches, conversation, and writing. The saying has also been credited to Richard Nixon, though far less often than to Cuomo. (A journalist who attributed the line to Nixon later noted that in the 2000 campaign "George Bush campaigned in nursery rhymes.") In an episode of NBC's *West Wing*, President Jed Bartlet's chief of staff used the poetry-prose line without attribution. Wherever it originated, this saying owes an unacknowledged debt to an observation

credited to British writer Beverley Nichols (1898–1983): "Marriage is a book in which the first chapter is written in poetry and the remaining chapters in prose."

Verdict: Credit Mario Cuomo, with a nod to Beverley Nichols for source material.

"It is better to light a CANDLE than curse the darkness." When Eleanor Roosevelt died in 1962, Adlai Stevenson observed that the former First Lady had been one who "would rather light a candle than curse the darkness, and her glow has warmed the world." Stevenson was widely praised for this eloquent tribute. In time "I'd rather light a candle than curse the darkness" was attributed to Eleanor Roosevelt herself. Long before Adlai's eulogy, however, the well-established motto of the Christopher Society—a Catholic humanitarian group organized after World War II—was "It is better to light one candle than to curse the darkness." The Christophers say their motto came from a Chinese proverb, although they don't know where their founder, Fr. James Keller, found it. Father Keller told Leo Rosten that he'd heard the proverb a long time before founding the Christophers, although he couldn't remember where or when. The Christophers' founder might well have read it in the American press, where that saying showed up frequently during the early 1940s, usually without attribution. A 1940 news report from China quoted one of that country's leaders as saying, "I had rather light a candle in the darkness than to curse the darkness." In a 1952 compilation of sayings, quote compiler Evan Esar credited this one to Confucius, but gave no source. Others have also attributed that saying to Confucius, who is one of history's leading flypaper figures. In 1961 the proverb helped motivate London lawyer Peter Benenson to found Amnesty International, and inspired Amnesty's logo of a candle within barbed wire.

Verdict: Proverbial wisdom, probably of Asian origin.

"CAN'T we all just get along?" During the 1992 Los Angeles protests triggered by the acquittal of four police officers accused of beating speeding motorist Rodney King, King himself pleaded, "People, I just want to say, you know, can we all get along? Can we get along? . . . Please, we can get along here. We all can get along." King's plainspoken eloquence resonated widely and was long remembered in condensed, altered form.

Verdict: Revised Rodney King.

"CHANCE favors the prepared mind." So said Louis Pasteur in an 1854 lecture. Pasteur's full statement was "In the fields of observation chance

favors only the prepared mind." (*"Dans les champs de l'observation le hasard ne favorise que les esprits préparés."*) Similar observations have been made repeatedly, before and since, by those who don't want to believe that random events can influence their lives. (See "Luck is the residue of design.")

Verdict: Abridged Pasteur.

"The CHATTERING classes." This characterization of those who like to natter on about the state of the world is especially popular in the British press. The *Oxford English Dictionary* defines "chattering classes" as "members of the educated metropolitan middle class, esp. those in academic, artistic, or media circles, considered as a social group freely given to the articulate, self-assured expression of (esp. liberal) opinions about society, culture and current events." *Oxford* traces this catchphrase back only to 1985. Some think it originated with journalist Auberon Waugh (the son of Evelyn). More often the phrase is associated with Waugh's colleague Alan Watkins, who has used it repeatedly in the column he's written for various London newspapers. Watkins does not claim to have originated the phrase, however. He credits fellow journalist Frank Johnson, whom he first heard use these words in the late 1970s. In 1890, on the other hand, an article in *The Chautauquan* included this line: "One who has belonged to the chattering class will find his task harder."

Verdict: A longstanding Anglo-American catchphrase.

"Too much CHECKING on the facts has ruined many a good news story." When he was chief justice of the Supreme Court, Warren Burger wrote in a libel decision, "Consideration of these issues inevitably recalls the aphorism of journalism attributed to the late Roy Howard that 'too much checking on the facts has ruined many a good news story.'" Staff members of Indiana University's Roy Howard Memorial Center could find no evidence that the late editor-in-chief of Scripps-Howard newspapers ever made such an observation. They let Burger know. In Burger's revised opinion, this saying was cited as an unattributed aphorism.

Verdict: Apocryphal aphorism attributed to journalists by debunkers.

"He can't walk and CHEW GUM at the same time." In the midst of the 2004 campaign, Democratic vice-presidential nominee John Edwards said, "The president of the United States has to actually be able to walk and chew gum at the same time." During the same campaign, Senator Jim Bunning (R-Ky.) told an audience, "I want everybody to look and see that I can walk and chew gum . . ." Both were alluding to a famous put-down of Gerald

Ford by Lyndon Johnson. When Ford became president in 1974, it was widely recalled in the press that Lyndon Johnson once said Ford was so dumb he couldn't walk and chew gum at the same time. According to Washington insiders, what the earthy LBJ *really* said was that Jerry Ford couldn't "fart" and chew gum at the same time.

Verdict: Credit LBJ for the earthier version.

"A CHICKEN in every pot." Although the Republican Party used this slogan in some of their 1928 advertising (at times adding, "a car in every garage"), their presidential candidate Herbert Hoover himself made no such promise. No reference to a chicken in every pot or a car in every garage has ever been found in Hoover's speeches or writing. The culinary part of that thought originated with King Henry IV of France, who said, "I desire that every laborer in my realm should be able to put a fowl in the pot on Sundays." (*"Je veux que chaque laboureur de mon royaume puisse mettre la poule au pot le dimanche."*)

Verdict: A Republican adaptation of Henry IV, not adopted by Herbert Hoover.

"CHILDREN learn what they live." In 1954, teacher-writer Dorothy Nolte wrote the prose poem "Children Learn What They Live." It began, "If children live with criticism, they learn to condemn. / If children live with hostility, they learn to fight," and continued in this vein for seventeen more lines. During the 1970s, abridgments of Nolte's words became popular on posters, bookmarks, coffee mugs, and the like. In 1972 *Reader's Digest* published a remarkably similar twelve-line prose poem called "Lessons from Life," by one Ronald Russell, © 1971 by AA Sales, Inc. Nolte herself subsequently published a twelve-line "author-approved short version." *Chicken Soup for the Soul* (1993) included her full version. In 1998 Nolte coauthored a book called *Children Learn What They Live*, which expanded on her original version.

Verdict: Credit Dorothy Nolte.

"If you bungle raising your CHILDREN, I don't think whatever else you do well matters very much." Jacqueline Kennedy Onassis's most memorable quotation was a spontaneous remark made during a 1960 TV interview shortly before her husband was elected president. In *It Takes a Village,* Hillary Clinton cited Jackie's words. Since then this comment has sometimes been misattributed to Hillary herself.

Verdict: Credit Jacqueline Kennedy Onassis.

WINSTON CHURCHILL

As a young man, Britain's future prime minister observed that reading *Bartlett's Familiar Quotations* was a capital way to expand one's intellectual horizons. Throughout his long career the eloquent politician paid careful attention to the quotability of his own public statements, with the unintended result that he is often misquoted.

In 1943, Churchill supposedly said of his Labor Party counterpart, Sir Stafford Cripps, **"There, but for the grace of God, goes God."** Richard Langworth, editor of the Churchill Centre, cannot find this among many comments Sir Winston made about Sir Stafford. In the United States, screenwriter Herman Mankiewicz was lionized for saying the same thing about Orson Welles two years earlier, as they filmed *Citizen Kane*. Whoever said this first was echoing a remark most often attributed to the English religious martyr John Bradford (1510–1555) as he watched a group of prisoners about to be hanged: "There, but for the grace of God, goes John Bradford." Shortly thereafter Bradford himself was burned at the stake.

Churchill is also renowned for saying of Clement Attlee, his successor as prime minister, **"Attlee is a very modest man . . . who has much to be modest about."** This comment is based on Churchill's reported exchange with Harry Truman after Truman observed that Attlee was a modest man. Churchill supposedly responded, "He has much to be modest about!" Archivists at the Truman Library can find no evidence that such an exchange took place. Richard Langworth doubts the authenticity of another supposed Churchill observation about Attlee, that he was **"a sheep in sheep's clothing."** When asked about that one, Churchill said it was based on a more pointed remark he'd once made about another prime minister, Ramsey Macdonald. Quotographer Nigel Rees notes earlier uses of the same put-down by others.

Countless anecdotes involving Churchill's gift for repartee are bruited about. In one of the most famous, a hefty Labor MP named Bessie Braddock accused him of being drunk at a dinner party. Churchill responded, **"And you, madam, are ugly. But I shall be sober tomorrow."** Members of Churchill's family question this one because Sir Winston held his liquor well, and was gallant to women. Yet Churchill's Scotland Yard bodyguard told Richard Langworth that

he overheard this exchange between Braddock and Churchill outside
the House of Commons in 1948:

> BRADDOCK: Winston, you are drunk, and what's more you
> are disgustingly drunk.
> CHURCHILL: Bessie, my dear, you are ugly, and what's
> more you are disgustingly ugly; but tomorrow I shall be
> sober and you shall still be disgustingly ugly.

Langworth thinks that Churchill was more likely tired than drunk on
this occasion, but perhaps played along for the sake of a good zinger. If
so, his rejoinder almost certainly was derivative. In the 1934 W. C.
Fields movie *It's a Gift* (whose screenplay was written by Jack Cun-
ningham, based on the Broadway revue *The Comic Supplement* by
J. P. McEvoy, and a story by Charles Bogle), when told "You're drunk,"
Fields's character responds, "Yeah, and you're crazy. But I'll be sober
tomorrow, and you'll be crazy for the rest of your life."

In a similar exchange, tart-tongued Lady Astor, the first woman
elected to the House of Commons, allegedly told Churchill, "If you
were my husband, I'd put poison in your coffee" (in his tea, more likely).
"Madam," Churchill is said to have responded, **"If you were my wife,
I'd drink it."** Many biographers of both Churchill and Astor report that
some form of this exchange took place. However, the researcher for a biography of Churchill being written by his son Randolph discounted the
comment as uncharacteristic of the rather prim prime minister. In any
event, the same story has been told about many another prominent
party, including baseball player Dizzy Dean, umpire Jack Sheridan,
Churchill's close friend F. E. Smith (whose acerbic wit and capacity for
alcohol matched Sir Winston's), and Churchill's predecessor as prime
minister, David Lloyd George. In that version, Lloyd George had this
exchange with a heckler while campaigning:

> HECKLER: If you were my husband I would give you poison.
> LLOYD GEORGE: Dear lady, if you were my wife I would
> take it.

According to Churchill's history of World War II, one of his more
famous observations, **"In wartime, truth is so precious that she**

should always be attended by a bodyguard of lies" was what he told Soviet dictator Joseph Stalin during their 1943 meeting in Tehran, about the need for the "Overlord" disinformation operation, which was designed to deceive the Germans about the Allies' D day plans. According to the Soviets themselves Churchill said, "Sometimes truth has to be safeguarded with the aid of untruth." British General Alan Brooke, who took part in the Tehran conference, recalled Churchill saying that in war, "truth must have an escort of lies."

In an early edition of his single-volume biography of Churchill, Martin Gilbert reported that his subject said of Charles de Gaulle, during World War II, **"The greatest cross I have to bear is the Cross of Lorraine."** Shortly after his book was published, more than one reader pointed out to Gilbert that this was actually said by Gen. Edward Spears, Churchill's liaison with de Gaulle. Gilbert and others also discredit another comment widely attributed to Sir Winston: that the only traditions of the Royal Navy were **"rum, sodomy and the lash."** In a 1985 speech, Churchill's assistant, Anthony Montague-Browne, said Sir Winston once told him that although he'd never said this, he wished he had. **"Golf is a game in which you try to put a small ball in a small hole with implements singularly unsuited to the purpose"** is commonly attributed to Winston Churchill in different forms, without a source. Richard Langworth can't find it in his extensive database of work by and about Churchill. He can find Churchill's depiction of golf as being "Like chasing a quinine pill around a cow pasture," credited to an "earwitness."

Although Churchill is famous for responding, **"This is the sort of ENGLISH up with which I will not put"** to an officious editor who corrected a sentence of his that ended with a preposition, no evidence exists that he actually did so.

Churchill is a leading flypaper figure, stuck with all manner of words he never said. Quotations commonly misattributed to him include, **"A LIE can travel halfway around the world before the truth gets its boots on," "There is nothing better for the inside of a man than the outside of a HORSE,"** and **"Any man who is not a SOCIALIST at age twenty has no heart. Any man who is still a socialist at age forty has no head."** Churchill is also among the many credited with Wilde's "We have really everything in common with America nowadays, except, of course, language." (See sidebar "Oscar Wilde.")

Like most members of his profession, Churchill was not above adopting and adapting other people's words. **"BLOOD, toil, tears, and sweat"** had a long literary pedigree by the time Churchill used his version of that phrase in 1940, as did **"IRON CURTAIN."** One of Churchill's most eloquent statements was made in the House of Commons as British forces fled Dunkirk in 1940: **"We shall fight on the beaches. We shall fight on the landing grounds. We shall fight in the fields, and in the streets, we shall fight in the hills. We shall never surrender!"** These words drew on ones used by Georges Clemenceau in the midst of a German offensive late in the First World War. By one account the French premier said, "We will fight them on the Loire, we will fight them on the Garonne, we will fight them in the Pyrenees." In his book *The World Crisis* (1931), Churchill himself gave Clemenceau's words as "I shall fight in front of Paris. I shall fight in Paris. I shall fight behind Paris."

Another popular Churchillism, **"DEMOCRACY is the worst form of government except for all those other forms that have been tried from time to time,"** is one for which he did not take credit. Churchill introduced this observation with the phrase "it has been said that . . ."

In his 1937 book *Great Contemporaries* Churchill wrote, **"Courage is rightly esteemed the first of human qualities, because, as has been said, it is the quality which guarantees all others."** This observation, considered one of his most memorable, usually appears without the phrase "as has been said." Churchill presumably was referring to Samuel Johnson's comment, "Sir, you know courage is reckoned the greatest of all virtues; because, unless a man has that virtue, he has no security for preserving any other." (See sidebar "Samuel Johnson.")

Memorable comments of Churchill's own invention include **"We shape our BUILDINGS, and afterwards our buildings shape us,"** and, with reference to the Soviet Russia, **"It is a RIDDLE wrapped in a mystery inside an enigma. . . ."**

Others are:

"Today we may say aloud before an awe-struck world: 'We are still masters of our fate. We are still captain of our souls.'" So said Churchill in a 1941 speech to the House of Commons (paraphrasing William Ernest Henley's 1875 poem *Invictus*).

"This was their finest hour." The full sentence that included this memorable phrase was part of a speech Churchill gave in the

House of Commons after France fell to the Nazis: "Let us therefore brace ourselves to our duties, and so bear ourselves that if the British Empire and Common-wealth last for a thousand years, men will still say, This was their finest hour."

During the Battle of Britain in August 1940, when so many British pilots were shot down while defending their homeland against the German Luftwaffe, Churchill said in Commons, **"Never in the field of human conflict was so much owed by so many to so few."** Citing an old quotation collection, quotographer Nigel Rees points out that after the fall of Calpi, Sir John Moore (1761–1809) said, "Never was so much work done by so few men."

"In war, resolution; in defeat, defiance; in victory, magnanimity; in peace, good will." Although Churchill first published these words in his history of World War II, his post–World War I private secretary wrote in a 1939 book that Churchill originated this declaration in the aftermath of World War I.

"Close, but no CIGAR." This catchphrase has been common in the United States since the 1930s, when it appeared in novels and at least one movie ("Close, Colonel, but no cigar!"—*Annie Oakley,* 1935). Presumably that expression could be heard in Depression-era fairs and carnivals, addressed to those who didn't win cigars for, say, trying to ring the bell with a sledgehammer.

Verdict: Catchphrase most likely born in Depression-era carnivals.

"Sometimes a CIGAR is just a cigar." University of California/Davis psychology professor Alan Elms has spent years trying to verify this celebrated observation by Sigmund Freud. He's had no success. Nor has the Freud Museum in London (whose website asks anyone with leads to please contact them). Elms believes this assertion is so at odds with Freud's actual views—essentially that nothing is *just* anything—that it's highly unlikely he ever said it. The earliest attribution of these words to Freud that Elms could find was in a paper published by historian Peter Gay in 1961. No source was given. When Elms queried Gay about his source, the historian said it wasn't clear (which was why he gave none). Gay's 1988 biography of Freud, which discusses his love of cigars at length, makes no reference to him saying that sometimes cigars were just cigars. Nor does Elizabeth Bruehel-Young's biography of Freud's daughter Anna, to

whom psychiatry's patron saint supposedly made the remark. (By other accounts Freud's remark was made in response to a question from the audience about the symbolic significance of all the cigars he smoked, following
a lecture Freud gave at Clark University in Massachusetts.) As best Alan
Elms can determine, this comment made its printed debut in Peter Gay's
1961 paper. Where it originated is anyone's guess. Elms wonders if Freud's
most famous remark might actually be twisted Kipling ("And a woman
is only a woman, but a good Cigar is a Smoke"), or perhaps the invention of
a comedian imitating the father of psychoanalysis. Alternatively, when a
character in Ivan Turgenev's *Fathers and Sons* is offered a cigar, he responds, "A cigar's a cigar, but do let's have some lunch."

Verdict: Apocryphal Freud.

"What this country needs is a good five-cent CIGAR." Woodrow Wilson's
vice president Thomas Riley Marshall (1854–1925) is famous for making this
remark on the eve of America's entry into World War I. After extensive research, biographer Charles M. Thomas concluded that Marshall did say
these words—while presiding over the Senate—in the midst of a speech by a
senator from Kansas about "what this country needs." Thomas thought it unfortunate that the onetime governor of Indiana should be remembered primarily for a single jest. In fact, the comment was not original to him. As early
as 1875 the *Saturday Evening Post* ran this item in its "Facetiae" feature: "The
Danbury News says: 'What this country really needs is a good five cent cigar.'"
A biographer of Indiana humorist Kin Hubbard said Hubbard used the quip
in conversation long before his fan and fellow Hoosier Tom Marshall did.

Verdict: Thomas Marshall made this remark, in jest, but did not originate it.

CIVIL RIGHTS

The Civil Rights Movement of the 1960s was the source of many
memorable sayings and slogans whose provenance is not always familiar.

"We shall overcome." The roots of this protest song can be
found in nineteenth-century slave songs, particularly one that declared, "I'll be all right someday." In 1901 Charles Albert Tindley, pas-
tor of the Calvary Methodist Episcopal Church in Philadelphia,
copyrighted a hymn called "I'll Overcome Some Day." In 1945, striking

tobacco workers in Charleston, South Carolina, sang a version of this hymn. Two strikers took their version to the Highlander Folk Center in Tennessee, where it became "We Will Overcome." (Members of black church congregations at that time recall hearing gospel versions of this hymn as both "We" and "I Will Overcome.") Folksinger Pete Seeger, who learned the song from Highlander's music director, is credited with changing "will" to "shall." Seeger himself said credit for this change should be shared with Septima Clark, Highlander's director of education. Folksinger Guy Carawan learned the song from a colleague of Seeger's in the 1950s, and, after becoming Highlander's music director, taught it to civil rights activists in 1960. Since the basis for this song is a Negro spiritual, some of these activists were bemused by Carawan's presentation. "We'd been singing the song all our lives," recalled scholar-singer Bernice Johnson-Reagan, who was a member of the SNCC Freedom Singers when Carawan sang them "We Shall Overcome," "and here's the guy who just learned the song and he's telling us how to sing it. And you know what I said to myself? 'If you need it, you got it.'" Regardless of who deserves credit, "We Shall Overcome" became the anthem of the 1960s Civil Rights Movement.

"Tell it like it is," the signature line of sportscaster Howard Cosell, was originally shouted by black protesters during the 1960s.

"I have a dream." Martin Luther King used this memorable phrase in several speeches before making it the set piece of his Lincoln Memorial address during the 1963 march on Washington. According to Drew Hansen, author of a book on that speech, antecedents can be found in the King James Bible. Although "I have a dream" may have been part of the prayers of other civil rights activists before King incorporated it into his own oratory, Hansen himself thinks King's inspiration was primarily biblical.

"Black is beautiful." Often mistakenly attributed to Martin Luther King, this phrase was put in play by Student Nonviolent Coordinating Committee (SNCC) leader Stokely Carmichael at a 1966 rally in Memphis. Its genesis may be The Song of Solomon 1:5: "I am black, but comely . . ." / "I am black but beautiful, O ye daughters of Jerusalem."

Carmichael was the most prominent civil rights leader to advocate **"black power,"** in 1966. However, that slogan was fed to him by a less prominent member of SNCC named Willie Ricks, who used it while exhorting a Mississippi crowd the year before. Well before that, SNCC workers had already been advocating "black power for black people." In 1954, Richard Wright published a book called *Black Power*. This phrase was also used by Paul Robeson, Adam Clayton Powell, and other postwar African-American leaders.

While being introduced as the new head of SNCC in 1967, H. "Rap" Brown told reporters, **"I say violence is necessary. It's as American as cherry pie."** Brown, of course, was adapting the old saw "as American as apple pie." His assertion has been mistakenly attributed to Stokely Carmichael, among others.

"CLOSE your eyes and think of England." This sexual advice for English wives is so Victorian that it is routinely attributed to Queen Victoria herself. Some believe that its actual originator was Lady Alice Hillingdon (for whom the "Lady Hillingdon" strain of roses is apparently named). She was married to a onetime Conservative member of parliament named Charles. Lady Hillingdon, who died in 1940, is said to have written in her diary in 1912, "I am happy now that Charles calls on my bedchamber less frequently than of old. As it is, I now endure but two calls a week, and when I hear his steps outside my door I lie down on my bed, close my eyes, open my legs and think of England." These journals were never published, however, and no one seems to know where this entry was found. Lexicographer Eric Partridge was skeptical about the attribution, and speculated that this advice may have been given seriously to British expatriate wives before it became a jokey catchphrase in more-liberated times. According to a 1943 news account, the son of British Prime Minister Stanley Baldwin (1867–1947) said his mother advised his sister that if a suitor wanted to kiss her, she should just close her eyes and think of England. When he was having doubts about his impending marriage to Lady Diana Spencer, Prince Charles was said to have been given the same advice by his sister, Anne.

Verdict: Origins lost in the mists of English erotic history.

"Let's get out of these wet CLOTHES and into a dry martini." Although this quip is routinely misattributed to Alexander Woollcott, the theater critic did not coin it and never claimed he had. *Bartlett's* gave it to Woollcott in 1968 (citing *Reader's Digest*), humorist Robert Benchley thereafter.

A decade of checking convinced biographer Howard Teichmann that Benchley deserved the credit. Bennett Cerf's 1944 book *Try and Stop Me* even included an anecdote about Benchley coming in from a driving rain and delivering the witticism. After Benchley died, columnist Earl Wilson said that in 1944 the humorist told him he'd used this line, but did not originate it. Benchley's son Nathaniel thought the quip began as a joke in a newspaper column, then was put in Robert Benchley's mouth by a press agent. Based on his own interview with Nathaniel Benchley, Teichmann reached a somewhat different conclusion: that a press agent working on Robert Benchley's behalf came up with the line, then passed it along to a columnist, giving credit to Benchley. In the 1942 film *The Major and the Minor,* Robert Benchley himself said to Ginger Rogers, "Why don't you slip out of those wet clothes and into a dry martini?" That film was written by Charles Brackett and director Billy Wilder. When *Los Angeles Times* columnist Jack Smith, who considered the wet clothes/dry martini quip "one of the most durable and rootless lines in the language," asked Wilder about its origin, the director said he'd always assumed it originated with Benchley himself. But during shooting, Benchley told Wilder it was coined by his friend Charles Butterworth. Jack Smith considered the case closed until a reader pointed out to him that the 1937 film *Every Day's a Holiday* featured this exchange between the characters played by Butterworth and Charles Winninger:

> WINNINGER (while anxiously awaiting the opening of a theatrical production he's bankrolled): I'm hot. Soaked all over.
> BUTTERWORTH: You oughta get out of those wet clothes and get into a dry martini.

Mae West, who starred in this movie, is sometimes said to have delivered Butterworth's line. Although she was listed as its screenwriter, West was notorious for taking credit for material she didn't write.

Verdict: If not Charles Butterworth, then some anonymous press agent.

"The COLDEST winter I ever spent was a summer in San Francisco." This popular remark has been attributed to Robert Louis Stevenson, Arthur Conan Doyle, H. L. Mencken, and, most often, Mark Twain. Despite extensive searching no one has ever found the comment in any of Mark Twain's works. In *Roughing It,* Twain called San Francisco's climate "mild and singularly equable. . . . It is no colder, and no warmer, in the one month than the other." The source of the coldest-winter comment could be an 1880 letter in which Twain quoted an eighteenth-century wit who, when asked if he'd ever *seen* such a winter, replied, "Yes. Last summer." Concluded Twain: "I judge he spent his summer in Paris."

Verdict: Author unknown; conceivably adapted Twain.

"Why don't you COME up and see me some time?" What Mae West actually said to Cary Grant in *She Done Him Wrong* (1933) was "Why don't you come up sometime, see me?" This provocative suggestion caught the public's fancy in its revised form. West herself used the popular version in her next movie, *I'm No Angel.* That movie was based on the 1928 play *Diamond Lil,* which included the line "Why don't you come up some time?" Six years before that, in 1922, an African-American blues song was published called "He May Be Your Man, but He Comes to See Me Sometimes," a song with which West was said to be familiar. She herself thought the line probably dated back to Delilah.

Verdict: Various sources, including the public's editing ear, gave Mae West her signature line—one rooted in African-American vernacular.

"The world is a COMEDY to those who think, a tragedy to those who feel." Although this observation has been attributed to Shaw and others, it was Horace Walpole who wrote in a 1776 letter, "I have often said, this world is a comedy to those that think, a tragedy to those that feel." His aphorism was one of many "Detached Thoughts" in *The Works of Horatio Walpole, Earl of Oxford* (1798), with the word "who" replacing "that."

Verdict: Credit Horace Walpole.

"COMFORT the afflicted and afflict the comfortable." In the 1960 movie *Inherit the Wind,* an H. L. Mencken–like newspaper editor says, "It is the duty of a newspaper to comfort the afflicted and afflict the comfortable." Credit for this credo gets passed around. In his 1942 quotation collection, Mencken attributed the saying to "Author unidentified." Mencken himself is sometimes thought to have been that author. (He was prone to quoting himself anonymously.) Four decades before Mencken's collection was published, however, Finley Peter Dunne wrote this observation by his philosophizing bartender, Mr. Dooley: "The newspaper does ivrything f'r us. It runs th' polis foorce an' th' banks, commands th' milishy, conthrols th' ligislachure, baptizes th' young, marries th' foolish, comforts th' afflicted, afflicts th' comfortable, buries th' dead an' roasts thim aftherward."

Verdict: Credit Mr. Dooley.

"Never COMPLAIN, never explain." In 1974 Henry Ford II was arrested for driving under the influence in Santa Barbara, California, accompanied by a young woman who was not his wife. Asked for an explanation, Ford said, "Never complain, never explain." These words were fed to him by his English public relations adviser. It was the motto of Benjamin Disraeli (1804–1881), and was subsequently picked up by Stanley Baldwin (1867–1947), Disraeli's successor as Britain's prime minister, then passed along to others. Variations on this theme—especially "Never apologize. Never explain."—have been attributed to everyone from Oxford University's Benjamin Jowett through British Admiral Jacky Fisher to John Wayne. And, of course, Henry Ford II.

Verdict: Credit Disraeli.

"Nothing CONCENTRATES the mind so wonderfully as the prospect of being hanged." This thought is usually attributed correctly to Samuel Johnson (though it has been attributed incorrectly to Camus and to Twain). Nonetheless, we are more likely to get the gist of Dr. Johnson's sentiment correctly than his actual words. According to James Boswell, what Johnson said, with reference to the unusually vigorous writing of a condemned forger, was "Depend upon it, Sir, when a man knows he is to be hanged in a fortnight, it concentrates his mind wonderfully."

Verdict: Credit Samuel Johnson for the thought, and his version of the words.

"CONSISTENCY is the hobgoblin of small minds." This popular saying is an oversimplified excerpt from Emerson's more nuanced thought in his 1841 essay "Self-Reliance": "A foolish consistency is the hobgoblin of little minds, adored by little statesmen and philosophers and divines."

Verdict: Simplified Emerson.

"CONTEMPT prior to investigation." This popular observation is widely attributed to philosopher Herbert Spencer: "There is a principle which is a bar against all information, which is proof against all arguments, and which cannot fail to keep a man in everlasting ignorance—that principle is contempt prior to investigation." What makes this observation so popular is that it justifies those with all manner of "alternative" approaches: homeopaths, chiropractors, herbalists, and the like. To encourage those who are skeptical of its faith-based approach to substance abuse, since 1939 Alcoholics Anonymous has included this quotation, attributed to Spencer, in twenty million copies of its book *Alcoholics Anonymous.* In a remarkable

piece of research, writer Michael StGeorge made exhaustive efforts to locate the original expression of this thought by Herbert Spencer. Despite the fact that various sources, including scholarly ones, cited works by Spencer as the source of this quotation, StGeorge could find it nowhere in any work they cited, or in anything else written by Spencer. StGeorge did find this passage in *A View of the Evidences of Christianity,* a 1794 book by British theologian William Paley: "The infidelity of the Gentile world, and that more especially of men of rank and learning in it, is resolved into a principle which, in my judgment, will account for the inefficacy of any argument, or any evidence whatever, *viz.* contempt prior to examination." StGeorge subsequently found a revision of Paley's words in an 1879 book that was close to the version usually attributed to Spencer. The earliest attribution to Spencer he found was in separate 1931 publications written by two homeopaths. (Their version was identical to the one Alcoholics Anonymous subsequently attributed to Spencer.) George Seldes included the erroneous Spencer attribution in his 1960 book *The Great Quotations.* By now this ascription is so taken for granted that StGeorge even found it in a 1995 book written by a Columbia University Ph.D. A search of the Internet turned up more than forty-two hundred hits attributing the quotation to Spencer, only seven attributing it to its actual author, William Paley. Others to whom variations on the "contempt prior to investigation" theme have been attributed include Chaucer, Franklin, Emerson, Edison, Einstein, and Hemingway.

Verdict: Credit William Paley as the originator of this thought, not Herbert Spencer.

"As long as I COUNT the votes, what are you going to do about it?" This arrogant response to those who questioned his political methods is the legacy of William Marcy "Boss" Tweed (1823–1878). During his lifetime the corrupt leader of New York's Tammany Hall repeatedly disavowed that statement, and with good reason. *Harper's Weekly* cartoonist Thomas Nast put the words in Tweed's mouth. One Nast cartoon showed Boss Tweed's thumb resting heavily on New York City. Its caption read: "The Boss. 'Well, what are you going to do about it?'" Another portrayed a tiger ravaging innocents in a stadium as Tweed and his cronies, dressed in Roman garb, enjoyed the spectacle. The caption of this cartoon was "THE TAMMANY TIGER LOOSE—'What are you going to do about it?'" In time, reporters, historians, and the public at large assumed these words were actually Tweed's. *Bartlett's* still does.

Verdict: Absolve Tweed; credit Nast.

"My COUNTRY, right or wrong, but my country." According to an 1848 biography of Commodore Stephen Decatur (1779–1820), the American naval officer gave this toast at an 1816 gathering in Norfolk, Virginia: "Our country! In her intercourse with foreign nations, may she always be in the right; but our country, right or wrong." In the same year that Decatur made his toast, a magazine reported his words as *"Our country—In her intercourse with foreign nationals may she always be in the right, and always successful, right or wrong."* (Italics in the original.)

   Verdict: Credit Stephen Decatur for some version of this famous vow.

"One man with COURAGE makes a majority." When he nominated Robert Bork to the Supreme Court in 1987, Ronald Reagan noted, "Andrew Jackson once said that one man with courage makes a majority. Obviously, Bob Bork has that courage." In his foreword to a young people's edition of *Profiles in Courage,* Robert Kennedy had so quoted Jackson, but without a citation. After World War II, Robert's brother John scribbled this Jackson quotation in his notebook, without a source. By tradition, in some form this is something the seventh U.S. president said. Each volume of a three-volume 1860 biography of Jackson includes as an epigraph "Desperate courage makes one a majority," implying that this was its subject's credo. Two decades later an 1881 publication called this a "Jacksonian motto." According to some sources that declaration can be found in Jackson's 1832 message to Congress vetoing renewal of a national bank charter. It can't. The genesis of this motto can be found in an inscription on the Reformation Monument in Geneva, which credits John Knox with saying, "A man with God is always in the majority." (*"Un homme avec Dieu est toujours dans la majorité."*) Over time many others picked up that beat ("One, on God's side, is a majority," Wendell Phillips; "Any man more right than his neighbors constitutes a majority of one," Henry David Thoreau; "One man with the law is a majority," Calvin Coolidge). Although Andrew Jackson is no less likely than anyone else to have adopted and adapted the Knox maxim, we have no conclusive proof that he did.

   Verdict: Modular old saw, possibly adapted by Andrew Jackson.

"Two o'clock in the morning COURAGE." Historian Emmanuel, Comte de Las Cases, recorded the former emperor's last conversations during his exile on St. Helena. According to de las Cases, "As for moral courage, Napoleon said, he had rarely encountered the 'courage of 2 A.M.'—that is, the extemporaneous courage which, even in the most sudden emergencies, leaves one's freedom of mind, judgment, and decision completely unaf-

fected. He asserted unequivocally that he had known himself to possess that 2 A.M. courage to a higher degree than any other man." Nearly four decades after Napoleon made this observation, Thoreau wrote in *Walden* of "The three-o'-clock-in-the-morning courage which Bonaparte thought was the rarest." In the inflationary 1980s, a character in Paul Theroux's novel *Mosquito Coast* twice referred to "four-o'clock-in-the-morning courage," without making reference to Napoleon. In *Civil War,* the book accompanying their PBS special on that topic, Geoffrey Ward with Ric and Ken Burns also referred to "four-o'clock-in-the-morning courage."

Verdict: Credit Napoleon, at two A.M.

"There is no limit to the good a man can do, if he doesn't care who gets the CREDIT." Variations on this theme have been attributed to Ronald Reagan (who put a sign with that saying on his desk), an aide to Gen. George Marshall (who also had the saying on his desk), Harry Truman, Dwight Eisenhower, Deepak Chopra, Rev. Dwight Moody, and others. Most often it is attributed to Benjamin Jowett (1817–1893), master of Oxford's Balliol College, though without a source. A version of the adage appeared without attribution in a 1903 issue of *The Friend: A Religious and Literary Journal,* and as "a saying" in C. E. Montague's book *Disenchantment* (1922).

Verdict: Credit Jowett, tentatively.

"Organized CRIME is bigger than U.S. Steel." When mobster Meyer Lansky died in 1983, the *New York Times* reported: "In a moment of triumph, Mr. Lansky once boasted to an underworld associate, 'We're bigger than U.S. Steel.'" That familiar quotation has a foggy history. While watching a 1962 television program on organized crime, Lansky might have murmured these words to his wife. The tape on which that comment allegedly appeared was recorded by FBI agents monitoring Lansky's hotel suite. Because this tape was later erased, we will never know if Lansky actually made that remark. Biographer Robert Lacey discovered in FBI files that Lansky's famous phrase was only the paraphrase of an agent reporting what he thought he'd heard on the tape. Over time this paraphrase was made into a direct quote and given dramatic play in *Life, Time,* and many other publications. In *The Godfather II,* the Lansky-inspired Hyman Roth (played by Lee Strasberg) says of his criminal operation, "We're bigger than U.S. Steel!" Lansky himself denied saying any such thing. Lacey doubted that he did. But those compelling words became a quote that wouldn't die.

Verdict: Probably a figment of an FBI agent's overactive imagination.

"When I hear the word CULTURE, I reach for my gun." Although commonly attributed to Hitler henchman Hermann Goering, this line appeared in a clumsier form in *Schlageter,* a 1933 play by Nazi poet Hanns Johst: "Wenn ich Kulture hore . . . entsichere ich meinen Browning." Two translations of the line in question are "Whenever I hear the word culture . . . I release the safety-catch of my Browning [pistol]," and "When I hear the word culture, I uncock my revolver's safety catch."

Verdict: Credit Hanns Johst, not Hermann Goering, for a clumsy original version of this line.

"CUT to the chase." In classic Hollywood Westerns, a static scene would quickly shift to an active one when a group of mounted good guys threw up furious clouds of dust as they chased a group of mounted bad guys. This was called "cutting to the chase," a phrase that dates back to the early days of moviemaking. (*Hollywood Girl,* a 1929 novel by sometime screenwriter J. P. McEvoy, included a brief mock movie script that directed, "Cut to chase" three times.) In recent decades "cut to the chase" has jumped the fences of moviemaking to become synonymous with "Get to the point." Rare in the 1970s, this usage became more and more common as show-business terminology grew increasingly ubiquitous in everyday discourse. In the 1980s "Cut to the chase" was cited as moviemaker parlance when films were being discussed, then became a phrase commonly used by members of the cultural avant-garde. By the 1990s this catchphrase was ubiquitous in its generic, multipurpose form.

Verdict: Vintage moviemaking terminology of uncertain parentage.

"No matter how CYNICAL you get, you can't keep up." Sometimes misattributed to Woody Allen, this much-quoted insight comes from a line written by Lily Tomlin's longtime collaborator Jane Wagner and delivered by Tomlin herself in *The Search for Signs of Intelligent Life in the Universe.* In that play, Tomlin's bag lady, Trudy, says, "I worry no matter how cynical you become, it's never enough to keep up."

Verdict: Credit Jane Wagner for the words, Lily Tomlin as their spokesperson.

"If I can't DANCE, it's not my revolution." Although it is generally attributed to Emma Goldman (1869–1940), the festive anarchist never made this assertion. After extensive research, biographer Alix Kates Shulman concluded that the closest words Goldman ever wrote were in her 1931 autobiography: "At the dances I was one of the most untiring and gayest.

One evening a cousin of Sasha, a young boy, took me aside. With a grave face, as if he were about to announce the death of a dear comrade, he whispered to me that it did not behoove an agitator to dance. Certainly not with such reckless abandon, anyway. It was undignified for one who was on the way to become a force in the anarchist movement. My frivolity would only hurt the Cause. . . . I was tired of having the Cause constantly thrown into my face. I did not believe that a Cause which stood for a beautiful ideal, for anarchism, for release and freedom from conventions and prejudice, should demand the denial of life and joy. I insisted that our Cause could not expect me to become a nun and that the movement should not be turned into a cloister." So where did the bumper-stickered version come from? Shulman thinks she herself may have been its source, indirectly. In 1973, an anarchist printer named Jack Frager asked the feminist writer for a slogan to accompany a picture of Red Emma on T-shirts he planned to sell as a fund-raiser. Shulman referred him to the passage above. The T-shirts that resulted read, "If I can't dance, I don't want to be in your revolution." Since the cause was just, and the sentiment "pure Emma," Shulman didn't point out its historical inaccuracy. Little did she know that this small seed would bloom into a thousand flowers of posters, bumper stickers, and sundry other applications of the apocryphal Goldman quotation.

Verdict: Credit Jack Frager, with help from Alix Kates Shulman, for a condensation of Emma Goldman's sentiments.

"There's a DANCE in the old dame yet." This was the oft-repeated motto of Mehitabel, an aging alley cat who claimed to have been Cleopatra in an earlier life. Mehitabel and her friend Archy the cockroach were created by humorist Don Marquis (1878–1937). The cat's signature line appeared often in *archy and mehitabel* (1927). That book includes "the song of mehitabel." This piece of free verse is written ee cummings–like in lowercase, as is the book as a whole, because its feline author couldn't reach her typewriter's shift key. Mehitabel's poem includes this stanza: "my youth i shall never forget / but there s nothing i really regret / wotthehell wotthehell / there s a dance in the old dame yet / toujours gai toujours gai."

Verdict: Credit Don Marquis.

"It was a DARK and stormy night." The first few words of the 1830 novel *Paul Clifford* by Edward Bulwer-Lytton have become so synonymous with banal writing that an annual "Bulwer-Lytton Fiction Contest" rewards those who come up with the most hackneyed opening to a novel.

The entire first sentence of *Paul Clifford* reads, "It was a dark and stormy night; the rain fell in torrents—except at occasional intervals, when it was checked by a violent gust of wind which swept up the streets (for it is in London that our scene lies), rattling along the house-tops, and fiercely agitating the scanty flame of the lamps that struggled against the darkness."

Verdict: Credit Edward Bulwer-Lytton.

"Murder your DARLINGS." This common admonition to writers (suggesting that they excise the parts of their work that most delight them) is widely misattributed to the likes of Samuel Johnson, Oscar Wilde, George Orwell, F. Scott Fitzgerald, Dorothy Parker, and William Faulkner. Its actual author was Sir Arthur Quiller-Couch, who wrote in *The Art of Writing* (1916), "Whenever you feel an impulse to perpetrate a piece of exceptionally fine writing, obey it—whole-heartedly—and delete it before sending your manuscript to press. *Murder your darlings.*" (Italics in original.)

Verdict: Credit Arthur Quiller-Couch.

"In the long run, we are all DEAD." In his 1924 book *A Tract on Monetary Reform,* John Maynard Keynes debunked economic theories based on extended timelines, ones often introduced with the phrase "in the long run." "But this *long run* is a misleading guide to current affairs," Keynes wrote. *"In the long run* we are all dead." (Italics his.) That observation by Keynes is continually requoted. Although usually attributed to him, it has been misattributed to economist John Kenneth Galbraith.

Verdict: Credit Keynes.

"A single DEATH is a tragedy. A million deaths is a statistic." In his 1965 novel *The Spy Who Came in from the Cold,* John le Carré quoted Joseph Stalin as having said, "Half a million liquidated is a statistic, but one man killed in a traffic accident is a national tragedy." Seven years earlier, in 1958, similar words were attributed to Stalin in a *New York Times* book review: "A single death is a tragedy, a million deaths is a statistic." Various versions of this cynical observation are typically attributed to Stalin, one of history's great cynics. No source is usually given, however, presumably because none exists. It doesn't show up in credible biographies of Stalin, and the editor of a book of his letters said not only that he'd never seen this saying in Stalin's writing but that it didn't even sound like him. Lenin has also been credited with the observation, as has Hitler henchman Heinrich Himmler. In a 1961 speech Robert Kennedy said, "Killing one man is

murder. Killing millions is a statistic." Twelve years later George McGovern applied this conclusion to the "body counts" that were popular during the Vietnam War.

Verdict: Words put in Stalin's mouth.

"The reports of my DEATH are greatly exaggerated." In 1897, Mark Twain's cousin, Jim Clemens, lay gravely ill (but survived). Confusing Twain with his cousin, the *New York Journal* sent a reporter to find out whether Twain himself was dying, or was already dead. Twain sent the reporter back with this note: "James Ross Clemens, a cousin of mine, was seriously ill two or three weeks ago in London but is well now. The report of my illness grew out of his illness; the report of my death was an exaggeration." A decade later, the author wrote that what he'd told a reporter about his alleged fatal illness was: "Say the report is exaggerated." Twain subsequently retyped this recollection, now scribbling "greatly" in front of "exaggerated" before mailing it to *The North American Review,* where it was published. According to this memoir, he had originally advised press inquirers to "Say the report is greatly exaggerated." Twain hadn't, of course. He was misquoting himself. But the revised version is more compelling than the original. It's the one that has lasted, typically said to have been a cable Mark Twain sent to the newspapers in New York.

Verdict: Credit Twain for both coining and improving this witticism.

"No one on his DEATHBED ever said, 'I wish I had spent more time on my business.'" In the early 1980s, a Massachusetts lawyer named Arnold Zack made this observation to his friend Paul Tsongas. Tsongas, then a U.S. senator, was suffering from the lymphoma that eventually killed him. Zack believes the thought was original to him. Tsongas repeated his friend's observation in a 1984 book. Although reviewers of this book often noted Zack's words, few mentioned his name. Tsongas himself sometimes got credit for the saying. Today this popular maxim, usually ending "more time at the office," is sometimes simply called "an old saying," "an old joke," or is introduced with the phrase "as they say . . ." It has also been attributed to or claimed by many others, including author H. Jackson Brown, Jr., presidential aide Vincent Foster, ex-congresswoman Pat Schroeder, executive-author Harvey MacKay (who calls the "office" version "MacKay's Moral"), Rabbi Harold Kushner (who quoted Zack's line in a 1986 book, crediting a friend of Tsongas), and sundry other members of the clergy. No attribution has more credibility than the one to Arnold Zack.

Verdict: Credit Arnold Zack.

"No good DEED goes unpunished." This epigram has floated about for decades in search of an author. Playwright-diplomat Clare Boothe Luce sometimes gets credit. So do Oscar Wilde, Gore Vidal, banker Andrew W. Mellon, and seventeenth-century English minister Thomas Brooks. A biographer attributed the quip to playwright and wit Noel Coward. In *Here at The New Yorker,* Brendan Gill said the thought originated with his uncle Arthur Knox. A wide range of other possible authors has been suggested. None are definitive.

    Verdict: Author yet to be determined.

"DEMOCRACY is the worst form of government except for all those other forms that have been tried from time to time." Winston Churchill said this during a 1947 speech to the House of Commons, and is generally credited with the remark. However, Churchill introduced his observation with the words "it has been said." His full statement was "Many forms of government have been tried, and will be tried in this world of sin and woe. No one pretends that democracy is perfect or all-wise. Indeed, it has been said that democracy is the worst form of government except all those other forms that have been tried from time to time."

    Verdict: Credit Churchill as publicist for the words of an unknown aphorist.

"We had to DESTROY the village in order to save it." This is by far the most familiar quotation to emerge from the Vietnam War. These few words seemed to capture perfectly the absurd futility of America's presence in Vietnam. They were originally reported by Peter Arnett of the Associated Press, who quoted an unidentified American officer on why the village of Ben Tre was leveled during the Tet Offensive in early 1968: "It became necessary to destroy the town in order to save it." A two-paragraph version of the AP dispatch was buried on page 14 of the *New York Times,* with no byline. Other newspapers substituted the word "village" for "town." Due to Peter Arnett's solid reputation as a reporter, this quotation was not questioned at the time. Eventually, however, doubts were expressed about its authenticity. For one thing, Ben Tre was not a town but a provincial capital of fifty thousand. For another, although heavily damaged by fighting, Ben Tre was not leveled. Only a handful of American soldiers took part in combat there. Their senior officer, army major Phil Cannella, later recalled telling Arnett that it was unfortunate that some of Ben Tre was destroyed in the course of its defense. Canella thought he might have said at most, "It was a shame the town was destroyed." Cannella, who later turned

against the war, believes Arnett may have embellished this comment by him. Arnett himself has steadfastly refused to identify the source of this famous quotation. He did tell writer Peter Braestrup it was one of four officers he'd interviewed on that day in 1968. As Braestrup pointed out in his book *Big Story,* the day before Arnett's story ran, columnist James Reston wrote in his *New York Times* column, "How do we win by military force without destroying what we are trying to save?" Reston's column concluded, "How will we save Vietnam if we destroy it in battle?"

Verdict: A quotation this seminal needs better confirmation.

"The DEVIL is in the details." Architect Mies van der Rohe (1886–1969) was fond of observing that "God is in the details." He may have picked up the saying from Aby Warburg (1866–1929), a distinguished German art historian who liked to say, "The good God is in the details." This may be no more than a traditional German proverb. A French version, *"Le bon Dieu est dans le détail,"* has been attributed to Flaubert, but without a source. In the mid-seventeenth century, Amsterdam professor Caspar Barleaus wrote, "Believe me that in the smallest particle God is enshrined." The Christian conviction that God resided in every detail of the world antedated this observation. In recent times, Lucifer replaced the Lord in what's become the more common version of van der Rohe's credo. One disseminator of this version, Adm. Hyman Rickover (1900–1986), liked to say, "The devil is in the details, and everything we do in the military is a detail." A 1978 news article called this variant "an old German saying." That saying, *"Der Teufel steckt im Detail,"* shows up in books of German idioms. (An English variant is "The devil is in the dice.") In *Your Own Words* (2004), language maven Barbara Wallraff noted that before presidential aspirant H. Ross Perot began using the devil version in the early 1990s, neither saying was especially common or favored in the United States. Since then the "devil" version has become more widespread. The unanswered question is, which came first: God or the Devil?

Verdict: Proverbial wisdom.

"The greatest trick the DEVIL ever pulled was convincing the world he didn't exist." This line from the 1995 movie *The Usual Suspects* owes an unacknowledged debt to Charles Baudelaire's 1864 story "The Generous Gambler." That story depicts a preacher who shouts from his pulpit, "My dear brothers, when you hear the progress of the enlightenment extolled, never forget that the devil's cleverest trick is to persuade you that he does not exist!" Whether the French writer originated this comment is unknown.

In the years since his story was published, that thought has been borrowed by sundry preachers, theologians, and screenwriters.

Verdict: Credit Baudelaire as propagator of this quotation, and possibly as its author.

"Better to DIE on our feet than live on our knees." Franklin D. Roosevelt made that vow while accepting an honorary degree from Oxford University in 1941. Republican firebrand Dolores Ibarruri ("La Pasionaria") said this repeatedly during the 1936–1939 Spanish Civil War. Ibarruri may have been inspired by Mexican revolutionary Emiliano Zapata, who reportedly said two decades earlier, "Better to die on your feet than live on your knees." (*"Es mejor morir de pie que vivir de rodillas."*) Although it is unlikely that Zapata spoke Yiddish, "Better to die upright than to live on your knees" is called a Yiddish proverb by proverb scholar Wolfgang Mieder. In 1866, a Quaker teacher in Virginia quoted a recently freed slave as saying, "It 'pears like, miss, we should *live* on our knees, for this great blessed freedom we now have."

Verdict: Too old and too obvious an idea for specific attribution.

"I DISAPPROVE of what you say, but will defend to the death your right to say it." This most familiar of quotations is usually attributed to Voltaire. However, the closest known words of Voltaire's that anyone has ever found are from his essay "Tolerance": "Think for yourself, and let others enjoy the privilege to do so, too." The more memorable sentence originated with Voltaire biographer Evelyn Beatrice Hall (using the pen name S. G. Tallentyre), who composed it in 1906 to characterize Voltaire's attitude toward a colleague's writing. For added weight, Hall put her composition in quotation marks, as if this sentence came straight from Voltaire's mouth, or pen. Twenty-eight years later, the *Reader's Digest* published the biographer's words over her subject's name as a "Quotable Quote."

Verdict: Credit Evelyn Beatrice Hall, not Voltaire.

"A house DIVIDED against itself cannot stand." Abraham Lincoln's famous "House Divided" speech drew on biblical antecedents, especially Mark 3:25: "And if a house be divided against itself, that house cannot stand." But the genesis of this saying is not just scriptural. As Wolfgang Mieder has explored meticulously in *"A House Divided": From Biblical Proverb to Lincoln and Beyond* (1996), this New Testament advisory had become secularized long before Lincoln made it the centerpiece of his 1858 speech in Springfield, Illinois. As early as 1704, a New England

Quaker recorded in a journal his mother's frequent admonition that "A house divided could not stand." Thomas Paine's *Common Sense* (1776) included the phrase "a house divided against itself." In 1793, America's ambassador to France, Gouverneur Morris, wrote to George Washington, "I am induced to quote a sound maxim from an excellent book;—'A house divided against itself cannot stand.'" By the early nineteenth century, different versions of this proverb were used frequently in political discourse, especially by Andrew Jackson. In 1850 Texas senator Sam Houston warned that "a nation divided against itself cannot stand," the earliest known application of the proverb to America's growing fissure over slavery. A year later Daniel Webster said in an antislavery speech, "If a house be divided against itself, it will fall, and crush every body in it." Similar observations were increasingly common in the run-up to the Civil War. Presumably Abraham Lincoln was familiar with at least some of them by the time he too warned of "a house divided." As Wolfgang Mieder points out, Lincoln admired Webster, and used an earlier speech by the Massachusetts senator as source material for his own in 1858.

Verdict: Biblical wisdom with many iterations before Lincoln took it over.

"*Those who can, DO. Those who can't, teach.*" The "Maxims for Revolutionists" in George Bernard Shaw's *Man and Superman* (1903) included "He who can, does. He who cannot, teaches." In his usual ham-handed revision style, turn-of-century aphorist Elbert Hubbard (1856–1915) transformed this to "Folks who can, do; those who can't, chin." Shaw's version has been misattributed to H. L. Mencken. In our gender-neutral times, this thought is more often expressed as "Those who can, do. Those who can't, teach."

Verdict: Credit Shaw.

"*It's not that he DOES it well, but that he does it at all.*" According to a *TV Guide* writer "A critic once wrote of a one-legged tap dancer: 'The miracle is not that he does it well, but that he does it at all.'" If this is so, that critic borrowed liberally from Samuel Johnson's classic observation about a Quakeress who gave a sermon: As James Boswell wrote of a 1763 exchange in his *Life of Johnson*: "I told him I had been that morning at a meeting of the people called Quakers, where I had heard a woman preach. Johnson: 'Sir, a woman's preaching is like a dog's walking on his hinder legs. It is not done well; but you are surprised to find it done at all.'" In some versions Johnson is misremembered as having referred to a dog talking, or playing the fiddle.

Verdict: Adapted Johnson.

"If you want a friend in Washington, get a DOG." Truman Library archivists question the common attribution of this quip to the thirty-third U.S. president. They point out that Truman spent much of his young manhood on a farm, where dogs were helpers more than pets. Harry and his wife, Bess, had no particular fondness for dogs, and gave away the two that were given to them while they lived in the White House. So why is "If you want a friend in Washington, get a dog" so routinely attributed to Harry Truman? Because the script of Samuel Gallu's 1975 play, *Give 'em Hell, Harry,* had Truman saying, "You want a friend in life, get a dog!" This script was subsequently published in book form. A few years later *New York Times* correspondent Maureen Dowd attributed the remark to Truman (with "Washington" taking the place of "life"), as did President Bill Clinton. Clinton's predecessor, George H. W. Bush, more accurately credited the quip to "some cynic."

Verdict: An old saw put in Harry Truman's mouth.

"Any man who hates DOGS and children can't be all bad." W. C. Fields's credo was actually said *about* the comedian, not *by* him. At a 1939 Masquers banquet in Fields's honor, Leo Rosten, at the time a young sociologist studying the movie industry, was invited to say a few words about the featured guest. Rosten blurted out, "The only thing I can say about Mr. W. C. Fields, whom I have admired since the day he advanced upon Baby LeRoy with an ice pick, is this: Any man who hates babies and dogs can't be all bad." Two weeks later Rosten's quip was mentioned in *Time* magazine. Since so few people had heard of Leo Rosten at the time, it didn't take long for his words to land in Fields's own mouth, where they've stayed ever since. Rosten wasn't the first one to use this line, however. Nearly two years before the Masquers banquet, *Harper's Monthly* ran a column by Cedric Worth about a 1930 New York cocktail party that featured a man who had a case against dogs. After leaving the party, Worth found himself in an elevator with *New York Times* reporter Byron Darnton. As the elevator made its way to the ground, Darnton observed, "No man who hates dogs and children can be all bad."

Verdict: Credit Byron Darnton as originator, Leo Rosten as publicist.

"The better I get to know men, the more I find myself loving DOGS." ("Plus je apprend à connaître l'homme, plus je apprend à estimer le chien.") This observation is generally credited to Charles de Gaulle, apparently on the basis of a 1967 attribution in a *Time* magazine article about a collection of the French president's remarks. In centuries past

many other French natives have been credited with the same basic thought. They include the inimitable letter-writer Madame de Sévigné (Marie de Rabutin-Chantal, Marquise de Sévigné, 1626–1696), the revolutionary writer Madame Roland (Marie-Jeanne Philipon, 1754–1793), author-politician Alphonse de Lamartine (1790–1869), author Alphonse Toussenel (1803–1885), and author Louise de la Ramée (1839–1908).

Verdict: Charles de Gaulle was the most recent spokesperson for a long-standing Gallic take on humanity.

"He marches to a different DRUMMER." In the last chapter of *Walden* (1854), Henry David Thoreau (1817–1862) wrote, "If a man does not keep pace with his companions, perhaps it is because he hears a different drummer." According to a literary review published in 1880, an unpublished manuscript Thoreau once read to a group of listeners in Concord included a more personalized version: "If I do not keep step with my companions it is because I hear a different drummer."

Verdict: Credit Thoreau, for a longer assertion than the more common, more compressed version.

"There's more old DRUNKARDS than there are old doctors." Poor Richard's "There's more old drunkards than old doctors" echoed an earlier comment by François Rabelais (circa 1483–1553), "A hundred devils leap into my body, if there are not more old drunkards than old physicians." (*"Cent diables me saultent au corps s'il n'y a plus de vieux hyurognes, qu'il n'y a de vieux medecins."*) The quip later showed up in a 1963 Willie Nelson song: "But there's more old drunks than there are old doctors / So I guess we'd better have another round."

Verdict: Credit Rabelais.

"The DUSTBIN of history." This is where Bolshevik Leon Trotsky consigned rival Mensheviks during the Russian Revolution in 1917. "You are pitiful isolated individuals," Trotsky told them. "You are bankrupts; your role is played out. Go where you belong from now on—into the dustbin of history!" A different translation of Trotsky's history of the Russian Revolution substituted the term "rubbish-can of history." According to Russian-speaking writer Keith Gessen, the term Trotsky used, *svalka,* was originally translated by John Reed as "garbage heap," but was toned down to "dust heap," or "dustbin" over time. Although Trotsky's exclamation thrust the term "dustbin of history" into the vernacular, it was not original to him. In an 1884 essay, English author-statesman Augustine Birrell (1850–1933)

referred to "that great dust-heap called 'history.'" This suggests either that Trotsky read Birrell, or, more likely, that this catchphrase was in popular play at the time.

Verdict: Trotsky's popularization of a preexisting concept.

"DUTY, then, is the sublimest word in our language. Do your duty in all things. . . . You cannot do more, you should never wish to do less." For years after Robert E. Lee's death in 1870, this thought—said to have been excerpted from an 1852 letter to his son G. W. Custis Lee—was considered one of the Confederate general's most eloquent statements. Questions were raised soon after its 1864 appearance in print, however, and in 1914 University of Virginia law professor Charles Graves gave a long paper summarizing the evidence that this supposed piece of writing by Lee was spurious. Since then no serious scholar has taken Lee's "Duty Letter" seriously.

Verdict: Apocryphal Lee.

"DYING is easy. Comedy is hard." In the 1982 movie *My Favorite Year,* an aging movie star played by Peter O'Toole says, "Dying is easy. Comedy is hard." Some think that this famous observation originated with English actor Edmund Kean (1789–1833). More often it is attributed to Welsh actor Edmund Gwenn (1875–1959). On his deathbed, in response to the comment, "It must be very hard," Gwenn supposedly responded, "It is. But not as hard as farce." In another version Gwenn responded, "Oh, it's hard, very hard indeed. But not as hard as doing comedy," when Jack Lemmon observed that facing death must be hard. Yet another account had director George Seaton playing straight man in that exchange. (Lemmon's biographer gave the nod to Seaton.) Others to whom the deathbed quip has been attributed include Groucho Marx, Stan Laurel, Marcel Marceau, Noel Coward, Oscar Wilde, David Garrick, and Sir Donald Wolfit. This exchange almost certainly comes under the heading of spurious "famous last words" that were later put in the mouth of the deceased.

Verdict: Invented "last words" making the show business rounds.

"DYING is no big deal, the least of us will manage that. Living is the trick." Sportswriter Red Smith is famous for having said this during a eulogy for a friend. In his exhaustive encyclopedia of world proverbs, Wolfgang Mieder cites "To die is easy, to live is hard" as a Japanese proverb, and "It is hard to die but it is harder to live" as one from the Philippines. In 1942, Bulgarian-British author Elias Canetti wrote, "Dying is too easy. It

ought to be much harder to die," and in 1769 Samuel Johnson said, "It matters not how a man dies, but how he lives."

Verdict: Red Smith's take on an old idea.

"You are what you EAT." During the 1960s, this became a counterculture catchphrase, sometimes misattributed to Karl Marx. It was German philosopher Ludwig Feuerbach, however, who in 1850 punned in his own language *"Man ist was man isst."* ("Man is what he eats.") A quarter century earlier, French politician Anthelme Brillat-Savarin wrote, "Tell me what you eat, and I will tell you what you are." (*"Dis-moi ce que tu manges, je te dirai ce que tu es."*)

Verdict: A collaboration between Ludwig Feuerbach and Anthelme Brillat-Savarin.

"An EDITOR is one who separates the wheat from the chaff and prints the chaff." This witticism is routinely attributed to Adlai Stevenson (1900–1965). However, when Stevenson was still a child, aphorist Elbert Hubbard (1856–1915) defined "Editor" as "A person employed on a newspaper, whose business it is to separate the wheat from the chaff, and to see that the chaff is printed." Since Hubbard was a chronic thief of other people's ideas, it's unlikely that this thought began with him. He may have been inspired by Oscar Wilde's observation in *The Ballad of Reading Gaol* (1898) that every man-made law "straws the wheat and saves the chaff."

Verdict: An old notion applied to editors, by Elbert Hubbard in any event.

ALBERT EINSTEIN

Albert Einstein had his secretary give this definition of "relativity" to the many reporters who inquired: **"An hour sitting with a pretty girl on a park bench passes like a minute; but a minute sitting on a hot stove seems like an hour."** Since he expressed himself in such plain, vivid language, Einstein was an eminently quotable figure. The brilliant physicist also played an important iconic role by being so intellectually accessible. When the human embodiment of genius made comprehensible observations, we felt reassured. Einstein's many warnings about the perils of unbridled technological advance confirmed our own suspicions. His compelling commentary on a wide range of subjects made the German-born physicist a sort of Emerson with an accent. We loved and love to quote Albert Einstein.

As a result, since his death in 1955, Einstein has become a primary source of things he never said. The physicist himself noted, "Many things which go under my name are badly translated from the German or are invented by other people." Because Einstein's name is synonymous with brilliance, any orphan quotation that sounds genius-like is liable to end up in his mouth. Because he so improbably believed in the power of imagination, spiritual reverence, clear expression, and the limits of technology, Einstein's comments along these lines are often quoted, along with a wide range of comments he never made.

Fortunately, based on more than two decades of work with Einstein's papers, Alice Calaprice has been able to verify or debunk a wide range of his quotations. In some cases the German-speaking editor has done her own translations. Calaprice's results are gathered in *The New Quotable Einstein*. The following assessment of Einstein's most popular quotations, and misquotations, draws on that resource, and others as well.

"God does not play dice." This is a condensation of Einstein's 1926 observation about God in a letter to Max Born: "I, at any rate, am convinced that He is not playing at dice." (Calaprice's translation is "I, in any case, am convinced that *He* does not play dice.") Sixteen years later, in 1942, Einstein reiterated this conviction in different words: "It is hard to sneak a look at God's cards. But that he would choose to play dice with the world . . . is something I cannot believe for a single moment." Biographer Phillip Frank quotes Einstein as having said, "I shall never believe," and "I cannot believe that God plays dice with the world." Obviously this thought was much on Einstein's mind. Frank also quoted Einstein as having said, "God is sophisticated, but he is not malicious."

"Science without religion is lame, religion without science is blind." Einstein made this observation during a 1941 New York symposium titled "Science, Philosophy and Religion." He subsequently observed that "Epistemology without contact with science becomes an empty scheme. Science without epistemology is—insofar as it is thinkable at all—primitive and muddled." Noting that Einstein was not above adapting ideas already expressed by others, Alice Calaprice called attention to this antecedent from Immanuel Kant, a philosopher Einstein admired: "Notion without intuition is empty, intuition without notion is blind."

"The unleashed power of the atom has changed everything save our modes of thinking, and thus we drift toward unparalleled catastrophe." Various versions of this 1946 comment by Einstein are tossed about, usually in crisper form. In 1991, for example, Sen. Daniel Patrick Moynihan referred to "something Einstein said once: 'Everything is changed, except our way of thinking.'"

"I do not know how the Third World War will be fought, but I can tell you what they will use in the fourth—rocks!" Einstein said this in a 1949 interview.

"I have no special talents. I am only passionately curious." Einstein observed this about himself to biographer Carl Seelig, among others.

"Imagination is more important than knowledge." Einstein was so quoted in a 1929 *Saturday Evening Post* profile.

Like Lincoln, Twain, Churchill, and others, Einstein has had many quotations put in his mouth by those who believe that a few words on their behalf by the world's leading genius might bolster their cause. One particularly egregious example is a spurious Einstein quotation making favorable reference to astrology. The physicist has been widely, and inaccurately, quoted as saying that compounded interest, or the income tax, is harder to understand than his own theory of relativity. He is one among many who are credited with defining insanity as doing the same thing over and over, hoping for a different result. Einstein has also been mistakenly credited with **"God (or the DEVIL) is in the details."** Since he himself once quoted "a wit" as saying that education is what remains after one has forgotten everything learned in school, that commonplace is sometimes attributed to him and to many others as well. (The "wit" might have been humorist Kin Hubbard, who wrote, "It's what we learn after we think we know it all that counts." See sidebar "Humorists.")

Among a multitude of Einstein misquotations in circulation, these are the most common:

"Only twelve people in the world can understand my theory." When he visited the United States in 1921, Einstein made a point of denying that he ever made this uncharacteristic remark, which was often attributed to him.

"There is no hitching post in the universe." Einstein asked George Seldes to delete this observation from his compilation *Great Thoughts,* noting that it was a classic illustration of how he'd been misquoted. The quip was said to have been Einstein's response to a reporter's request for a one-line definition of his theory of relativity upon his arrival in New York in 1930. According to the *New York Times*'s account of that shipboard press conference, when asked to define his theory of relativity in one sentence, Einstein responded, "It would take me three days to give a short definition of relativity."

"If only I had known, I should have become a watchmaker." ("Plumber" is sometimes substituted for "watchmaker.") The obvious implication of this popular misquotation is that Einstein felt remorseful about a career in which he helped invent the atomic bomb. Einstein said no such thing. In a 1954 letter to the editor, the physicist did use similar words to make a very different point. Einstein's letter, in response to a series of articles in *The Reporter* magazine about scientists in America, included these lines: "If I would be a young man again and had to decide how to make my living, I would not try to become a scientist or scholar or teacher. I would rather choose to be a plumber or a peddler in the hope to find that modest degree of independence still available under present circumstances." On other occasions, the reclusive, violin-playing physicist said he might rather have been a musician, or lighthouse keeper.

"Heaven is like a library." Einstein was so quoted in the movie *IQ.* The more likely source of this analogy is Jorge Luis Borges's observation "I have always imagined that Paradise will be a kind of library."

"If you are out to describe the truth, leave elegance to the tailor." In the preface to his 1916 book *Relativity,* Einstein said he never concerned himself with elegance when trying to present his ideas clearly. "I adhered scrupulously to the precept of that brilliant theoretical physicist L. Boltzmann," he explained (referring to Austrian physicist Ludwig Boltzmann, 1844–1906), "according to whom matters of elegance ought to be left to the tailor and the cobbler." Boltzmann's precept is often attributed to Einstein himself.

"We use only 10 percent of our brains." According to Alice Calaprice, this commonly cited Einsteinism is apocryphal.

Other widely circulated quotations that Calaprice has concluded did not come from Einstein's mouth or pen include:

If you think intelligence is dangerous, try ignorance.

There is no hope for an idea that at first does not seem insane.

Common sense is the collection of prejudices acquired by age eighteen.

If the facts don't fit the theory, change the facts.

In the middle of every difficulty lies opportunity.

Not everything that counts can be counted, and not everything that can be counted counts.

There are only two ways to live your life. One is as though nothing is a miracle. The other is as though everything is a miracle.

"ELEMENTARY, my dear Watson." In the collected works of Sir Arthur Conan Doyle, these words are never uttered by Sherlock Holmes, or by anyone else. In Doyle's *The Crooked Man,* Dr. Watson does have this exchange with Holmes: "'Excellent!' I cried. '"Elementary," said he." The more familiar version first appeared in *The Return of Sherlock Holmes.* In this 1929 film (whose screenplay was written by Garrett Fort and Basil Dean), actor Clive Brook, who played Holmes, said, "Elementary, my dear Watson, elementary."

Verdict: Credit Arthur Conan Doyle for the inspiration, Garrett Fort and Basil Dean for the actual words.

"ELEVEN O'CLOCK Sunday morning is the most segregated hour in America." Martin Luther King, Jr., often made this observation in speeches and sermons during the 1950s and 60s. It is among his most famous quotations. But in one speech King prefaced the remark by saying, "*Still* the most segregated hour" (emphasis added), indicating that the thought had a longer provenance. In a 1960 *Reader's Digest* article, Billy Graham wrote, "It has become a byword that 'the most segregated hour of the week is still eleven o'clock Sunday morning.'" The use of the word "still" by both King and Graham suggests their awareness of how long this comment had been in circulation. Indeed, it appeared in the American press throughout the 1950s, as when Dr. Kenneth Miller, executive secretary of the New York Mission Society, told a 1953 conference, "What we have to do is practice brotherhood every day and stop having the 11 o'clock hour on Sunday [be] the most segregated hour of the week."

Verdict: King said it, as did Graham, and others before them.

RALPH WALDO EMERSON

A wise, but accessible, dead philosopher is bound to be a popular source of things he never said. Such is the case with Ralph Waldo Emerson. The transcendental clergyman-philosopher-essayist made so many quotable observations on such a wide range of subjects that he lends himself to misquotation. Emerson's writing teems with insightful comments—just not as many as we think. Since his death in 1882, this people's philosopher has been the subject of more than one controversy involving quotations he may or may not have originated. (See especially **"Build a better MOUSETRAP and the world will beat a path to your door."**)

Emerson himself was ambivalent about quoting others. "I hate quotations," he once wrote. "Tell me what you know." Yet Emerson himself was a constant quoter. "By necessity, by proclivity—and by delight, we all quote," he observed. And: "Next to the originator of a good sentence is the first quoter of it." In the process of quotation Emerson himself didn't always get it right. In his essay "Experience," the philosopher mistakenly attributed **"It's WORSE than a crime, it's a blunder!"** to Napoleon. Emerson also perpetrated this minor misquotation in alluding to an observation by Walter Scott: "Wherever Macdonald sits, there is the head of the table." Scott's own words were "Where MacGregor sits, there is the head of the table."

Emerson was not above borrowing thoughts from others. For example, he once wrote in his journal an observation now commonly attributed to him that begins, **"A man is known by the BOOKS he reads, by the company he keeps, by the praise he gives. . . ."** This drew on an earlier thought by one William Law: "We commonly say, that a man is known by his Companions; but it is certain, that a Man is much more known by the Books that he converses with."

According to a biographer, Emerson once told Oliver Wendell Holmes, **"When you strike at a king you must kill him."** Some sources say that "Never strike a king unless you are sure you shall kill him" can be found in Emerson's journal for September 1843, but it can't. In any event, this thought could well have been inspired by an English proverb from the early seventeenth century: "Whosoever draws his sword against the prince must throw the scabbard away."

In his essay "Worship," Emerson wrote, **"The louder he talked of his honor, the faster we counted our spoons."** The kernel of this remark apparently came from something Johnson told Boswell a century earlier: "If he does really think that there is no distinction between virtue and vice, why, sir, when he leaves our houses let us count our spoons." In *The Biglow Papers*, written in 1848, several years before Emerson wrote his essay, James Russell Lowell portrayed a semi-literate Massachusetts private in the Mexican War who writes home, "Ef these creeturs / Thet stick an Anglosaxon mask onto State-prison feeturs / Should come to Jaalam Centre fer to argify an' spout on 't, / The gals 'ould count the silver spoons the minnit they cleared out on 't." This suggests that "count your spoons" was a saying in common use long before it was requisitioned by Emerson.

Many of Emerson's own observations have entered the vernacular in a condensed form that alters their meaning. The phrase "a foolish," for example, is routinely omitted from his observation that **"A foolish CONSISTENCY is the hobgoblin of little minds. . . ."** **"What you do speaks so loud that I cannot hear what you say,"** often credited to Emerson, apparently is a condensation of something he wrote in *Letters and Social Aims:* "Don't say things. What you are stands over you the while, and thunders so that I cannot hear what you say to the contrary."

"Do not go where the path may lead; go instead where there is no path and leave a trail" is commonly attributed to Emerson. No source of this quotation has ever been found in his works or those of anyone else. Nor has **"What lies behind us / And what lies before us / Are tiny matters / Compared to what lies WITHIN us,"** also regularly attributed to Emerson without any evidence. The mini-essay beginning **"He has achieved SUCCESS, who has lived well, laughed often, and loved much . . ."** is routinely misattributed to him. Other quotations sometimes misattributed to Emerson include: **"We do not INHERIT the earth from our ancestors, we borrow it from our children,"** and **"I expect to PASS through this world but once. Any good therefore that I can do or any kindness that I can show to any fellow creatures, let me do it now."**

"We have met the ENEMY and he is us." In his foreword to *The Pogo Papers* (1953), cartoonist Walt Kelly wrote, "Resolve then, that on this very ground, with small flags waving and tinny blasts on tiny trumpets, we shall meet the enemy, and not only may he be ours, he may be us." Kelly later extracted the smoother, terser version, which became one of the most requoted lines of modern times after it appeared on a 1970 poster promoting the first Earth Day. In 1971 he drew a two-panel cartoon that depicted Pogo and his friend Porkypine examining junk littering their Okefenokee swamp. "It *is* hard walking on this stuff," says Porkypine. "Yep, son," responds Pogo. "We have met the enemy and he is us." To better suit gender-neutral sensibilities, the ending of this quotation is often altered to conclude "and it is us."
Verdict: Credit Walt Kelly.

"We have met the ENEMY and they are ours . . ." Following his 1813 victory over the British on Lake Erie, Adm. Oliver Hazard Perry scribbled in pencil on the back of an old letter, "Dear General: We have met the enemy and they are ours: Two ships, two Brigs one Schooner & one Sloop," then sent this message to Gen. William Henry Harrison and the history books.
Verdict: Credit Admiral Perry.

"ENGLAND and America are two countries separated by the same language." *Reader's Digest* attributed this thought to George Bernard Shaw, in 1942, but gave no source. The comment subsequently showed up in many quote collections over Shaw's name. The Library of Congress could not find this observation in any of the playwright's published works. Its genesis may be Oscar Wilde's earlier line in *The Canterville Ghost* (1887), "We have really everything in common with America nowadays, except, of course, language." Similar observations have been credited to Bertrand Russell, Dylan Thomas, and Winston Churchill.
Verdict: Adapted Wilde.

"This is the sort of ENGLISH up with which I will not put." Winston Churchill is famous for making this response to an officious grammarian who corrected a sentence of his that ended with a preposition. No one has a reliable citation, however, and the context in which Churchill's comment was supposedly made varies widely. So does the wording of his purported remark. Washington State English professor Paul Brians has found at least fourteen variations circulating on and off the Internet. The source most commonly cited for the Churchill attribution is Sir Ernest Gowers, who wrote in *Plain Words* (1948), "It is said that Mr. Winston Churchill once made this marginal comment against a sentence that clumsily avoided a prepositional ending: 'This is the sort of English up with which I will not put.'" Brians could find no index reference to "prepositions" in any Churchill biography. He did find on the Internet an astonishing array of narrative versions of his attributed rejoinder that gave the supposed context. In Brians's account, "Sometimes the person rebuked by Churchill is a correspondent, a speech editor, a bureaucrat, or an audience member at a speech and sometimes it is a man, sometimes a women, and sometimes even a young student. Sometimes Churchill writes a note, sometimes he scribbles the note on the corrected manuscript, and often he is said to have spoken the rebuke aloud. The text concerned was variously a book manuscript, a speech, an article, or a government document." Another quotographer, Ben Zimmer, found a 1942 *Wall Street Journal* item that attributed a variation of this comment ("offensive impertinence, up with which I will not put") to an anonymous government memo writer. The *Journal's* source was *The Strand*, magazine of London. Since Churchill was a *Strand* contributor, Zimmer noted, would they not have identified him if he were the author of this witticism? Zimmer found that it was only after the war ended that this quip began to be attributed to Churchill in the press—including, ironically, the *Wall Street Journal*. This process culminated in Gowers's 1948 attribution. Since then it's been Churchill all the way.

Verdict: An old joke put in Winston Churchill's mouth.

"Peace, commerce, and honest friendship for all nations, ENTANGLING alliances with none." Although the phrase "entangling alliances" is more associated with George Washington than with Thomas Jefferson, Jefferson first used that term in the above portion of his first inaugural address. In his farewell address, the first president of the United States did say, "It is our true policy to steer clear of permanent alliance with any portion of the foreign world," and "Why, by interweaving our destiny with that of any part of Europe, entangle our peace and prosperity in the toils of

European ambition, rivalship, interest, humor or caprice?" But Washington referred to "entangling alliances" only in our memories. This hook phrase made it easier for us to recall Washington's warning, even though the words belonged to Jefferson. Martin Van Buren echoed them when he said in his 1840 message to Congress that the United States was "Bound by no entangling alliances . . ."

Verdict: Credit Jefferson.

"The only thing necessary for the triumph of EVIL is that good men do nothing." In a poll conducted by Oxford University Press as the new millennium got underway, a version of this quotation was the most popular of one hundred candidates. It circulates widely in various forms (scores of variations can be found in thousands of postings on the Internet), and is usually attributed to Edmund Burke. That attribution appeared in the American press as early as 1950. John Kennedy liked to use this quotation in his speeches, crediting Burke. In their fourteenth edition (1968) *Bartlett's Familiar Quotations* not only attributed the comment to Burke but cited a 1795 letter in which he supposedly wrote it. The preface to *Bartlett's* fifteenth edition (1980) admitted the error, and said no valid source of this familiar quotation could be located. Despite diligent searching by librarians and others, no one has ever found these words in the works of Edmund Burke, or anyone else.

Verdict: Author unknown.

"Whenever I feel an urge to EXERCISE I lie down until it goes away." This observation is often attributed to Mark Twain. It certainly "sounds like" the sedentary author. Others who get credit for the witticism include W. C. Fields, animator Paul Terry, and—most often—former University of Chicago president Robert Maynard Hutchins. According to biographer Harry S. Ashmore, this line originated with humorist J. P. McEvoy and was one of many that Hutchins squirreled away to use at appropriate moments. In a 1938 profile of Hutchins, McEvoy himself wrote in *American Mercury,* "He holds with that hero who confessed: 'The secret of my abundant health is that whenever the impulse to exercise comes over me, I lie down until it passes away.'" If "that hero" was McEvoy himself, he wouldn't be the first writer to put his own words in an anonymous mouth. A version of this line ("Every time I think of exercise, I have to lie right down 'til the feeling leaves me.") appeared in the 1939 movie *Mr. Smith Goes to Washington,* whose screenplay was written by Sidney Buchman.

Verdict: Not Twain, not Hutchins, more likely J. P. McEvoy.

"EXPERIENCE is the name every one gives to their mistakes." Oscar Wilde liked this thought so much that he used different forms of it in his novel *The Picture of Dorian Gray* (1891) and two plays: *Vera, or the Nihilists* (1882) and *Lady Windermere's Fan* (1892). According to Leo Rosten, George Bernard Shaw, G. K. Chesterton, Sydney Smith, Samuel Butler, and Voltaire have also been given credit for a version of these words. Rosten himself thought they began as an old Jewish folk saying.

Verdict: Credit Wilde for putting a widespread hunch into words.

"We're EYEBALL to eyeball, and I think the other fellow just blinked." This was how Secretary of State Dean Rusk depicted the denouement of the Cuban Missile Crisis. The *Saturday Evening Post* thought so much of Rusk's comment that they put it on their cover, to tease a 1962 article about the crisis. "Eyeball to eyeball" was common military lingo during the Korean War. Former Army Chief of Staff Harold Johnson told William Safire that the phrase originated early in that war when the Twenty-fourth Infantry Regiment was confronted by a furious enemy attack. MacArthur's headquarters asked if they'd had contact with the enemy. Their widely reported reply was that they and the enemy were "eyeball to eyeball." In an anthology called *Wild Blue,* a 1953 depiction of Korean War air combat by Capt. Jack Jordan reported that he and his fellow pilots sometimes dived close enough to see enemy ground soldiers "eyeball to eyeball." In a 1959 movie about Korean War combat called *Pork Chop Hill,* an American Army officer played by Gregory Peck orders his soldiers to fix bayonets, then observes, "The Chinese love this eyeball-to-eyeball stuff." Perhaps Dean Rusk saw *Pork Chop Hill.*

Verdict: A Korean War catchphrase popularized by Dean Rusk.

"At fifty, everyone has the FACE he deserves." The last words George Orwell wrote in his notebook, on April 17, 1949, were "At fifty, everyone has the face he deserves." Orwell was hardly the only one to whom this thought had occurred. Some think Lincoln thought we were responsible for our face after the age of thirty, or forty (there is no evidence that he did). *The Viking Book of Aphorisms* attributes "A man of fifty is responsible for his face" to Lincoln's war secretary, Edwin Stanton. A century later, Albert Camus wrote in *The Fall* (1960), "Alas, after a certain age every man is responsible for his face." Nearly three decades after that, in *The American Ambassador* (1987), novelist Ward Just wrote of a character, "If at forty everyone has the face he's earned . . ."

Verdict: A popular thought put in modern play by George Orwell.

"FAMOUS for being famous." In his 1962 book *The Image,* historian Daniel Boorstin wrote that "The celebrity is a person who is known for his well-knownness." In its more popular form—"famous for being famous"—this thought gets passed around, most often landing in the lap of Andy Warhol (presumably on the assumption that someone who said one famous thing about fame must have said another).

Verdict: Credit the concept to Daniel Boorstin, the words to time.

"The only thing we have to FEAR is fear itself." Shortly before his first inauguration Franklin Delano Roosevelt was given an anthology of Henry David Thoreau's writings. This volume included Thoreau's 1852 thought that "Nothing is so much to be feared as fear." Thoreau's book was in FDR's hotel suite as he wrote his inaugural address. An aide thought *Walden's* author was the probable source of Roosevelt's most memorable line, "The only thing we have to fear is fear itself," which did not appear until a late draft of his inaugural address. But Thoreau's thought itself had antecedents: "The thing of which I have most fear is fear" (Michel de Montaigne, 1580), "Nothing is terrible except fear itself" (Francis Bacon, 1623), and "The only thing I am afraid of is fear" (Duke of Wellington, circa 1832).

Verdict: Credit the thought to Montaigne, its improvement to Bacon, and the final version to FDR, with help from Thoreau.

FEMINISM

Like the Civil Rights Movement, feminism has been the source of many comments whose authenticity or origins aren't always clear.

"Burn your bra." This presumed feminist exhortation has its roots in a 1968 protest against the Miss America pageant. Protesters were invited to discard symbols of restriction, such as brassieres. None went up in flames. During the era of draft card burning and flag burning, however, it wasn't hard to imagine that the skies were bright with the flames of bras ablaze. This remains a popular, and exciting, mismemory.

Because she edited a 1970 collection of feminist writing called **Sisterhood Is Powerful,** many quote collections (including *The Oxford Dictionary of Quotations*) attribute this phrase to onetime *Ms.* editor Robin Morgan. Morgan herself called it "a slogan we use on marches . . ." Before Morgan's book was published, however, that slo-gan had already been used as the title of a magazine article by Susan Brownmiller. Brownmiller said she'd seen it on a button. According to one history of feminism, "sisterhood is powerful" first appeared in print in a January 1968 pamphlet written by radical feminist Kathie Amatniek.

"A WOMAN needs a man like a fish needs a bicycle." Al-though this piece of feminist humor is commonly attributed to Gloria Steinem, she herself disavows authorship. A more accurate attribution is to Australian activist Irina Dunn, who says that in 1970 she based the slogan on an atheist observation about man needing God like a fish needs a bicycle.

A 1973 *Ms.* magazine profile of activist lawyer Florynce Kennedy (1916–2000) by Gloria Steinem included a compendium of Kennedy's salty observations. One was **"If men could get pregnant, abortion would be a sacrament."** Since then, this feminist truism has gener-ally been attributed to Kennedy. However, a decade after making this attribution, Steinem admitted that the quip's real author was an Irish cabdriver, an elderly woman, who—while ferrying her and Kennedy around Boston in the early 1970s—said, "Honey, if men could get preg-nant, abortion would be a sacrament."

"Good FENCES make good neighbors." Although Robert Frost did write this in "Mending Wall" (1914), the thought is clearly attributed to a neigh-bor of that poem's narrator. In any event, it's an adage with a long history. In 1846, *Dwight's American Magazine, and Family Newspaper* included "Good fences make good neighbors" in its "Farmer's Calendar" feature. That saying subsequently appeared in other American publications, al-manacs especially. In 1864 the *Ecclesiastical Register* called this saying "an old adage." The earliest known appearance of an analogue was in a 1640 letter from Rev. Ezekiel Rogers to Massachusetts governor John Winthrop, which included the phrase "a good fence helpeth to keepe peace betweene neighbours . . ." Proverb scholar Wolfgang Mieder notes similar sayings from other cultures, such as "There must be a fence between good neighbors" (Norway), and "Build a fence even between intimate friends" (Japan).

Verdict: Robert Frost was the most prominent publicist of a very old adage.

"FIFTEEN minutes of fame." This is among the most quoted, and mis-quoted, observations of modern times. How long we think everyone is famous for ranges from five seconds to fifteen hours, and many amounts in between. The quotation's wording also varies in the retelling. What Andy Warhol actually said, in a 1968 catalog accompanying an exhibition of his work at the Moderna Muséet in Stockholm, was "In the future everybody will be world-famous for fifteen minutes." According to curators at the Andy Warhol Museum in Pittsburgh, even though Warhol himself subsequently used different versions, this is the original form of his most famous quotation.

Verdict: Credit Andy Warhol with the full version.

"I have not yet begun to FIGHT!" Did John Paul Jones really give this defiant response to a request for surrender as his ship, the *Bonhomme Richard,* started leaking during a 1779 battle? It's not clear. Jones's retort was first reported by an eyewitness, 1st Lt. Richard Dale, nearly half a century later. Ten days after the engagement, Jones himself described the battle in a letter to Benjamin Franklin. In this letter the naval officer said he responded to an English surrender request "in the most determined negative," but didn't convey his actual words. Two decades later Benjamin Rush reported that a couple of years after the battle, Jones told him he'd said, "No, Sir, I will not [surrender], we have had but a small fight as yet." A sailor on the *Bonhomme Richard* recalled that when one of his own men pleaded with him to strike his colors, Jones responded, "No, I will sink, I will never strike!"

Verdict: Whatever John Paul Jones did say, it probably wasn't "I have not yet begun to fight."

"I propose to FIGHT it out on this line if it takes all summer." On the sixth day of the savage battle of Spotsylvania, two months after he was given overall command of Union forces in 1864, Ulysses S. Grant sent Secretary of War Edwin M. Stanton a brief status report. It concluded, "I propose to fight it out on this line if it takes all summer." That same day Grant sent Army Chief of Staff Maj. Gen. Henry W. Halleck a longer report. In this May 11, 1864, letter, Grant wrote, "I am now sending back to Belle Plaines all my wagons for a fresh supply of provisions, and Ammunition, and propose to fight it out on this line if it takes all Summer." The key idea here, "I propose to fight it out on this line if it takes all summer," caught the Northern public's fancy, making them think that a tenacious fighter was finally in charge of their forces. For some reason Grant's memoirs included a

somewhat different version of his original letter to Halleck. There, the word *propose* has been changed to *purpose* in his 1864 letter. As a result, it is quite common in works of history and collections of quotations (including *The Oxford Dictionary of Quotations*) to cite Grant as having written, "I purpose to fight it out on this line if it takes all summer." This doesn't make a whole lot of sense, and is almost certainly due to a mistake on the part of the book's author, editor, or printer. Alternatively, Grant the memoirist might have thought "purpose" was a tonier word than "propose." Historian John Y. Simon, who has devoted much of his career to editing Grant's papers, has no idea how the discrepancy originated. So which is it, *propose* or *purpose*? During the Civil War, Grant continually used the phrase "I propose" in his dispatches (e.g., "I propose to move immediately upon your works."). This suggests that the correct version of his most famous statement is the original one, and includes the word "propose," not "purpose."

Verdict: Credit Grant, saying, "I propose."

"Never pick a FIGHT with anyone who buys ink by the barrel." Sometimes including "and newsprint by the ton," this piece of advice usually gets passed around without an attribution ("As they say," "In the old adage," etc.). When credit is given to anyone at all, it most often goes to Mark Twain, sometimes to Ben Franklin, or Oscar Wilde, Winston Churchill, H. L. Mencken, Will Rogers, Franklin Delano Roosevelt, Bill Clinton, New York mayor Jimmy Walker, University of Texas football coach Darrell Royal, or Los Angeles Dodgers manager Tommy Lasorda. William Greener, a press aide to President Gerald Ford and other political and corporate figures in the 1970s–1980s, called the admonition "Greener's Law." According to Barbara P. Semonche, director of the Park Library at the University of North Carolina School of Journalism and Mass Communication, no one has ever determined the origins of this commonly cited quotation. "Ink by the barrel" was a phrase often used in the late nineteenth century.

Verdict: Author undetermined.

"Don't FIRE until you see the whites of their eyes!" By tradition this is what Col. William Prescott told his men at the Battle of Bunker Hill. Others attribute the words to Prescott's colleague Gen. Israel ("Old Put") Putnam. An 1849 history of the battle listed this command as one of several that American officers gave, but didn't attribute it to anyone in particular. If such an order was given at Bunker Hill, there was ample precedent. In 1745, Prince Charles of Prussia was said to have ordered his men, "Silent till you see the whites of their eyes." Twelve years later, Frederick the

Great elaborated, "By push of bayonets, no firing till you see the whites of their eyes." Others contend that the order originated with Andrew Jackson.

Verdict: Probably a common military command following the invention of gunpowder.

"If you give a man a FISH, he will eat for a day. If you teach him to fish, he will eat all his life." The origins of this popular precept have been hashed over ad nauseam by librarians, with no resolution in sight. It has been attributed to (among others) Confucius, Lao Tzu, Mark Twain, and Jesus. Some sources call this a Native American proverb, or one of African or Asian origin. It is most often cited as a Chinese proverb, possibly from statesman-philosopher Kuan Tzu, though the adage has not been found in his works. In 1885 an American magazine published a short story that included this observation by a character named Max: "He certainly doesn't practice his precepts, but I suppose *the patron* meant that if you give a man a fish he is hungry again in an hour; if you teach him to catch a fish you do him a good turn."

Verdict: Longstanding proverbial wisdom whose source has yet to be determined.

"Only those are FIT to live who are not afraid to die." So said Douglas MacArthur at a 1935 reunion of combat veterans from the Forty-second Infantry Division. A few decades earlier Theodore Roosevelt wrote, "Only those are fit to live who do not fear to die. . . ."

Verdict: On loan from Theodore Roosevelt to Douglas MacArthur.

"The FOG of war." In his classic 1832 book *Vom Kriege (On War),* Karl von Clausewitz (1780–1831) wrote, "War is the realm of uncertainty; three-quarters of the factors on which action in war is based are wrapped in fog of greater or lesser uncertainty." He added that "all action takes place, so to speak, in a kind of twilight, which, like fog or moonlight, often tends to make things seem grotesque and larger than they really are." Over time all of these words were boiled down to three: "fog of war." Von Clausewitz himself never used that phrase, but we have for him.

Verdict: Von Clausewitz's idea, our words.

"FOLLOW the money." After scouring the book *All the President's Men* by Bob Woodward and Carl Bernstein, as well as the Watergate coverage on which it was based, commentator Daniel Schorr could not find this pithy admonition. Nor could *Newsday*'s Rita Ciolli. It first entered the vernacular

via the movie based on Woodward and Bernstein's book. In this movie Hal
Holbrook, who plays "Deep Throat," does use the line. "Follow the money,"
he advises Robert Redford and Dustin Hoffman, who play Woodward and
Bernstein, when they meet in a parking garage. "Always follow the money."
Woodward and Bernstein both thought this line came from Mark Felt, the
FBI official who was the real Deep Throat, and that it appeared in their
book. (In *All the President's Men,* an unnamed lawyer does tell Bernstein,
"The money is the key to this thing.") Since the line is not in Woodward
and Bernstein's book, the movie's screenwriter, William Goldman, presumably coined it. Goldman thought the admonition derived from his extensive contact with Bob Woodward. But Woodward can't find it in any of
his notes. Nor can he recall if he shared this thought verbally with Goldman. There the matter rests. Except that, after William Safire mentioned
this mystery in his *New York Times* column, a former *Newsweek* correspondent named Stephan Lesher wrote Safire to say that in early 1973 an
assistant attorney general named Henry Peterson told him he'd advised
Watergate investigators to "follow the money. If they followed the money,
they'd get to the bottom of the case." Long before Woodward met Bernstein the phrase "follow the money trail" had appeared in the press. That
concept was probably floating about Washington in the Watergate era, and
got picked up by Woodward, Bernstein, Goldman, or all three.

Verdict: An investigative adage that William Goldman probably picked
up in conversation with Bob Woodward, who heard it he can't remember
where.

**"You can FOOL all of the people some of the time; you can fool some of
the people all of the time; but you can't fool all of the people all of the
time."** By tradition Abraham Lincoln made this observation during an
1858 speech at Clinton, Illinois. Other dates and locations have been
cited. These words do not appear in any of Lincoln's published works,
however, nor does any known press account of his speeches report this observation. Our only evidence that Lincoln might have said such a thing is
the memory of those who—long after the fact—recalled hearing Lincoln
give a speech in which he discussed fooling people. In a 1904 book called
Abe Lincoln's Yarns and Stories, Pennsylvania Republican leader Alexander
K. McClure said the president made this remark during a conversation
with a visitor. McClure's book put the maxim on our rhetorical map. However, Lincoln scholars don't give much credence to his memory or that of
anyone else when it comes to Honest Abe having made this remark.

Verdict: Author unknown; probably not Lincoln.

"*FOOTBALL is a mistake. It combines the two worst elements of American life: violence and committee meetings.*" George Will's much-repeated critique of football took this form in his *Newsweek* column in 1976: "It is, I know, naughty to commit sociology promiscuously, but if you hold up football to the bright light of the social sciences you will see that it mirrors modern life. It is committee meetings, called huddles, separated by outbursts of violence." Two years later Will wrote in his newspaper column, "Long ago I earned the pelting abuse of football fans by observing that football is popular and (semi-yucky) because it mirrors modern life. It is a mixture of violence and committee meetings (called huddles), and it is the moral equivalent of the President's energy problem: unnecessary complexity." Twenty years after that, Will said on Fox News, "I'm on record as saying football combines the two worst features of American life. It's violence punctuated by committee meetings." In its pithier form, this has become Will's most-cited observation. It is possible, of course, that the erudite columnist read Winston Churchill's reported response to watching his first American football game: "Actually, it is somewhat like rugby. But why do they have to have all those committee meetings?"

Verdict: Credit George Will, with a probable handoff from Winston Churchill.

"*FORM follows function.*" Although Frank Lloyd Wright sometimes gets credit for this design truism, it was architect Louis Sullivan who wrote in an 1896 magazine article, "Whether it be the sweeping eagle in his flight, or the open apple-blossom, the toiling work-horse, the blithe swan, the branching oak, the winding stream at its base, the drifting clouds, over all the coursing sun, *form ever follows function,* and this is the law." The italics are Sullivan's. Does that suggest the concept isn't?

Verdict: Credit Sullivan, for now.

"*Behind every great FORTUNE is a great crime.*" Mario Puzo used this quotation as the epigraph for his novel *The Godfather,* attributing it to Balzac. (Victor Hugo has also been given credit for that remark.) The closest words by Honoré de Balzac that anyone has ever found are in his novel *Père Goriot:* "The secret of a great fortune made without apparent cause is soon forgotten, if the crime is committed in a respectful way." ("*Le secret des grandes fortunes sans cause apparente est un crime oublié, parce qu'il a été proprement fait.*") (Alternatively, "The secret of a great success for which you are at a loss to account is a crime that has never been found out, because it was properly executed.") Where did Puzo's pithier version come from?

Most likely *The Power Elite* by C. Wright Mills (1916–1962). As quotographer Fred Shapiro discovered, in this 1956 book the sociologist referred to "Balzac's assertion that behind every great fortune there lies a crime."

Verdict: Concept by Balzac, paraphrase by Mills, publicity by Puzo.

BENJAMIN FRANKLIN

Benjamin Franklin is unusually prominent in the annals of quotation and misquotation for at least three reasons: 1. He was highly quotable. 2. Many words have been put in his mouth. 3. He put many words in his own mouth, or that of Poor Richard. When researching a Ph.D. thesis on the original sources of Poor Richard's sayings, Robert Newcomb found that a good three-quarters of them had been published elsewhere, in similar or identical form. Not that Franklin would have minded Newcomb's exposé. "Why should I give my Readers *bad lines* of my own," Franklin once asked, "when *good ones* of other People's are so plenty?" He admitted that less than 10 percent of his published sayings were original, calling the rest "gleanings that I made of the sense of all the ages and nations." Proverb scholar Wolfgang Mieder estimates that no more than 5 percent of Poor Richard's 1,044 proverbs were Franklin's creations. Franklin apparently found **"A word to the wise is enough"** in an old book of proverbs, which in turn adapted it from similar observations dating back to the Roman playwright Plautus. (Over time our ears changed "enough" to "sufficient.") In varying forms, **"There are no GAINS without pains"** had already appeared in several proverb collections by the time Poor Richard took credit for it in 1745. Even an adage so associated with Franklin as **"Early to bed and early to rise, makes a man healthy, wealthy, and wise"** had appeared in a proverb collection nearly a century before it ran in *Poor Richard's Almanack* in 1735.

In the process of expropriating other people's sayings, Franklin often improved them. Mark Twain called him "The immortal axiom-builder, who used to sit up nights reducing the rankest old threadbare platitudes to crisp and snappy maxims that had a nice, varnished, original look . . ." Thus a predecessor's "Success has blown up, and undone, many a man" became, with the help of Franklin's pen, **"Success has ruined many a Man."** Plautus had said that no guest is welcome after three days, and Lyly, in 1580, "Fish and guests in three days are stale." Franklin's version was, **"Fish and visitors smell in three days."** In *Poor Richard's Almanack,* Benjamin Franklin wrote, **"For want of a Nail the Shoe is lost; for want of a Shoe the Horse is lost; for want of a Horse the Rider is lost."** More than a century earlier, poet-aphorist George Herbert (1593–1633) wrote, "For want of a nail the shoe is lost, for want of a shoe the horse is lost, for want of a horse the rider is lost." Herbert also wrote, "A man in Passion rides a horse that runs away from him." Franklin's version was **"A Man in a Passion rides a mad HORSE."** Franklin borrowed **"Love your NEIGHBOR, yet don't pull down your hedge,"** from Herbert too, who had written, "Love your neighbor, yet pull not down your hedge." **"Don't throw stones at your neighbors, if your own windows are glass"** was Franklin's version of either Herbert's "Whose house is of glass, must not throw stones at another," or "Who hath glass-windows of his own, let him take heed how he throws stones at those of his Neighbor," by proverb compiler James Howell (1594–1666). He also wrote, in a 1789 letter, **"Our new Constitution is now established, and has an appearance that promises permanency, but in this world nothing can be said to be certain, except death and taxes."** Six decades earlier, in *History of the Devil* (1726), Daniel Defoe had made reference to "Things as certain as death and taxes. . . ."

Franklin didn't even attempt to claim credit for **"An OUNCE of prevention is worth a pound of cure,"** an adage generally attributed to him. He called this "an old saying," or "an English proverb."

Anyone as quotable as Franklin attracts lots of orphan quotes and ones coined by others. He is a primary flypaper figure. In a speech to the National Press Club, economist Lester Thurow said, "Remember the advice of Benjamin Franklin in *Poor Richard's Almanack,* 1755: **"Build a better MOUSETRAP and the world will beat a path to your door.'"** (See sidebar "Ralph Waldo Emerson.")

The quotation most commonly misattributed to Franklin is **"We must all HANG together, or most assuredly we shall all hang separately."** Others include **"Where there is LIBERTY, there is my country," "Never pick a FIGHT with anyone who buys ink by the barrel," "If you want to know what people are like, share an INHERITANCE with them," "INSANITY consists of doing the same**

> **thing over and over, hoping for a different result,"** and "Charac-
> ter is what you do when no one is looking."
>   One of Franklin's own most requoted statements, apparently orig-
> inal to him, is **"Those who desire to give up FREEDOM in order to
> gain security will not have, nor do they deserve, either one."** In
> two separate 1783 letters he wrote, the memorable words **"There
> never was a good war or a bad peace."**

"There's no such thing as a FREE lunch." Because he published a book
by this title in 1975, economist Milton Friedman is often credited with
coining the popular adage. But Friedman never claimed to have originated
this saying and had no idea who did. The conclusion that free lunches
aren't really free is so obvious that it's hard to imagine it wasn't articulated
soon after the first plate of hard-boiled eggs was set out for paying drinkers
at a New Orleans saloon in the 1830s. Lexicographer Stuart Berg Flexner
dated common use of the phrase "free lunch" to the 1840s, when it worked
its way to both coasts along with the institution itself. Some credit Robert
Heinlein with propagating the idea that there's no such thing as a free
lunch because the phrase is so central to his 1966 novel *The Moon Is a
Harsh Mistress* that it's abbreviated as "tanstaafl." ("'Oh,'" explained one of
Heinlein's characters, "'"tanstaafl." Means "There ain't no such thing as a
free lunch." And isn't,' I added, pointing to a FREE LUNCH sign across
room, 'or these drinks would cost half as much. . . .'") Robert Heinlein
was far from the first person to reach this conclusion, however. Extensive
database searching by *Yale Dictionary of Quotations* editor Fred Shapiro
turned up a reference to "Professor Alvin Hansen's 'famous TINSTAAFL
formula—There is no such thing as a free lunch'" in a 1952 issue of *Ethics*
magazine. This acronym had already appeared in a 1949 newspaper column. Two years before that, a 1947 column by economics commentator
Merryle S. Rukeyser (father of Louis Rukeyser) advised retail executives to
"instruct their buyers that there is no free lunch, but that their role is creative selection of goods which will please their customers quality-wise and
price-wise."
    Verdict: This thought is so obvious and so shopworn that trying to
attribute it to anyone in particular is an exercise in futility.

*"Those who desire to give up FREEDOM in order to gain security will
not have, nor do they deserve, either one."* (Wording varies.) So many

quotations are misattributed to Benjamin Franklin that it's refreshing to consider something Franklin actually said but for which he rarely gets credit. His actual words, in the Pennsylvania Assembly in 1755, were "Those who would give up essential Liberty, to purchase a little temporary Safety, deserve neither Liberty nor Safety." Twenty years later, in 1775, Franklin wrote in a political critique, "They who can give up essential liberty to obtain a little temporary Safety, deserve neither Liberty nor Safety." This thought of Franklin's is sometimes credited to Jefferson.

Verdict: Credit Franklin.

"FRIENDS are God's apology for relations." Jay McInerney began his 1996 novel *Last of the Savages*, "The capacity for friendship is God's way of apologizing for our families." McInerney neglected to credit this provocative thought to its originator, British essayist Hugh Kingsmill (1889–1949). In recognition of this attribution, Richard Ingrams's 1978 biography of Kingsmill was titled *God's Apology*. Across the Atlantic, Wilson Mizner's brother Addison (1872–1933) once observed, "God gives us our relatives— thank God, we can choose our friends." That echoed an earlier observation by French poet Jacques Delille (1738–1813): "Fate chooses your relations, you choose your friends." Obviously this basic idea has been floating about for some time, in various forms.

Verdict: Credit Hugh Kingsmill for the most familiar version.

"Are we having FUN yet?" In the 1981 movie *The Four Seasons,* Carol Burnett asked this question repeatedly. It subsequently became T-shirt common. Long before *The Four Seasons* appeared, however, "Are we having fun yet?" was the signature line of Bill Griffith's cartoon character Zippy the Pinhead. Griffith himself told an inquiring librarian that "Zippy was prone to asking the obvious on many occasions from the time I started drawing him in 1970—it also probably spins off from the kids' perennial nagging, 'Are we there yet?' . . . kind of an existential question, in Zippy's case. It's been interpreted (unauthorized bumper stickers, plaques, T-shirts) as, kind of, 'Let's Party' by generations of brainless hedonists, but its real intention is to question the very nature of the 'fun' concept." We all get one sound bite, Griffith concluded, and just as $E=MC^2$ was Einstein's, "Are we having fun yet?" would undoubtedly be his.

Verdict: Credit Bill Griffith.

"That was the most FUN I've had without laughing." In *Annie Hall,* Woody Allen said this about making love with Diane Keaton. It has been recycled often since that movie appeared in 1977, and was the title of a 1990 book of quotations about sex. Thirty-five years before Allen's movie premiered, in the more inhibited World War II era, H. L. Mencken's book of quotations included "Love is the most fun you can have without laughing." This was attributed to "Author Unidentified," typically a euphemism for Mencken himself. Bennett Cerf later said that publishing was the most fun you could have with your clothes on. Following that, British fashion arbiter Peter York said the same thing about critiquing other people's outfits. Apparently this is one of those modular quotations with lots of mix 'n' match possibilities.

Verdict: Not Woody Allen's invention, possibly Mencken's, more likely a modular old saw.

"Git thar FUSTEST with the mostest." Confederate General Nathan Bedford Forrest is best remembered for this bit of homespun military philosophy. Since he was an ill-educated former slave trader from southern Tennessee, these words sounded about right—to Northern ears anyway. Isn't that how they talk down there? Apparently not, at least not in this case. According to biographer Ralph Selph Henry, "Forrest would have been totally incapable of so obvious and self-conscious a piece of literary carpentry." (Given the diction of the time, Forrest's pronunciation might have been "Git thar fust with the most men," Henry thought.) Memoirs written by Union and Confederate officers who talked with Forrest reported these versions of his credo: "I always make it a rule to get there first with the most men"; "I just took the short cut and got there first with the most men"; and "I got there first with the most men," which was the version in a Confederate general's memoir published two years after Forrest's death in 1877, and the first to appear in print. Over time Forrest's words were embellished, first with "mostest," then with "fustest." ("The mostest" was a spoofy term popular in the post–Civil War period.) In 1918 the *New York Times* concluded, "The truth is, that somebody who was trying to make Forrest talk what he imagined to be Southern dialect evolved that incredible phraseology, and [it] has been followed slavishly ever since."

Verdict: Forrest's credo, someone else's words.

"I have seen the FUTURE, and it works." According to his autobiography, after returning from Russia in 1919, journalist Lincoln Steffens told financier Bernard Baruch, "I have been over into the future, and it works."

Baruch's own autobiography confirmed that exchange. Steffens frequently used different versions of this comment in conversation, and once wrote to a friend, "I have seen the future; and it works." According to biographer Justin Kaplan he'd begun developing the line while en route to Russia. It is sometimes misattributed to American communist John Reed.

Verdict: Credit Lincoln Steffens.

"A GAFFE is when a politician tells the truth." Michael Kinsley made this memorable observation in a somewhat different form in 1984. Here is the exact line, from Kinsley's "TRB from Washington" column: "A 'gaffe' is the opposite of a 'lie': it's when a politician inadvertently tells the truth."

Verdict: Credit Michael Kinsley for this idea.

"There are no GAINS without pains." In varying forms, this advisory had already appeared in several proverb collections by the time it ran in *Poor Richard's Almanack* in 1745. Thomas Fuller, for one, had written, "Without pains, no gains" decades before Franklin put the thought in Poor Richard's mouth, as had John Ray in *English Proverbs* (1670). In *Display of Dutie* (1589) Leonard Wright wrote, "No gaine without pain."

Verdict: Old saw.

"She ran the GAMUT of emotions from A to B." Dorothy Parker is famous for depicting Katharine Hepburn's acting this way, in her review of a play called *The Lake*. The actual genesis of the line can be found in a book by Alexander Woollcott. After quoting from Parker's review of *House Beautiful* (which she called "the play lousy"), Woollcott wrote, "And more recently she achieved an equal compression in reporting on *The Lake*. Miss Hepburn, it seems, had run the whole gamut from A to B." Readers were free to infer that this assessment appeared in a Parker review of the 1934 play. No such review has been found in any magazine Parker wrote for at the time. It's conceivable that she made this observation about Hepburn's acting in some other context, such as a conversation with Woollcott. Hepburn reported in her own autobiography that Parker had said, "Go to the Martin Beck [Theater] and see K.H. run the gamut-t-t of emotion from A to B." According to Hepburn biographer Gary Carey, Parker made a similar remark during *The Lake*'s intermission, but Carey gave no source.

Verdict: Until further notice, credit Dorothy Parker for this remark (though in conversation, not in print).

MAHATMA GANDHI

A Palestinian living in Holland once wrote a mock memo from Mahatma Gandhi to *New York Times* columnist Thomas Friedman in the manner often favored by Friedman (who was born five years after Gandhi was assassinated). In time this "memo" circulated on the Internet with the name of its actual author deleted, his words now attributed to Gandhi alone. One passage in particular, **"When I despair, I remember that, all through history, the way of truth and love has always won,"** is now widely, and mistakenly, assumed to be an authentic quotation from Mahatma Gandhi.

In recent years Gandhi has become an increasingly prominent fly-paper figure. A wide range of quotations that call for a saintly source with a familiar name end up in his mouth. Gandhi is frequently credited with different versions of **"The TEST of a civilization, . . ."** such as **"The greatness of a nation and its moral progress can be judged by the way its animals are treated."** (A vegetarians' website gives a 1931 Gandhi speech as the source of this comment, but those words cannot be found within that speech.)

While playing Gandhi in the eponymous 1982 movie, whose script was written by John Briley, Ben Kingsley said, **"An eye for an eye only ends up making the whole world blind."** This line now routinely appears in quotation compilations over Gandhi's name. A similar line had already been used by dairyman Tevye in the 1971 movie *Fiddler on the Roof,* which director Norman Jewison and Joseph Stein adapted from Stein's stage musical by the same title, which was based on stories by Sholom Aleichem:

> VILLAGER: We should defend ourselves! An eye for an eye and a tooth for a tooth!
> TEVYE: Very good. That way the whole world will be blind and toothless.

Virtually the same words have also been attributed to Kahlil Gibran (1883–1931): "An eye for an eye, and the whole world would be blind." In *Stride Toward Freedom* (1958), Martin Luther King, Jr., wrote, "The old law of an eye for an eye leaves everybody blind." (The year before that book was published, King's associate Harris Wofford

said the same thing in a lecture.) Screenwriter John Briley freely admitted that he himself was the source of this observation in the movie
about Gandhi. According to Briley the entire movie included only two
sentences actually spoken by the Indian leader.

During his first visit to England, when asked what he thought of
modern civilization, Gandhi is said to have told news reporters, **"That
would be a good idea."** *The Oxford Dictionary of Quotations* cites
E. F. Schumacher's *Good Work* as its source for this Gandhiism, as
does Nigel Rees in the *Cassell Companion to Quotations*. In that 1979
book, Schumacher said he saw Gandhi make this remark in a filmed
record of his quizzing by reporters as he disembarked in Southampton
while visiting England in 1930. Gandhi did not visit England in 1930.
He did attend a roundtable conference on India's future in London
the following year. Standard biographies of Gandhi do not report his
making any such quip as he disembarked. Most often it has been revised to be Gandhi's assessment of "Western" civilization: "I think it
would be a good idea." A retort such as this seems a little flip for
Gandhi, and must be regarded as questionable. A comprehensive collection of his observations includes no such remark among twelve entries for "Civilization." The closest were "Civilizations have come and
gone and, in spite of our vaunted progress, I am tempted to ask again
and again, 'To what purpose?'", and "Modern civilization has taught us
to convert night into day and golden silence into brazen din and
noise." Not that Gandhi lacked wit. During his 1931 visit to London,
reporters questioned his scant apparel of loincloth, sandals, and
shawl. Gandhi responded, "You people wear plus-fours, mine are minus fours." When asked if he'd had on enough clothing while visiting
King George V, Gandhi said, "The king had enough on for both of us."

"Be the change you wish to see in the world" is a quotation
that often appears over Gandhi's name. Despite diligent searching, no
one has ever found this saying in his published works. It is included on
"The Official Mahatma Gandhi eArchive and Reference Library," but
without a source (as is "Imitation is the sincerest flattery," attributed
to Gandhi). This website's version is "You must be the change you
wish to see in the world." Gandhi's descendants say he made that observation in person.

During her childhood in northern India, novelist Meena Nayak often heard the Christian admonition **"If someone slaps you on one**

cheek, present the other one" misattributed to Gandhi. Gandhi is also one among the many who are mistakenly credited for saying, **"I shall PASS through this world but once. Any good thing therefore I can do, or any kindness that I can show to any human being, let me do it now. Let me not defer it, or neglect it, for I shall not pass this way again."**

"There go the PEOPLE. I must follow them, for I am their leader" is sometimes attributed to Gandhi, rather than to the mid-nineteenth-century Frenchman to whom it's more often ascribed. An admonition to salesclerks that reads, **"A customer is the most important visitor on our premise. He is not dependent on us. We are dependent on him. He is not an interruption in our work. He is the purpose of it. He is not an outsider in our business. He is part of it. We are not doing him a favor by serving him. He is doing us a favor by giving us an opportunity to do so"** has been credited to Gandhi (presumably because he believed in "service to humanity").

Some other quotations that are frequently attributed to Gandhi with scant evidence include:

Hate the sin, love the sinner.

I like their Christ, but I do not like their Christians.

Live as if you were to die tomorrow. / Learn as if you were to live forever.

There is more to life than increasing its speed.

"What's good for GENERAL MOTORS is good for the country." While testifying about his nomination as secretary of defense before the Senate Committee on Armed Services in 1953, General Motors head Charles E. Wilson was asked whether he could make a decision on behalf of the government that would adversely affect his company. "Yes, sir," Wilson replied, "I could. I cannot conceive of one because for years I thought what was good for our country was good for General Motors, and vice versa." This resembles the commonly misquoted version, but doesn't mean the same thing at all. Fourteen years earlier, in the 1939 movie *Stagecoach,*

whose screenplay was written by Dudley Nichols, a corrupt banker said, "And remember this: what's good for the bank is good for the country." That line does not appear in the short story by Ernest Haycox on which Nichols's screenplay was based.

Verdict: An unfair adaptation of Charles Wilson's words, with a cinematic antecedent.

"GENIUS is 1 percent inspiration and 99 percent perspiration." Thomas Edison's motto was a long time a-borning. In 1898, a *Ladies Home Journal* article about Edison included the inventor's response when he was asked for his definition of genius: "Two percent is genius and 98 percent is hard work." The article added that on another occasion he'd said, "Bah! Genius is not inspired. Inspiration is perspiration." Four years later, in 1902, *Scientific American* reported about Edison, "'Genius is 2 percent inspiration and 98 percent perspiration,' is the incisive, epigrammatic answer he once gave to a man who thought that a genius worked only when the spirit moved him." A 1934 biography of the inventor also cited the 2:98 ratio. In a 1919 speech, an associate of Edison said he'd once asked him what genius was. "Well," Edison replied, "about 99 percent of it is a knowledge of the thing that will not work. The other 1 percent may be genius, but the only way that I know to accomplish anything is everlastingly to keep working, with patient observation." Biographer Ronald Clark thinks this statement represented Edison's views better than the snappier aphorism generally attributed to him. Apparently the pithiest, most memorable version of this saying evolved over time, perhaps with the help of news reporters. In a 1932 interview, Edison said the motto was indeed his.

Verdict: Credit Thomas Edison for the basic idea, and some version of the words.

"GINGER ROGERS did everything Fred Astaire did. She just did it backwards and in high heels." Texas Treasurer Ann Richards pointed this out in her keynote address to the 1988 Democratic convention. Richards thought she got the line from television journalist Linda Ellerbee. Ellerbee said she might have gotten it from a fellow passenger on an airplane. Ronald Reagan used the gag long before Richards did. It has also been attributed to Republican politician Faith Whittlesey, and Ginger Rogers herself. In her autobiography the actress said she first saw it in a comic strip. Indeed, in a 1982 "Frank and Ernest" comic strip panel, one character says of Fred Astaire, "Sure he was great, but don't forget Ginger Rogers did everything he did, . . . backwards, and in high heels!" Some think this line

predated the panel by several decades, and may have been a gag on early television. "Frank and Ernest" creator Bob Thaves believes it originated with him. "I am not aware of the 'Ginger Rogers' line appearing anywhere before it appeared in Frank and Ernest," he wrote in an e-mail. "I did not take it from another source."

Verdict: Unless and until an earlier source comes along, credit Bob Thaves.

"Win one for the GIPPER." As Notre Dame was about to play Army in 1928, football coach Knute Rockne invoked the name of former player George Gipp. Gipp's deathbed request eight years earlier supposedly had been to use his memory to motivate the Fighting Irish for a big game. "'Rock,'" the coach said Gipp told him, "'some day when things look real tough for Notre Dame, ask the boys to go out there and win one for me.' Well, I've never used Gipp's request until now. This is the time." Notre Dame won. A *New York Daily News* writer later reported Rockne's emotional locker room speech in a feature story headed, "Gipp's Ghost Beat Army / Irish Hero's Deathbed Request Inspired Notre Dame." Two years later Rockne embellished the legend when he wrote in a magazine that Gipp told him, "'Some time, Rock, when the team's up against it, when things are wrong and the breaks are beating the boys—tell them to go in there with all they've got and win just one for the Gipper." In 1940, an adaptation of these words, "Tell 'em to go out there with all they got and win just one for the Gipper," provided the dramatic denouement of a movie in which Ronald Reagan played George Gipp. That movie (whose script was written by Robert Buckner), and Reagan's lifelong identification with this role, made "Win one for the Gipper" a permanent part of America's athletic-political lore.

Verdict: Bumper-stickered Rockne.

"The GLOBAL village." Although this concept is indelibly associated with Marshall McLuhan, he got it from the 1948 book *America and Cosmic Man* by his friend Wyndham Lewis. In that book Lewis wrote, "The earth has become one big village, with telephones laid from one end to the other, and air transport, both speedy and safe."

Verdict: Marshall McLuhan's words, Wyndham Lewis's idea.

"Think GLOBALLY, act locally." Microbiologist René Dubos (1901–1982) advocated this way of thinking in 1972, while chairing an advisory panel for the first United Nations Conference on the Human Environment, held in Stockholm. Dubos later recalled using words to this effect in subse-

quent speeches. In a 1977 *American Scholar* column he wrote, "While certain natural constraints make it imperative to think globally, in practice each social group must work out its own fate and act locally." A 1979 essay by Dubos that appeared in the *Wall Street Journal* and in *Newsweek* as a full-page advertisement sponsored by SmithKline was headlined, "Think Globally, Act Locally." That phrase appeared in a 1980 book by Dubos, and was a chapter title in a 1981 book he authored. These words have also been attributed to environmentalist David Brower. Credit for a variant is claimed by Canadian futurist Frank Feather, who chaired a 1980 conference in Toronto titled "Thinking Globally, Acting Locally" and says he came up with that phrase in 1979.

Verdict: Credit René Dubos.

"GOD *always favors the big battalions.*" (**"Dieu est toujours pour les gros bataillons."**) This aphorism is routinely misattributed to Napoleon. Long before Napoleon's rise, Voltaire wrote in a 1770 letter, "They say that God always favors the big battalions." Voltaire's use of "they say" suggests this thought was already in play when he wrote his letter. And indeed it was. More than a decade earlier, Frederick the Great wrote in a letter, "God is for the big squadrons." (*"Dieu est pour les gros escadrons."*) In 1673, the inimitable letter writer Madame de Sévigné told a correspondent that "de Turenne" used to say that fortune was for the big battalions. This referred to the Vicomte de Turenne, a French military officer who, a century before Voltaire, was said to have observed that "God always favors the big battalions." (*"Dieu est toujours pour les gros bataillons."*) Roger de Rabutin, the Comte de Bussy, subsequently wrote in a 1677 letter, "As a rule God is on the side of the big squadrons against the small ones." (*"Dieu est d'ordinaire pour les gros escadrons contre les petits."*)

Verdict: An old saying, favored especially by the French.

"GOD *helps those who help themselves.*" Despite a widespread misconception that these words come straight from the Bible, Aesop wrote, five centuries before the birth of Christ, "The gods help them that help themselves." Two millennia later, James Howell included in a 1659 collection of proverbs, "God helps him, who helps himself." In 1698 this became "God helps those who help themselves," from the pen of British politician Algernon Sidney. Thirty-five years after that, Benjamin Franklin's Poor Richard observed, "God helps them that help themselves."

Verdict: Credit Aesop for recording an early version of this thought, which was probably commonplace even in his time.

"This is the way GOD would have built it if he'd had the money." Theater critic Alexander Woollcott supposedly said this about the country home of playwright Moss Hart, in the late 1930s. George Bernard Shaw reportedly made the same remark after visiting William Randolph Hearst's opulent San Simeon ranch in 1933. According to the *Macmillan Dictionary of Quotations,* four years before that, Ian Fleming's brother Peter Fleming reported to their brother Rupert in a 1929 letter, "Long Island represents the American's idea of what God would have done with Nature if he'd had the money." Variations on this theme have also been attributed to George S. Kaufman, Wolcott Gibbs, and Frank Case, manager of the Algonquin Hotel. That type of comment was obviously making the rounds in the 1920s and 30s, available for whoever could get away with claiming authorship.

Verdict: A post–World War I quip of uncertain origin.

"We'll win, because GOD'S on our side." This thought is as ancient as the Crusades, as modern as Osama bin Laden and George W. Bush. It is what Joe Louis is often credited with saying during a 1942 speech at Madison Square Garden, soon after Pearl Harbor was bombed. The boxer's actual words were a bit more modest: "We're gonna do our part, and we will win, because we are on God's side."

Verdict: An old conviction put in modern play by Joe Louis.

SAMUEL GOLDWYN

Like Yogi Berra, Samuel Goldwyn gets credit for a few malaprops that he did utter, and many that he didn't. As with his baseball counterpart, inventing mangled comments to put in the mouth of the Polish-born movie mogul was a popular pastime during Goldwyn's lifetime. In his case, a group of studio screenwriters actually held a contest to see who could come up with the best "Goldwynism." (The winner was: "It rolls off my back like a duck." A 1993 book called *The 776 Stupidest Things Ever Said* included this one over Goldwyn's name.)

After Samuel Goldwyn died in 1974, Frances Goldwyn identified those malaprops she thought her husband actually uttered. Her list included "I was on the brink of an abscess," "I had a monumental idea this morning, but I didn't like it," "I don't care if my pictures don't make a dime, so long as everyone comes to see them," and "In this business it's dog eat dog, and nobody's gonna eat me."

Scores of other malaprops attributed to Goldwyn on slimmer evidence include **"I'll give you a definite maybe," "Let's have some new clichés,"** and, **"It's more than magnificent, it's mediocre."**

In a few cases evidence exists with which the validity of specific Goldwynisms can be assessed. For example:

"Include me out." Goldwyn is said to have made this statement before storming out of a heated discussion about a labor dispute. Though he denied saying it, in later years the producer grew philosophical about this classic Goldwynism, going so far as to write, "Include me out" as his own epitaph during a parlor game. Most Goldwyn watchers consider it authentic, in part because his language-mangling was most frequent during times of stress. Whether the line is authentic or not, according to biographer Scott Berg at least a dozen people said they heard Goldwyn make this comment, in twelve different settings.

"I can answer you in two words: 'im possible.'" Goldwyn vehemently denied ever saying this, and with good reason. Charlie Chaplin later admitted that it was an old gag he pinned on the producer.

"A verbal contract isn't worth the paper it's written on." Goldwyn also denied ever saying that a verbal contract wasn't worth the paper it was written on. According to movie industry chronicler Norman Zierold, Goldwyn did say of fellow mogul Joe Schenck, "His verbal contract is worth more than the paper it's written on," and reporters gave his words a polish.

"I read part of it all the way through." According to Goldwyn biographer Alva Johnston, a Goldwyn rival once made this remark to a team of writers, then pleaded with them to "Tell it on Sam."

"Anyone who sees a psychiatrist ought to have his head examined." Attributed to Goldwyn in a 1948 issue of *Reader's Digest,* without a source, this Goldwynism may have been coined by playwright-screenwriter Lillian Hellman. It's unlikely that the producer himself said it. In 1946 Goldwyn told a reporter that he'd occasionally seen a psychiatrist himself.

"GOLF is a good walk spoiled." Mark Twain's purported put-down of golf provided the title for three books. *Peter's Quotations* (1977) credited the quip to Twain without citing a source. In 1948, *Reader's Digest* also attributed this thought to Twain, citing the *Saturday Evening Post,* but without a date. No scholar has ever been able to confirm that Twain said this. Most doubt that he did. The witticism appeared anonymously in American newspapers as early as 1913. From mid-century on "Golf is a good walk spoiled" was attributed most often to Mark Twain, but also to George Bernard Shaw and W. C. Fields. According to an expert on German writer Kurt Tucholsky (1890–1935), this was one of the many aphorisms that Tucholsky called "Schnipsel" and that appeared in *Die Weltbuhne* in 1931: *"Golf, sagte einmal jemand, ist ein verdorbener Spaziergang."* ("Golf, somebody said, is a walk spoiled.") The question is, who said it?

Verdict: Author yet to be determined; probably not Twain.

"How can you GOVERN a nation that has 246 kinds of cheese?" According to a French collection of his mots, Charles de Gaulle once said of his native land, "How can you govern a nation that has 246 kinds of cheese?" Or was it 243? Or 265? The number varies in the retelling. Maybe de Gaulle himself wasn't quite sure how many cheeses were made in France. (By now it's well over 400.) Nonetheless, following a political setback in 1951, he did say, "Nobody can simply bring together a country that has 265 kinds of cheese." (*"On ne peut rassembler á froid un pays qui compte 265 spécialités de fromages."*) This echoed an earlier observation attributed to French wit and gastronome Alexander de La Reynière (1758–1838): "One knows in France 685 ways of preparing eggs." (*"On connoit en France 685 manières differentes d'accomoder les oeufs."*)

Verdict: Credit de Gaulle for a somewhat clunkier version than the more popular one.

"I would rather be GOVERNED by the first hundred names in the Boston phone book than by the Harvard faculty." William Buckley is renowned for saying he'd rather be governed by X number of names in the Boston phone book than by Harvard's entire faculty. In the retelling, the number of phone book names varies from 100 to 200, 300, 400, 435, 500, 600, "several hundred," 1,000, 2,000, or 3,000. During a 1965 *Meet the Press* appearance, Buckley said, "I've often been quoted as saying I would rather be governed by the first two thousand people in the Boston telephone directory than by the two thousand people on the faculty of Harvard University." Two years earlier he wrote, "I am obliged to

confess that I should sooner live in a society governed by the first two thousand names in the Boston telephone directory than in a society governed by the two thousand faculty members of Harvard University." So let's go with 2,000.

Verdict: Credit William Buckley for saying he'd rather be governed by the first 2,000 names in the Boston phone book than by that number of Harvard professors.

**"GOVERNMENT *of the people, by the people, for the people . . ."* According to a biographer, in the late eighteenth century, playwright-politician Richard Sheridan (1751–1816) belonged to a London group called the Westminster Association for Reform, whose slogan was "Government for the people, through the people, by the people." In 1794 an English book on America by one Thomas Cooper included this observation about its political system: "The government is the government *of* the people, and *for* the people." Variations on this theme were common in nineteenth-century America. Thirty-three years before Abraham Lincoln delivered the Gettysburg Address, Daniel Webster spoke of "people's government, made for the people, made by the people and answerable to the people." An 1841 essay on the American Revolution by Asher Robbins concluded that "the most powerful, the most prosperous, and the most happy of all governments is the government of the people, by the people." During the 1850s, Rev. Theodore Parker included several versions of this credo in his abolition lectures. One, in 1850, referred to "government of all the people, by all the people, for all the people." In the early stages of the Civil War, Lincoln's law partner, William Herndon, gave the president a copy of Parker's published speeches. According to Herndon, before composing his Gettysburg Address Lincoln marked these words in an 1858 Parker sermon: "Democracy is direct self-government, over all the people, by all the people, for all the people." Because it dispensed with all the "alls," Lincoln's own version, "Government of the people, by the people, for the people," was more harmonious. As proverb scholar Wolfgang Mieder points out, deleting the "alls" also acknowledged implicitly that America's slaves were not yet free, and its women were not allowed to vote.

Verdict: A longstanding conception of democracy that culminated in Lincoln's famous version, based on one by Theodore Parker.

**"That GOVERNMENT *is best which governs least."* This observation is often misattributed to Thomas Jefferson. It became a common part of public discourse when Thoreau quoted the line without attribution in his

1849 essay "Civil Disobedience." Its original author may have been John L. O'Sullivan, editor of the *United States Magazine and Democratic Review.* When that magazine was founded in 1837, the introduction to its first issue included the line "The best government is that which governs least." O'Sullivan, incidentally, later coined the term *manifest destiny.*

Verdict: Credit John L. O'Sullivan.

"GRACE under pressure." Newscaster Ted Koppel once misattributed this classic definition of courage to John F. Kennedy. Kennedy did use the line, at the outset of his book *Profiles in Courage,* correctly attributing it to Ernest Hemingway. When asked to define courage, the swashbuckling novelist had responded, "Guts." Asked what he meant by "guts," Hemingway said, "I mean, grace under pressure." In a 1929 *New Yorker* article, Dorothy Parker reported this exchange between Hemingway and an unnamed interlocutor.

Verdict: Credit Ernest Hemingway.

"I'd walk over my own GRANDMOTHER if necessary to get Richard Nixon elected." Former presidential aide Charles Colson is notorious for having said, "I'd walk over my own grandmother if necessary to get Richard Nixon elected." In fact, this was said *about* Colson, not by him. In a 1971 *Wall Street Journal* profile of Colson, a former aide to then-senator Leverett Saltonstall (R-Mass.) observed that Nixon's henchman "would walk over his own grandmother if he had to." Before long the words of this unnamed aide wended their way to Colson's own mouth. Colson didn't help himself by issuing a tongue-in-cheek memo to his staff in which he concurred that he'd walk over his grandmother if necessary to elect Richard Nixon—a memo that was leaked to the press. Despite Charles Colson's vigorous attempts to correct the record in subsequent years, "walk over my own grandmother" remains his verbal legacy.

Verdict: Credit a senator's aide, not Charles Colson.

"The GRAVEYARDS are full of indispensable men." This mordant observation is commonly recited by politicians on the verge of leaving office. Most often attributed to Charles de Gaulle, it has also been credited to Winston Churchill, English soccer coach Geoff Cooke, American political operative James Carville, Nebraska senator Chuck Hagel, Pennsylvania senator Rick Santorum, and the grandmother of former Texas senator Phil Gramm. Others simply call it a proverb, of French or Spanish origin. On the eve of his departure as Olympic Committee president, Spain's Juan

Antonio Samaranch recited this saying as if it were proverbial and familiar. Others simply call the adage "an old saying."

Verdict: An old saying.

"I am the GREATEST." Muhammad Ali never claimed to have coined his own signature line. Late in his boxing career Ali told a reporter that he didn't even believe he was the greatest. Ali explained that wrestler Gorgeous George, whose boasting filled stadium seats, inspired him to follow suit. "So I started the 'I am the greatest' thing," said Ali. However, biographer Thomas Hauser pointed out that Ali was bragging long before he saw Gorgeous George wrestle. Wilfrid Sheed, another Ali biographer, thought this famous boast may have originated with the boxer's father.

Verdict: Although it is too generic for a specific attribution, credit Muhammad Ali for being the most energetic publicist of this boast.

"GREED is good." Often thought to typify the narcissistic 1980s, this statement is a simplified version of something financier Ivan Boesky said in a 1986 commencement address at the University of California's School of Business Administration: "Greed is all right. . . . Greed is healthy. You can be greedy and still feel good about yourself." Boesky later went to prison for financial malfeasance. His philosophy inspired the memorable assertion by Michael Douglas as stockbroker Gordon Gekko in the 1987 movie *Wall Street* (whose screenplay was cowritten by Stanley Weiser and director Oliver Stone): "Greed, for lack of a better word, is good." *Bartlett's* and many other sources include the bumper-stickered version of this line: "Greed is good."

Verdict: Simplified Boesky, condensed *Wall Street.*

"Never doubt that a small GROUP of thoughtful, committed citizens can change the world." This comment—sometimes including the coda "In fact it's the only thing that ever has"—is so widely attributed to anthropologist Margaret Mead (1901–1978) that it's become her most familiar quotation. It is the only quotation posted on the home page of the Institute for Intercultural Studies, an organization devoted to keeping Mead's ideas alive. No one, however, including members of this institute, knows when or where she might have uttered these words. Diligent searching by them and others has never found an original source. A similar quotation, "We must remember that one determined person can make a significant difference, and that a small group of determined people can change the course of history," has been attributed to feminist Sonia Johnson, though without a source.

Verdict: Possibly Margaret Mead, in conversation or in a speech.

"The GUARD dies, but never surrenders." ("La Garde meurt, mais ne se rend pas.") When he commanded the Imperial Guards at Waterloo, Lt. Gen. Pierre Jacques E. Comte de Cambronne (1770–1842) was renowned for this proud response to the English demand for their surrender. Count Cambronne himself denied ever saying it. Since he was taken prisoner at Waterloo, prima facie evidence supports his case. As Cambronne remarked at an 1835 banquet in his honor, "In the first place, we did not die, and in the second, we did surrender." In *Les Misérables,* Victor Hugo incorporated what many think Cambronne actually responded to the English: *"Merde!"* ("Shit!") In France it is so generally assumed this is what the count actually said that *"Merde!"* is known as *"le mot de Cambronne,"* and the term *Cambronne* is sometimes used as a euphemism for *merde.* The source of his more eloquent response is thought to have been a journalist named Basilon de Rougemont. Known in his time for an ability to compose stirring phrases, Rougemont is said to have attributed this one to Cambronne the day after his defeat at Waterloo.

   Verdict: More likely Basilon de Rougemont than Count Cambronne.

"Up, GUARDS, and at 'em!" This order was supposedly given at Waterloo by the Duke of Wellington (Arthur Wellesley, 1769–1852). Various other versions of his command have also been reported. "People will invent words for me," the Duke reportedly told a sculptor who was working on a bust of him in 1841, "but I really don't know what I said." Eleven years later he responded to a letter of inquiry, "What I must have said, and possibly did say, was, 'Stand up, guards!' and then gave the commanding officers the order to attack."

   Verdict: Melodramatized Wellington.

"Better that ten GUILTY persons escape than one innocent person suffer." The English jurist Sir William Blackstone made this point in his *Commentaries on the Laws of England* (1769). It became such a bedrock principle of Western law that, in legal parlance, 10 guilty to 1 innocent is known as the "Blackstone ratio." In a thorough exploration of the background of this concept, Harvard Law School Professor Alexander Volokh has shown that (a) this concept long antedates its most familiar expression by Blackstone, and (b) ratios vary widely in its various iterations, from 1,000:1 to 1:1. According to Volokh, Roman emperor Trajan (A.D. 53–117) thought it "preferable that the crime of a guilty man should go unpunished than an innocent man be condemned." Eleven centuries later, Jewish-Spanish legal philosopher Moses Maimonides (1135–1204) wrote, "It is better and more satisfactory to acquit a thousand guilty persons than to

put a single innocent man to death...." In his 1693 publication *Cases of Conscience concerning evil SPIRITS Personating Men, Witchcrafts, infallible Proofs of Guilt in such as are accused with that Crime,* Increase Mather (the father of Cotton) anticipated Blackstone's ratio when he concluded it "were better that ten suspected witches should escape than one innocent person should be condemned." And this is just a small sampling of many expressions of this kind.

Verdict: Credit William Blackstone for the most familiar expression of a historic legal concept.

"Any good prosecutor can get a grand jury to indict a HAM sandwich." When a high-profile public figure is on the verge of being indicted by a grand jury, the Ham Sandwich Theory is invariably trotted out. According to this theory any good prosecutor can get a grand jury to indict a ham sandwich. That usually is called "an old saying," "an old saw," or "an adage," because no one seems quite sure where this axiom originated. Sol Wachtler, the onetime Chief Judge of New York's State Court of Appeals, is the first person known to have observed that most grand juries would "indict a ham sandwich" if asked to do so by a district attorney. Wachtler said this in January 1985. In 1992 Wachtler himself was indicted for harassing a former girlfriend and spent eleven months in prison after being convicted.

Verdict: Credit Sol Wachtler.

"If the only tool you have is a HAMMER, everything looks like a nail." Credit for this familiar quotation has been given to everyone from Buddha to Bernard Baruch. Mark Twain is the most common recipient, based on no evidence whatsoever. One surgeon says it is an old saying in his profession. Computer programmers are also fond of the adage, as is author-speaker Steven Covey. The earliest known appearance of this basic idea is in *The Conduct of Inquiry,* a 1964 book by philosopher Abraham Kaplan. To illustrate what he called the "law of the instrument," Kaplan wrote, "Give a small boy a hammer, and he will find that everything he encounters needs pounding." Two years later, in his 1966 book *The Psychology of Science,* psychologist Abraham Maslow wrote, "I suppose it is tempting, if the only tool you have is a hammer, to treat everything as if it were a nail."

Verdict: For now, credit two Abrahams: Kaplan for the basic idea, Maslow for the more popular version.

"We must all HANG together, or most assuredly we shall all hang separately." Benjamin Franklin supposedly made this observation as he signed

the Declaration of Independence (in response to a colleague who warned, "We must be unanimous. There must be no pulling different ways; we must all hang together."). No contemporary account attributed this quip to Franklin, however, and for good reason. Well into the nineteenth century Franklin's erstwhile pun was attributed to William Penn's grandson Richard Penn, the lieutenant governor of Pennsylvania and a strong supporter of the revolution. According to Penn family history and Philadelphia lore, when told by his revolutionary colleagues that "they must all hang together," Richard responded, "If you do not, gentlemen, I can tell you that you will be very apt to hang separately." This version appeared in an 1830 book, and an 1841 press account. An 1839 joke book and an 1840 biography moved the quip from Penn's mouth to that of Ben Franklin, however, and there it has stayed.

Verdict: If anyone said this, it was Richard Penn, not Benjamin Franklin.

"If you can't stand the HEAT, get out of the kitchen." To explain his decision not to run for reelection in 1952, Truman quoted the advice of an old friend: "If you can't stand the heat, get out of the kitchen." At the time, it was assumed that Truman was referring to his wisecracking pal Harry Vaughan, who still gets credit for this line in *The Oxford Dictionary of Quotations*. More often Truman himself is assumed to be its author. A few months after he first put this aphorism into the vernacular, Truman called it "a saying I used to hear from my old friend and colleague on the Jackson County [Missouri] Court." According to biographer Robert Ferrell, Jackson County politician Eugene "Buck" Purcell, a fellow judge of Truman's, said in 1931, "If a man can't stand the heat he ought to stay out of the kitchen." In his bestselling biography of Truman, David McCullough also credited Purcell for this saying, though he gave no source. (Presumably his source was Ferrell.)

Verdict: Credit Buck Purcell as author, Harry Truman as publicist.

"HELL hath no fury like a woman scorned." Often misattributed to Shakespeare, this thought first appeared in William Congreve's 1697 play *The Mourning Bride*: "Heaven has no rage, like love to hatred turned, / Nor hell a fury like a woman scorned." Congreve, in turn, undoubtedly was familiar with Colley Cibber's *Love's Last Shift,* a play produced the year before *The Mourning Bride*. Cibber's play included the lines "No Fiend in Hell can match the fury of a disappointed woman!—Scorned! Slighted; dismissed without a parting Pang!"

Verdict: Credit Cibber for the idea, Congreve for its better expression, and time for compression and polish.

"The hottest place in HELL is reserved for those who do not speak out in times of moral crisis." Variations of this comment are popular among idealistic politicians, who invariably cite Dante, because John Kennedy did. In a 1959 speech, Kennedy said, "For, as the poet Dante once said: 'The hottest places in hell are reserved for those who in a time of great moral crisis maintain their neutrality.'" Shortly after World War II he'd recorded a slightly different version of this saying as Dante's in his notebook. Dante did say some things about hell, but apparently this wasn't among them. The closest words anyone has found in Dante's *Inferno* are: "They are mixed with that repulsive choir of angels . . . undecided in neutrality. Heaven, to keep its beauty, cast them out, but even Hell itself would not receive them for fear the wicked there might glory over them." Winston Churchill is sometimes credited with having said during the run-up to World War II, "The hottest part of hell is reserved for those who, at a time of grave moral crisis, steadfastly maintain their neutrality," but Churchill scholar Richard Langworth cannot find that comment in any speech given by his subject from 1938 on. The phrase "hottest place in hell" was a commonplace in nineteenth-century religious exhortations.
    Verdict: Author unknown, not Dante, not Churchill.

"He who HESITATES is lost." The original wording in Joseph Addison's 1713 play *Cato* is "The woman that deliberates is lost." Over time "the woman" became "she," then "he."
    Verdict: Polished, gender-bent Addison.

"HIGH SCHOOL is closer to the core of the American experience than anything else I can think of." This could be Kurt Vonnegut's most re-quoted line, from his introduction to the 1970 collection *Our Time Is Now: Notes from the High School Underground.*
    Verdict: Credit Kurt Vonnegut.

"HISTORY is bunk." In 1916, on the eve of America's entry into World War I, *Chicago Tribune* reporter Charles N. Wheeler asked Henry Ford about the historical context of his prodisarmament views. Ford responded, "What do we care what they did five hundred or one thousand years ago? . . . History is more or less bunk. It's tradition. We don't want tradition. We want to live in the present and the only history that is worth a tinker's dam is the history we make today." Ford's full thought—including his "more or less" qualifier—soon gave way to the three-word version for which he's best remembered.

Verdict: One more unflattering abridgement of a prominent man's words.

"HISTORY is written by the victors." Because he said that history is written by the winners in a 1972 interview, *Roots* author Alex Haley sometimes gets credit for this thought. Winston Churchill and Joseph Stalin do too. Some think it actually began with Napoleon. The French emperor made other observations about history, but not this one. In a critique of "historicism," written shortly before he died in 1940, German literary critic Walter Benjamin wrote that if one should ask with whom its adherents empathize, "The answer is inevitable: with the victor." Subsequently, India's first prime minister, Jawaharlal Nehru, wrote in *The Discovery of India* (1946), "History is almost always written by the victors and conquerors and gives their viewpoint." This maxim feels older than that, however, and probably is. In 1879, a brief article in *Potter's American Monthly* described pieces of bark discovered in Kansas that apparently depicted a defeat inflicted on local Indians by ones from what is now Mexico. "The records were evidently written by the victors," this article concluded. While hardly conclusive, that observation suggests that this basic concept was in play well over a century ago.

Verdict: An old idea given modern expression by Nehru, Haley, and many others.

"HOLD the fort! I am coming!" This is what we like to think a determined William Tecumseh Sherman wired the beleaguered defenders of a Union supply depot in Georgia's Allatoona Pass in 1864. What General Sherman actually semaphored from Kenesaw Mountain was more mundane: "Hold out; relief is coming," according to one report, or "Sherman says hold fast. We are coming," according to another. Popular retelling melodramatized this message. The improved version was riveted into popular lore when it became the first line of a postwar hymn by Philip Paul Bliss that was popularized by evangelists Dwight L. Moody and Ira Sankey.

> *"Hold the fort, for I am coming."*
> *Jesus signals still;*
> *Wave the answer back to heaven,*
> *"By the grace we will."*

Sherman himself always disavowed the melodramatized version of his message from Kenesaw Mountain, but by 1887 he had concluded, "It makes little difference and we had better allow Moody and Sanky's hymn of 'Hold the Fort, for I am Coming' to stand uncontradicted."

Verdict: Romanticized Sherman.

"All is lost save HONOR." ("Tout est perdu fors l'honneur.") After losing the Battle of Pavia in 1525, Francis I of France wrote to his mother, "Madame, I have begged to be allowed to write you this letter, to inform you what hope I have of recovering my present misfortune, in which all that remains is my honor, and my life which is safe," etc., etc. The thought went on and on. Over time the French king's words were abridged and polished into the more popular version.

Verdict: Condensed Francis I.

"A man in passion rides a mad HORSE." Another Franklin-Herbert collaboration. In 1640 George Herbert wrote, "A man in Passion rides a horse that runs away from him." Franklin's version, a century later, was "A Man in a Passion rides a mad Horse."

Verdict: Franklin's improvement of Herbert.

"There is nothing better for the inside of a man than the outside of a HORSE." The cover of a trade magazine once credited this observation to Winston Churchill. Other individuals—including Woodrow Wilson's physician Dr. Cary Grayson and Ronald Reagan—peddled that tribute to horses as if it originated with them (leading George W. Bush to say in his eulogy for Reagan, "He believed in taking a break now and then, because as he said, there is nothing better for the inside of a man than the outside of a horse"). In fact, this observation has a long pedigree, dating back well into the nineteenth century. Clergyman Henry Ward Beecher (1813–1887) is one person to whom the thought was attributed in his time. Oliver Wendell Holmes is another, along with several others of lesser renown. In England, Winston Churchill's predecessor as prime minister, Lord Palmerston (1784–1865) is credited with saying that nothing is better for the inside of a man than the outside of a horse.

Verdict: Longtime male equestrian wisdom.

"I don't care what you do as long as you don't do it in the street and frighten the HORSES." This popular expression of sexual tolerance is generally attributed to Mrs. Patrick Campbell (the actress Beatrice Stella Tanner,

1865–1940). Even though her many biographers usually credit "Mrs. Pat" with making that observation, their wording varies, and no rock-solid source is ever cited. According to biographer Alan Dent, around 1910 Mrs. Campbell—the first woman to play Eliza Doolittle in Shaw's *Pygmalion*—told a young actress who complained about the affection one male actor showed for another, "Does it *really* matter what these affectionate people do—so long as they don't do it in the streets and *frighten the horses!*" Margot Peters's biography has her saying, "I don't care what people do, as long as they don't do it in the street and frighten the horses!" after being told of a homosexual love affair between two actors. In his biography of Somerset Maugham, Ted Morgan improbably credits the line to King Edward VII.

Verdict: Credit Mrs. Patrick Campbell, tentatively.

HUMORISTS

Mark Twain and Will Rogers are America's premier humorists, and the sources of many of its most quoted quips. But in the late nineteenth and early twentieth centuries, a strong bench backed them up.

Artemus Ward

(Charles Farrar Browne, 1834–1867). Wildly popular in antebellum and Civil War–era America, the writer-lecturer from Maine was best known for telling funny stories in dialect, with fractured grammar. Abraham Lincoln was partial to Ward, and sometimes read the humorist's yarns aloud to his cabinet. One, sometimes attributed to Lincoln himself, depicted a young man who, having killed his parents, pleads for mercy as an orphan. Another Ward creation featured a "Wise Man" telling a little girl, "Ah! You poor foolish little girl—here is a dollar for you." Responded the girl, "Thank you sir; but I have a sister at home as foolish as I am; can't you give me a dollar for her?" Even though he was not known for coining aphorisms, Ward nonetheless is sometimes given credit for ones coined by others, such as Josh Billings's about knowing what just ain't so.

Josh Billings

(Henry Wheeler Shaw, 1818–1885) was among the most prominent American humorists of his time, possibly the most prominent, even being invited by Lincoln to perform at the White House. Though he eventually published several books, the New Yorker's primary forum was the lecture podium, where his spoofy speeches were a form of prior-day stand-up comedy. (One result of his prolific lecturing is that several different versions of noted Billings lines can sometimes be found.) Like Finley Peter Dunne, Artemus Ward, and many other American humorists of an earlier era, Billings expressed himself in a fractured phonetic dialect. Billings's most quoted line, often polished up and put in other humorists' mouths, was **"It is better to kno less than to kno so much that AIN'T so."** Nearly as well-known in his own time was "I hav finally cum to the konklusion that a good reliable set of bowels iz worth more to a man than any quantity ov branes." Billings also said, "Flattery iz like Colone water, tew be smelt ov, not swallowed." Mark Twain's famous line about the difference between the right word and the wrong word being the difference between lightning and a lightning bug was inspired by Billings, as Twain himself suggested when saying in a 1901 speech, "Josh Billings defined the difference between humor and wit as that between the lightning bug and lightning."

Kin Hubbard

(Frank McKinney "Kin" Hubbard, 1868–1930). In the early twentieth century, Kin Hubbard's droll observations had a devoted following. "No man in our generation was within a mile of him," said Will Rogers. Hubbard's humor writing for the *Indianapolis News* was nationally syndicated as two lines in modified dialect from a bumpkin named Abe Martin, with a caricature drawn by his creator. Eventually Hubbard began writing comic essays as well. His most enduring line—seldom attributed to him—was **"When a feller says, 'It hain't th' MONEY, but th' principle o' th' thing,' it's th' money."** Other Hubbard sayings showed the seventh-grade dropout to be a keen observer of human foibles:

Th' feller that don't know what he's talkin' about allus wants t' bet you.

Th' feller that say's 'I may be wrong, but—' does not believe ther kin be any such possibility.

Some folks are too polite t' be up t' any good.

It seems like th' less a statesman amounts to th' more he loves th' flag.

Th' feller that's mean around home is allus th' life an' sunshine o' some lodge.

A never failin' way t' git rid of a feller is t' tell him somethin' for his own good.

It's pretty hard t' be efficient without bein' obnoxious.

Nobuddy ever forgets where he buried a hatchet.

Th' hardest kind o' prosperity to stand is a neighbor's.

It's what we learn after we think we know it all that counts.

Hubbard biographer Fred C. Kelly believed that Thomas Marshall borrowed his line **"What this country needs is a good five-cent CIGAR"** from his fellow Hoosier, but offered no conclusive evidence. (That saying was already circulating when Hubbard was a boy.) On the other hand, Abe Martin's observation **"T'AIN'T what a man don't know that hurts him; it's what he knows that just ain't so"** owed an unacknowledged debt to Josh Billings.

Mr. Dooley

Finley Peter Dunne (1867–1936). Through his mouthpiece "Mr. Dooley," Finley Peter Dunne continues to be one of the most quoted American folk oracles. Expressed in the brogue of his fictional Irish-American bartender, Dunne's most requoted lines include, **"Th' supreme coort follows th' illiction returns," "POLITICS ain't bean bag,"** and—on the proper role of a newspaper—**"COMFORTS th' afflicted, afflicts th' comfortable."** Mr. Dooley is also renowned for advising, **"Thrust ivrybody, but cut the caards."**

Other comments by Mr. Dooley that aren't quite as renowned but still sometimes get cited include: "A fanatic is a man that does what he thinks th' Lord wud do if He knew the facts in th' case," "A vote on the tallysheet is worth two in the box," and "Most vigitaryans I iver see looked enough like their food to be classed as cannibals."

Although some think Dunne originated the maxim **"All POLITICS is local,"** no evidence has ever been produced to confirm this attribution. Dunne biographer Edward Bander is sure he was not the source of this saying. In *Mr. Dooley and Mr. Dunne,* Bander points out how many ersatz Dooleyisms have been put into circulation, often to promote a cause. In one Mr. Dooley ridicules the "open shop" (a workplace that isn't unionized) as a place "where they kape the doors open to accommodate th' constant stream of min comin' t' take jobs chaper than the min that has the jobs . . ." This made-up Dooleyism achieved such wide circulation and credibility that economist Paul Samuelson included it in his classic textbook, *Economics.*

Fred Allen

(John Florence Sullivan, 1894–1957). Between the wars, sardonic, droopy-eyed Fred Allen was one of America's best-known humorists. Allen began as a stage actor and vaudevillian after World War I, then segued to radio, where he hosted an enormously popular weekly comedy show. After the Second World War Allen had a mercifully short-lived television show that provided him with the grist for some of the most biting observations ever made about that medium. According to Allen the reason they called television a medium was because nothing on it was well done. (This quip is also attributed to comedian Ernie Kovacs.) Allen added that "Imitation is the sincerest form of television."

What set Allen apart from his many colleagues was that he wrote his own material, drawing largely on native wit. Fred Allen is remembered today primarily for a few quotations that stayed in play long after his death in 1957. **"California is a wonderful place to live, if you're an orange"** is perhaps the most often cited ("Los Angeles" or "Hollywood" replaces "California" in some versions). That line is sometimes attributed to Dorothy Parker, or Herman Mankiewicz. Allen also called Hollywood **"a place where people from Iowa mistake each other for stars,"** adding, **"You could take all of the sincerity there is in Hollywood, stuff it into a flea's navel, and you'd still have room for six caraway seeds and an agent's heart."** (Some think it was a flea's nose Allen referred to, a firefly's navel, or a gnat's, and that only three caraway seeds were involved, or four.) Variations on this theme have been expressed by many others. Allen once called a conference of radio executives **"a meeting at which a group of men who, singly, can do nothing, agree collectively that nothing can be done."** This classic remark is often applied to committee meetings in general. An unverified, but frequently quoted, Allenism is **"A celebrity is one** who works hard to become well-known, then goes through back-streets wearing dark glasses so he won't be recognized." Fred Allen also is one of the many who are credited with characterizing a man as someone "who can brighten a room by leaving it."

"Don't worry about people stealing an IDEA. If it's original, you will have to ram it down their throats." According to Robert Slater's book *Portraits in Silicon,* Harvard computer pioneer Howard Aiken gave this advice to a graduate student who was concerned about ideas in his thesis being stolen.
   Verdict: Credit Howard Aiken.

"There is one thing stronger than all the armies of the world, and that is an IDEA whose time has come." According to *Great Thoughts* compiler George Seldes, Mussolini's house newspaper *Il Popolo d'Italia* repeated this maxim regularly. No original source has ever been found for the classic declaration. (*The Oxford Dictionary of Quotations* cites a nonexistent 1943 issue of the *Nation* as its source. It turns out that this quotation actually appeared on a *Nation* advertising flier.) Apparently this most familiar of quotations is an adaptation of a line Victor Hugo wrote in 1852, also referenced by *Oxford*: *"On résiste á l'invasion des armées; on ne résiste pas à l'invasion des idées."* ("An invasion of armies can be resisted; an invasion of ideas cannot be resisted.")
   Verdict: Pithier Hugo.

"Immature poets IMITATE; mature poets steal." T. S. Eliot made this assertion in a thoughtful essay about literary debts. Eliot contended that it was not the borrowing from someone else's work that should concern us, but the manner in which this transaction is negotiated. "One of the surest of tests is the way in which a poet borrows," he wrote. ". . . bad poets deface what they take, and good poets make it into something better, or at least something different. The good poet welds his theft into a whole of feeling which is unique, utterly different from that from which it was torn; the bad poet throws it into something which has no cohesion." Eliot's glib-sounding, out-of-context assertion is the one that survived as a quotation. Due to a spoof feature in *Esquire* magazine in 1962, "Immature artists imitate. Mature artists steal." is sometimes misattributed to Lionel Trilling. Pablo Picasso has been credited with "Mediocre artists borrow, great artists steal," and Igor Stravinsky with "A good composer does not imitate; he steals."
   Verdict: Credit T. S. Eliot.

"All the things I like to do are either IMMORAL, illegal, or fattening." This popular catchphrase is often attributed to Alexander Woollcott, though without a specific source. According to biographer Howard Teichmann, the rotund theater critic frequently made this observation to others. In 1933, *Reader's Digest* attributed the comment to Woollcott without a citation. In a movie made the next year, W. C. Fields told a woman, "According to you, everything I like to do is either illegal, immoral or fattening."

Verdict: Credit Alexander Woollcott, in conversation.

"The only good INDIAN is a dead Indian." Whether Gen. Phil "Fightin' Phil" Sheridan actually said that the only good Indians were dead has never been determined. Documentary filmmaker Ken Burns thought he did. "It has the ring of typical Sheridan rhetoric," wrote biographer Paul Hutton. The genesis of our assumption that General Sheridan made this statement is his 1869 meeting with a Comanche chief in Oklahoma. This chief reportedly told Sheridan, "Me good Indian." Sheridan allegedly replied, "The only good Indians I ever saw were dead." Sheridan later denied having said any such thing. Even if he did say that the only good Indians were dead, Sheridan would hardly have been the first American to do so. On May 28, 1868—some months before Fightin' Phil was supposed to have made this remark—Montana congressman J. M. Cavanaugh said on the floor of the House, "I have never in my life seen a good Indian (and I have seen thousands) except when I have seen a dead Indian." A 1926 history of postwar America reported that in the immediate aftermath of the Civil War, "the proverb that the only good Indian was a dead one was subscribed to in every ranch house, military post, overland stage station and mining gulch in the Western states and territories." Proverb scholar Wolfgang Mieder thinks that in different forms this folk saying expressed sentiments that were especially common on the American frontier. Mieder gives little credence to its attribution to Phil Sheridan.

Verdict: An old canard put in Phil Sheridan's mouth, possibly by himself.

"No one can make you feel INFERIOR without your consent." Some consider this Eleanor Roosevelt's signature line. *Bartlett's* and other sources say her famous quotation can be found in *This Is My Story,* Roosevelt's 1937 autobiography. It can't. Quotographer Rosalie Maggio scoured that book and many others by and about Roosevelt in search of this line, without success. In their own extensive searching, archivists at the Franklin D. Roosevelt Library in Hyde Park, New York, have not been able to find the

quotation in *This Is My Story* or any other writing by the First Lady. Nor have they been able to find two other quotations commonly attributed to Eleanor Roosevelt: "The future belongs to those who believe in the beauty of their dreams," and "Women are like tea bags. You never know how strong they are until you put them in hot water." According to Maggio the latter is an old saw that has been applied to women and men alike.

    Verdict: No proof exists that Eleanor Roosevelt ever said or wrote this.

"We do not INHERIT the earth from our ancestors, we borrow it from our children." Former Secretary of State James Baker once attributed this thought to Emerson. According to a Celestial Seasonings tea box, it's actually an Amish proverb. More often this popular saying is said to come from American, or Canadian, Indians. It has also been attributed to members of other indigenous groups. Alternatively, the proverb's birthplace has been located in Africa, in one case specifically in Kenya. Its more likely place of origin is a bar in North Carolina. That was where, after his third martini, environmentalist David Brower (1912–2000) said he observed, "We do not inherit the earth from our fathers, we are borrowing it from our children." In a 1995 book Brower said that after being told these words were chiseled in stone at the National Aquarium in Baltimore over his name, he found them in a record of the North Carolina interview buried in his files.

    Verdict: David Brower is as good a guess as any.

"If you want to know what people are like, share an INHERITANCE with them." This comment has been widely attributed to Benjamin Franklin—by advice columnist Ann Landers especially—but never with a source. It's unlikely that one exists. On the other hand, in *Aphorisms on Man* (1788), Swiss clergyman Johann Caspar Lavater wrote, "Say not you know another entirely, till you have divided an inheritance with him."

    Verdict: Credit Reverend Lavater.

"INSANITY consists of doing the same thing over and over, hoping for a different result." This popular definition of insanity (or "neurosis") has been attributed to Ben Franklin, Rudyard Kipling, and "Anonymous"; it has also been called a "Chinese proverb." Albert Einstein most often gets credit for the remark, perhaps because he is often credited with a similar observation: "The world we've made, as a result of the level of thinking we have done thus far, creates problems we cannot solve at the same level of thinking." (Various versions of this thought are attributed to Einstein, most reliably "The unleashed power of the atom has changed everything save

our modes of thinking, and thus we drift toward unparalleled catastrophe.") Author Rita Mae Brown became another credit contender after a
character mouthed this definition of insanity in her 1983 novel *Sudden
Death*. Twelve-step groups have long warned about doing the same thing
over and over hoping for a different result, without giving any specific
source for their warning. After seeing this depiction of insanity in a book
his wife gave him, Bill Clinton used it during his 1992 campaign for the
presidency. Comedienne Jackie "Moms" Mabley (1897–1975) was famous
for a variation on this theme attributed to her: "If you always do what you
always did, you will always get what you always got." Some version of those
words has been attributed to others as well, including Yogi Berra, Dale
Carnegie, motivational speaker Zig Ziglar, and cookie maker Wally Amos.

   Verdict: Originator yet to be determined.

"INSANITY is hereditary; you get it from your children." Humorist Sam
Levenson (1911–1980) included this thought in his 1975 book *You Can Say
That Again, Sam!* (after being so quoted twelve years earlier, in the *Diner's
Club Magazine*). This witticism circulates widely and anonymously. A
bumper sticker is sometimes cited as its source, or a wall plaque. Comedian
Joey Adams used the line in his own routines. *Forbes* magazine attributed it
to "Lillian Holstein." Shortly before she died in a car crash, actress Grace
Kelly was quoted as saying, "Premature graying of the hair is hereditary.
Parents inherit it from their children."

   Verdict: Credit Sam Levenson.

*"The test of a first-rate INTELLIGENCE is the ability to hold two op-
posed ideas in the mind at the same time, and still retain the ability to
function."* This appears in "The Crack-Up," an essay F. Scott Fitzgerald
wrote in 1936 that was published posthumously in a book with the same
title. Fitzgerald's full thought was "Let me make a general observation—
the test of a first-rate intelligence is the ability to hold two opposed ideas
in the mind at the same time, and still retain the ability to function." In his
1949 book *1984* George Orwell subsequently wrote, "*Doublethink* means
the power of holding two contradictory beliefs in one's mind simultaneously, and accepting both of them."

   Verdict: Credit F. Scott Fitzgerald.

"May you live in INTERESTING times." Robert Kennedy put this mini-
curse in modern play when he said during a 1966 speech in South Africa,
"There is a Chinese curse which says, 'May he live in interesting times.'

Like it or not, we live in interesting times. . . ." Although the curse caught on, as one of Chinese origin, nobody has ever been able to confirm those roots. In *Report from Greco* (1961), a fictionalized memoir written in the late 1950s, *Zorba the Greek* author Nikos Kazantzakis (who spent time in China) wrote, "The Chinese have a strange malediction: 'I curse you; may you be born in an important age.'" Professor Stephen DeLong of the State University of New York has doggedly explored this saying's provenance. The earliest use DeLong has discovered is in a 1950 story in *Astounding Science Fiction* that included this line: "For centuries the Chinese used an ancient curse: 'May you live in interesting times.'" DeLong and others have queried Chinese acquaintances about this saying. None were familiar with the "ancient Chinese curse," including a group of Hong Kong professionals. One inquirer discovered that a Chinese acquaintance was the first person he'd ever asked about this quotation who had never even heard of it. Others said they had heard it only in English. A Chinese immigrant in Canada cited his country's proverb "It's better to be a dog in a peaceful time rather than a man in a chaotic period" as a possible source of the "interesting times" curse. Dr. Torrey Whitman, president of New York's China Institute and a specialist in Chinese proverbs, has concluded that "May you live in interesting times" did not originate in China. Whitman thinks the saying was created by a Westerner, probably an American, who called the saying "Chinese" to enhance its mystique. It has also been called a curse of Jewish origin, or one used by the Scots, or by the Russians.

Verdict: Most likely a Western creation put in eastern mouths.

"*. . . an IRON CURTAIN has descended across the continent.*" In a famous 1946 speech at Fulton, Missouri, Churchill said of the emerging political map, "From Stettin in the Baltic to Trieste in the Adriatic, an iron curtain has descended across the continent." That sentence thrust the term "iron curtain" into public discourse. It did not originate with Churchill, however. "Iron curtain" was the name given fireproof metallic curtains that were first installed in theaters during the late eighteenth century. As early as 1819, an Englishman traveling in India used the term metaphorically when he wrote, "As if an iron curtain had dropped between us and the Avenging Angel, the deaths diminished." In his 1904 novel *The Food of the Gods,* H. G. Wells noted of one character, "An iron curtain had dropped between him and the outer world." On the eve of World War I, Belgium's Bavarian-born Queen Elizabeth said of the invading Germans, "Between them and me there is now a bloody iron curtain which has descended forever!" A year later, in *A Mechanistic View of War and Peace* (1915), George Crile asked Americans to imagine how they would react if Mexico "were a rich, cultured, and brave nation of forty million with a deep-rooted grievance, and an iron curtain at its frontier." In that same year, a New York resident wrote *The Dial* that "the great war, like an iron curtain . . . has measurably interrupted our communication with Europe." After the successful Bolshevik revolution of 1917, Russian author Vasily Rozanov wrote, "With a clang, thud, and bang the iron curtain is dropping down on Russian history." In a 1919 assessment of Bolshevik Russia's prospects, German commentator Hans Vorst wrote of the need to "have a glance behind the iron curtain which separates us from the future." The following year a British visitor named Ethel Snowden said of her arrival in the Soviet Union: "We were behind the 'iron curtain' at last!" In 1921 an American magazine article reported, "Bolshevik Russia lay concealed behind an iron curtain. . . ." During the 1930s, Russians themselves repeatedly warned that the West was trying to seal itself off from the Communist world with an iron curtain of contempt. Three years before Churchill's Fulton speech, Nazi propagandist Joseph Goebbels warned that if Russia defeated Germany, "Behind an iron curtain mass butcheries of people would begin." On the eve of Germany's defeat, Foreign Minister Count Lutz Schwerin von Krosigk talked of Bolshevism's "Iron Curtain." The speech in which von Krosigk used this term was reported by the *Times of London* on May 3, 1945. Nine days later Winston Churchill sent Harry Truman a telegram in which he wrote, "An iron curtain is drawn down upon their [Russian] front." A month later he used the phrase again in another telegram to Truman. On July 24, 1945, Churchill gave a speech in which he said that due to Soviet machinations in Eastern Europe, the British mission in Bucharest was cut off—"An iron fence has come down around them . . ." On October 21, 1945, one year before Churchill used the phrase in Fulton, London's *Sunday Empire News* ran an article headlined "An Iron Curtain Across Europe."

Verdict: Many authors, one key publicist—Winston Churchill.

THOMAS JEFFERSON

Thomas Jefferson came down on so many sides of so many issues that he's easily invoked by those who need a good quotation to buttress their cause. Jefferson himself complained that "Every word of mine which they can get hold of, however innocent, however orthodox even, is twisted, tormented, perverted, and, like the words of holy writ, ... made to mean everything but what they were intended to mean."

As one of America's most quoted figures, Jefferson inevitably became one of its most misquoted. Sayings as unlikely as "Never put off until tomorrow what you can do today," and "The harder I work, the more luck I have," have been put in Jefferson's mouth. Ted Kennedy thought it was Jefferson who said, **"All that is necessary for EVIL to strive over good is for good to remain silent"** (a variation on the quotation that Kennedy's brother John misattributed to Edmund Burke). Jefferson also has been cited for observing, **"That GOVERNMENT is best which governs least,"** a quotation better attributed to editor John L. O'Sullivan. And, of course, David McCullough did mistakenly attribute the phrase "colossus of independence" to Jefferson in his biography of John Adams. (See "Introduction.")

In recent years Jefferson's words have been particularly beloved by right-wing zealots. Timothy McVeigh wore a T-shirt that featured a Jefferson quotation (**"The TREE of liberty must be refreshed from time to time with the blood of patriots and tyrants."**) on the day he bombed the Oklahoma City Federal Building. Conservative talk show hosts are fond of quoting the author of the Declaration of Independence about the right to bear arms, the need to keep religion in public life, and other topics. On the Internet it is common to see Jefferson's actual words, "No freeman shall ever be debarred the use of arms," with a second sentence spliced on: "The strongest reason for the people to retain the right to keep and bear arms is, as a last resort, to protect themselves against the tyranny in government." Another spurious Jefferson quotation, expressing concern about the power of private banks to control monetary policy, includes the word "deflation," a term that did not enter the lexicon until a century after Jefferson's death.

Other quotations commonly misattributed to Jefferson include: **"Eternal VIGILANCE is the price of liberty," "Those who desire to give up FREEDOM in order to gain security will not have, nor do they deserve, either one,"** and some variation of **"I am a SOLDIER so that my son may be a poet."** On the other hand, it was Jefferson, not Washington, who put the phrase **"ENTANGLING alliances"** on America's agenda when he spoke of **"Peace, commerce, and honest friendship for all nations, ENTANGLING alliances with none"** in his first inaugural address. Jefferson also wrote, **"I tremble for my country when I reflect that God is just."** This comment, taken from Jefferson's 1785 observation on slavery in *Notes on the State* *of Virginia,* "Indeed, I tremble for my country when I reflect that God is just: that his justice cannot sleep forever," was favored by Ronald Reagan and others.

Jefferson later wrote in a letter, "The basis of our governments being the opinion of the people, the very first object should be to keep that right; and **were it left to me to decide whether we should have a government without newspapers, or newspapers without a government, I should not hesitate a moment to prefer the latter.**" Illustrating his penchant for contradicting himself, Jefferson also commented, **"The man who never looks into a newspaper is better informed than he who reads them, inasmuch as he who knows nothing is nearer to truth than he whose mind is filled with falsehoods and errors."** Late in life Jefferson wrote a correspondent, **"I read no newspaper now but Ritchie's, and in that chiefly the advertisements, for they contain the only truths to be relied on in a newspaper."** This comment is sometimes abridged to read, "Advertisements contain the only truths to be relied on in a newspaper."

Another authentic Jefferson comment, "If a due participation of office is a matter of right, how are vacancies to be obtained? Those by death are few, by resignation none," is typically condensed into the more felicitous **"Few die and none resign."** Jefferson's comment about Shay's Rebellion in Massachusetts, "God forbid we should ever be twenty years without such a rebellion," is often generalized into some form of observation that we should have a revolution every couple of decades. He wrote James Madison about that uprising, **"I hold it, that a little rebellion, now and then, is a good thing, and as necessary in the political world as storms in the physical."** The first part of this authentic Jefferson quotation is often requoted in various forms.

In his last letter, Jefferson famously argued that "The general spread of the light of science has already laid open to every view the palpable truth, that **the mass of mankind has not been born with saddles on their backs,** nor a favored few booted and spurred, ready to ride them legitimately, by the grace of God." This may have been inspired by a famous 1685 scaffold speech by Richard Rumbold, who was condemned to death for plotting against James II. According to a 1734 account, Rumbold said that, "he did not believe that God had made the greater part of mankind with saddles on their backs and bridles in their mouths, and some few booted and spurred to ride the rest."

"If JESUS Christ had taken a poll, he never would have preached the Gospel." Rep. Henry Hyde (R-Ill.) was especially fond of making this observation, as if the thought were original to him. Other politicians have done the same thing. But in an undated memo to himself written some time after the 1948 election, Harry Truman mused, "I wonder how far Moses would have gone if he had taken a poll in Egypt? What would Jesus Christ have preached if He had taken a poll in the land of Israel? Where would the Reformation have gone if Martin Luther had taken a poll?" This memo was later published in various collections of Truman's writing.

Verdict: Credit Harry Truman.

"JOHN MARSHALL has made his decision. Now let him enforce it." Although these words may represent Andrew Jackson's attitude toward the 1832 Supreme Court decision barring relocation of Cherokee Indians from Georgia, no credible evidence exists that he said them. This oath was put on the record two decades after Jackson's death, when, in an 1864 book, Horace Greeley reported his contemptuous retort to Chief Justice Marshall. (A three-volume biography of Jackson published in 1860 included only two references to Marshall, neither involving this retort.) According to Greeley, a former congressman told him of hearing about Old Hickory's challenge to Marshall, when he was in Washington during Jackson's presidency. Such a familiar quotation deserves a better source.

Verdict: There is no reliable evidence that Andrew Jackson ever said this.

SAMUEL JOHNSON

Due primarily to his chronicler-biographer James Boswell, Samuel Johnson is one of our richest sources of quotable quotes—and misquotes. Ranked with Wilde and Shaw as a conversationalist, Johnson had the great fortune to have someone present to record his many quips and comments. He also was a prolific writer. As a result, Samuel Johnson is the second-most-quoted Englishman (after Shakespeare). It did not hurt that he was a gifted aphorist, and a master of the English language who produced one of its first dictionaries. As with so many highly quotable figures, Johnson's words are often altered in the retelling, and apocryphal words or those of others are put in his mouth.

Familiar quotations that can reliably be attributed to Samuel Johnson (because they appear in Boswell's *Life of Samuel Johnson*) include:

"Depend upon it, no man was ever written down but by himself." This remark by Johnson, which he attributed to "old Bentley," (Thomas Bentley, the nephew of prominent classicist Richard Bentley, who in fact wrote in 1735, "No Man is demolished but by himself.") could be the genesis of a maxim routinely attributed to Eleanor Roosevelt, without verification: **"No one can make you feel INFERIOR without your consent."**

"Depend upon it, sir, when a man knows he is to be hanged in a fortnight, it CONCENTRATES his mind wonderfully." (Often recalled as "The prospect of being hanged focuses the mind wonderfully.")

"Sir, a woman's preaching is like a dog's walking on his hind legs. It is not done well; but you are surprised to find it done at all." (Said to Boswell about the preaching of a Quaker woman.)

"Sir, you know courage is reckoned the greatest of all virtues; because, unless a man has that virtue, he has no security for preserving any other." (The wording of this comment is often altered in retelling.) Churchill introduced a similar observation with the words "as has been said." (See sidebar "Winston Churchill.")

Other examples of authentic Johnsoniana include:

". . . a decent provision for the poor is the true TEST of a civilization."

". . . it was the TRIUMPH of hope over experience." (Johnson's assessment of a second marriage.)

"Patriotism is the last refuge of a scoundrel."

"No man but a blockhead ever wrote, except for money."

"I am willing to love all mankind, *except an American.*"

"He who praises everybody praises nobody." (This observation was included in a posthumous gathering of Johnsoniana, based on the recollection of a contemporary.)

"I would say to Robertson what an old tutor of a college said to one of his pupils: 'Read over your compositions, and wherever you meet with a passage which you think is particularly fine, STRIKE it out.'" (The tutor's words are routinely credited to Johnson himself.)

Quotations sometimes misattributed to Johnson include:

"Murder your DARLINGS." Sir Arthur Quiller-Couch's line is often misattributed to Samuel Johnson, probably because Johnson did say **"STRIKE it out."**

"Easy WRITING makes hard reading." Richard Sheridan's line is also a misattribution.

"Your manuscript is both good and original. But the part that is good is not original, and the part that is original is not good." Commonly thought to be a splendid put-down by Johnson, this cannot be found in his writing.

"The road to hell is paved with good intentions." According to Boswell, Johnson did say, "Hell is paved with good intentions," but that thought was hardly original to him, nor did he imply that it was.

"It is better to keep your MOUTH shut and appear stupid than to open it and remove all doubt." (Alternatively, **"It is better to remain silent and be thought a fool than to open your mouth and remove all doubt."**) Johnson is one among many to whom this warning is attributed, based on no evidence.

"A fishing pole has a hook at one end and a fool at the other." This dig at fishing is attributed to both Johnson and Jonathan Swift, without evidence in either case. There is no mention of fishing in Boswell's life of Johnson.

"Golf: A game in which you claim the privileges of age and retain the playthings of youth." According to Frank Lynch, who hosts a website devoted to Johnson quotations, the closest observation he actually made, in Rambler No. 50, was "It is a hopeless endeavor to unite the contrarieties of spring and winter; it is unjust to claim the privileges of age, and retain the play-things of childhood."

"The true measure of a man is how he treats someone who can do him absolutely no good." Both Abigail Van Buren and Ann Landers peddled this thought in their advice columns, Landers attributing it to Johnson. No evidence exists that he ever said, or wrote, these words. This saying has also been attributed to French aphorist François la Rochefoucauld (1613–1680).

"The next best thing to knowing something is knowing where to find it." Frank Lynch believes this is a corruption of Johnson's observation that "Knowledge is of two kinds. We know a subject ourselves, or we know where we can find information upon it."

"You don't have to eat the whole ox to know that it is tough." Although it can be found in no published work by or about Johnson, Lynch thinks this could be based on something Johnson did say about a book on Shakespeare: "I have indeed, not read it all. But

when I take up the end of a web, and find it packthread, I do not expect, by looking further, to find embroidery."

**"I did not have the time to write you a short LETTER, so I
wrote you a long one instead."** Pascal is the source of this thought,
in a different form, in a letter.

"TRUTH is the first casualty of war." At best this is an adaptation of what Johnson wrote in *The Idler* in 1758: "Among the calamities of war may be justly numbered the diminution of the love of truth
by the falsehoods which interest dictates and credulity encourages."

"JOURNALISM is the first draft of history." Journalists are very partial to this
depiction of what they do. Some think it originated with former *Washington
Post* editor Ben Bradlee. Others credit *Washington Post* publisher Katharine
Graham. In fact it was Philip Graham, Bradlee's boss, Katharine's husband
and her predecessor as *Post* publisher, who made a somewhat more turgid exhortation to *Newsweek* correspondents soon after his newspaper acquired that
magazine in 1963: "So let us today drudge on about our inescapably impossible task of providing every week a first rough draft of a history that will never
be completed about a world we can never understand. . . ."
     Verdict: Credit Philip Graham for the genesis of this thought.

"A JOURNEY of a thousand miles begins with a single step." Commonly
misattributed to Confucius, at times to Mao Zedong, or called simply a
"Chinese proverb" (by John Kennedy and many, many others), this adage appears in some translations of Lao Tzu's *Tao Teh Ching*. Some have questioned that translation, saying a more accurate version would be "The
journey of a thousand miles begins beneath one's feet." To complicate matters still further, it's a "thousand li" that Lao Tzu refers to, which is approxi-
mately four hundred miles. (The version in the most recent *Oxford
Dictionary of Quotations* is "The journey of a thousand li starts from where
one stands.") Therefore, according to one translator, the most accurate translation would be "A walk of four hundred miles begins beneath one's feet."
     Verdict: Credit Lao Tzu for the basic idea.

"Don't JUDGE a man until you have walked a mile in his shoes." This is
generally thought to be an update of an American Indian saying: "Don't
judge another man until you have walked two moons in his moccasins."
Although some say that this saying originated with the Nez Perce, the

Cherokee, or the Sioux, or more broadly with Northern Plains Indians, no solid evidence exists to confirm its actual origins. Since at least the 1950s the maxim has circulated in different forms, sometimes as a prayer ("Oh, Great Spirit . . ."), and with the distance to be walked ranging from "a mile" through "two moons," "three moons," or "two months." A similar proverb—"Don't criticize a man's gait until you are in his shoes"—is said to have originated in Ontario. According to lawyer Atticus Finch in Harper Lee's novel *To Kill a Mockingbird* (1962), "You never really understand a person until you consider things from his point of view—until you climb in his skin and walk around in it." And in the Talmud, Rabbi Hillel advised, "Do not judge others until you stand in their place."

Verdict: An old proverb, probably of North American Indian origin, and an even older basic idea.

JOHN F. KENNEDY

John F. Kennedy loved to pepper his speeches and public statements with quotations. This not only perked up his prose but improved his press by giving him an air of erudition. JFK depended for speech material not only on his erudite speechwriter Theodore Sorensen (who may have ghostwritten Kennedy's Pulitzer Prize–winning *Profiles in Courage*) but also on other well-educated aides, such as Arthur Schlesinger, Jr., John Kenneth Galbraith, and Richard Goodwin. Kennedy's main resource for quotations, however, was his memory and the notebook in which he'd spent years jotting quotations and other material, usually without a source. From his Senate days on, according to Sorensen, Kennedy "was the chief source of his own best quotations." Some came from his journal, some from his favorite books, most from inside his head. As a result, he was an endless source of half-remembered quotations from forgotten sources that his own aides and Library of Congress staffers scurried to try to confirm.

With such a haphazard approach to quote-confirmation, JFK was not always as knowledgeable as he tried to sound. Until his wife, Jacqueline, corrected him, Kennedy combined Emerson and Frost to conclude some of his speeches by saying:

> *I'll hitch my wagon to a star*
> *But I have promises to keep*
> *And miles to go before I sleep.*

Even though JFK routinely got his quotations wrong, it took years for us to figure this out. Meanwhile the young president launched any number of misworded, misattributed, or completely mystifying quotations into the public conversation, where they've stuck around to this day. The most glaring example is **"The only thing necessary for the triumph of EVIL is that good men do nothing,"** which Kennedy attributed to Edmund Burke and which recently was judged the most popular quotation of modern times (in a poll conducted by editors of *The Oxford Dictionary of Quotations*). Even though it is clear by now that Burke is unlikely to have made this observation, no one has ever been able to determine who did.

During his presidency, John Kennedy had a reputation as an original wit and elegant stylist. Some of this reputation was deserved, some not. Kennedy's oratory was not always as fresh as it seemed. Even his most famous phrases turned out to have long, unacknowledged pedigrees. **"The New Frontier"** was the title of a chapter in a 1936 book written by Sen. Alf Landon (R-Kan.), who ran for president that year. Two years earlier, in 1934, Franklin Roosevelt's onetime vice president, Henry Wallace, wrote a book titled *New Frontiers*. When Kennedy said **"LIFE is unfair,"** no mention was made that Oscar Wilde once wrote, **"Life is never fair."** (See sidebar "Oscar Wilde.") The most stirring line of JFK's inaugural address, **"ASK not what your country can do for you, ask what you can do for your country,"** echoed similar exhortations made by Oliver Wendell Holmes, Warren Harding, and the headmaster of Kennedy's prep school, among others. The inspiration for Kennedy's famous observation **"For of those to whom much is given, much is required"** can be found in Luke 12:48: "For unto whomsoever much is given, of him shall be much required. . . ."

When the United States made Winston Churchill an honorary citizen in 1963, Kennedy said of Britain's former prime minister: **"He mobilized the English language and sent it into battle."** Nine years earlier, on the occasion of Churchill's eightieth birthday in 1954, journalist Edward R. Murrow had said, "He mobilized the English language and sent it into battle to steady his fellow countrymen and hearten those Europeans upon whom the long dark night of tyranny had descended."

Even when he did try to cite his sources, Kennedy routinely got them wrong. For example, **"The hottest places in HELL are reserved for those who in a period of great moral crisis maintain**

their neutrality" is a quotation he attributed to Dante. (It is recorded in JFK's notebook over Dante's name, without a source.) Dante did say some things about hell, but this wasn't among them. On another occasion Kennedy quoted Emerson as having said, **"What we are speaks louder than what we say,"** a condensation of Emerson's actual thought on this subject: "Don't say things. What you are stands over you the while, and thunders so that I cannot hear what you say to the contrary." (See sidebar "Ralph Waldo Emerson.")

Journalist Sander Vanocur said that Kennedy liked to quote British statesman Lord Morley's observation that **"Life in politics is one continuous choice between second bests."** No source can be found for this attribution. To make the point that we must plan not just for our time but for posterity, Kennedy would often quote "the great French Marshal Lyautey" who he said once asked his gardener to plant a tree. When the gardener cautioned Lyautey that this tree was slow-growing and wouldn't mature for a century, according to JFK the marshal replied, "In that case there is no time to lose, plant it this afternoon." Library of Congress researchers were never able to verify this story or its source. Nor could they find in Nikita Khrushchev's speeches or writings **"The survivors will envy the dead,"** an observation about nuclear war that Kennedy attributed to the Soviet premier during a 1963 press conference. (Three years before Kennedy so quoted Khrushchev, Herman Kahn had published a book on nuclear war in which he repeatedly asked, "Will the living envy the dead?")

"I know that there is a God and I see a storm coming. If he has a place for me, I am ready." John Kennedy's secretary Evelyn Lincoln retrieved a scrap of paper on which he'd written these words. Later they were interpreted as a premonition of his fate. Kennedy had used the words more than once in speeches, however, attributing them to Abraham Lincoln. A longer version of the same thought had been attributed to Abraham Lincoln for decades. (See sidebar "Abraham Lincoln.")

Whether or not the phrase was original to him, in a 1961 executive order John Kennedy referred to the need for "affirmative steps." This was the precursor of what came to be known as "affirmative action." JFK also was the first American official to talk about **"LIGHT at the end of the tunnel"** with reference to Vietnam, though the phrase was hardly original to him. In a mid-1963 speech, Kennedy referred to the economic notion that **"a rising tide lifts all boats,"** prefacing this thought with the words "As they say on my own Cape Cod . . ."

One quip by JFK that has no known antecedent is his comment at a White House dinner for winners of the Nobel Prize: **"I think this is the most extraordinary collection of talent, of human knowledge, that has ever been gathered together at the White House—with the possible exception of when Thomas Jefferson dined alone."** Arthur Schlesinger, Jr., told author Thurston Clarke that his draft of a speech for this dinner had included a tortured passage on Jefferson's many talents and achievements, and that Kennedy himself came up with the pithier, more memorable remark.

Without claiming they were his own words, Kennedy put a number of quotations into play that were subsequently attributed to him. When taking responsibility for the Bay of Pigs fiasco, Kennedy said, **"There's an old saying that VICTORY has a hundred fathers and defeat is an orphan."** Similarly, in a 1961 speech, Kennedy said, **"Somebody once said that WASHINGTON was a city of Northern charm and Southern efficiency,"** another thought now routinely credited to him.

A 1961 speech by Kennedy heightened interest in what he called an old Chinese proverb: **"To begin a voyage of a thousand miles requires the first step."** In his notebook Kennedy attributed this proverb to its probable author, Lao Tzu. In the same journal he called the Persian saying **"I had no SHOES—and I murmured until I met a man who had no feet"** a "Hindu proverb," and attributed **"In war, TRUTH is the first casualty"** to the Greek playwright Aeschylus.

Though not as promiscuous as their older brother when it came to misquotation, JFK's younger brothers did their bit to confuse the wording and attribution of quotations.

During a tribute to his brother Robert, Ted thought it was Jefferson who said, "All that is necessary for evil to strive over good is for good to remain silent." In his foreword to a young people's edition of *Profiles in Courage,* Robert quoted Andrew Jackson as having said, **"One man with COURAGE makes a majority,"** but gave no citation. (John Kennedy had recorded this Jacksonism in his notebook, without a source.) No conclusive evidence exists that Jackson ever said this.

"My views on birth control are somewhat distorted by the fact that I was the seventh of nine children" is thought to be one of Robert Kennedy's best quips. Several decades before the president's brother made that rueful observation, lawyer Clarence Darrow was quoted as saying, "Whenever I hear people discussing birth control, I always remember that I was the fifth."

In a 1961 speech Robert said, **"Killing one man is murder. Killing millions is a statistic,"** a thought adapted from one commonly misattributed to Joseph Stalin. (See sidebar "Joseph Stalin.")

Although in a 1963 speech John Kennedy correctly attributed **"You see things and you say, 'W**HY**?' But I dream things that never were; and I say: 'Why not?'** to George Bernard Shaw, Robert used an altered version of Shaw's lines as the theme of his 1968 presidential campaign without citing anyone.

In a 1966 speech in South Africa, Robert said, "There is a Chinese curse which says, **'May he live in** INTERESTING **times.'** Like it or not, we live in interesting times." Although the curse caught on as one of Chinese origin, no one has ever been able to confirm its origins, Asian or otherwise. The same thing is true of another "old Chinese saying" Bobby Kennedy liked to cite, about one generation building a road for the next. In the same 1966 speech Robert said, **"Only those who dare to fail greatly, can ever achieve greatly."** Three decades later this comment circulated widely on the Internet over Robert Kennedy's name—accurately for once.

"We are all KEYNESIANS now." Although it is often attributed to Richard Nixon, Milton Friedman is the actual source of this comment (a play on the purported observation by Edward VII that "We are all socialists nowadays," itself probably apocryphal). Friedman says he was misquoted, however, or quoted out of context in the 1965 *Time* cover story that reported he'd said, "We're all Keynesians now." According to the conservative economist, what he really said was "In one sense, we are all Keynesians now; in another, no one is a Keynesian any longer."

Verdict: Oversimplified Friedman.

"What does not KILL me makes me stronger." Although this saying has been attributed to Camus, actually it is one of the many "Maxims and Arrows" that Nietzsche included in *Twilight of the Idols.* The Nazis were

partial to this saying, and in recent years it has shown up in the script of more than one movie.

Verdict: Credit Nietzsche.

"KINDER, gentler . . ." This phrase was common long before speech-writer Peggy Noonan inserted her version into George H. W. Bush's 1988 inaugural address. Although we tend to remember that version as "a kinder, gentler nation," what Bush actually said about his vision for America was "It is to make kinder the face of the nation and gentler the face of the world." Since at least the early nineteenth century, "kinder, gentler" has been a poetic commonplace. ("The panting soil that warms my heart / No kinder, gentler sun can know," 1804; "But you with kinder, gentler hearts are blest," 1814.) In 1848 Horace Greeley wrote that anyone who wished to live a more rewarding life "should be kinder, gentler, and more elastic in spirits, as well as firmer and truer." Ten years later a commentator said of Thomas Carlyle, "Nothing in the main can be kinder, gentler or more honest, than the spirit in which he judges even those whom he least likes." In 1911 a reviewer wrote that a character in a novel "was kinder and gentler to his wife than ever before." Thomas Wolfe used the phrase "kinder, gentler," in one novel, and "I never knew a kinder or a gentler man" in another. In his 1978 memoir *A Childhood,* writer Harry Crews wrote about his stepfather, "The stronger the smell of whiskey on him, though, the kinder and gentler he was with me and my brother." New York governor Mario Cuomo subsequently urged Barnard's class of 1983 to "be wiser than we are, kinder, gentler, more caring." Two years after that, singer Roy Orbison observed that Elvis Presley had "made gentler and kinder souls of us all." Three years later Peggy Noonan suggested George Bush follow in the footsteps of Orbison, Cuomo, Wolfe, Crews, and Greeley, et al. in articulating his vision.

Verdict: Too generic a phrase for specific attribution to George Bush, Peggy Noonan, or anyone else.

"There, I guess KING GEORGE will be able to read that!" Legend and paintings to the contrary, on July 4, 1776, there was no dramatic group signing of the Declaration of Independence during which John Hancock made this exclamation as he exuberantly scrawled his name extra large. Those who signed the Declaration did so over several days' time. Various accounts have been given of what, if anything, Hancock said on the day he wrote his ornate signature (which had taken this form for years). The most popular version is given above. According to another report, Hancock said, "There!

John Bull can read my name without spectacles and may now double his reward of five hundred pounds on my head. That is my defiance." Since no colleague joined John Hancock on the day he signed the Declaration, most likely he wrote his name in silence.

Verdict: Patriotic apocrypha.

"A little KNOWLEDGE is a dangerous thing." In a 1711 essay, Alexander Pope actually wrote, "A little learning is a dangerous thing."

Verdict: Credit Pope, for "learning."

"LAFAYETTE, we are here." After American troops landed in France in 1917, Gen. John J. Pershing was celebrated for honoring the Marquis de Lafayette's service to the American Revolution with this stirring declaration. Pershing denied that he'd said "anything so splendid." He thought the words were spoken by the more eloquent Col. Charles E. Stanton, chief disbursing officer of the American Expeditionary Force. Historians generally agree, and credit Stanton with saying, "Lafayette, we are here" at Lafayette's tomb on July 4, 1917. Stanton himself concurred. Nearly four decades later, however, in 1954, an American correspondent who was present at the July 4 ceremony recalled hearing Pershing himself say, "Lafayette, we are here" at Lafayette's tomb on June 14. In *The Dictionary of Misinformation,* Tom Burnam wondered if this remark might have been current at the time our forces arrived in France and not original to either man.

Verdict: Credit Charles E. Stanton for uttering and possibly originating this eloquent remark.

ANN LANDERS AND ABIGAIL VAN BUREN

During their heyday as advice columnists, Ann Landers (1918–2002) and her twin sister Abigail Van Buren (1918–) were primary purveyors of misquotes. Their columns were a revolving fund of sayings that more often than not were misworded, misattributed, or both. Sometimes the sisters would run other people's comments over their own names. At other times they published quotations or entire essays without crediting the actual author. To their credit, both routinely ran corrections submitted by readers.

Landers once published as her "Gem of the Day" **"Too many people know the PRICE of everything and the value of nothing,"** without crediting Oscar Wilde, or anyone else. Another Gem of the Day was "I have never heard a man who was diagnosed with a fatal illness say, 'Gee, **I wish I had spent more time at the office,**'" credited to "a physician." Until he disabused her, Ann quoted Harvard president Derek Bok as having said, **"If you think education is expensive, try ignorance."** (Several years after Bok disowned authorship of the sentence, Landers informed her readers of this fact, adding that she'd since discovered a related thought from Sir Claus Moser: "Education costs nothing. But then, so does ignorance." Moser, Britain's onetime Chief Statistician, is famous in his native land for having said, "Education costs money, but then so does ignorance.") Landers also once concluded a column that dealt with dancing, "So, dear readers, this wraps it up. But before we leave the subject, let's have a long round of applause for Ginger Rogers. She did everything Fred Astaire did . . . only she did it backwards and in high heels." The last sentence, of course, has various plausible originators, not including Ann Landers.

Like many, Ann Landers credited Douglas MacArthur with writing an essay called "Youth," which was actually written by Samuel Ullman of Birmingham, Alabama. Ann became a leading propagator of the popular admonition to **"Practice RANDOM kindness and senseless acts of beauty,"** after a reader told her that a friend had seen this on a warehouse wall. As this reader informed the columnist, she subsequently discovered that it was actually the brainchild of an unnamed "writer in California." (Her name is Anne Herbert.)

Landers continually advised readers who were squabbling over estates to bear in mind what Ben Franklin said: **"If you want to know what people are like, share an INHERITANCE with them."** Although no evidence exists that Franklin ever said this, in 1788 the Swiss clergyman Johann Caspar Lavater did write, "Say not you know another entirely, till you have divided an inheritance with him." The advice columnist repeatedly exhorted readers with what she called the "Ann Landers admonition": **"No one can take advantage of you without your permission."** More often Eleanor Roosevelt is credited with saying, **"No one can make you feel INFERIOR without your consent,"** an attribution that has never been confirmed.

More than once Ann ran pieces of writing by Erma Bombeck that readers sent her, only without Bombeck's name. In various forms, **"I would rather have my column on one thousand refrigerator**

doors than win a Pulitzer" (or "hang in the Louvre") is an observation Ann made often, as did Bombeck and author Robert Fulghum.

Landers sometimes got credit for saying that lies traveled halfway around the world before the truth got its boots on because she once so advised a reader, introducing the thought with "It has been said that . . ." Many websites (those that don't credit Samuel Johnson) mistakenly credit the columnist with saying, **"The true measure of a man is how he treats someone who can do him absolutely no good."** Ann's sister Abby once wrote, "The best index to a person's character is (a) how he treats people who can't do him any good, and (b) how he treats people who can't fight back." (See sidebar "Samuel Johnson.")

Ann and Abby both thought Emerson wrote the essay "Success," which begins **"He has achieved success, who has lived well, laughed often, and loved much . . ."** The actual author of that essay was Bessie Anderson Stanley.

Shortly before she stopped writing her column, Abby advised a reader, "Never be afraid to try something new. Remember, **amateurs built the ark. professionals built the *Titanic*."** (Submitted by David Broome.) This is a new saw that floats about in search of an originator.

Years earlier Abby made this observation in her advice column: **"A man who does not read good books has no advantage over the man who can't read them."** Although some readers told her that this thought originated with Mark Twain, it did not. Perhaps it originated with Abigail Van Buren.

LAST WORDS

Mark Twain thought that "last words" should not be left to the vagaries of fate. Rather, Twain concluded, they should be carefully composed well in advance by one approaching the end. "He should never leave such a thing to the last hour of his life," wrote Twain, "and trust to an intellectual spurt at the last moment to enable him to say something smart. . . . There is hardly a case on record where a man came to his last moment unprepared and said a good thing—hardly a case where a man trusted to that last moment and did not make a solemn botch of it and go out of the world feeling absurd."

Many so-called last words read as if the person who mouthed them took Twain's advice. Either that or someone else composed these words after the fact. Exit lines provide a great opportunity to rewrite the historical record. We want noted people to say something notable as they leave this life, and we aren't shy about giving them a hand. Not surprisingly, the final words put in famous mouths usually typify that person's persona. Does anyone really believe that Theodore Roosevelt said on his deathbed, **"Only those are FIT to live who do not fear to die"**? He didn't. Roosevelt did write those words, long before he died. Henry James is alleged to have declared, "Ah, here it is, that distinguished thing!" as he lay dying. Biographer Leon Edel called these words "a beautiful bit of apocrypha." So, of course, were Nathan Hale's famous "last words" about regretting he had only one life to give for his country. **"Don't give up the SHIP!"**, supposedly the dying words of Capt. James Lawrence as his frigate lost a battle during the War of 1812, were apparently put in his mouth by an imaginative newspaper editor. **"What is the answer?"** is what we like to think were Gertrude Stein's next-to-last words, followed by **"In that case, what is the question?"** when her first inquiry went unanswered. According to Stein's companion, Alice B. Toklas, the two did have this exchange as Stein lay dying, but Toklas did not claim they were her friend's "last words."

On her own deathbed, witty Lady Astor is said to have opened her eyes one last time, seen herself surrounded by family, and murmured, **"Am I dying or is this my birthday?"** According to her son Jakie, his mother did say this (to him) as the end drew near. But two biographers agree that Lady Astor's actual last word was the name of her late husband: "Waldorf!"

In his introduction to a collection of deathbed statements, Gyles Brandreth pointed out that "The last words of many of the most famous and interesting and important figures of history were simply never recorded, while many of those that were recorded are often of such a bleak banality as to be really of no interest at all." Then there are the multitude of unlikely clever exit lines. In the course of his research, Brandreth discovered that, when asked by a clergyman to renounce the devil, at least six dying wits are said to have responded, **"This is no time for making enemies!"**

It seems only fitting for history's great wits to expire with a quip on their lips. By legend that is exactly how Oscar Wilde died. Wilde's

putative last quip varies, however. Some think that before expiring Wilde
said he was dying as he lived, beyond his means. The playwright did say
this, but it was several days before he died. In other recountings Wilde
murmured, **"Either the wallpaper goes or I go,"** then went. In fact,
well before the end Wilde told a visitor to his tacky Paris hotel room, **"My
wallpaper and I are fighting a duel to the death. One or the other
of us has to go."** According to biographer Richard Ellman, the playwright's words were unintelligible during his final hours. Wilde's friend
Robert Ross, who was at his bedside, said that after spending some time
in a silent semicoma, Oscar Wilde heaved a deep sigh, then died.

"Only when I LAUGH." The genesis of this catchphrase is an old joke in
which rescuers discover the lone survivor of a wagon train massacre with
an arrow in his back. When asked if it hurts, the man moans, "Only when
I laugh." (The British version of this story features a colonial in Africa.)
Harry Truman's secretary of state, Dean Acheson, was fond of telling this
story, using its punch line to describe how he felt about the constant vitriol
aimed in his direction. That line subsequently became a gag in *MAD* magazine, and provided the title for a novel and two movies.

Verdict: Punch line of an old joke.

"LEAD, follow, or get out of the way." Because he had a sign with that
slogan displayed prominently on his desk in the 1980s, media mogul Ted
Turner is often given credit for this admonition. Christian Williams even
used it as the title of his 1981 biography of Turner. Another Turner biographer, Porter Bibb, called the admonition "an old Marine cliché." Laurence
Peter dubbed it "Peter's Survival Principle" in his 1979 book *Peter's People*.
The advisory has also been attributed to Thomas Edison. Chrysler used it
as an ad slogan in the early 1990s, sometimes mouthed personally by their
chairman, Lee Iacocca. Whatever its source, this macho maxim has long
been a popular poster and sign slogan.

Verdict: Yet another sloganeer's adaptation of street talk.

"When you have a LEMON, make lemonade." Dale Carnegie included
this thought in his classic work *How to Stop Worrying and Start Living*
(1948), saying he got it from University of Chicago president Robert
Maynard Hutchins, who got it from Sears, Roebuck president Julius
Rosenwald. (Carnegie's version was "When you have a lemon, make

a lemonade.") Well before that, an optimist was commonly defined as someone who made lemonade out of all the lemons life handed him. In 1927 *Reader's Digest* credited aphorist Elbert Hubbard with "A genius is a man who takes the lemons that fate hands him and starts a lemonade stand with them." Master salesman Elmer Wheeler called one chapter of his 1940 book *Sizzlemanship* "Turn Your 'Lemons' into 'Lemonade.'" In 1974 former *Ramparts* editor Warren Hinckle published a book called *If You Have a Lemon, Make Lemonade.* Hinckle said he got the title from a friend. Obviously this saying has been floating about for quite some time, landing here and there along the way.

Verdict: Longtime common wisdom.

"Can the LEOPARD change his spots?" This is a condensation of Jeremiah 13:23: "Can the Ethiopian change his skin, or the leopard his spots?"

Verdict: Condensed Jeremiah.

"LESS is more." Although generally attributed to Mies van der Rohe, this phrase appeared thirty-three years before the architect was born. In his 1855 poem *Andrea del Sarto,* Robert Browning wrote, "Well, less is more, Lucrezia; I am judged."

Verdict: Credit Browning as author, van der Rohe as publicist.

"There is LESS in this than meets the eye." In 1922, theater critic Alexander Woollcott attended a revival of Maurice Maeterlinck's play *Aglavaine and Selysette.* In the next day's *New York Times,* Woollcott reported that this performance "was best summed up by the beautiful lady in the back row: 'There is less in this than meets the eye.'" The "beautiful lady in the back row" turned out to be Tallulah Bankhead. At the time Bankhead was an obscure young actress. According to biographer Lee Israel, Bankhead's mot was actually a malaprop. The twenty-year-old actress meant to say "more than meets the eye," but blew her line. After the remark stormed New York with Tallulah as its source, she knew better than to claim it was anything less than intentional. "I wasn't aware I'd said anything devastating," Bankhead later admitted, ". . . it is only fair to say that most of the wisecracks I have mothered have been accidental quips." Her accidental quip has also been attributed to Dorothy Parker and Robert Benchley.

Verdict: Credit Tallulah Bankhead as inadvertent author.

"Since I did not have time to write you a short LETTER, I wrote you a long one instead." In an epilogue to the paperback edition of his lengthy

memoir *My Life,* Bill Clinton wrote that its undue size was due to his being rushed to meet a deadline. "Thomas Jefferson once said," Clinton explained, "that if he had had more time he could have written shorter letters." Jefferson didn't say that. Nor did Samuel Johnson, Henry Thoreau, Abraham Lincoln, Mark Twain, Voltaire, or any of the many others who have received credit for this basic thought. It can be found in a 1656 letter written by French philosopher Blaise Pascal: *"Je n'ai fait celle-ci plus longue que parce que je n'ai pas eu le loisir de la faire plus courte."* ("The present letter is a very long one, simply because I had no leisure to make it shorter.")
   Verdict: Credit Pascal.

"Give me LIBERTY, or give me death!" Patrick Henry's immortal exclamation was supposedly made to fellow members of the second Virginia Convention in March 1775. In fact it was reconstructed by biographer William Wirt from the recollection of two of Henry's contemporaries. Although George Washington and Thomas Jefferson were also present at Henry's oration, neither considered this stirring call worth mentioning in their own writing, assuming it was made at all. In his biography of Washington, Douglas Southall Freeman said it was his "thankless duty" to conclude that Henry's historic oath most likely was apocryphal. Presumably William Wirt was familiar with Joseph Addison's 1713 play *Cato,* which included the lines "It is not now a time to talk of aught / But chains or conquest; liberty or death."
   Verdict: Credit William Wirt, with an assist from Joseph Addison.

"Where there is LIBERTY, there is my country." According to *Bartlett's,* in its Latin form (*Ubi libertas ibi patria*), this was James Otis's motto. The Library of Congress has been unable to find such a motto in any writing by or about Otis. (There is a Latin proverb that says, "Ube bene, ibi patria." / "Where it is well with me, there is my country.") Other sources say the motto was that of libertarian philosopher Algernon Sidney (1622–1683). Still more think it originated with Benjamin Franklin. In his 1941 quote collection, H. L. Mencken said Franklin used this phrase in a March 14, 1783, letter to Benjamin Vaughan. The editors of Franklin's papers could find no such letter. A tradition among biographers of Thomas Paine is that Franklin once told Paine, "Where liberty is, there is my country." Paine responded, "Where liberty is not, there is mine." This unlikely exchange was first reported in an 1819 book that never actually said the two men were together when they took their respective stands. According to Paine biographer Alfred Owen Aldridge, "The story must be written off as apocryphal."
   Verdict: Still looking.

"A LIE can travel halfway around the world before the truth gets its boots on." In various forms this familiar quotation sometimes gets attributed to Mark Twain, sometimes to Will Rogers, or Edward R. Murrow, or Ann Landers, or Winston Churchill, or Churchill's successor as prime minister, James Callaghan, or a host of lesser lights. In fact this is proverbial wisdom dating back at least to the early nineteenth century. In an 1855 sermon, the popular English clergyman Charles Haddon Spurgeon said, "If you want truth to go round the world you must hire an express train to pull it; but if you want a lie to go round the world, it will fly: it is as light as a feather, and a breath will carry it. It is well said in the old proverb, 'A lie will go round the world while truth is pulling its boots on.'" Three years later this passage was reprinted in an 1858 American volume titled *Spurgeon's Gems.* Even though he indicated that it was not original to him, Spurgeon thrust this saying into general discourse. Others had already put it on the record, however. While verifying quotes for *The Yale Dictionary of Quotations,* editor Fred Shapiro found "Falsehood travels seven leagues while truth is putting her boots on" in an 1854 edition of the *Gettysburg Republican Compiler.* Researcher Bonnie Taylor-Blake subsequently found "falsehood will fly from Maine to Georgia, while truth is pulling her boots on" in an 1820 edition of the *Boston Commercial Gazette* (reprinting material from the *Portland Gazette*). Taylor-Blake also found similar sayings in earlier publications, including Jonathan Swift's 1710 declaration that "Falsehood flies and truth comes limping after it."

Verdict: Proverbial wisdom popularized by Rev. Charles Haddon Spurgeon.

"A LIE is an abomination unto the Lord and an ever present help in times of trouble." Because he made this observation in a 1951 speech, Adlai Stevenson routinely gets credit for the line that Mark Twain had already used in a 1901 speech. Twain's exact words were: "Another instance of unconscious humor was of the Sunday school boy who defined a lie as 'An abomination before the Lord and an ever present help in time of trouble.' That may have been unconscious humor, but it looked more like hard, cold experience and knowledge of facts."

Verdict: Credit Twain.

"I cannot tell a LIE." America's bedrock parable of honesty, in which little George Washington confessed he'd cut down a cherry tree, was invented by biographer Mason Locke Weems (1759–1825). Weems's bestselling biography of Washington (*The Life and Memorable Actions of George Washington,* 1800) contained more fiction than fact, including the story about

little George being caught red-handed next to a fallen cherry tree with a hatchet in his hand. ("Looking at his father with the sweet face of youth brightened with the inexpressible charm of all-conquering truth, he bravely cried out, 'I cannot tell a lie. I did cut it with my hatchet.'") Parson Weems, whose fictionalized account of Washington's life went through multiple editions, himself claimed to have been "Rector of Mount-Vernon Parish." There was no such church.

Verdict: More Weems than Washington.

"If they will stop telling LIES about us, we will stop telling the truth about them." While running for president in 1952, Adlai Stevenson said of his Republican opponents, "If they will stop telling lies about the Democrats, we will stop telling the truth about them." This was thought to be a superb example of Adlai Stevenson's sharp wit. Nearly half a century earlier, while running against Charles Evan Hughes for governor of New York in 1906, William Randolph Hearst said, "If Mr. Hughes will stop lying about me, I will stop telling the truth about him." Chauncey Depew, who was a Republican senator from New York from 1899 to 1911, often said, "If you will refrain from telling any lies about the Republican Party, I'll promise not to tell the truth about the Democrats." This line probably antedates both Hearst and Depew (to say nothing of Stevenson).

Verdict: An old political saw.

"LIES, damned lies, and statistics." In a 1907 essay, Mark Twain wrote that the statement "There are three kinds of lies: lies, damned lies, and statistics" was a "remark attributed to Disraeli . . ." As a result, this famous line appears often in quote collections over Benjamin Disraeli's name (and sometimes over Twain's). A dispatch from London that appeared in an Iowa newspaper in 1896 had already credited Disraeli with saying there were three kinds of lies: "lies, d_____d lies and statistics." After consulting a Disraeli biographer, British statistician John Bibby concluded that the British prime minister probably never made this remark. So who did? That remains unclear. By the late-nineteenth century this expression was familiar in both Britain and America. An 1892 *Living Age* article written by "Mrs. Andrew Crosse," reprinted from the London literary journal *Temple Bar,* included this passage: "It has been said by some wits that there are three degrees of unveracity: 'lies, d_____d lies, and statistics." In a paper read to an 1894 gathering of the Philadelphia County Medical Society, a doctor named M. Price referred to "the proverbial kinds of falsehoods, 'lies, damned lies, and statistics.'" The fact that Dr.

Price called this saying "proverbial" implied that it was familiar to his listeners. A year later, in an 1895 speech delivered in Saratoga Springs, New York, British MP and election reformer Leonard Courtney said, "After all, facts are facts, and although we may quote one to another with a chuckle the words of the Wise Statesman, 'Lies—damned lies—and statistics,' still there are some easy flaws the simplest must understand, and the astutest cannot wriggle out of." A year later, in early 1896, the U.S. commissioner of labor attributed the "lies, damned lies, and statistics" expression to "a recent president of Harvard." In 1901 a London correspondent for the *Washington Post* said this was the way Conservative leader Arthur Balfour characterized newspaper commentary. The catchphrase has also been attributed to politicians Henry Labouchere and Abraham Hewitt, and to poet Alfred, Lord Tennyson.

Verdict: Author yet to be determined; not Twain, and probably not Disraeli.

"LIFE begins at forty." Because she sang a song by that title so often, Sophie Tucker is sometimes credited with originating this phrase. But the song she sang was inspired by a 1932 book with the same title whose author was named Walter B. Pitkin (1878–1953). (Quotographer Nigel Rees and others mistakenly give Pitkin's first name as "William.") The book's title also became that of a 1935 movie and more than one television series, besides providing us with a lasting catchphrase.

Verdict: Credit Walter B. Pitkin.

"LIFE is unfair." After he called up military reservists during the 1962 Cuban Missile Crisis, John Kennedy made this much-noted observation during a press conference. In *An Ideal Husband,* Oscar Wilde wrote, "Life is never fair." Undoubtedly this thought has occurred to many over the millennia besides Wilde and Kennedy.

Verdict: JFK's reiteration of a longtime suspicion.

"LIFE is what happens to you while you're busy making other plans." Because this line is part of John Lennon's song "Beautiful Boy," it is sometimes attributed to him. Before Lennon recorded that song in 1980, the same idea in various forms had already been credited to less-well-known figures such as ex–political wife Betty Talmadge, quip-writer Thomas La Mance, and mystery-writer Margaret Millar, who put the saying in the mouth of one of her characters in a 1970 novel. ("I read that somewhere," the character adds.) This line has also been ascribed to Lily Tomlin, based

on no discernible evidence, and to author William Gaddis (1922-1998). Another contender is Allen Saunders (1899–1986), writer of the comic strip *Mary Worth,* who was given credit for "Life is what happens to us while we are making other plans" by *Reader's Digest* in 1957.

Verdict: Possibly Allen Saunders, based on chronology alone.

"Some say LIFE is the thing, but I prefer reading." Because she used this line in a 1977 novel, Ruth Rendell sometimes gets credit for it. However, as quotographer Rosalie Maggio discovered, in his 1931 book *Afterthoughts,* aphorist Logan Pearsall Smith had already written, "People say that life is the thing, but I prefer reading."

Verdict: Credit Logan Pearsall Smith.

"There is LIGHT at the end of the tunnel." This optimistic assessment of our early prospects in Vietnam is usually credited to Secretary of State Dean Rusk, Secretary of Defense Robert McNamara, or Gen. William Westmoreland. In fact it was John Kennedy who said during a 1962 press conference, "So we don't see the end of the tunnel, but I must say I don't think it is darker than it was a year ago, and in some ways lighter." That wasn't the first time this phrase was applied to fighting in Indochina, however. On the eve of the 1954 French debacle at Dien Bien Phu, Gen. Eugene-Henri Navarre said, "A year ago none of us could see victory. There wasn't a prayer. Now we can see it clearly—like light at the end of a tunnel." According to the *Oxford English Dictionary,* the phrase "light at the end of the tunnel" dates back at least to 1922. British politicians saw this light often during the 1920s and 30s. In 1932 the governor of the Bank of England, discussing gloomy economic conditions, said, "We may all see and approach the light at the end of the tunnel. . . ." Following World War II, British and French leaders alike made frequent use of the term.

Verdict: A catchphrase of long standing.

"For those who LIKE that sort of thing I should think it just the sort of thing they would like." This piece of droll tact—considered by some to be the perfect book review—is said to have been Abraham Lincoln's response to an author's work. (Longtime Stanford president David Starr Jordan loved quoting Lincoln to this effect.) Who that author was and in what context Lincoln said these words varied in the retelling. Thirty-eight years after Lincoln was assassinated, George Bernard Shaw wrote in *Man and Superman* (1903), "Very nice sort of place, Oxford, I should think, for people that like that sort of place." Eight years after that, in 1911, Max Beerbohm put a Greek version of Lincoln's words in the mouth of ancient Athenian "Clio the muse" in his novel *Zuleika Dobson,* then translated Clio's words for readers: "For people who like that kind of thing, this is the kind of thing they like." The prankish Beerbohm claimed that the words were his own invention. This provoked a heated controversy about where the comment originated. Lincoln buff David Mearns concluded that it actually originated with humorist Artemus Ward. As Mearns discovered, in late 1863 a spoofy newspaper advertisement for Ward included this testimonial: "I have never heard any of your lectures, but from what I can learn I should say that for people who like the kind of lectures you deliver, they are just the kind of lectures such people like. Yours respectfully, O. Abe."

Verdict: Credit Artemus Ward.

"I never met a man I didn't LIKE." According to his friend Homer Croy, Will Rogers began composing his own epitaph in the early 1920s. An early version of the one Rogers finally chose was "He joked about every prominent man of his time, but he never met one he disliked." This line first appeared in print after Rogers's mid-1920s trip to the Soviet Union, where Stalin would not let the American humorist meet with Leon Trotsky. As Rogers told readers of the *Saturday Evening Post* in 1926, "But I bet you if I had met him and had a chat with him, I would have found him a very interesting and human fellow, for I have never yet met a man I dident like." (Misspelling in original.) After that, Rogers experimented with many variations on this theme in his writing and speeches. During a talk he gave at a Boston church in 1930, Rogers said, "I've got my epitaph all worked out. When I'm tucked away in the old graveyard west of Oologah [Oklahoma], I hope they will cut this epitaph—or whatever you call them signs they put over gravestones—on it, 'Here lies Will Rogers. He joked about every prominent man in his time, but he never met a man he didn't like.'" When the Associated Press reported this remark, it caused a national stir. Rogers's saintly self-epitaph made the popular humorist that much more beloved. According to Croy, Rogers recognized his own hyperbole. "In reality there were many men he couldn't abide," wrote Croy. Rogers knew a good epitaph when he composed one, however, and gladly suffered fools as its price.

Verdict: Credit Will Rogers.

ABRAHAM LINCOLN

Because Lincoln's popularity soared so high following his assassination, the decades after 1865 saw a rush to publish recollections of quotable observations by America's martyred president. For a time it seemed as though anyone who had so much as shaken the president's hand was publishing the many memorable remarks Lincoln made before their hands parted. Although little of this effusion is taken seriously by Lincoln scholars, some of these recorded comments caught the public's fancy. Many still do. Fortunately, Lincoln scholar Don Fehrenbacher and his wife, Virginia Fehrenbacher, have published a book called *Recollected Words of Abraham Lincoln* (1996), in which they assess the probable authenticity of what they call "recollective quotations" attributed to Lincoln. Many, the Fehrenbachers found, if not most, proved to be more quotable than credible.

The bane of reference librarians is spurious Lincoln quotations they're routinely asked to verify. Lincoln is the most misquoted president largely because he's the one most quoted. The fact that America's sixteenth president didn't say much of what we want him to have said hasn't stopped us from misquoting him anyway. Spurious Lincoln quotes have long been used by management, labor, free-traders, protectionists, wets, dries, and sundry others to promote their various causes.

Actor Warren Beatty once made a speech in which he quoted Lincoln as saying that "the money power preys upon the nation in times of peace, and it conspires against it in times of adversity." This comment has been attributed to Lincoln for more than a century but was debunked long before Beatty put it back in play. On the other side of the political aisle, a conservative paean to self-sufficiency consisting of ten points that begins "1. You cannot bring about prosperity by discouraging thrift. 2. You cannot strengthen the weak by weakening the strong. . . ." is an outright misattribution to Lincoln of words written in 1916 by an American clergyman named William J. H. Boetcker.

By his own admission, many of the president's most memorable comments did not originate with him. At least three Lincoln acquaintances said that after losing his 1858 race for the U.S. Senate to Stephen Douglas, Lincoln observed that it hurt too much to laugh but he was too old to cry. Lincoln did not claim to have coined this comment, however, but attributed it to a boy who had just stubbed his toe. In general he did not hesitate to borrow material as needed: proverbs, jokes, yarns. "I remember a good story when I hear it," Lincoln once said, "but I never invented anything original. I am only a retail dealer."

LINCOLN'S BORROWED WORDS:
"A house DIVIDED against itself cannot stand." This line from Lincoln's famous "House Divided" speech of 1858 drew on Mark 3:25, "If a house be divided against itself, that house cannot stand," and many other versions of this saying that were widespread in antebellum America.

"GOVERNMENT of the people, by the people, for the people . . ." drew on similar expressions by Daniel Webster and Theodore Parker, among others.

"With MALICE toward none, with charity for all." John Quincy Adams said essentially the same thing decades before Lincoln did.

WORDS PUT IN LINCOLN'S MOUTH:
"You can FOOL all of the people some of the time; you can fool some of the people all of the time; but you can't fool all of the people all of the time." Historians doubt that Lincoln said this.

"If I ever get a chance to hit that thing, I'll hit it hard." This is what we'd like Lincoln to have said about slavery, but there is no reliable evidence that he did. The Fehrenbachers give this alleged vow their lowest grade for credibility.

"Tell me what brand of WHISKEY Grant drinks. I'll send a barrel to my other generals." (Wording varies.) No one who has taken a serious look at this amusing remark thinks it originated with Lincoln, or that he said it at all.

"Is this the little woman who wrote the book that made this great war?" It is commonly thought—even by some historians—that Lincoln made this remark to the diminutive Harriet Beecher Stowe when they met a decade after her novel *Uncle Tom's Cabin* was published. Stowe herself recorded no account of their 1862 meeting. Because the only evidence that Lincoln said this to the author consists of "unverified family tradition," the Fehrenbachers did not even consider the credibility of this comment to be worth assessing.

"He reminds me of the man who killed his parents, then

pleaded for mercy because he was an ORPHAN." Lincoln is one of many to whom this quip has been credited, with very little credibility in his case.

"A lawyer who represents himself has a fool for a client." Lincoln also is one of a number of parties to whom this commonplace is attributed, primarily because we have no idea where it actually originated.

"For those who LIKE that sort of thing I should think it just the sort of thing they would like." Said to have been Lincoln's response to an author's work, this pluperfect review is more likely an Artemus Ward invention.

While running for the presidency in 1988, George H. W. Bush told an audience, "As Abraham Lincoln said, 'Here I stand, **WARTS and all.**'" No evidence can be found that the gnarly Lincoln said such a thing, though Oliver Cromwell did make a similar remark.

A Jimmy Carter television spot once quoted Lincoln as saying, **"A statesman thinks of the future generations, while a politician thinks of the coming election."** This is more commonly attributed to nineteenth-century clergyman James Freeman Clarke.

"I know that there is a God and I see a storm coming. If he has a place for me, I am ready." According to an 1866 biography of Abraham Lincoln, he'd made this observation to a visitor in 1860: "I know there is a God and that He hates injustice and slavery. I see the storm coming, and I know that His hand is in it. If He has a place and work for me—and I think He has—I believe I am ready. I am nothing, but truth is everything. I know I am right because I know that liberty is right, for Christ teaches it and Christ is God." Lincoln's friend and law partner William Herndon doubted the authenticity of this comment (though spiritual, Lincoln was not formally religious in the way these words suggest), and most Lincoln scholars agree with him. In an abridged form, the quotation took on a new life when used by John Kennedy. (See sidebar "John Kennedy.")

PROBABLY AUTHENTIC:

"The LORD prefers common-looking people. That is the reason he makes so many of them." Enough Lincoln contemporaries say they heard the president say this in different forms that most likely he did.

YET TO BE DETERMINED:

"I should think that a man's legs ought to be long enough to reach from his body to the ground." No credible source has been found for this popular observation by Lincoln.

"It is more important to know that we are on God's side." This was Lincoln's reported response to a delegation that visited him during the Civil War, and suggested that God was "on our side." By another account, in an 1868 book by artist Francis B. Carpenter (who painted the famous picture of Lincoln reading the Emancipation Proclamation to his cabinet), when a clergyman told Lincoln that he hoped "the Lord was on our side," the president responded that his greater concern was that he and the nation "should be on the Lord's side." The Fehrenbachers do not consider Carpenter a reliable source.

"If I were to try to read, much less answer, all the attacks made on me, this shop might as well be closed for any other business." This declaration also appeared in Carpenter's book. Lincoln buffs do not consider it authentic. In his last public address Lincoln did say, "As a general rule I abstain from reading the reports of attacks upon myself, wishing not to be provoked by that to which I cannot properly offer an answer."

"People are about as happy as they make up their minds to be." This popular Internet quotation is usually attributed to Lincoln. It doesn't sound like him, however, and no evidence has been offered that he ever said or wrote this. It has appeared in unreliable collections of Lincolniana, and was attributed to Lincoln in the 1960 film *Pollyanna*.

"The LION shall lie down with the lamb." The origin of this proverb can be found in Isaiah 11:6: "The wolf also shall dwell with the lamb, and the leopard shall lie down with the kid."

Verdict: Revised Isaiah.

"If I'd known I was going to LIVE this long, I'd have taken better care of myself." Baseball great Mickey Mantle said this just before he died in 1995 at the age of sixty-three. Well before that, in 1983, jazz pianist Eubie Blake was quoted to this effect five days before he died at 100. Seven years earlier, impresario Adolph Zukor had been quoted as saying that if he'd known how long he'd live, he'd have taken better care of himself (Zukor died in 1976, at 103). Others to whom the comment has been attributed include Mark

Twain, George Burns, actor William Demarest, labor leader George Meany, football player Bobby Layne, and umpire Cal Hubbard. While serving as Lord Chancellor of Great Britain from 1757 to 1766, Robert Henley, the first Earl of Northington (1708–1772), was celebrated for commenting, "Damn these legs! If I had known they were to carry a Lord Chancellor, I would have taken better care of them."

Verdict: An old saw that gets passed around.

"LIVE fast, die young, and have a good-looking corpse." Often misattributed to actor James Dean, as quotographer Anthony Shipps discovered, this motto is repeated continually by the protagonist of Willard Motley's 1947 novel *Knock on Any Door,* a criminal on the road to execution. His motto reappeared in the 1949 movie of the same title, which was based on Motley's novel.

Verdict: Credit Willard Motley, possibly recycling street talk.

"LIVING well is the best revenge." This was the title of Calvin Tomkins's 1971 biography of Gerald and Sara Murphy, who made that saying their credo. Gerald thought it was a Spanish proverb. Friends of Scott and Zelda Fitzgerald, the Murphys were the model for Dick and Nicole Diver in *Tender Is the Night.* Scott and Zelda themselves are sometimes thought to have been the source of the Murphys' motto. In fact, these exact words are proverb no. 524 in George Herbert's 1640 publication *Outlandish Proverbs.* Herbert may have been inspired by John Lyly's earlier aphorism "The greatest harm that you can do unto the envious, is to do well."

Verdict: Credit Lyly and Herbert as source, the Murphys as modern publicists.

"Mark Hopkins on one end of a LOG and a student on the other." The classic American definition of higher education is generally attributed to James Garfield. The future president attended Williams College in the mid-1850s, when Mark Hopkins was its president. Years later, at an 1871 gathering of Williams alumni, Garfield (then an Ohio congressman) argued passionately against an ambitious building program proposed for the college. Although no one recorded his remarks, a number of those present later recalled different versions of Garfield's defense of the human element in education. This meeting was generally assumed to be the setting in which Garfield observed that an ideal college consisted of Mark Hopkins and a student sharing a log. Earwitnesses varied widely in their memory of Garfield's actual words, however, and nobody recalled hearing him mention any log. Several decades after the Williams alumni met, a quotographer named Carroll Wil-

son thoroughly investigated James Garfield's memorable quotation. Wilson determined that, (a) Garfield's words only became a commonplace long after they were uttered; (b) it was the hook word *log* that captured our imagination and made this quote so memorable; but that (c) this word was grafted on to Garfield's purported remarks after he'd died and couldn't correct the record. Wilson concluded that what Garfield actually said in 1871 was "A log cabin (in the woods), with a pine bench in it with Mark Hopkins at one end and me at the other, is a good enough college for me." So where did the log version come from? Its source was a prominent lecturer and friend of Garfield named John Ingalls. One of Ingalls's lectures was titled "Garfield: The Man of the People." In that speech, delivered late in the century, Ingalls said of the late president, "He always felt and manifested a peculiar interest in his alma mater and in President Hopkins, whom he regarded as the greatest and wisest instructor of the century. 'A pine log,' he said, 'with the student at one end and Doctor Hopkins at the other, would be a liberal education.'"

Verdict: Garfield's sentiments, Ingalls's words.

ALICE ROOSEVELT LONGWORTH

When Theodore Roosevelt warned about the danger of "race suicide" if American mothers did not have at least four children, his young daughter Alice organized a Race Suicide Club whose members discussed birth-control methods. Throughout her life Alice Roosevelt Longworth was known for having a strong will and sharp tongue. Her father once observed that he could be president of the United States or control Alice, but he couldn't do both. (See sidebar "Theodore Roosevelt.") Later in life, a throw pillow in Mrs. Longworth's sitting room was embroidered, IF YOU CAN'T SAY SOMETHING GOOD ABOUT SOMEONE, SIT RIGHT HERE BY ME (supposedly something she'd once said). She lived by this credo. Of Republican presidential nominee Wendell Willkie, a folksy Wall Street lawyer who ran against Franklin Roosevelt in 1940, Longworth observed that he'd "sprung from the grass roots of the country clubs of America." Of her own husband, the bon vivant House Speaker Nicholas Longworth, she said, "He'd rather be tight than president." When Joseph McCarthy put his arm around her at a party, called her his "date," and said he was going to call her Alice, Mrs. Longworth's response achieved instant renown: "No, Senator McCarthy, you are *not* going to call me Alice. The truckman, the trashman, and the policeman on the block may call me Alice but you may not." Years later, after she underwent a double mastectomy in her eighties, Mrs. Longworth called herself "the only topless octogenarian in Washington."

Alice Roosevelt Longworth is one of many to whom this assessment of her father has been attributed: "He wanted to be the bride at every wedding, and the corpse at every funeral." (Some accounts add, "and the baby at every christening.")

When British author Rebecca West visited Washington in 1935, she observed, "Intellectually, spiritually, the city is dominated by the last good thing said by Alice Roosevelt Longworth." As with so many wits, Mrs. Longworth's actual quips were augmented by others that she tried to disown. The line most often misattributed to her was this portrayal of Thomas Dewey: **"He looks like the little man on a wedding cake."** Some thought the unsuccessful 1944 Republican candidate for president never recovered from that devastating put-down. But Teddy Roosevelt's daughter didn't coin this phrase, and never claimed she had. A few years before her death in 1980, Longworth told William Safire that it was her friend Grace Hodgson Flandrau who had said Dewey looked like the bridegroom on a wedding cake. Longworth repeated this line so often that she eventually got credit for its invention. (Others to whom the line has been attributed include Franklin D. Roosevelt, Harold Ickes, Walter Winchell, Dorothy Parker, and Ethel Barrymore.)

Earlier, Mrs. Longworth was celebrated for observing that Calvin Coolidge looked as though he'd been **"weaned on a pickle."** Once again she was merely publicizing someone else's quip. During the Coolidge presidency, Longworth later explained, her doctor greeted her one day with a malicious grin. "The patient who has just left said something that I am sure will make you laugh," he said. "We were discussing the President, and he remarked, 'Though I yield to no one in my admiration for Mr. Coolidge, I do wish he did not look as if he had been weaned on a pickle.' Of course I shouted with pleasure and told every one," Longworth reported, "always carefully giving credit to the unnamed originator, but in a very short time it was attributed to me." This line has also been credited to H. L. Mencken (by columnist George Will). In 1929, a newspaper called the "weaned on a pickle" line an "ancient wheeze."

Two other renowned comments attributed to Longworth were ones she told biographer Michael Teague originated elsewhere. One was her comment after giving birth to a daughter: "Having a baby is like trying to push a grand piano through a transom." Her famous warning about Gen. Douglas MacArthur, "Never trust a man who combs his hair straight from his left armpit," was merely an old joke, Longworth added.

Alice Roosevelt Longworth is famous for having called her cousin Franklin Roosevelt, whose wife Eleanor was also her cousin, a combination of mush and Eleanor. The proportions varied in the retelling. Some thought it was "90 percent mush and 10 percent Eleanor," or else "90 percent Eleanor and 10 percent mush," or 80 mush / 20 Eleanor, or "one part mush and two parts Eleanor." Whatever the exact ratio, Longworth denied this one too. Fastidious about her language, Longworth said she'd never use a pedestrian word like "mush." As Theodore Roosevelt's daughter told *Eleanor and Franklin* author Joseph Lash, she considered mush "a bad, a silly word. There's no ring to 'mush.'" Perhaps that was why the *New York Times* obituary of Mrs. Longworth had her calling FDR "one-third sap and two-thirds Eleanor." Whoever said it, this quip owes a literary debt to James Russell Lowell. In 1848 Lowell wrote in a poem, "There comes Poe, with his raven, like Barnaby Rudge, / Three-fifths of him genius and two-fifths sheer fudge."

"Don't LOOK back. Something might be gaining on you." This was the last of the six rules for "How to Stay Young" coined by pitcher Leroy "Satchel" Paige, one of the first black players in the major leagues. Paige's famous advisory was part of a sidebar to a 1953 profile of the pitcher that ran in *Collier's* magazine.

Verdict: Credit Satchel Paige.

"You could LOOK it up." Casey Stengel remains famous for saying this, repeatedly, during his decades as a baseball manager after World War II. "You Could Look It Up" was the title of a James Thurber short story that ran in the *Saturday Evening Post* in 1941. This story, about a manager named Squawks Magrew (who adds a midget to his roster), included lines like "This was thirty, thirty-one year ago; you could look it up. . . ." and "Well, sir, it'll all be there in the papers of thirty, thirty-one year ago, and you could look it up." Thurber's story was popular among sportswriters, who may have fed Stengel the line.

Verdict: Credit James Thurber as author, Casey Stengel as publicist.

"The LORD prefers common-looking people. That is the reason he makes so many of them." Some investigators have concluded that Lincoln said no such thing. They point out that this observation and its attribution to Lincoln appeared without evidence in a 1928 book on U.S. presidents. Twenty years earlier, however, in 1908, that comment had already appeared in John Hay's published letters and diary. Hay, Lincoln's private secretary, wrote in his diary on December 23, 1863: "The President tonight has a dream:—He was in a party of plain people, and, as it became known who he was, they began to comment on his appearance. One of them said:—'He is a very common-looking man.' The President replied:—'The Lord prefers common-looking people. That is the reason he makes so many of them.'" While not conclusive, Hay's diary entry suggests persuasively that this was a genuine Lincoln comment. Lincoln scholars Don and Virginia Fehrenbacher consider it legitimate.

Verdict: Credit Lincoln.

"The LORD works in mysterious ways." In "Light Shining Out of Darkness," one of his *Olney Hymns,* most of which were written in 1771 and 1772, British poet and hymnist William Cowper (1731–1800) wrote, "God moves in a mysterious way." T. S. Eliot (1888–1965) subsequently wrote, "God works in a mysterious way," in his 1920 poem "The Hippopotamus." Since "The Lord" rings a little better in our ears, in tandem with "mysterious ways," that's how we've most commonly remembered this popular thought.

Verdict: Credit Cowper for the idea, Eliot for a polish, and time for the final version.

"Show me a good LOSER and I'll show you a loser." Although it is rarely credited to Knute Rockne, biographer Jerry Brondfield thought Notre Dame's legendary coach might be the source of this line. Brondfield was told that during a conversation Rockne had with a colleague in the 1920s, after that man complimented a fellow coach for being "such a good and gracious loser," Rockne responded, "You show me a good and gracious loser and I'll show you a loser." In terser form, this became a bedrock American adage. In the 1930s, Richard Nixon was told good losers were losers by his Whittier College football coach, Wallace "Chief" Newman. Like Nixon, Jimmy Carter was fond of this slogan. So are many American men. The thought is commonly attributed to Leo Durocher, for no better reason than that it "sounds like him." It has also been attributed to Boston Celtics coach Red Auerbach, and, of course, Vince Lombardi.

Verdict: Credit Knute Rockne, tentatively, in conversation.

"You are a LOST generation." ("Vous êtes une génération perdue.") Gertrude Stein is famous for saying this about Ernest Hemingway and his peers. Hemingway used that line as the epigraph for *The Sun Also Rises,* crediting "Gertrude Stein in conversation." In an unpublished foreword to that novel, Hemingway said Stein borrowed the term *une génération perdue* from the owner of a Paris auto repair shop, who used it to describe dysfunctional World War I veterans whom he couldn't train as mechanics. (Hemingway later recounted a different version of this story in *A Movable Feast.*) Stein herself said she'd first heard the term *génération perdue* used by the proprietor of the Hotel Pernollet in Belley, in 1924. "He said that every man becomes civilized between the ages of eighteen and twenty-five," wrote Stein. "If he does not go through a civilizing experience at that time in his life he will not be a civilized man. And the men who went to war at eighteen missed the period of civilizing, and they could never be civilized. They were a lost generation." What neither Stein nor Hemingway may have realized is that "lost generation" is a concept with a long heritage. As early as 1834, Russian czar Nicholas I said in a Warsaw speech, "The current generation is lost. . . ." The *New-York Mirror* headlined their report of his speech "A lost generation."

Verdict: Credit Stein as reporter and Hemingway as publicist of a French tradesman's recycling of a long-standing notion.

"If you LOVE somebody, set them free." This popular poster and greeting card saying became the title of a Sting song on his 1985 album *Dream of the Blue Turtles.* A decade before that, in his 1974 book *I Ain't Much, Baby—but I'm All I Got,* Jess Lair depicted a college student who—when asked to record some provocative thought, which needn't be original— wrote on an index card: "If you want something very very badly, let it go free. If it comes back to you it's yours forever. If it doesn't, it was never yours to begin with." Prior to this, a poem called "If You Love Something"— one that was incorporated on trinkets worldwide—said essentially the same thing. Its author is usually given as "Unknown." (According to one source that is because the poem was originally written for a charity fundraiser but not copyrighted.) This thought has also been attributed to psychotherapist Fritz Perls, but without a source.

Verdict: Author yet to be determined.

"LOVE and work." These two words depicting life's proper goals are routinely attributed to Sigmund Freud. Evidence that he actually said them is vague at best. Freud's alleged observation was publicized by Erik Erikson's 1963 book *Childhood and Society.* After referring to "Freud's shortest

saying," Erikson wrote, "Freud was once asked what he thought a normal person should be able to do well. The questioner probably expected a complicated answer. But Freud, in the curt way of his old days, is reported to have said: *'Lieben und arbeiten'* (to love and to work)." Erikson was scrupulous enough to say that this was something Freud was "reported to have said." He gave no source. University of California/Davis professor Alan Elms contacted Erikson to ask for his source. The Swedish psychiatrist said he'd heard this Freud comment in Vienna before the Second World War, although he couldn't remember the context. Erikson conceded that he might have made it up. Elms himself believes the phrase more or less reflects Freud's views, albeit in an oversimplified way. A German-speaking analyst once referred Elms to several passages in Freud's work in his native tongue that support the "love and work" concept, but none of them included the words "lieben" or "arbeiten." Nor has "love and work" been located in the work of analyst Theodore Reik, where some think that phrase can be found. Even if Freud (or Reik) ever did express a belief that love and work were life's aims, that thought was hardly original. In an 1856 letter, Tolstoy wrote to Valerya Arsenyev, "One can live magnificently in this world, if one knows how to work and how to love. . . ."

Verdict: Freud's belief, if not his actual words.

"LOVE me, love my dog." ("**Qui me amat, amat et canem meam.**") This has been identified as an old proverb, possibly Italian, or Spanish, or French, or English, or all of them. It is commonly thought to come from an 1150 sermon by St. Bernard of Clairvaux (1090–1153), who referred to the saying as a proverb. (The dog breed was named after an earlier St. Bernard.) Sir Joshua Reynolds later painted a picture inspired by this saying, and P. G. Wodehouse wrote a story using it as his title.

Verdict: Proverbial wisdom publicized by St. Bernard of Clairvaux.

"'Tis better to have LOVED and lost / Than never to have loved at all." So wrote Alfred, Lord Tennyson, in *In Memoriam,* published anonymously in 1850. A century and a half earlier, Congreve wrote in his play *The Way of the World* ". . . 'tis better to be left, than never to have been loved." Others expressed similar ideas in print before Tennyson did. His was the most felicitous version, however, and the one we remember best.

Verdict: Credit Tennyson.

"LUCK is the residue of design." This was the most famous of many maxims attributed to baseball mogul Branch Rickey. His biographers routinely

report that Rickey said this, but none give a specific time or place. Branch B. Rickey—his namesake's grandson—believes Rickey did make that noted observation. "Knowing my grandfather," adds the president of the Pacific Coast League, "he probably honed it around the family for years before mentioning it publicly." A 1946 newspaper article reported that "The other day Rickey discoursed at length on 'luck—the residue of design.'"

Verdict: Credit Branch Rickey.

"Give me the LUXURIES of life and I will willingly do without the necessities." In his 1853 book *The Autocrat of the Breakfast-Table,* Oliver Wendell Holmes quoted "my friend, the Historian" (now known to be John Lothrop Motley, 1814–1877) as saying, "Give us the luxuries of life, and we will dispense with its necessaries." Holmes himself sometimes gets credit for this thought, as do Oscar Wilde and architect Frank Lloyd Wright. It echoes an earlier observation by Scopas of Thessaly, as quoted by Plutarch: "We rich men count our felicity and happiness to lie in those superfluities, and not in those necessary things."

Verdict: Credit John Lothrop Motley.

"MAD, bad, and dangerous to know." After she met Lord Byron, but before she became his mistress, Lady Caroline Lamb wrote in her journal that the poet was "Mad, bad and dangerous to know." Evelyn Waugh later used the same expression to describe his associates at Oxford in the 1920s. Mordecai Richler repeated the phrase twice in nearly identical passages separated by more than one hundred pages in the 1980 novel *Joshua Then and Now.* (*Time*'s reviewer chided Richler for borrowing from Waugh.)

Verdict: Credit Lady Caroline.

"Call me MADAM." When, in 1933, Secretary of Labor Frances Perkins became the first woman to join a president's cabinet, journalists were puzzled about how to address her. She suggested, "Miss Perkins." After a reporter pointed out that they called male cabinet members "Mr. Secretary," Perkins deferred to the incoming Speaker of the House. The Speaker suggested, "Madam Secretary." Some press accounts reported that this suggestion came from Perkins herself. It quickly morphed into "Call me madam." In 1950 that became the title of a successful Broadway musical with songs by Irving Berlin. Eleanor Roosevelt herself perpetuated the misquote when she wrote about Secretary Perkins in a 1954 book (coauthored with Lorena Hickock), "Some fool reporter wanted to know what to call her. . . .

"'Call me Madam,' she replied."

Verdict: Misremembered version of a House Speaker's words, with a hand from the press, Irving Berlin, and Eleanor Roosevelt; not Frances Perkins's own words.

"MAKE my day." In 1985, President Ronald Reagan dared Congress to send him a tax increase to veto by saying, "Go ahead and make my day!" Reagan borrowed the line from Clint Eastwood's taunting of a criminal in the 1983 movie *Sudden Impact*. *Bartlett's* credits that movie's screenwriter, Joseph Stinson, for Reagan's version. Although Stinson and Eastwood gave it an ironic spin, as a sincere, positive expression "make my day" had been floating around for well over a century. "Thy presence makes my day," read an 1825 poem in *The Christian Journal*. An 1840 poem in the *New-York Mirror* included the lines "Can Death have robbed the radiance from my brow, / Or dimmed the eyes whose light did make *my day*."
Verdict: Longtime catchphrase.

"With MALICE toward none, with charity for all." In an 1838 letter declining an invitation to help celebrate slavery's abolition in the British West Indies, John Quincy Adams wrote, "In charity to all mankind, bearing no malice or ill-will to any human being, and even compassionating those who hold in bondage their fellow-men, not knowing what they do." Lincoln expressed this thought better in his second inaugural address, but Adams said it first.
Verdict: Credit Lincoln for the phrase, Adams for the thought.

"A MAN in America is a failed boy." So wrote John Updike in a celebrated observation by a character in his novel *The Coup* (1978). Updike later admitted that he "stole" the line from a story by John Cheever.
Verdict: Credit Cheever as originator, Updike as publicist.

"A MAN'S got to do what a man's got to do." Lexicographer Eric Partridge dated this catchphrase to the World War II era. Just before the war, however, John Steinbeck's 1939 novel *The Grapes of Wrath* included the line "A man got to do what he got to do." This observation subsequently, and inaccurately, has been attributed to John Wayne in the movie *Stagecoach*, and to Alan Ladd in *Shane*.
Verdict: Catchphrase put in circulation by John Steinbeck.

"MARRIAGE is a fortress besieged. Outsiders want to get in. Insiders want to get out." This saying inspired the title of Qian Zhongshu's classic

1947 novel *Fortress Besieged*. According to its introduction, the saying was thought to be a French proverb. And sure enough, an 1845 collection of French proverbs included "Marriage is like a beleaguered fortress; those who are without want to get in, and those within want to get out." (*"Le mariage est comme une forteresse assiégée; ceux qui sont dehors veulent y entrer et ceux qui sont dedans en sortir."*) The provenance of this saying is quite diverse. After noting the 1595 essay in which Montaigne wrote of marriage, "It may be compared to a cage: the birds without despair to get in, and those within despair to get out." (*"Il en advient ce qui se veoid aux cages: les oyseaux qui en sont dehors, desperent d'y entrer: et d'un pareil soing en sortir, ceuix qui sont au dedans."*), quotographer Burton Stevenson cited an Arab proverb that made much the same point. John Webster included this observation about marriage in his 1612 play *The White Divel*: "'Tis just like a summer bird-cage in a garden, the birds that are without, despaire to get in and the birds that are within despaire and are in a consumption for feare they shall never get out." In the same year poet John Davies wrote, "Wedlock, indeed, hath oft compared been / To public feasts, where meet a public rout, / Where they that are without would fain go in / And they that are within would fain go out." Over a century later, in 1734, Ben Franklin borrowed this thought for *Poor Richard's Almanack*. A century after that, in an essay on Montaigne, Emerson asked, "Is not marriage an open question, when it is alleged, from the beginning of the world, that such as are in the institution wish to get out and such as are out wish to get in?" To complicate matters even further, according to Stevenson an old Arab proverb states that "Wedlock is like a place besieged; those within wish to get out; those without wish to get in."

Verdict: A thought too old and too obvious for specific attribution.

"I MARRIED him for better or worse, but not for lunch." In the United States this widely repeated mot has been attributed variously to the wife of Ohio State's retiring football coach Woody Hayes and the wife of retiring New York Yankees general manager George Weiss In Great Britain, the quip is credited to the Duchess of Windsor. According to lexicographer Eric Partridge it's an old saw of Australian origin.

Verdict: Old saw.

"MARRY in haste, repent at leisure." Admonitions not to marry in haste have been around at least since the Talmud. In *Henry VI*, Shakespeare wrote, "Hasty marriage seldom proveth well." As for regretting this act, when asked whether or not a man should marry, Socrates replied, "Whichever you do you will repent it." Late in the sixteenth century Robert Greene

wrote of a woman, "She was afrayde to match in haste least shee might repent at leisure." This basic idea was in common proverbial circulation in
Elizabethan England. But it took aphorist John Ray to compress the
thought into one crisp proverb in 1670: "Marry in haste and repent at
leisure." In *The Old Bachelor* (1693), playwright William Congreve put his
own spin on this saying by having one character say, "Married in haste, we
may repent at leisure," and another respond, "Some by experience find
those words misplaced. At leisure married, they repent in haste."

Verdict: Proverbial wisdom expressed best by John Ray.

*"Down these MEAN streets a man must go who is not himself mean, who
is neither tarnished nor afraid."* Raymond Chandler's most celebrated single
sentence appeared not in one of his novels but in his 1944 essay "The Simple
Art of Murder." As quotographer Nigel Rees points out, the hook phrase in
that sentence dates back at least to 1894, when Arthur Morrison published a
book about London's East End called *Tales of Mean Streets*. A 1920 book
about Oscar Wilde depicted him wandering about the "mean streets" of Paris
late in the nineteenth century. This phrase obviously has a long history.

Verdict: Credit Raymond Chandler for originating this sentence, but
not the phrase "mean streets."

"The MEDIUM is the message." This saying became Marshall McLuhan's
signature line, the title of a 1969 book by him, and a chapter heading in his
earlier book *Understanding Media* (1964). McLuhan had used the phrase
for years before that, however, most notably in a 1958 speech to the National Association of Educational Broadcasters in Omaha, Nebraska.

Verdict: Credit McLuhan.

*"The Right Honorable Gentleman is indebted to his MEMORY for his
jests, and to his imagination for his facts."* Richard Sheridan (1751–1816)
said this on the floor of the House of Commons, about a parliamentary
colleague. According to Thomas Moore, who edited Sheridan's memoirs,
the British politician spent years honing that observation before launching
it from his sling during parliamentary debate. After Sheridan's death,
Moore found this entry in Sheridan's journal: "He employs his fancy in his
narratives, and keeps his recollections for his wit."

Verdict: Credit Richard Sheridan.

"Poor MEXICO! So far from God and so close to the United States."
("Pobre México! Tan lejos de Dios y tan cerca de los Estados Unidos.")
A 1940 magazine article translated from Mexico's *Hoy* included the

sentence "There is certainly reason for the words attributed to our greatest statesman: 'Poor Mexico, so far from God and so near to the United States!'" Presumably this statesman was dictator Porfirio Díaz (1830–1915), to whom this remark is generally attributed (though some credit the lament to revolutionary icon Benito Juárez). No source is usually given for either attribution, however. Even Díaz biographer Paul Garner can only say the quotation is attributed to him. In a book on revolutionary Mexico, author Frank McLynn concluded that the observation was uncharacteristic of the dour Díaz, and probably not his. There is even less evidence that it belongs to Juárez.

Verdict: Most likely words moved from an obscure mouth to a more famous one.

"MILLIONS for defense but not one cent for tribute." American envoy Gen. Charles Cotesworth Pinckney is famous for this firm response to French leaders who demanded a substantial bribe to stop attacking American ships late in the eighteenth century. Pinckney denied that he said any such thing. According to him, his actual words were "Not a sixpence, sir." Pinckney attributed the more popular version to Robert Goodloe Harper, a Maryland congressman whose claim to fame was that he coined the name "Liberia" for that African country. At a 1798 dinner honoring John Marshall, the returning U.S. ambassador to France, Harper was one of sixteen present who offered toasts. The next day a newspaper reported his toast as: "Millions for Defense but not a cent for Tribute." At the same banquet, Pinckney's toast to Marshall was: "'Tis not in mortals to command success. He has done more—deserved it" (adapted from Joseph Addison's play *Cato*). It didn't take long for Harper's words to migrate to Pinckney's mouth, where they stayed thereafter.

Verdict: Credit Robert Goodloe Harper.

WILSON MIZNER

After Irving Berlin dedicated his song "Black Sheep Has Come Back to the Fold" to Wilson Mizner (1876–1933), Mizner commented, "It's the first time anything but a dinner check has ever been dedicated to me, but somehow I can't get happy over it. The title seems to indicate that I've been hanging around, bleeding with remorse over my misspent life. I have returned to no fold whatsoever. I'm the most unfolded guy I've ever known."

In his time Wilson Mizner was considered one of America's premier raconteurs and wits. After spending his early life as a gambler in
California and Alaska, Mizner settled in Manhattan, where he regaled
eager listeners at tables reserved for him in prominent restaurants.
Like Samuel Johnson and Oscar Wilde, Wilson Mizner sparkled even
more in conversation than he did on the page. Unlike them, Mizner
was too indolent to write more than an occasional play or movie script.
He also was none too fastidious about borrowing other people's words
and making them his own. Nonetheless, many sayings that still circu-
late were put into circulation by Wilson Mizner. H. L. Mencken said
that Mizner contributed more humorous observations to the national
dialogue than any other man of his time. Screenwriter Anita Loos—
who modeled the character played by Clark Gable in *San Francisco* after Mizner—predicted accurately that "generations yet to come will
be quoting Mizner without ever having heard his name."

Mizner's reputation as a wit was spread largely by an army of at-
tentive Boswells who eagerly recorded his many epigrams and passed
them along to newspaper columnists. They included such observations
as "A fellow who's always declaring he's no fool usually has his suspicions," and "I hate careless flattery, the kind that exhausts you in your
effort to believe it." Mizner also is credited with saying, "Be urbane to
everybody. You can never tell in which pool the next sucker will bite."
The gambler-playwright-raconteur had an abiding disdain for "suckers." Mizner figured that those who volunteered to be fleeced in card
games deserved whatever they got. His trademark salutation, **"Hello,
Sucker!"** was adopted by flamboyant speakeasy hostess Texas Guinan
(later played by Betty Grable in *Incendiary Blonde*) as her own signature line. The greeting enjoyed a national vogue for a time. Mizner also
popularized and may have coined the phrase **"Never give a SUCKER
an even break."**

Many other Miznerisms are still in play, sometimes attributed to
him, sometimes to others, or to no one in particular. His epithet **"just
some mouse studying to be a rat"** is often applied to the cad of the
hour, with no acknowledgment that Mizner said this nearly a century
ago. Mizner's **"If you steal from one person it's PLAGIARISM; if
you steal from several it's called research"** also gets bruited
about, though seldom with credit given to its originator. New York
mayor Jimmy Walker adapted Mizner's **"Living in Hollywood is
like floating down a sewer in a glass-bottom boat"** when he said,

"A reformer is a guy who rides through a sewer in a glass-bottom boat."
Many others have also adapted this analogy, to various ends.

Mizner sometimes gets credit for **"Be NICE to people on your way up because you'll meet them on the way down,"** as do entertainer Jimmy Durante and columnist Walter Winchell. **"Life's a tough proposition—and the first hundred years are the hardest"** is attributed both to Mizner and cartoonist Tad Dorgan (a fellow migrant from San Francisco to New York). Along with Dorothy Parker, Wilson Mizner is credited with asking, **"How can they tell?"** when told that Calvin Coolidge had died. On his own deathbed, when asked if he wanted to see a priest, Mizner was said to have responded, "I want a priest, a rabbi, and Protestant clergyman. I want to hedge my bets." When a priest appeared at his bedside and asked if he wished any counsel, Mizner reportedly told him, "Much obliged, Padre, much obliged. But why bother? I'll be seeing your boss in a few minutes."

"Bad MONEY drives out good." "Gresham's Law" was not actually authored by sixteenth-century English financier Sir Thomas Gresham. It originated with an 1857 misinterpretation of Gresham's ideas by Scottish economist Henry Dunning MacLeod. MacLeod thought the financier had concluded that "bad coin invariably and necessarily drives out good coin from circulation," and that this should be known as "Gresham's Law." However, Copernicus and others had already noted that when too much base money was in circulation, legitimate coins tended to be hoarded, sent abroad, or melted down. Generalizing from that point to the broader observation that bad money drives out good was MacLeod's doing, not Gresham's. The most popular form of this conviction has been traced back to a 1902 collection of proverbs.

Verdict: Credit Henry MacLeod, not Thomas Gresham, for a modern version of an old idea.

"Because that's where the MONEY is." Bank robber Willie Sutton is famous for this response to an interviewer who asked why he robbed banks. Sutton denied having said it. "The credit belongs to some enterprising reporter who apparently felt a need to fill out his copy," wrote Sutton in his autobiography. "I can't even remember when I first read it. It just seemed to appear one day, and then it was everywhere." Today it's so commonplace that some social scientists espouse what they call "Sutton's Law": Consider the obvious first.

Verdict: Words put in Willie Sutton's mouth.

"MONEY is the mother's milk of politics." This axiom gets recycled a lot—particularly during high-rolling election seasons—but no one seems sure who said it first. Some give credit to House Speaker Thomas P. "Tip" O'Neill. In fact it was Jesse Unruh, the tall, rotund speaker of California's Assembly during the early 1960s, who made this remark. In a 1962 interview with T. George Harris for *Look* magazine, Unruh observed that "Money is the mother's milk of politics." Unruh, a flamboyant figure known as "Big Daddy," put into cynical words what many already suspected. Harris says Unruh later thanked him for getting him into *Bartlett's*. Big Daddy's axiom outlived his own reputation. Few remember Jesse Unruh, but many are familiar with his immortal seven words.

    Verdict: Credit Jesse Unruh.

"MONEY is the root of all evil." In 1 Timothy 6:10 "the love of money," not money itself, is called "the root of all evil."

    Verdict: Cite Timothy; include "love of."

"When somebody says, 'This is not about MONEY, it's the principle of the thing,' it's about money." Indiana humorist Frank McKinney "Kin" Hubbard observed, "When a feller says, 'It hain't th' money, but th' principle o' th' thing,' it's the money." Hubbard's axiom gets repeated often in various forms, and attributed to a wide variety of sources ranging from H. L. Mencken to Bill Clinton, Rush Limbaugh, and sundry Hollywood cynics.

    Verdict: Credit Kin Hubbard.

"You pays your MONEY and you takes your choice." Because Twain used this phrase in *Huckleberry Finn,* it's easy to assume it originated with him. However, in 1846, nearly four decades before *Huckleberry Finn* was published (1884), *Punch* magazine ran a cartoon called "The Ministerial Crisis," in which a character who asks "Which *is* the prime minister?" is told, "Which ever you please, my little dear. You pays your money, and you takes your choice." It is probably safe to assume that this was a common showman's pitch at the time, along the lines of "Step right up!" In 1852, six years after the *Punch* cartoon appeared, an American magazine referred to "the old showman spirit of 'whichever you please, my little dear, you pays your money and you takes your choice.'" In years to follow, that catchphrase showed up regularly enough in print to suggest how familiar it was to readers. When asked about the difference between expert testimony and perjury, Mr. Dooley responded, "Ye pay ye're money an' take ye're choice." The familiarity of this catchphrase was not limited to the

English-speaking world. In *Wit and Its Relation to the Unconscious* (1905), Sigmund Freud wrote about an 1897 German novel that included a scene set in Madame Tussauds. After being told by a guide that she was looking at a wax statue of the Duke of Wellington and his horse, a little girl asks which was which. "Just as you like, my pretty child," responds the guide. "You pay your money and you take your choice." Freud called this an example of "representation through the opposite."

Verdict: An old showman's pitch.

"Build a better MOUSETRAP and the world will beat a path to your door." This beloved American adage is routinely attributed to Ralph Waldo Emerson. Emerson did once write, "If a man has good corn, or wood, or boards, or pigs to sell, or can make better chairs or knives, crucibles or church organs, than anybody else, you will find a broad hard-beaten road to his house, though it be in the woods." The more popular version does not appear in his published works, however. When dimestore aphorist Elbert Hubbard claimed in 1911 that it was he, not Emerson, who composed the catchy saying, considerable effort was devoted to discovering its actual author. Eventually this search led to *Borrowings,* a collection of sayings published in 1889 by members of the First Unitarian Church in Oakland, California. Several observations by Emerson in this volume included, "If a man can write a better book, preach a better sermon, or make a better mouse-trap than his neighbor, though he builds his house in the woods, the world will make a beaten path to his door." In 1912, one of *Borrowings'* compilers—Sarah S. B. Yule—said she'd jotted this sentence in her notebook after hearing Emerson lecture in Oakland in the early 1870s, when she was a girl of sixteen. Emerson did speak in Oakland on May 18, 1871, about "Hospitality and How to Make Homes Happy." Whether he discussed mousetraps and beaten paths will probably never be known. No written copy of Emerson's lecture exists, and press reports of this talk were sketchy. After conducting exhaustive research in the early 1930s, quotographer Burton Stevenson concluded that Emerson most likely did say the words Mrs. Yule jotted in her notebook.

Verdict: Credit the idea to Emerson, and some form of the wording.

"It is better to keep your MOUTH shut and appear stupid than to open it and remove all doubt." This popular piece of advice has been credited to Samuel Johnson, Mark Twain, and many others (Confucius, Galileo, Franklin, Lincoln, George Eliot, Sam Rayburn, etc.). Its actual provenance has yet to be determined. The genesis of this saying may be found in

Proverbs 17:28: "Even a fool, when he holdeth his peace, is counted wise: and he that shutteth his lips is esteemed a man of understanding." Alternatively, Woodrow Wilson once said, "If a man is a fool, the best thing to do is to encourage him to advertise the fact by speaking."

Verdict: Author yet to be determined.

"But it does MOVE." (**"Eppur si muove."**) Galileo's suggestion that the Earth moved around the Sun was considered heretical by reactionary clerics. Unless the astronomer recanted, they threatened to torture him. In 1633 Galileo did recant, agreeing with his inquisitors that the Earth was the stationary center of the universe. He is famous for then whispering, *"Eppur si muove."* ("But it does move.") Galileo's disclaimer first appeared in print more than a century after his death in 1642. "The moment he was set at liberty," reported a 1757 Italian history book, "he looked up to the sky and down to the ground, and, stamping with his foot, in a contemplative mood, said, Eppur si muove; that is, still it moves, meaning the earth." As a comment murmured before his inquisitors, this remark gained widest circulation in a French book published in 1761. The remark was then repeated so often that it became central to Galileo's intellectual legacy. However, no serious student of the astronomer's life thinks he was reckless enough to actually whisper, *"Eppur si muove"* or anything of the kind with thumbscrews and body racks hovering in the background.

Verdict: What we wish Galileo had said.

MOVIE LINES

No movie has been the source of more memorable lines than *Casablanca* (1942). They include: "We'll always have Paris," "Here's looking at you, kid," "I stick my neck out for nobody," "I'm shocked. Shocked!" "Round up the usual suspects," and "Louis, I think this is the beginning of a beautiful friendship." These lines were a product of inspired screenwriting by Julius and Philip Epstein and Howard Koch. The Epstein twins said that "Round up the usual suspects" occurred to them simultaneously as they drove to the studio one day. "Here's looking at you, kid" was penciled into the script at the last moment (simply adding one word to the traditional toast, "here's looking at you)." In the movie itself, Ingrid Bergman told Dooley Wilson, "Play it, Sam. Play 'As Time Goes By,'" but neither she nor Humphrey

Bogart said, **"PLAY it again, Sam."** Bogart did say, "Not so fast, Louis," in *Casablanca,* but he denied ever saying, **"Drop the gun, Louis,"** in that movie or any other. Bogart also disavowed **"Tennis, anyone?"** supposedly the only words he uttered in his first Broadway play. This phrase may have its roots in a line from Shaw's 1914 play *Misalliance:* "Anybody on for a game of tennis?"

Like Bogart, James Cagney was the subject of more than one apocryphal attribution. Before receiving the American Film Institute's Life Achievement Award in 1975, Cagney had someone check all of his films to see if he'd ever said, **"You dirty rat!"** He hadn't. In *Blonde Crazy* (1931), the actor did say, "That dirty, double-crossin' rat!" This could be the line Cagney impersonators condensed into the more popular version. In his autobiography, Cagney wrote, "Most of my imitators also say, **'All right, you guys!'** which I don't remember ever saying." He thought that line sounded more like something the Bowery Boys would have said, and that his impersonators might have gotten it from them. Cagney subsequently advised Frank Gorshin, a leading Cagney impersonator, "Oh Frankie, I never said 'MMMMmmm, you dirty rat!' What I actually said was **'Judy, Judy, Judy.'**" These three words, of course, were routinely mouthed by impersonators of Cary Grant. Grant once had some soundmen listen to the soundtracks all of his movies to see if he'd ever said them. He hadn't. Where did the actor think it came from? "I vaguely recall," said Grant, "that at a party someone introduced Judy Garland by saying, 'Judy, Judy, Judy,' and it caught on, attributed to me." Alternatively, a 1960 *New Yorker* ad for several Garland albums was titled "Judy! Judy! Judy!"

As with Cagney and Grant, the line best beloved by Charles Boyer impersonators, **"Come with me to the Casbah,"** was never uttered by the French actor in *Algiers* or any other movie. Boyer thought it was invented by his press agent.

Like many other quotation collections, *Bartlett's* reports that Johnny Weissmuller said, **"Me Tarzan, you Jane"** in *Tarzan the Ape Man* (1932). That could be because Weissmuller himself said in a 1932 interview, "I didn't have to act in *Tarzan the Ape Man*—just said, 'Me Tarzan, you Jane.'" He didn't. Judge Jon Newman of the U.S. Court of Appeals called this "perhaps the most widely used quotation of a nonexistent line from movie dialogue." A copyright decision handed down by the Second Circuit court in Hartford, Connecticut, incorporated an excerpt from *Tarzan the Ape Man*'s screenplay to show the actual dialogue that ensued after Tarzan chased off an ape that was bothering Jane. This included:

> JANE: (pointing to him) You? (Tarzan does not respond; she points to herself) Jane.
> TARZAN: (tapping her) Jane.
> JANE: (pointing to him) And you? You?
> TARZAN: (tapping himself) Tarzan. Tarzan.

Here is the correct wording and context of some famous movie lines whose origins or exact words are not always clear:

"You ain't heard nothin' yet!" from *The Jazz Singer* (1927), was Al Jolson's signature line and among the first words spoken in a talkie: "Wait a minute! Wait a minute! You ain't heard nothin' yet. Wait a minute, I tell ya, you ain't heard nothin'! Do you wanna hear 'Toot, Toot, Tootsie!'?" The line sounded spontaneous, but had been used by Jolson during live performances long before *The Jazz Singer* was produced, and it inspired Jolson's 1919 song "You Ain't Heard Nothing Yet" (cowritten with Gus Kahn and Buddy De Sylva).

"It ain't a fit night out for man or beast." W. C. Fields's celebrated remark in *The Fatal Glass of Beer* (1928) was generally attributed to him. Fields disavowed authorship, however, writing in a 1944 letter, "I do not claim to be the originator of this line as it was probably used long before I was born in some old melodrama."

"Would you be shocked if I put on something more comfortable?" Jean Harlow asked this provocative question in *Hell's Angels* (1930), which had four screenwriters and uncredited dialogue contributions by future *Frankenstein* director James Whale.

"It seemed like a good idea at the time" was said by Richard Barthelmess, in *The Last Flight* (1931), a film about American flyers after World War I that was based on a story by John Monk Saunders, who also wrote the screenplay. The line was delivered to explain why some American airmen abroad tried bullfighting, losing one of their ranks to a bull.

"We have ways to make men talk." Playing the suave, sinister Mohammed Khan, Douglass Dumbrille made this ominous observation to three members of the Bengal Lancers (including one played by

Gary Cooper) whom his soldiers had taken prisoner, in *The Lives of a Bengal Lancer* (1935). (The full line is "Well, gentlemen [smile, pause, scowl], we have ways to make men talk.") Reportedly Adolf Hitler's favorite movie, *The Lives of a Bengal Lancer* was adapted by Grover Jones and William Slavens McNutt and three screenwriters from Francis Yeats-Brown's novel by the same title.

"We could have made beautiful music together." Gary Cooper said this to Madeleine Carroll in *The General Died at Dawn* (1936), a movie written by playwright Clifford Odets, based on a story by Charles G. Booth.

"Toto, I have a feeling we're not in Kansas anymore." Judy Garland made this observation to her little dog as black-and-white turned to Technicolor, in *The Wizard of Oz* (1939), whose script was written by three screenwriters.

"Frankly, my dear, I don't give a damn." Films' most famous exit line, conveyed by Clark Gable as Rhett Butler in *Gone with the Wind* (1939), added one word to the version in Margaret Mitchell's 1936 bestseller by the same title ("My dear, I don't give a damn."). Presumably screenwriter Sidney Howard inserted "Frankly." Fortunately, film censors lost their struggle to have the line changed to "Frankly, my dear, I don't care," or "Frankly, my dear, I don't give a darn."

"You know how to whistle, don't you, Steve? You just put your lips together and blow." Another provocative question, this time posed by Lauren Bacall as Marie "Slim" Browning in *To Have and Have Not* (1944). Bacall's full thought, conveyed to Humphrey Bogart's character, was "You know, you don't have to act with me, Steve. You don't have to say anything, and you don't have to do anything. Not a thing. Oh, maybe just whistle. You know how to whistle, don't you, Steve? You just put your lips together and blow." That movie's script was written by Jules Furthman and William Faulkner, and was loosely based on the eponymous 1937 novel by Ernest Hemingway.

"We don't need no stinkin' badges." This is how we're most likely to remember the retort of a Mexican bandit pretending to be a police officer, when Humphrey Bogart asks to see the badges of him and his men, in *The Treasure of the Sierra Madre* (1948), in part because Mel Brooks included this version in his spoofy *Blazing Saddles* (1974). What the bandit actually said in John Huston's movie (Huston wrote the screenplay and directed) was "Badges? We ain't got no badges. We don't need no badges. I don't have to show you any stinkin' badges." This was adapted from the original lines in B. Traven's 1935 novel by the same title, on which the movie was based: "Badges, to god-damned hell with badges! We have no badges. In fact, we don't need badges. I don't have to show you any stinking badges, you god-damned cabrón and ching' tu madre!"

"What a dump!" Bette Davis said this in *Beyond the Forest* (1949), whose screenwriter was Lenore J. Coffee. Her line was later quoted by Elizabeth Taylor in *Who's Afraid of Virginia Woolf* (1966). According to quotographer Nigel Rees, this catchphrase had been around since early in the twentieth century, and had already been used in the movie *Fallen Angel* (1945).

"Fasten your seat belts. It's going to be a bumpy night." Screenwriter-director Joseph Mankiewicz wrote Bette Davis's notable warning in *All About Eve* (1950, based on a radio play and short story by Mary Orr). Understandably, the conclusion of this line is often misremembered as "a bumpy ride."

"I am big! It's the pictures that got small." Gloria Swanson's most famous line in *Sunset Boulevard* (1950) was made in response to a man who observed about her character, faded actress Norma Desmond, "You used to be big." *Sunset Boulevard*'s script was written by director Billy Wilder and two collaborators. It also included **"We didn't need dialogue. We had faces,"** Gloria Swanson's next-most-famous line.

"I coulda had class! I coulda been a contender. I coulda been somebody, instead of a bum, which is what I am." Marlon Brando's character, washed-up boxer Terry Malloy, made this poignant lament to his brother, Charley, played by Rod Steiger, in *On the Water-front* (1954), whose screenplay was written by Budd Schulberg.

"This is the West. When the legend becomes fact, print the legend." That is the creed of Western newspaperman Carleton Young in John Ford's *The Man Who Shot Liberty Valance* (1962), whose script was written by James Warner Bellah and Willis Goldbeck, based on a short story by Dorothy M. Johnson (which does not include this line).

"I just want to say one word to you. Just one word." / "Yes, sir." / "Are you listening?" / "Yes, sir. I am." / **"Plastics."** This famous ex-change took place between the characters played by Walter Brooke and Dustin Hoffman in *The Graduate* (1967). It does not appear in Charles Webb's novel by the same title, on which the movie is based.

Buck Henry, who cowrote the screenplay with Calder Willingham, says the dialogue was his invention, inspired by a professor he had at Dartmouth who railed against America's "plastic" society. Long after "Plastics" became a classic cinema line, and iconic of *The Graduate* as a whole, director Mike Nichols admitted that he'd initially questioned whether this word belonged in the movie. He and Buck Henry played around with alternative terms to portray a stultifying conversation stopper used by one generation when talking to another. They could not improve on "Plastics."

"What we've got here is failure to communicate." Our memories understandably add an "a" to Strother Martin's memorable line in *Cool Hand Luke* (1967), but this is what he actually said. Martin was a superb actor who, rather than include the "a" in his peroration as a prison warden who has just clubbed prisoner Paul Newman for making a sarcastic remark, says, "What we've got here is (pause) *failure to communicate.*" *Cool Hand Luke* was based on a novel by Donn Pearce, who cowrote the screenplay with Frank Pierson.

"When you've got it, flaunt it!" In Mel Brooks's 1968 movie *The Producers,* whose screenplay he wrote, theatrical producer Max Bialystock (played by Zero Mostel) makes this observation as he watches a white Rolls Royce drive by.

"I'm going to make him an offer he can't refuse." Marlon Brando's most memorable line as Don Vito Corleone in *The Godfather* (1972) drew on the novel by that title, which was written by Mario Puzo. In Puzo's novel Don Corleone says, "He's a businessman. I'll make him an offer he can't refuse." Puzo cowrote the movie's screenplay with director Francis Ford Coppola. In different forms Puzo's catchphrase, apparently original to him, was repeated in both *Godfather I* and *II,* by Don Corleone and his son Michael.

"What do we do now?" Playing novice political candidate Bill McKay, a perplexed Robert Redford raises this question after he is unexpectedly elected to the U.S. Senate in *The Candidate* (1972), whose screenplay was written by Jeremy Larner. Redford's question is often recalled when inexperienced figures such as George W. Bush or Canada's Brian Mulroney are elected to high office. Its genesis may have been a comment John Kennedy reportedly made to an aide several minutes into his first day in the Oval Office: "What the hell do I do now?"

"I'm as mad as hell, and I'm not going to take this anymore!"

So said newscaster Howard Beale, played by Peter Finch, in *Network* (1976), whose screenplay was written by Paddy Chayefsky. This line caught on quickly because it expressed the way many were feeling about lots of things. "This" is commonly replaced by "it" in popular usage.

"It's showtime!" Roy Scheider's mantra in *All That Jazz* (1979) presumably was that of screenwriter-director Bob Fosse, on whom Scheider's character was based.

"There are simply too many notes." This criticism of a Mozart opera was expressed by Jeffrey Jones, playing Emperor Joseph II in *Amadeus* (1984), whose script was written by Peter Shaffer, based on his play by the same title.

"Greed, for lack of a better word, is good." The most memorable line in *Wall Street* (1987) is often condensed by public memory into **"GREED is good."**

"If you build it, he will come." Ray Liotta's voice said this in *Field of Dreams* (1989), often. The memorable line is not from W. P. Kinsella's book *Shoeless Joe,* on which that movie—with a screenplay written by Phil Alden Robinson—was based. It is commonly misquoted as "they will come."

"I'll have what she's having." So says an unnamed older woman played by Estelle Reiner, mother of producer-director Rob Reiner, to the waiter in Katz's Deli, as Meg Ryan fakes an orgasm at the next table, in *When Harry Met Sally* (1989). Although the movie's script was written by Nora Ephron, Reiner said its costar, Billy Crystal, suggested this line.

"You can't handle the truth!" Jack Nicholson's explosive statement was made in *A Few Good Men* (1992). Aaron Sorkin, who later created and wrote the hit TV series *The West Wing,* based that movie's screenplay on his play by the same title. The full courtroom exchange, between Nicholson and Tom Cruise, is: "You want answers?" "I want the truth." "You can't handle the truth!"

"SHOW me the money!" Cuba Gooding's mantra in *Jerry Maguire* (1996) was written by screenwriter-director Cameron Crowe, says Crowe, but supplied by sports agent Drew Rosenhaus, says Rosenhaus, or a client of agent Leigh Steinberg, says Steinberg. In fact it's an old sports saw. Renée Zellweger's admission to Tom Cruise, "You had me at hello," is *Jerry Maguire*'s second-most-notable line.

"MUSIC has charms to soothe the savage beast." The actual wording of this line, in William Congreve's 1697 play *The Mourning Bride,* is "Music has charms to soothe a savage breast."

    Verdict: Credit Congreve; don't forget the "r."

"It's like trying to NAIL Jell-O to the wall." This is an update of "like trying to nail currant jelly to the wall," Theodore Roosevelt's depiction of negotiations with Colombian leaders in 1903 about a canal-enabling treaty. "You could no more make an agreement with them than you could nail currant jelly to a wall," he later wrote, "—and the failure to nail currant jelly to a wall is not due to the nail; it is due to the currant jelly."

    Verdict: Credit Theodore Roosevelt for currant jelly version.

"NASTY, brutish, and short." In *Leviathan* (1651), Thomas Hobbes depicted primitive human existence with this breathtaking sentence: "In such condition there is no place for industry, because the fruit thereof is uncertain: and consequently no culture of the earth; no navigation, nor use of the commodities that may be imported by sea; no commodious building; no instruments of moving and removing such things as require much force; no knowledge of the face of the earth; no account of time; no arts; no letters; no society; and which is worst of all, continual fear, and danger of violent death; and the life of man, solitary, poor, nasty, brutish, and short." The last four words of this run-on sentence were the ones that stuck.

    Verdict: Credit Hobbes.

"Love your NEIGHBOR, yet don't pull down your hedge." Yet another loan to Ben Franklin from George Herbert, who included "Love your neighbor, yet pull not down your hedge" in his 1640 collection of proverbs.

    Verdict: Improved Herbert (though proverbial wisdom, not original to him).

"NEVER play cards with a man named Doc. Never eat at a place called Mom's. Never sleep with a woman whose troubles are worse than your own." This popular piece of folk wisdom is attributed to Nelson Algren by *Bartlett's, Oxford,* and many other collections of quotations. In his best-selling 1956 novel *A Walk on the Wild Side,* Algren put these rules in the mouth of a prison convict. During a subsequent interview, Algren said he'd got them from an old black woman. On other occasions the novelist said this advice was his own invention. Biographer Bettina Drew thought the "rules" didn't sound like Algren, and might have originated with his friend

Dave Peltz. Sure enough, Peltz recalled cooking up the rules and including them in a letter to Algren, attributed to a black whorehouse madam to give them added credibility with his wild-walking friend. According to Peltz, "Never play cards with a man named Doc" is an old gambler's expression. "Never eat at a place called Mom's" reflected the fact that there were so many restaurants called "Mom's" in midcentury America, few of them any good. " 'Never go to bed with somebody whose troubles are worse than your own" was his own invention, based on the fact that Algren had a history of getting involved with people who were in worse straits than he. Peltz said the novelist never responded to his "rules," but began using them in lectures even before they achieved quote-book status as a result of appearing in *A Walk on the Wild Side.*

Verdict: Credit Dave Peltz as author, Nelson Algren as publicist.

"Be NICE to people on your way up because you'll meet them on the way down." Columnist Walter Winchell sometimes gets credit for this line, as do entertainer Jimmy Durante and rocker Frank Zappa. It's become a show business and sports commonplace, usually repeated with no attribution at all. Playwright-quipster Wilson Mizner used this line early in the century, and may have been its author.

Verdict: Credit Wilson Mizner for now.

"NICE guys finish last." As his league-leading Brooklyn Dodgers were about to play the seventh-place New York Giants in July 1946, irascible manager Leo Durocher talked with a group of sportswriters. Although the Giants had beaten his team the day before, Durocher ridiculed their pathetic record and dinky home runs. Red Barber, the Dodgers' radio announcer, asked Durocher why he couldn't be a nice guy for a change. After scoffing at the very notion, Durocher waved contemptuously toward the Giants' dugout. "The nice guys are all over there," he said. "In seventh place." The next day, Frank Graham of New York's *Journal-American* devoted his entire column to the Dodger manager's views on nice guys. "Leo Doesn't Like Nice Guys," it was titled. When Graham's column was reprinted in *Baseball Digest,* Durocher's reference to "seventh place" as the proper haven for nice guys had been changed to "last place," and, "in the second division." Before long his words were condensed and polished into the terse version that became the most familiar of American quotations. At first Durocher denied ever saying that nice guys finish last. Finally he gave up and said yes, he'd said it, though in two sentences, not one. ("Nice guys. Finish last.") The single-sentence version eventually became the title of his autobiography and was routinely cited by quotation collections as what Durocher actually said.

Verdict: Credit the concept to Durocher, its pithy version to the press.

"If NOMINATED, I will not run. If elected, I will not serve." Under pressure to run for president in 1871, William Tecumseh Sherman responded, "I hereby state, and mean all that I say, that I never have been and never will be a candidate for president; that if nominated by either party I should peremptorily decline; and even if unanimously elected I should decline to serve." Thirteen years later, when Sherman-for-president fever revived, the general received a telegram from the Republican convention in Chicago telling him that, like it or not, he was about to be nominated. Sherman's son Tom later recalled his father's response to this telegram: "Without taking his cigar from his mouth, without changing his expression, while I stood there trembling by his side, my father wrote the answer, 'I will not accept if nominated and will not serve if elected.'" This is as close as the historical record gets to the edited, more popular "Shermanesque" statement of noncandidacy.

Verdict: Poeticized Sherman.

"NUTS!" Since reporters routinely clean up soldiers' profanity, it's easy to assume that "Nuts!", Gen. Anthony McAuliffe's bold response to a German request for surrender of his position in the Belgian town of Bastogne during the Battle of the Bulge, is a euphemism. However, a history of that battle, *The Men of Bastogne* (with a foreword by McAuliffe), has an extended account of how he came up with this response and conveyed it to the Germans. During a lengthy interview with *Look* magazine editor David Maxey, McAuliffe never wavered in his contention that "Nuts!" was exactly what he had said. Since McAuliffe never used profanity during their long, liquid lunch, Maxey concluded that he was probably telling the truth.

Verdict: Wording accurate; credit Gen. Anthony McAuliffe.

"You can't make an OMELET without breaking eggs." This centuries-old proverb—found in many languages in a variety of forms—is commonly misattributed to revolutionary egg-breaker Joseph Stalin. In France, Robespierre and Napoleon get credit for saying, *"On ne fait pas d'omelette sans casser des oeufs,"* but according to quotographer Burton Stevenson that saying predated them both. An Italian version is *"Chi non rompe le uova, non fa la frittata,"* and one in Spanish goes *"No se hacen tortillas sin romper huevos."* Proverb scholar Wolfgang Mieder cites two related maxims: "Eggs

cannot be unscrambled" (American) and "To eat an egg, you must break the shell" (Jamaican).

Verdict: Historic common wisdom put in uncommon mouths.

"I see ONE-THIRD of a nation ill-housed, ill-clad, ill-nourished." According to speechwriter Samuel Rosenman this memorable line in Franklin Delano Roosevelt's second inaugural address came from the president's own pencil. It followed by three decades the publication of H. G. Wells's 1906 novel *In the Days of the Comet.* That novel included a passage that began, "I was ill clothed, ill fed, ill housed, ill educated and ill trained. . . ."

Verdict: Credit FDR, with help from H. G. Wells.

"The OPERA ain't over 'til the fat lady sings." During 1978's National Basketball Association playoffs, the Washington Bullets took a commanding lead over the Philadelphia 76ers. Asked about their prospects, Bullets coach Dick Motta cautioned, "The opera ain't over 'til the fat lady sings." This aphorism quickly caught the public's fancy. It was used by a character on the television program *Dallas,* by George H. W. Bush on the hustings, all manner of sportscasters, endless political commentators, and countless secondhand wits. When credited to anyone at all, it was usually credited to Dick Motta. Motta himself never claimed to have coined this line, however. Motta said he'd first heard it used by a TV sportscaster in San Antonio named Dan Cook. Cook, a longtime columnist for the *San Antonio Express-News,* may simply have been taking part in a great southern tradition: peddling shopworn Dixieisms to unsuspecting Yankees as fresh merchandise. An obscure 1976 pamphlet called *Southern Words and Sayings* included this entry: "Church ain't out 'till the fat lady sings." An informal poll of longtime southerners confirmed that many had heard this saying long before Dan Cook mouthed it and Dick Motta put the words into national discourse. During his coverage of the 2000 election, Texas-born CBS news anchor Dan Rather used a more grammatical, more sensitive version: "The opera isn't over until the heavy lady sings."

Verdict: A southern-fried old saw.

"He reminds me of the man who killed his parents, then pleaded for mercy because he was an ORPHAN." Abraham Lincoln is one of many to whom this quip is credited (in particular by his friend Ward Hill Lamon, whom Lincoln scholars Don and Virginia Fehrenbacher say routinely put words into the president's mouth). The gag has also been attributed to Vice President Alben Barkley and President William Howard Taft. Its actual

point of origin seems to be a much longer yarn called "A Hard Case," a newspaper sketch written in the early 1860s by one of Lincoln's favorite humorists, Artemus Ward. In this yarn Ward told the story of a baby-faced fourteen-year-old Arkansan who killed his parents with a meat ax. After being convicted by a jury, this boy was asked by the judge if he had anything to say before sentence was passed. "Why no," the boy replied. "I think I haven't, though I hope yer Honor will show some consideration FOR THE FEELINGS OF A POOR ORPHAN!"

Verdict: Credit Artemus Ward.

"An OUNCE of prevention is worth a pound of cure." Although it is generally attributed to him, Ben Franklin didn't even attempt to take credit for this adage. He called it "an old saying," or "an English proverb." Variations on "Prevention is the better cure" have been cited as proverbs for centuries, in English and in Spanish.

Verdict: A global old proverb, improved by Franklin.

"PARIS is worth a mass." ("**Paris vaut bien une messe.**") Questioning the common attribution of this cynical statement to France's Protestant King Henry IV, biographer Ronald S. Love noted that Henry's Huguenot-turned-Catholic adviser Maximillien de Béthune, duc de Sully, claimed credit for the comment. Among historians Sully is a more popular choice than Henry. Love himself thought it more likely that ultra-Catholic enemies of the king put these words into his mouth.

Verdict: King Henry probably never said it; who did remains a mystery.

DOROTHY PARKER

Before World War II, Dorothy Parker was considered America's leading wisecracker. Her quips were a columnist's delight. There just weren't enough of them to meet the demand. That's one reason so many comments were put in her mouth. "I say hardly any of those clever things that are attributed to me," Parker once insisted. "I wouldn't have time to earn a living if I said all those things."

In one famous story, playwright-politician Clare Boothe Luce waved Dorothy Parker through a door, saying, "Age before beauty." As Parker glided through the door, she was said to have trilled, **"Pearls before swine."** (In another version of this exchange, Parker delivered the setup line, actress Beatrice Lillie the retort.) Luce denied that this encounter ever took place. Parker biographer John Keats concurred. The genesis of this legend might have been in a short story written by Parker's friend Alexander Woollcott called "The Pearl," in which the heroine explains that she got her name "because I'm cast before swine."

Some of Parker's most famous sayings can be traced back to Woollcott's fawning profile of her in his 1935 bestseller *While Rome Burns*. (She reciprocated by writing a puff piece about Woollcott for *Vanity Fair*.) Woollcott's profile included a widely repeated story about Parker painting MEN on the door of her rented office when she grew too lonely inside. As Parker herself confirmed, this mystique-building prank took place only in her head, and in a letter she wrote to a friend.

Other Parkerisms put in play by Woollcott include her legendary tombstone inscription **"Excuse My Dust"** (these words were included as Parker's "epitaph" in a spoofy 1925 *Vanity Fair* feature), and her unverified depiction of Katharine Hepburn's acting as running **"the GAMUT of emotions from A to B."**

The huge volume of lines misattributed to Parker includes **"There is LESS to this than meets the eye," "You can never be too RICH or too thin,"** "Nobody goes there anymore—it's too crowded," "She was the original good time that was had by all," "The only difference between men and boys is the cost and number of their toys," "Hogamous, Higamous, men are polygamous, Higamous, Hogamous, women monogamous," "It's a wonderful country if you're an orange [California]," and—about Thomas Dewey—"He looks like the little man on a wedding cake."

Authentic Parkerisms include two lines from *New Yorker* reviews, **"*The House Beautiful* is, for me, the play lousy,"** and, about *The House at Pooh Corner*, **"Tonstant Weader fwowed up."** (Parker's *New Yorker* book reviews were signed "Constant Reader.")

Early in her career, while working at *Vogue*, Parker composed a caption for an underwear layout. The caption's last six words remain one of her most quoted quips: "From these foundations of the autumn wardrobe, one may learn that **brevity is the soul of lingerie.**"

"I expect to PASS through this world but once. Any good therefore that I can do or any kindness that I can show to any fellow creatures, let me do it now." Many books and magazines in the post–Civil War period recorded

different versions of this popular saying, sometimes unattributed, sometimes attributed to "a worthy Quaker" or "an old Quaker." Members of the Society of Friends were especially partial to these words. As early as 1869 they began to appear in Quaker publications, but without any specific attribution. In 1895 a query was posted to *Friends Intelligencer* about the origins of the quotation, noting that it was commonly credited to an unnamed Quaker, and once to Stephen Grellet. This was the French-American Quaker Stephen Grellet (Etienne de Grellet du Mabillier, 1773–1855), to whom this saying is attributed more than to any other individual (*The Oxford Dictionary of Quotations* credits Grellet), though never with an actual source. While conceding that this observation can't be found in Stephen Grellet's writing, quotographer Burton Stevenson gave him the nod in *The Macmillan Book of Proverbs, Maxims, and Famous Phrases*. Stevenson's British counterpart, W. Gurney Benham, reached the same conclusion in *Putnam's Dictionary of Thoughts*. The saying has also been credited to Marcus Aurelius, Joseph Addison, William Penn, John Wesley, Ralph Waldo Emerson, Thomas Carlyle, Mahatma Gandhi, and many, many others. Diligent searching for the actual author of these words for over a century has never discovered a reliable source. Noting how many authors have been credited with the exhortation, *Bartlett's* simply calls it "a proverbial saying." Considering that a character in Chaucer's *Canterbury Tales* makes reference to "an old proverbe . . . 'the goodness that thou mayest do this day, do it; and abyde nat ne delaye it nat til tomorowe,'" *Bartlett's* conclusion is the only credible one, for now.

Verdict: Proverbial wisdom.

"This too shall PASS." Abraham Lincoln popularized these comforting words of reassurance when, in an 1859 speech, he referred to "an Eastern monarch" who asked wise men to compose a sentence that would apply to all situations. Their composition was "And this, too, shall pass away." The same basic story, typically featuring "an Eastern monarch," had appeared in American periodicals since at least 1839. In 1852, Edward Fitzgerald's *Polonius: A Collection of Wise Saws and Modern Instances* included an entry titled "SOLOMON'S SEAL," in which "The Sultan asked Solomon for a signet motto, that should hold good for adversity or prosperity. Solomon gave him—'This too shall pass away.'" As a "Jewish folktale," some versions of this story feature Solomon as either the source or the recipient of this mot. Though he cited a source for many of his wise saws and modern instances, Fitzgerald gave none for this one. It is conceivable that the original source of the "Eastern monarch" version was Persian poet Sufi Farid al-Din

Attar of Nishapur (1142–1221), who was beheaded by Genghis Kahn's Mongols. In one of Attar's fables, a powerful king gathered a group of wise men and asked them to produce a ring that would make him happy when sad, and sad when happy. After much consultation among themselves, the wise men presented the king with a ring inscribed THIS, TOO, WILL PASS. Another twelfth-century Persian poet-philosopher, Sana'i of Ghazni, also used this phrase, as did others from that part of the world.

Verdict: A line from a Middle Eastern fable, Persian most likely.

"The PAST is never dead. It's not even past." So wrote William Faulkner in his 1950 play, *Requiem for a Nun.* (This line is sometimes misquoted as "In Mississippi, the past is never dead. . . .")

Verdict: Credit Faulkner.

"Those who cannot remember the PAST are condemned to repeat it." George Santayana made this much-repeated observation in *The Life of Reason* (1905).

Verdict: Credit George Santayana.

"PEACE with honor." After meeting with German Chancellor Otto von Bismarck at the Congress of Berlin in 1878, British Prime Minister Benjamin Disraeli announced, "[Foreign Minister] Lord Salisbury and myself have brought you back peace—but a peace, I hope, with honor." In his time, Disraeli was celebrated for coining this phrase. Today it is more commonly associated with a subsequent Prime Minister, Neville Chamberlain. After his ill-fated 1938 meeting with Hitler in Munich, Prime Minister Chamberlain told his countrymen, "This is the second time in our history that there has come back from Germany to Downing Street peace with honor. I believe it is peace for [not *in*] our time." Many antecedents existed for this phrase, including an 1853 speech in which Lord John Russell said, "But while we endeavor to maintain peace, I certainly should be the last to forget that if peace cannot be maintained with honor, it is no longer peace." Prior to Russell's speech these words had appeared often in English. In Shakespeare's *Corirolanus* (1608), Volumnia urges her son Coriolanus to "hold companionship in peace / With honor, as in war. . . ." In 1650, Sir Anthony Weldon wrote in *The Court and Character of King James,* "He had rather spend £100,000 on Embassies to keep or procure peace with dishonor, than £10,000 on an army that would have forced peace with honor."

Verdict: Too traditional an idea for specific attribution, to Chamberlain, Disraeli, or anyone else.

"There go the PEOPLE. I must follow them, for I am their leader." This ironic expression has been attributed to Disraeli, Gandhi, Boston mayor James Michael Curley, and British statesman Andrew Bonar Law. It is most often credited to Alexandre Ledru-Rollin, a prominent figure in the French Revolution of 1848. Ledru-Rollin—considered by some to be the father of universal suffrage—was thought to have been forced by circumstances to lead an insurrection he thought ill-advised. Those who made this point often quoted the French democrat as saying, "I am their chief; I must follow them," or words to that effect. After reviewing extensive evidence, biographer Alvin R. Calman concluded that this alleged remark was based on a single unreliable account and most likely was apocryphal. It might well have been a gag that was circulating at the time and landed in Ledru-Rollin's mouth.

Verdict: Words put in the mouth of Alexandre Ledru-Rollin during the mid-nineteenth century, and the mouths of many others since.

"Eighty PERCENT of success is showing up." Among many popular Woody Allen observations, this is the most quoted, and misquoted. However, the exact percentage that showing up accounts for, and what exactly showing up is good for, often get garbled. George H. W. Bush quoted Allen as saying, "Ninety percent of life is just showing up." Figures as low as 50 percent have also been cited, as well as 75 and 85 percent. Allen told William Safire that as best he could recall, 80 percent was what he'd first said was the percentage of success based on showing up. The simple need to "show up" is featured in many another saying (e.g., "The world is run by those who show up.").

Verdict: Credit Woody Allen, at 80 percent.

"On the whole, I'd rather be in PHILADELPHIA." Despite a widespread assumption that these words are on W. C. Fields's tombstone, what's actually written on the vault holding his ashes is w.c. FIELDS, 1880–1946. The more popular version originated in the same 1925 *Vanity Fair* gag feature that reported Dorothy Parker's epitaph as "Eat my Dust." Fields's was given as "I Would Rather Be Living in Philadelphia." Whether this spoof epitaph was his own invention wasn't made clear. (Fields often hired ghostwriters to compose magazine pieces that appeared under his byline.)

Verdict: Fields (or his ghostwriter) originated the thought, but not in the form or setting that we imagine.

PHONY FALSE FORECASTS

Mistaken forecasts are ever-popular because they seem so antiprescient. This genre is especially popular in the world of technology. Too few of such stunningly wrong predictions have been verified. Most should be treated as apocryphal until proven accurate. They include:

"Everything that can be invented has been invented." The U.S. commissioner of patents is said to have made this observation in 1899. Despite diligent research, no one has ever confirmed that he did. Supplementing a 1940 study by historian Eber Jeffery with his own research, librarian Samuel Sass concluded that not only did then-Patent Commissioner Charles Duell say nothing of the kind, but Duell actually believed that turn-of-the-century America was in the midst of a flowering of invention. The most recent version of this apocryphal remark appeared in an English book called *The Book of Facts and Fallacies: A Book of Definitive Mistakes and Misguided Predictions* (1981). Citing this work, Christopher Cerf and Victor Navasky included the prediction in *The Experts Speak: The Definitive Compendium of Authoritative Misinformation* (1984, republished in 1998), after which it appeared in full-page magazine ads sponsored by TRW, and in Bill Gates's 1995 book *The Road Ahead.* What is the source of this misquotation? Sass cites two possibilities. U.S. Patent Commissioner Henry L. Ellsworth wrote in his 1843 report to Congress, "The advancement of the arts, from year to year, taxes our credulity and seems to presage the arrival of that period when human improvement must end." This was merely a rhetorical flourish, however, in the midst of a report that predicted increased patenting of inventions. Seven decades later, in 1915, *Scientific American* reported, "Someone poring over the old files in the United States Patent Office in Washington the other day found a letter written in 1833 that illustrates the limitations of the human imagination. It was from an old employee of the Patent Office, offering his resignation to the head of the department. His reason was that as everything inventable had been invented the Patent Office would soon be discontinued and there would be no further need of his services. . . ." As Sass pointed out, this account too is far-fetched, not the least reason being that a fire in 1836 destroyed all Patent Office records.

"I think there is a world market for maybe five computers." IBM president Thomas Watson supposedly made this observation in

1943. It was popularized in *The Experts Speak,* whose compilers again cited as their source that book's English predecessor, *The Book of Facts and Fallacies.* Though many have tried to verify this remark, no one has succeeded. Diligent searching by biographer Kevin Maney turned up no such prediction in press coverage of IBM or in Watson's speeches and papers. IBM's own archivists can only tell the many who inquire about this prediction by Watson that it can't be found in their files (and they've looked). On the other hand, Harvard's Howard Aiken, who before World War II developed a mechanical calculator called Mark I, is known to have estimated after the war that the entire country's computing needs could be met with four or five electronic computers. (Aiken was not the only one to feel this way at that time.) According to Maney, Thomas Watson's son and successor, Thomas Watson, Jr., gave a speech in 1953 saying that in the 1940s IBM anticipated getting five orders for an early computer they developed. In 1951, British physicist Douglas Hartree told a visitor that in his opinion three computers would be sufficient to do all the calculations that Great Britain would ever need. Attributing a version of these forecasts to Tom Watson is one more case of a quotation seeking out the most prominent appropriate mouth.

"There is no reason anyone would want a computer in their home." Kenneth Olsen, president, chairman, and founder of Digital Equipment Corporation (DEC), is said to have made this comment at the World Future Society in Boston in 1977. This is the context given by Cerf and Navasky (who misspell Olsen's name in both editions of *The Experts Speak*), but it has not been verified. The authors cite as their source an interview with personal computer pioneer David Ahl. Ahl has told others that DEC's head made his bleak assessment of home computers during a midseventies meeting of his company's operations committee that Ahl attended as a DEC product developer working on small computers. According to *Fire in the Valley,* Paul Freiberger and Michael Swain's history of the personal computer, at this meeting "Olsen said that he could see no reason why anyone would want a home computer." David Ahl is apparently the authors' source for this comment. Based on his stormy relationship with DEC (from which he'd once been fired for protesting cutbacks in educational product development) and his role as a passionate advocate of personal computers, Ahl can hardly be considered an objective source.

Although shortsighted on the future of home computers, Kenneth Olsen, as Freiberger and Swaine note, was considered one of his industry's most astute executives overall. It seems unlikely that he would have made so categorical a statement on the prospects of computers in the home.

Bill Gates is widely quoted as having said in 1981 that **"640K ought to be enough** [computer memory] **for anybody"** No one has ever produced any evidence that he did. It is doubtful that any exists. Gates himself once told an interviewer, "I've said some stupid things and some wrong things, but not that. No one involved in computers would ever say that a certain amount of memory is enough for all time." The origins of this popular misquotation remain a mystery.

"Please do not shoot the PIANIST; he is doing his best." Though he didn't claim they were his, these words are often put into Oscar Wilde's mouth (when not being attributed to Mark Twain). In fact, as Wilde reported in *Impressions of America,* he saw this plea on a sign in a Leadville, Colorado, saloon during his 1882 tour of the United States.

Verdict: Credit a Leadville saloon owner, not Oscar Wilde.

"One PICTURE is worth a thousand words." According to a biographer of John Wanamaker, well before the twentieth century began, the desk of Philadelphia's department store magnate and advertising pioneer displayed "the Chinese motto 'One picture is worth ten thousand words.'" In different forms that thought was ubiquitous in the early twentieth century, but with little agreement about its origins. A 1914 realtor's ad in the *New York Times* began "'A look is worth a thousand words,' say the Japanese." Several months later a furniture manufacturer advertised in the *Chicago Tribune* that "The Chinese have a saying that one look is worth a thousand words." In 1921, adman Fred Barnard composed an advertisement for *Printer's Ink* magazine that attributed "One look is worth a thousand words" to "a famous Japanese philosopher." Five years later Barnard titled another ad in the same magazine "One picture is worth ten thousand words." He called this version "a Chinese proverb." This was the most common attribution at that time. In a 1924 test of facsimile transmission, the words "One picture is worth ten thousand words"—said to be "an old Chinese proverb"—were transmitted from London to New York. Questioning that attribution, proverb scholar Wolfgang Mieder points out that this maxim does not show up in the many

collections of Asian proverbs (though "Seeing it once is better than being told one hundred times" appears on a website, devoted to Chinese culture, attributed to Zhou Chongguo of the Han Dynasty). Furthermore, adds Mieder, the form of this saying is consistent with others circulating in mid-twentieth-century America such as "One smile is worth a thousand tears," and "One laugh is worth a thousand groans." Whether these variants originated before the "one picture" version is unclear. We do know that a character in Ivan Turgenev's 1862 novel *Fathers and Sons* observes, "A picture shows me at a glance what would take up all of ten pages in a book." Perhaps the most popular version of this notion is an amalgam of ancient Chinese wisdom and snappy American patter with a dash of Russian literary insight.

Verdict: Proverbial wisdom of uncertain origin.

"You furnish the PICTURES and I'll furnish the war." As the Spanish-American war was about to erupt, newspaper publisher William Randolph Hearst sent sketch artist Frederick Remington to portray the action in revolutionary Cuba. After spending a few days there, Remington wired that he could find no hostilities and wanted to return. Hearst is notorious for responding, "Please remain. You furnish the pictures and I'll furnish the war." There is no reliable evidence that the publisher sent any such telegram. He himself denied having done so. The wire in question has never been found. As Hearst biographer John K. Winkler pointed out, it is unlikely that such an inflammatory message would have gotten past Spanish censors. The source of Hearst's pithy telegram seems to have been a 1901 memoir by journalist James Creelman, a Hearst admirer who reported the publisher's order to Remington without giving any source. In the movie *Citizen Kane,* which was based on the life of William Randolph Hearst, a reporter sends Kane a telegram that concludes COULD SEND YOU PROSE POEMS ABOUT SCENERY BUT DON'T FEEL RIGHT SPENDING YOUR MONEY. STOP. THERE IS NO WAR IN CUBA. Kane responds, YOU PROVDE THE PROSE POEMS, I'LL PROVIDE THE WAR.

Verdict: Apocrypha.

"If you steal from one person it's PLAGIARISM; if you steal from several it's called research." This take on research is most often attributed to playwright-raconteur Wilson Mizner. As an unrepentant thief of other people's words, Mizner knew whereof he spoke. The question is, did Mizner plagiarize his classic observation on plagiarism?

Verdict: Credit Wilson Mizner, gingerly.

"No PLAN survives contact with the enemy." This wartime commonplace is attributed to all the usual suspects: Napoleon, Eisenhower, Omar

Bradley—anyone but its actual originator: Helmuth von Moltke the Elder (1800–1891). In a mid-nineteenth-century essay titled "On Strategy," the Prussian field marshal wrote, "Therefore no plan of operations extends with any certainty beyond the first contact with the main hostile force." Von Moltlke's windier words were compressed into pithier ones over time, his name no longer associated with them.

Verdict: Credit Helmuth von Moltke for the original idea, if not the final version.

"Make no little PLANS. They have no magic to stir men's blood." House Speaker Dennis Hastert made this admonition while opening the 109th Congress in 2005. He attributed the words to architect Daniel Burnham (1846–1912), who was instrumental in developing Chicago on a grand scale more than a century earlier. They are widely cited as Burnham's credo. Concerted efforts to find a source for the comment have been unsuccessful, however. Apparently it first appeared on a Christmas card composed by Burnham's associate Willis Polk six months after Burnham died in 1912. The quotation subsequently appeared in a 1921 biography of Daniel Burnham, and thereafter became central to his legacy. The architect's son, Daniel Burnham, Jr., thought Polk's version of the statement was cobbled together from parts of a 1910 speech given by his father. When Chicago architect Henry Saylor analyzed that speech, however, the closest passage he could find was "In city planning there is no limit to be fixed." Biographer Thomas Hines concluded that Willis Polk probably constructed the lines from ones Burnham told him in conversation, or wrote him in letters.

Verdict: Burnham's thoughts, Polk's words.

"Can't **anybody** *here PLAY this game?"* While managing the inept New York Mets, an exasperated Casey Stengel once said, "Can't *anybody* play this here game?" After reporters cleaned up his grammar, "Can't *anybody* here play this game?" became Stengel's signature line.

Verdict: Cleaned-up Stengel.

"PLAY it again, Sam." The most misquoted of all movie lines appears neither in the script nor the film of *Casablanca*. In that film, Ingrid Bergman, playing Ilsa, does say to the piano player played by Dooley Wilson, "Play it, Sam. Play 'As Time Goes By.'" Rick, played by Humphrey Bogart, later tells Sam, "You played it for her, you can play it for me," and, "If she can stand it I can. Play it!" After years of hearing his words misquoted, the cowriter of *Casablanca*'s script, Howard Koch, speculated that the word "again" was

simply added by nostalgic memory to the scene in which Bogart broods and Wilson plays "As Time Goes By." "Play it again, Sam" later became the title of a Woody Allen play and movie. Describing how, as a teenager, he imitated Bogart, Woody Allen recalled, "I was walking like Bogart, talking like Bogart, curling my lip and saying, . . . 'Play it again, Sam.' (I know he never actually said 'Play it again, Sam,' but I said it enough for both of us.)"

Verdict: Misremembered *Casablanca.*

"The great PLEASURE in life is doing what people say you cannot do." Sometimes thought to be a Chinese proverb, this line was part of an 1879 essay about Shakespeare written by economist-author Walter Bagehot.

Verdict: Credit Walter Bagehot.

"A POEM is never finished, only abandoned." This widely cited observation by Paul Valéry (1871–1945) takes different forms. Apparently it is a condensation of a longer, more complex thought expressed by the French poet and critic in his essay "Au Sujet du Cimetière Marin": "In the eyes of those who anxiously seek perfection, a work is never truly *completed*—a word that for them has no sense—but abandoned; and this abandonment, of the book to the fire or to the public, whether due to weariness or to a need to deliver it for publication, is a sort of accident, comparable to the letting-go of an idea that has become so tiring or annoying that one has lost all interest in it." (*"Aux yeux de ces amateurs d'inquiétude et de perfection, un ouvrage n'est jamais achevé, —mot qui pour eux n'a aucun sens, —mais* abandonné; *et cet abandon, qui le livre aux flammes ou au public (et q'il soit l'effet de la lassitude ou de l'obligation de livrer), leur est une sorte* d'accident, *comparable à la rupture d'une réflexion, que la fatigue, le fâcheux, ou quelque sensation viennent rendre nulle."*) In the preface to his 1947 novel, *A Fortress Besieged,* Qian Zhongshu struck a similar note: "Despite all the talk about handing it over, the book remains like the flying knife of the magician—released without ever leaving the hand." The derivative saying "A painting is never finished, only abandoned" has been attributed to Picasso and others, without any source.

Verdict: Condensed Valéry.

"A thousand POINTS of light." When speechwriter Peggy Noonan wrote these words for George H. W. Bush (who used them while running for president in 1988, then while in the White House), she assumed they were original. Noonan subsequently discovered that any assumption of originality is a risky proposition in the phrasemaking business. In 1987 Linda Sexton published a novel called *Points of Light,* which included this epigraph

from a letter by Vincent van Gogh: "The sight of stars always sets me dreaming just as naively as those black dots on a map set me dreaming of towns and villages. Why should these points of light in the firmament, I wonder, be less accessible than the dark ones on the map of France?" In 1955, C. S. Lewis wrote in *The Magician's Nephew,* "One moment there had been nothing but darkness, next moment a thousand points of light leaped out—single stars, constellations, and planets, brighter and bigger than any in our world." Thomas Wolfe used the phrase "a thousand points of friendly light" in his 1939 novel *The Web and the Rock.* In 1924, a visitor to a national forest in California wrote, "The sky was bright with a thousand points of light. . . ." An 1878 profile of the Empress of Austria said, "The sun set her dress a-sparkle in a thousand points of light. . . ." An 1872 travel article depicted the peaks of the Alps as "cold and blue in the shadow, but breaking into a thousand points of light in the sun." In 1866, a serialized novel described the surface of water beneath moonlight erupting "into a thousand points of light . . ." When William Safire sent Peggy Noonan a speech by a turn-of-the-century engineer urging the electrification of Venice so that it might be filled with "a thousand points of light," Bush's speechwriter said she had no conscious awareness of drawing on that source or any other. Noonan did recall reading *The Web and the Rock* as a teenager and admitted that its thousand points of friendly light might have burrowed dimly in her consciousness awaiting a George Bush speech to shine through.

Verdict: A neopoetic commonplace of unknown origins.

"*Forever POISED between a cliché and an indiscretion.*" The head of the U.S. Arms Control and Disarmament Agency once described someone in a position like his as being "poised between a cliché and an indiscretion." What he called an "adage" is considered a classic portrayal of the lot of a diplomat. British Prime Minister Harold Macmillan is the only serious candidate for authorship. A onetime foreign secretary, Macmillan said of one who holds that position, "He is forever poised between a cliché and an indiscretion." Macmillan was so quoted in a 1956 issue of *Newsweek* (the source given for this remark by *The Oxford Dictionary of Quotations*). The year before that, in 1955, Macmillan used the same terminology in at least two speeches. Twenty-six years later, in 1981, the Archbishop of Canterbury, Rev. Robert Runcie, said of his premarital counsel to the Prince of Wales and Lady Diana Spencer, "My advice was delicately poised between the cliché and the indiscretion."

Verdict: Credit Harold Macmillan.

"An honest POLITICIAN is one who when he's bought stays bought."
Even *Bartlett's* attributes this corrupt and cynical comment to Pennsylvania's cynical and corrupt political boss Simon Cameron (1799–1899). Although Cameron acknowledged the popular perception that he "bought" influence, biographer Erwin Stanley Bradley concluded that there was no basis for the attribution of this infamous remark to Lincoln's first secretary of war. The phrase "stays bought" was common in considerations of corruption during Cameron's time. In 1856, after noting a report that $50,000 was being spent in Pennsylvania to buy votes for Democratic presidential candidate James Buchanan, the *New York Times* observed, "If they are to be bought up so cheaply they will not stay bought long. . . ." An 1870 commentator in *Lippincott's* magazine noted that anyone who accepts bribes must be willing to display "some character, some conscience—something which when bought will stay bought." Most likely the wittier version of this thought was pinned on Cameron by one of his many enemies.
   Verdict: Familiar words put in Simon Cameron's mouth.

"A POLITICIAN is a person who approaches every subject with an open mouth." Quote collections most often attribute this witticism to Adlai Stevenson (who did say something similar). Variations have also been attributed to Oscar Wilde and Supreme Court Justice Arthur Goldberg. G. K. Chesterton wrote in 1908, "An open mind is really a mark of foolishness, like an open mouth." While calling the version defining politicians "another of those quotations that floats continually in search of a definite source," quotographer Nigel Rees gives a tentative nod to Stevenson. Adlai himself told an interviewer that he'd made this quip. As with so many of Stevenson's witticisms, however, one must be braced to discover them in earlier sources.
   Verdict: Credit Stevenson, tentatively.

"All POLITICS is local." Former House Speaker Thomas P. "Tip" O'Neill considered this his credo, and used it as the title of a book he cowrote. In that book the Boston politician said he first heard the adage used by his father. Where Thomas O'Neill, Sr., got it is anyone's guess. According to biographer John A. Farrell, this saying was a commonplace among politicians when the future House Speaker was cutting his political teeth in Depression-era Massachusetts. During the early 1930s it appeared often in the American press, without attribution. Farrell and others speculate that the adage originated with humorist Finley Peter Dunne (Mr. Dooley). Dunne biographer Edward J. Bander says it did not.
   Verdict: An old political saw adopted by Thomas P. "Tip" O'Neill.

"Being in POLITICS is like being a football coach. You have to be smart enough to understand the game, and dumb enough to think it's important." Former Minnesota senator and presidential aspirant Eugene McCarthy (1916–2005) is often so quoted. A 1967 newspaper profile of McCarthy led off with this comment by him. It is the first entry in Bill Adler's *The McCarthy Wit* (1969), though no source is given. McCarthy was known for his acerbic wit, and he liked to use sports analogies.

Verdict: Credit Eugene McCarthy.

"POLITICS ain't beanbag." So observed Mr. Dooley in the first authorized collection of Finley Peter Dunne's columns (*Mr. Dooley in Peace and in War,* 1898). The preface to that book included this comment by Dunne about his imaginary bartender-commentator: "His early experiences gave him wisdom in discussing public affairs. 'Politics,' he says, 'ain't bean bag. 'Tis a man's game; an' women, children, an' pro-hybitionists do well to keep out iv it.'"

Verdict: Credit Mr. Dooley via Finley Peter Dunne.

"POLITICS is the art of the possible." ("**Die Politik is die Lehre von Moglichen.**") Although sometimes attributed to British politician R. A. Butler (whose 1971 memoir was titled *The Art of the Possible*), this definition of politics is more reliably credited to Otto von Bismarck, as Butler himself acknowledged. Certainly it reflected the views of Prussia's Iron Chancellor, though in condensed form. One biographer quoted Bismarck as saying, "Politics is not a science, as the professors are apt to suppose. It is an art." (*"Die Politik is keine Wissenschaft, wie viele der Herren Professoren sieh einbilden, sondern eine Kunst."*) According to an early quotation collection, Bismarck said this in the Reichstag in 1884, echoing an earlier version of the same sentiment expressed by him in the Prussian upper house in 1863: "Politics is not an exact science." (*"Die Politik is keine exakte Wissenschaft."*) Another old collection concurs, adding that Bismarck made a similar observation in the Prussian Chamber of Deputies in 1884. *The Oxford Dictionary of Quotations* cites a 1918 biographer who quoted Bismarck as having made an observation to this effect during an 1867 conversation.

Verdict: Bismarck's sentiments, if not his exact words.

"POLITICS makes strange bedfellows." In *The Baviad and Maeviad* (1797), English editor-author William Gifford wrote, "I can only say that politics, like misery, 'bring a man acquainted with strange bedfellows.'" "Verily," agreed an American press commentator thirty-five years later, "politics *do*

make strange bedfellows." Seven years after that, in 1839, onetime New York mayor Philip Hone wrote in his diary that "party politics, like poverty, 'bring men acquainted with strange bedfellows.'" In 1851, a Wisconsin political analyst compressed this thought into "Politics makes strange bedfellows." The root of that saying can, of course, be found in *The Tempest* (1611), where Shakespeare wrote that "misery acquaints a man with strange bedfellows." Over time Shakespeare's phrase inspired many a saying in which all manner of antecedents made for "strange bedfellows" (adversity, money, etc.). The political version is the one that stuck. In 1870, American journalist Charles Dudley Warner applied the phrase to both horticulture and politics when he wrote, "I may mention here, since we are on politics, that the Doolittle raspberries had sprawled all over the strawberry-beds: so true is it that politics makes strange bed-fellows." ("Doolittle" referred to Wisconsin senator James Rood Doolittle.) *Bartlett's* condenses Warner's 1870 version to "Politics makes strange bedfellows," and attributes the saying to him. *The Oxford Dictionary of Quotations* more prudently, and more accurately, calls it a mid-nineteenth-century proverb, though the saying was apparently in play well before then.

Verdict: A modular saying built on Shakespeare's foundation.

"POWER corrupts, and absolute power corrupts absolutely." In an 1887 letter, British historian Lord Acton (John Dahlberg, 1834–1902) wrote, "Power tends to corrupt, and absolute power corrupts absolutely." This insight was Lord Acton's only contribution to most quotation collections (although in the same letter he made the notable observation that "Great men are never good men."). We tend to forget "tends," however, and can't always remember who actually said that power corrupts. (Texas senator Phil Gramm, a former college professor, attributed the thought to "ancient Greeks.") Nor do most of us realize that similar thoughts had already been expressed by, for example, William Pitt (1708–1778) when he said in a 1770 speech, "Unlimited power is apt to corrupt the minds of those who possess it."

Verdict: Credit Lord Acton for articulating an existing thought; don't forget "tends."

"POWER is the ultimate aphrodisiac." Although this observation has been attributed to Nancy Kissinger, most often it is credited to her husband, Henry. In the early 1970s the onetime secretary of state was often quoted as calling power the ultimate aphrodisiac, although it's hard to imagine no one reached this conclusion before then.

Verdict: Kissinger probably said it, but did he say it first?

"Freedom of the PRESS belongs to those who own one." When attributed at all, various forms of this popular observation are usually put in the mouth of some prominent journalist, especially H. L. Mencken. Its actual author, A. J. Liebling, wrote in the *New Yorker* in 1960, "(Freedom of the press is guaranteed only to those who own one.)." Liebling's use of parentheses suggests either that this thought was not new, or that it was a throwaway line, or both.

Verdict: Credit A. J. Liebling.

"Every man has his PRICE." This cynical maxim is most often attributed to British Prime Minister Sir Robert Walpole (1676–1746). According to biographers William Coxe and Lord Morley, what Walpole actually said (around 1740, about some nemeses) was "All those men have their price." On other occasions Sir Robert was said to have referred to knowing the price of various political figures. The more sweeping, more cynical version apparently was put in his mouth by political enemies. In any event, this version had been circulating widely long before it ended up in Walpole's lap. In 1734, Sir William Wyndham wrote, "It is an old maxim that every man has his price." A letter writer in a 1776 issue of *The Pennsylvania Magazine* observed that "The free-thinking gentry tell us upon this subject, that 'every man has his price.'" No mention was made of Sir Robert Walpole.

Verdict: An old saying put in Robert Walpole's mouth.

"Nowadays people know the PRICE of everything and the value of nothing." This version appeared in Oscar Wilde's 1891 novel, *The Picture of Dorian Gray.* A year later, in *Lady Windermere's Fan,* Wilde defined a cynic as "A man who knows the price of everything and the value of nothing." Several years after that aphorist Elbert Hubbard took credit for "Too many people nowadays know the price of everything and the value of nothing." In 1918, a *Puck* writer defined education as "That which knows the price of everything and the value of nothing." An unattributed "Gem of the Day" in Ann Landers's advice column in 1993 was "Too many people know the price of everything and the value of nothing."

Verdict: Credit Wilde.

"PRIDE goes before a fall." According to Proverbs 16:18, "Pride goes before destruction, and a haughty spirit before a fall." Many subsequent writers, including Jonathan Swift and Samuel Johnson, noted that pride preceded a fall.

Verdict: Condensed Proverbs.

"*PRIVACY is the right to be left alone.*" In their classic 1890 *Harvard Law Review* article "The Right to Privacy," Louis Brandeis and Samuel Warren called privacy "the right to be let alone" (not "left alone," as usually is assumed). Their full thought was "Gradually the scope of these legal rights broadened; and now the right to life has come to mean the right to enjoy life,—the right to be let alone; the right to liberty secures the exercise of extensive civil privileges; and the term 'property' has grown to comprise every form of possession—intangible, as well as tangible."
    Verdict: Condensed, revised Brandeis (and Warren).

"*For every PROBLEM there is always a solution that is simple, obvious, and wrong.*" This sounds like Twain, and has been attributed to him. H. L. Mencken is the more likely source, however, having written, "Explanations exist; they have existed for all times, for there is always an easy solution to every human problem—neat, plausible, and wrong."
    Verdict: Credit Mencken for this idea.

"*You're either part of the solution or you're part of the PROBLEM.*" Black activist Eldridge Cleaver said this in a 1968 speech. As a result, Cleaver generally gets credit for the Age of Aquarius slogan. It quickly became a counterculture cliché attributed to the likes of Abbie Hoffman and Stokely Carmichael. Variations on this theme had appeared in the American press for years, however. In 1956 an Ohio newspaper depicted an unnamed "advertising expert" who congratulated participants in a Washington, D.C., women's conference for "their obviously sincere effort to be part of the solution, not a part of the problem, of living in this changing world." In 1961 an Iowa newspaper included as an unattributed filler, "Every person is either part of the problem, or part of the solution." Three years later a member of the board of education in Oakland, California (where Eldridge Cleaver was later based), said, "I am here to be part of the solution—and not part of the problem."
    Verdict: A pre-existing thought popularized by Eldridge Cleaver.

"*PROFESSIONALS built the* Titanic. *Amateurs built the Ark.*" Since the early 1990s this comment has been all over the media, on the Internet, on posters, in speeches, and in at least one work of fiction. Its originator has yet to be determined. As an orphan quotation it is free for the taking. Some have taken it, as if the thought were original to them. More often the many retailers of this observation call it a "saying," "adage," or "maxim."
    Verdict: Author unknown.

"All PROFESSIONS are conspiracies against the laity." So wrote George Bernard Shaw in his 1906 play *The Doctor's Dilemma*. Several decades later economist Kenneth Boulding was quoted as saying that trades and professions were likely to organize themselves into "a conspiracy against the public."
     Verdict: Credit Shaw.

"PROMISES are like pie crust, made to be broken." Ronald Reagan was especially fond of quoting Lenin to this effect. Reagan thought he had read somewhere that the Bolshevik leader said this. In a 1905 article for the magazine *Proletarii*, Lenin did write, "The promises like pie crust are leaven to be broken," which he called "an English proverb." Lenin's point was not that he believed this proverb, but that his rivals did. This proverb appeared in Jonathan Swift's 1738 *Polite Conversation* in the form of a comment by a Lady Answerall: "I beg your Pardon, my Lord, Promises and Pye-Crusts, they say, are made to be broken." More than half a century earlier, a 1681 issue of the earliest periodical published in Britain, *Heraclitus ridens: or, a discourse between jest and earnest; where many a true word is pleasantly spoken, in opposition to all libellers against the government,* included this sentence: "He makes no more of breaking Acts of Parliaments, than if they were like Promises and Pie-crust, made to be broken." Presumably these passages articulated common wisdom. The fact that its historic English heritage had long been clear didn't prevent rabid anti-Communists—including Secretary of State John Foster Dulles—from attributing this old English proverb to Vladimir Ilyich Lenin as proof of the Bolshevik's perfidy.
     Verdict: An old English proverb misattributed to Lenin.

"PROSPERITY is just around the corner." Generations of Democratic orators notwithstanding, Herbert Hoover said no such thing after the stock market crash of 1929. This chins-up assurance appeared in the American press as early as 1909. By the 1920s, "prosperity is just around the corner" had become a cliché of a catchphrase. In the early years of the Depression, that phrase was used generically to ridicule those business and government leaders who kept making optimistic statements about the economy, if not this one exactly. Hoover himself made a lot of reassuring sounds about the imminence of better times, but this wasn't one of them.
     Verdict: A longstanding catchphrase; Hoover never said it.

"PUBLIC office is a public trust." Grover Cleveland's motto was meant to portray him in a statesmanlike light. Many took credit for suggesting this phrase to the twenty-second president. The most credible claim was that of

Cleveland campaign aide William C. Hudson, a former journalist. Unable to find a proper slogan for the title page of Grover Cleveland's first presidential campaign pamphlet in 1884, Hudson approached the matter as if he were writing a newspaper headline. "Public Office Is a Public Trust" is what he came up with. After persuading Cleveland that this was a précis of views he'd often expressed, Hudson wrote "G. Cleveland" under the headline, and sent his pamphlet copy off to the printer and history. Successful as it proved to be, Cleveland's 1884 slogan had a long heritage. In 1872, twelve years before Cleveland took it over, Sen. Charles Sumner observed in a speech that "The phrase, 'public office is a public trust,' has of late become common property." In his memoirs, William Hudson noted that the edition of *Bartlett's* current at the time he attributed this phrase to Cleveland cited its use by Sumner, and other antecedents as well. Hudson conceded that he might have read the phrase there or somewhere else, but couldn't recall doing so.

Verdict: An old political slogan publicized by Grover Cleveland, with help from a campaign aide.

"The PUBLIC be damned!" During the Gilded Age, railroad magnate William Henry Vanderbilt claimed to be the world's richest man. The public perceived him as a greedy robber baron. In the fall of 1882, as Vanderbilt traversed the Midwest in a private train, two journalists joined him in his car outside Chicago. One of them, Clarence Dresser, later reported that in the midst of a discourse on widespread ignorance about the railroad business, Vanderbilt said, "The public be damned!" This remark raced around the country, confirming a widespread perception of Vanderbilt as arrogant in the extreme. The railroad mogul claimed that Dresser put those words in his mouth. After a thorough assessment of various accounts of this episode, writer John Steele Gordon concluded that Vanderbilt probably did say the fateful words, or ones like them. Clarence Dresser later said that although Vanderbilt had indeed exclaimed, "The public be damned!" his tone was more bemused than contemptuous. If so, he was one of many in a long line of public figures who learned the hard way that irony vanishes in print.

Verdict: Credit Vanderbilt.

"A PURITAN is someone who can't sleep at night worrying that someone, somewhere is having a good time." In his 1992 State of the Union address, President George H. W. Bush referred to "the old definition of the Puritan, who couldn't sleep at night worrying that somehow someone somewhere was having a good time." Peggy Noonan wrote this speech. She may or may not have known the genesis of this line. In his 1949 collection

Mencken Chrestomathy, H. L. Mencken defined "Puritanism" as "The haunting fear that someone, somewhere, may be happy." In various forms this proved to be one of Mencken's most durable observations.

Verdict: Credit Mencken.

"Practice RANDOM kindness and senseless acts of beauty." California writer Anne Herbert says she came up with this phrase in 1982, and wrote it on a place mat at a Sausalito restaurant. "I knew it worked," Herbert later told *San Francisco Chronicle* columnist Adair Lara, "because people kind of wet their teeth when I used that phrase." Herbert subsequently published her suggestion in a 1985 article called "Random Kindness and Senseless Acts of Beauty" in the *Whole Earth Review.* Others picked up on this notion, especially after *Glamour* and *Reader's Digest* reprinted Adair Lara's revision of a 1991 *Chronicle* column she wrote touting Herbert's idea. (Ann Landers later published a truncated version of this column that a reader sent her, which did not mention either Adair Lara or Anne Herbert.) "Practice random kindness and senseless acts of beauty" subsequently became a commonplace of West Coast graffiti, posters, and bumper stickers. In 1993, Bakersfield College professor Chuck Wall initiated a "Random Acts of Kindness" movement, at first taking credit for the slogan itself. That same year Anne Herbert coauthored a book called *Random Kindness and Senseless Acts of Beauty.* The first part of her admonition has been misattributed to Lao Tzu. An antecedent can be found in William Wordsworth's lines "On that best portion of a good man's life, / His little, nameless, unremembered, acts / Of kindness and of love."

Verdict: Credit Anne Herbert.

"READ my lips." This saying had been street common long before George H. W. Bush used it repeatedly during his 1988 campaign for president (to emphasize that he would never, ever raise taxes). Three decades earlier, in 1957, songwriter Joe Greene copyrighted a song called "Read My Lips," which was recorded for a 1958 album. Politicians adopted the phrase throughout the 1980s, as did quite a few songwriters and sundry novelists. In Scott Turow's 1987 novel *Presumed Innocent,* one character tells another to "watch my lips." A William Safire correspondent thought "Read my lips," like so many other phrases, may have originated in the Borscht Belt. At a Catskills resort he'd once heard a comedian squelch a heckler by saying, "Can you read lips?" Then, without waiting for a response, the comic continued, "Well, read my lips," and gave the heckler a Bronx cheer.

Verdict: Postwar street talk put to tune, fiction, and political oratory.

"REALITY is nothing but a collective hunch." This is another creation of Lily Tomlin's writing partner, Jane Wagner. In *The Search for Signs of Intelligent Life in the Universe*, after saying, "I refuse to be intimidated by reality anymore," Trudy the bag lady (played by Lily Tomlin) adds, "After all, what is reality anyway? Nothin' but a collective hunch."

Verdict: Words by Wagner, delivery by Tomlin.

"A RECESSION is when a neighbor loses his job. A depression is when you lose yours." This gag was pretty shopworn by the time Ronald Reagan revived it during the 1980 campaign (adding the tag line, "And recovery is when Jimmy Carter loses his."). Harry Truman said this back in the 1950s. So did Teamsters president Dave Beck. Others have claimed credit for it as well, or had credit assigned to them. In 1954 the comment ran in American newspapers as a witticism "overheard on the street."

Verdict: Postwar gag of uncertain origin, credited to the most recent, most prominent user.

"I only REGRET that I have but one life to give for my country." Nathan Hale's famous last words (which vary in the retelling) were first reported in the memoirs of his friend Gen. William Hull. Hull—who wasn't present at Hale's hanging—said he heard about them from a British officer who was present. Another British officer who witnessed Hale's execution for spying wrote in his diary that the young patriot's final words were "It is the duty of every good officer to obey any orders given him by his commander-in-chief." During his days as a Yale student, Hale was known to be fond of Joseph Addison's 1713 play *Cato*. This play included the lines "What pity is it / That we can die but once to serve our country." Addison is a more likely source of this quote than Hale or Hull.

Verdict: Credit Joseph Addison for this thought, William Hull for the popular version.

"RELIGION is the opium of the people." According to historian Gertrude Himmelfarb this observation was common among young Hegelians when Karl Marx recorded it in the introduction to his *Critique of the Hegelian Philosophy of Right* (1844). In the introduction to that book, Marx wrote, "Religion is the sigh of the oppressed creatures, the heart of a heartless world, just as it is the soul of soulless conditions. It is the opium of the people." (*"Die Religion is der Seufzer der bedrangten Kreatur, das Gemut einer herzlosen Welt, wie sie der Geist geistloser Zustande ist. Sie ist das Opium des Volkes."*) Since Marx's use of the phrase is

the first one known to have appeared in print, he usually gets author's credit.

Verdict: A pithier version of an existing idea, put in print by Karl Marx.

"No one washes a RENTED CAR." Who you think made this popular observation may depend on your demographic cohort. Some attribute a version to former Harvard president Lawrence Summers. Thomas Friedman has so quoted Summers more than once in his *New York Times* column, in one case saying he'd heard Summers say this. An assistant to Summers said she believed he had made this observation, but her only source was Friedman. One member of an audience listening to speaker-author Steven Covey (*The Seven Habits of Highly Effective People*) recalls hearing him say in the mid-1990s that no one washed rented cars. During that decade "no one washes a rented car" became a business-world truism, shorthand for the virtues of ownership, and usually conveyed with no source at all.

Verdict: A new saw; author yet to be determined.

"I can RESIST everything except temptation." This observation gained broadest currency as a line in Oscar Wilde's play *Lady Windermere's Fan* (1892). It has also been attributed to Mark Twain, Mae West, and W. C. Fields. Whether or not the words originated with Wilde, he was their primary disseminator.

Verdict: Credit Oscar Wilde.

"I shall RETURN." According to biographer William Manchester, Douglas MacArthur's vow to return after the Japanese drove his forces from the Philippines was suggested by future Philippine president Carlos Romulo. The Office of War Information in Washington strongly urged the American commander to say, "*We* shall return." Romulo, at the time a journalist, argued that his countrymen trusted MacArthur personally more than they trusted Americans in general. MacArthur took Romulo's advice and stuck to the singular. In his autobiography, MacArthur quotes himself as saying, "I came through and I shall return," but mentions no coauthor. Among his troops, these egotistical words became a standing joke (e.g., "I'm going to the latrine, but I shall return."). MacArthur's vow echoed an earlier one common among French soldiers during Napoleon's exile in Elba: *"Il reviendra!"* ("He will return!")

Verdict: Credit Carlos Romulo for the words, Douglas MacArthur for their dissemination.

"I've been RICH and I've been poor. Rich is better." In 1937, a newspaper columnist portrayed the wife of playwright George S. Kaufman urging a theatrical figure to accept one of many movie opportunities he was being offered. "Don't overlook the money part of it," Bea Kaufman reportedly said. "I've been poor and I've been rich. Rich is better!" Sometimes misattributed to Mae West, Bessie Smith, Billie Holiday, Joey Adams, Joe Louis, Frank Sinatra, Irving Wallace, John Connally, or Pearl Bailey, this thought is most often credited to singer Sophie Tucker. Nonetheless, there is no reliable record of her ever having said it. A retired *Hartford Courant* editor named Henry McNulty once scoured his newspaper's coverage of the hometown celebrity from the beginning of her career in 1922 until she died in 1966. He found no reference to this comment. Nor could McNulty find it in obituaries about Tucker written elsewhere, or in her autobiography. Some think the thought originated with comedian Joe E. Lewis, or comedienne Fanny Brice. Since Tucker and Lewis sometimes performed together, they had many an opportunity to borrow each other's material. Tucker and Brice were contemporaries and friends. Most likely this was a show business commonplace free for the taking.

Verdict: An old entertainer's saw.

"The RICH are different from you and me." / "They have more money." In a celebrated exchange, F. Scott Fitzgerald told Ernest Hemingway, "The rich are not like you and me." Hemingway replied, "Yes, they have more money." Although that dialogue never took place (at least not between Fitzgerald and Hemingway), there's a reason for the widespread assumption that it did. In 1926 Fitzgerald published a short story called "The Rich Boy." The third paragraph of that story included these lines: "Let me tell you about the very rich. They are different from you and me. They possess and enjoy early, and it does something to them, makes them soft where we are hard, and cynical where we are trusting, in a way that, unless you were born rich, it is very difficult to understand." Ten years later, an early version of Hemingway's "The Snows of Kilimanjaro" ran in *Esquire* magazine. That story included this passage: "He remembered poor Scott Fitzgerald and his romantic awe of them [the rich] and how he had started a story once that began, 'The very rich are different from you and me.' And how someone had said to Scott, Yes, they have more money." Though Hemingway didn't say so, the reader was free to conclude that this rejoinder was his. *The Crack-Up,* Fitzgerald's posthumously published miscellany, included this jotting by its author: "'They have more money.' (Ernest's wisecrack.)" In a

footnote, editor Edmund Wilson explained, "Fitzgerald had said, 'The rich are different from us.' Hemingway had replied, 'Yes, they have more money.'" That's not exactly accurate. Here's what really happened: Several years before writing "Snows of Kilimanjaro," Hemingway had lunch with his editor, Maxwell Perkins, and critic Mary Colum. Perkins later wrote a relative that during this lunch Hemingway commented, "I am getting to know the rich." Colum responded, "The only difference between the rich and other people is that the rich have more money." When Hemingway's story suggested that Scott Fitzgerald was the actual target of this topper, Perkins wrote Fitzgerald, "I was present when that reference was made to the rich, and the retort given, and you were many miles away." In response to Fitzgerald's objection, Hemingway changed his name to "Julian" in the book version of "Snows of Kilimanjaro."

Verdict: Credit the setup line to F. Scott Fitzgerald, the topper to Mary Colum, its propagation and misattribution to Ernest Hemingway.

"*You can never be too RICH or too thin.*" This popular maxim has been attributed to Dorothy Parker, Joan Rivers, Rose Kennedy, Diana Vreeland, and—most often—either the Duchess of Windsor (Wallis Simpson) or Babe Paley. In the early 1970s the duchess even had these words embroidered on a throw pillow. No matter how rich and thin she may have been, Ms. Simpson was not particularly clever and is unlikely to have coined this phrase. Babe Paley is a more promising candidate. The comely wife of CBS founder William Paley was known for her tart tongue. Nonetheless, no credible evidence exists that she coined this remark. The most likely candidate of all is one to whom the observation is seldom attributed: author Truman Capote. According to quote compiler Alec Lewis, Capote said he observed that you can't be too rich or thin on *The David Susskind Show* in the late 1950s (probably 1959). Capote was close to Babe Paley and could have fed her the line.

Verdict: Credit Truman Capote as originator, tentatively, and Babe Paley as primary publicist.

"*A RIDDLE wrapped in a mystery inside an enigma.*" When Richard Burton called Elizabeth Taylor "a secret wrapped in an enigma inside a mystery," he neglected to cite his source. In the fall of 1939, following the Soviet occupation of East Poland, Winston Churchill told the British public in a radio broadcast, "I cannot forecast to you the action of Russia. It is a riddle wrapped in a mystery inside an enigma: but perhaps there is a key. That key is Russian national interests."

Verdict: Credit Churchill.

"I would rather be RIGHT than president." In 1839, when Kentucky senator Henry Clay was composing a centrist speech on issues surrounding slavery and its abolition (Clay condemned slavery but opposed abolition), his South Carolina colleague William Preston warned him that this approach would antagonize extremists on both sides. According to an account published at the time, Clay responded, "I trust the sentiments and opinions are correct; I had rather be right than be President." According to another contemporary version, he told Preston, "I did not send for you to ask what might be the effect of the proposed movement on my prospects, but whether it was right; I had rather be right than be President."

Verdict: Credit Clay with saying he had rather be right than president.

"The RIGHT stuff." These three words became an American catchphrase after Tom Wolfe published a bestselling 1979 book by this title that later became a hit movie. The phrase "right sort of stuff" had been used to describe manly virtues for centuries, however. In 1769, a British military officer on the verge of a career change fretted that he was "not of the right stuff for a merchant . . ." Seventy-one years before Tom Wolfe's book appeared, a 1908 novel by Scottish author Ian Hay (John Hay Beith, 1876–1952) had already been called *The Right Stuff*. In 1922, justifying his support of a Republican for marshal in Jackson County, Missouri, Harry Truman explained that the man had been his commanding officer in World War I, and he'd seen him and his men hold off a German attack when they were badly outnumbered. "He was of the right stuff," Truman concluded.

Verdict: An old Anglo-American catchphrase on loan to Tom Wolfe.

"We was ROBBED!" According to *Bartlett's* and other quote collections, boxing manager Joe Jacobs made this exclamation after heavyweight champion Max Schmeling (whom he managed) lost a 1932 title fight to Jack Sharkey. That could be true. In an oral history recorded some forty years after that fight, its referee, Gunboat Smith, said those were Jacobs's words. The *New York Times's* 1940 obituary of Jacobs recalled him saying, "We wuz robbed." But a survey of major New York newspapers turned up these contemporaneous reports of his manager's words after Schmeling lost the decision:

"Joe Jacobs . . . said his champion had been robbed." Daily Mirror

". . . Joe Jacobs said they were robbed. . . ." Daily Mirror

"I was robbed of the decision." Times

"He was robbed." Evening Post

"We've been robbed!" American (reported by Damon Runyon)

"It was a bare-faced robbery." American

"He was jobbed." American (reporting a postfight radio interview with Jacobs)

It's conceivable that every New York reporter gave Jacobs a hand with his diction. More likely the version that's gone down in history is the one we wanted to hear from this former-day Yogi Berra, and heard.
Verdict: Punched-up Jacobs.

WILL ROGERS

During the 1920s and 1930s, Will Rogers was America's humorist-in-chief. At one time there was even a semiserious movement to elect him president. The Oklahoma cowboy was shrewder, smarter, and better read than the rube persona he affected. Despite his drawl and slouch hat, Rogers was the most modern of men. The onetime rodeo performer was quick to jump from trick roping to telling jokes onstage (often banking barbs with his signature line, "All I know is just what I read in the papers."), then to writing a newspaper column and books, before proceeding on to the more contemporary arts of radio commentary and movie acting. In all such media, but especially in his daily column, Rogers contributed many enduring quips to the national discourse.

A favorite chuckle from the Cherokee-descended Rogers was **"My ancestors didn't come over on the *Mayflower*, but they met 'em at the boat."** (This is quoted often—in publications of the Will Rogers Memorial and Research Center and elsewhere—but without a source. Rogers biographer Ben Yagoda says he used the line onstage.) Rogers also said that he had just enough white blood in him to make his honesty questionable.

Other memorable Rogersisms include:

Now, everything is funny, as long as it is happening to somebody else.

A fanatic is always the fellow that is on the opposite side.

Half our life is spent trying to find something to do with the time we have rushed through life trying to save.

We'll hold the distinction of being the only nation in the history of the world that ever went to the poorhouse in an automobile.

You can't say that civilization didn't advance, however, for in every war they kill you in a new way.

The income tax has made more liars out of the American people than golf has.

But with Congress, every time they make a joke it's a law. You know. And every time they make a law it's a joke.

I tell you folks, all politics is applesauce.

Rogers's well-honed epitaph, **"He joked about every prominent man in his time, but he never met a man he didn't LIKE,"** is one he repeated often, in different forms. His famous observation **"I am not a member of any organized party—I'm a Democrat"** is sometimes misattributed to Mark Twain. (This observation is quoted by biographer P. J. O'Brien, who does not give a source; Yagoda confirms that it is authentic.) In a speech at Harvard, TV journalist Ted Koppel quoted Twain as having said, "We are all ignorant; just about different things." In fact, it was Will Rogers who said, **"You know, everybody is ignorant, only on different subjects."**

Like any other quotable figure Rogers is frequently misquoted. Realtors are fond of sharing this advice from Rogers: **"Buy land. They ain't makin' any more of the stuff."** In fact, the humorist did not consider land a particularly good investment. "There is nothing that can break a man quicker than land, unless it's running a grocery store or dealing in second-hand cars" is an actual quote from Rogers.

Rogers has also been erroneously credited with saying, **"A LIE can travel halfway around the world before the truth gets its boots on," "Never pick a FIGHT with anyone who buys ink by the barrel," "Everybody talks about the WEATHER, but no one does anything about it,"** and **"I don't care what they say about me as long as they SPELL my name right."** Along with Twain, Rogers has been miscredited with "We've got the best Congress money can buy." (See sidebar "Mark Twain.")

"When in ROME, do as the Romans do." This popular advisory improves on what St. Ambrose (circa 340–397) was said to have advised St. Augustine in 387: "If you are at Rome, live after the Roman fashion; if you are elsewhere, live as they do there." (*"Si fueris Romae, Romano vivito more; si fueris alibi, vivito sicut ibi."*) According to proverb scholar Wolfgang Mieder, "In a village do as the village does" is a Japanese proverb, though he does not indicate its era of origin.

Verdict: St. Ambrose's advice, edited and polished over time. Basic idea widespread.

THEODORE ROOSEVELT

Theodore Roosevelt was both more quotable and more inventive than the average president. The many phrases he contributed to our discourse include "hat in the ring," "pussyfooting," "loose cannon," and "lunatic fringe." Roosevelt became the first politician to throw his hat in the ring when he responded to a reporter's question about whether he planned to run for president in 1912, "My hat's in the ring. The fight is on, and I'm stripped to the buff." (This was based on a Western frontier custom of throwing one's hat in a boxing ring to indicate a willingness to take on all comers.) Roosevelt may also have coined "hearts and minds" during a conversation with his young military aide Douglas MacArthur in which he attributed his popularity among the citizenry to his ability to "put into words what is in their hearts and minds but not in their mouths." (See sidebar "Vietnam.") The contemporary line "It's like

trying to nail Jell-O to the wall" was inspired by Roosevelt's 1903 observation that attempting to conclude an agreement with the leaders of
Colombia was like trying to **"NAIL currant jelly to the wall."**

For all of his originality, Roosevelt was no less likely than any other
politician to appropriate existing material. Although he got credit for the
phrase "weasel word," this actually was coined by writer Stewart Chaplin in a 1900 magazine article, "Muckraker," from Roosevelt's 1906 description of overzealous journalists as "raking the muck." Roosevelt's
characterization drew on John Bunyan's depiction of a man with a
"muck-rake" in *Pilgrim's Progress* (1678). Thirty-five years before Roosevelt applied the term to journalists, an American politician had already
been described as raking in muck.

Theodore Roosevelt was especially fond of spinal similes, saying that
William McKinley had no more backbone than a chocolate éclair, and,
of Supreme Court Justice Oliver Wendell Holmes, Jr., **"I could carve
out of a banana a justice with more BACKBONE than that."** Such
similes were popular at the turn of the century, and hardly originated
with Roosevelt. His signature line, **"SPEAK softly, and carry a big
stick,"** was an old proverb that Roosevelt didn't even claim to have authored. In a 1901 speech that included this adage, Roosevelt also said, **"I
stand for the square deal,"** a phrase he repeated often. *Square deal*
was a gambling term TR may have picked up while cowboying out west.

Roosevelt did originate **"I wish to preach, not the doctrine of
ignoble ease, but the doctrine of the strenuous life,"** which was
part of a sentence he used in an 1899 speech. Several years later, Roosevelt said during a 1910 lecture at the Sorbonne, **"It is not the critic
who counts; not the man who points out how the strong man
stumbled, or where the doer of deeds could have done them better. The credit belongs to the man in the arena, whose face is
marred by dust and sweat and blood."** This is Roosevelt's celebrated
"man in the arena" remark, quoted by John Kennedy and many others.
After his son Quentin was killed in World War I, TR wrote, **"Only
those are FIT to live who do not fear to die . . . ,"** a phrase later
requisitioned by Douglas MacArthur. On the other hand, Roosevelt did
not call the Spanish-American conflict of 1898 **"a splendid little
war,"** as is sometimes thought. That was Secretary of State John Hay.

Like most prolific speakers and writers, Theodore Roosevelt was
not reluctant to recycle thoughts of his own that he especially liked.

For example, he was celebrated for the conclusion to his 1900 essay "The American Boy": **"In short, in life, as in a foot-ball game, the principle to follow is: Hit the line hard; don't foul and don't shirk, but hit the line hard!"** Three years before that appeared in *St. Nicholas* magazine, Roosevelt wrote in the preface to a volume of his collected works, "To borrow a simile from the football-field, we believe that men must play fair, but that there must be no shirking, and that success can come only to the player who 'hits the line hard.'" He had also published various versions of his "man in the arena" admonition before the one that stuck.

Teddy Roosevelt remains famous for having said of his unruly oldest daughter that he could govern the country or he could control Alice Roosevelt Longworth, but that he couldn't possibly do both. This comment is requoted in various forms. The *New York Times* obituary of Longworth included this version: "I can do one of two things. I can be President of the United States, or I can control Alice. I cannot possibly do both." A biographer reported that Roosevelt said those words to his friend Owen Wister, author of *The Virginian*. Wister himself wrote in his 1930 book *My Friendship with Roosevelt,* "'Why don't you look after Alice more?' a friend once asked Roosevelt. 'Listen,' he said. 'I can be President of United States—or I can attend to Alice.'"

"A ROSE is a rose is a rose." In her 1913 poem "Sacred Emily," Gertrude Stein wrote "Rose is a rose is a rose is a rose." To make that sentence more coherent, we usually add an "a" to the beginning and prune a blossom from the end. Stein subsequently used what became her signature line—sometimes shortened by a rose and with an "a" added to the beginning—in other pieces of writing, on her stationery, and on a signet ring she wore (which could be used to emboss sealing wax). What exactly did it mean? Some thought the line referred to Sir Francis Rose, a painter whose work Stein admired and collected. But Stein didn't meet Rose until several years after she wrote "Sacred Emily." That poem referred to a "Jack Rose." (Was this a person, or the cocktail Hemingway wrote about in *The Sun Also Rises*?) Stein's own middle name was Rose. So was the first name of the heroine of her 1939 children's book *The World Is Round*. The cover of the American edition of that book was rose-colored. Its English edition was illustrated by Sir Francis Rose, and printed on rose-colored paper. Both editions were dedicated "To a French rose / Rose, Lucy, Renée, Anne d'Aiguy."

In his own consideration of Stein's most famous line, literary critic Richard Poirier has pointed out that rose not only is a common euphemism for vagina (so used by Shakespeare and Dante), but that "a rose" repeated often enough can be heard as "eros." Gertrude Stein succeeded in befuddling us all with her "rose-is-a-rose" observation, and felt no need to resolve the confusion. She did say of her most famous words, "I made poetry and what did I do I caressed completely caressed and addressed a noun," and "in that line the rose is red for the first time in English poetry for a hundred years."

Verdict: Credit Gertrude Stein for the original version of this line, with one less "a" and one more flower.

"RUM, Romanism, and rebellion." In 1884, this slogan was thought to be a slanderous portrayal of the Democrats' credo by Republican presidential candidate James G. Blaine. The resulting uproar helped Grover Cleveland defeat Blaine. These words were not his, however, but those of a supporter: the Reverend Dr. Samuel D. Burchard. At a Blaine reception one month before the election, Burchard said, "We are Republicans, and don't propose to have our party identify ourselves with the party whose antecedents have been rum, Romanism and rebellion." The last part of this statement lodged in the public's ear. Before long it was as if the Republican candidate had said it himself, or so the Democrats successfully persuaded American voters.

Verdict: Credit Samuel D. Burchard, not James G. Blaine.

"He can RUN, but he can't hide." Toward the end of the 2004 presidential election, George W. Bush said this repeatedly about his opponent, John Kerry. The comment was hardly original. In fact, it's been beloved by politicians of every ideological stripe for decades. The taunt was first put in political play by Harry Truman when he told delegates to the 1948 Democratic convention that they could take heart from Joe Louis's remark about an opponent who could run away but couldn't hide. The president was a little vague on when and where the heavyweight fighter said this. A few days before his 1946 rematch with Irish-American boxer Billy Conn, Joe Louis was asked by a reporter whether he'd chase his faster opponent if Conn stayed in motion. "He can run," responded Louis, "but he can't hide." Louis knocked Conn out in the eighth round. Whether or not these words were original to Louis, his use of them caught the public's fancy.

Verdict: Credit Joe Louis, possibly repeating street talk.

"SATIRE is what closes on Saturday night." George S. Kaufman's most famous quip is quoted often, but never with an actual source. Kaufman's

daughter Anne has no doubt that he said this, but she does not know where or when. Nor do biographers Malcolm Goldstein and Jeffrey Mason, both of whom believe that Kaufman's line is authentic. Mason thought that this remark might have circulated in Manhattan after the playwright used it in conversation. According to Goldstein the "satire is what closes" line is so much a part of Kaufman's lore and sounds so much like him that it undoubtedly is legitimate.

Verdict: Kaufman probably said this, but in an unrecorded conversation.

"If you like laws and SAUSAGE, you should never watch either one being made." Various versions of this observation were especially popular during the 2000 presidential election debacle. By 2004 it was so familiar that Ted Kennedy could say, to laughter and applause, "The Medicare bill is a poster child for how not to write a law. Even a sausage maker would be offended by how this law was made." When attributed to anyone at all, different forms of the original remark are credited to Otto von Bismarck. The Library of Congress calls that attribution "unverified." Kaiser Wilhelm has also received credit for this line, as has Benjamin Disraeli, eighteenth-century French statesman Honoré Gabriel de Riqueti, the comte de Mirabeau, and Betty Talmadge, the former wife of Georgia senator Herman Talmadge. Variations on this theme were popular in post–Civil War America. In an 1869 lecture Vermont lawyer and author John Godfrey Saxe said, "Laws, like sausage, cease to inspire respect in proportion as we know how they are made." Others made much the same observation in subsequent years.

Verdict: An old political saw, possibly coined by Bismarck, or by John Godfrey Saxe.

"SAY it ain't so, Joe." In 1920, Shoeless Joe Jackson was one of eight Chicago White Sox players tried for intentionally losing the 1919 World Series (at the behest of gamblers). Their sin cast a pall over America's secular religion. Someone needed to tell these ballplayers how hurt Americans felt, how let down, and to plead that they deny the charges. That someone appeared in the form of a little boy whose question was put to Jackson as he emerged from a Chicago courthouse, in the account of sportswriter Hugh Fullerton:

" 'It ain't so, Joe, is it?'

" 'Yes, kid, I'm afraid it is.' "

This boy's plaintive question focused the "Black Sox Scandal." Along the way his words were given a polish, euphonized from the pedestrian "It ain't so, Joe, is it?" to the pithier, more poetic, "Say it ain't so, Joe." *Bartlett's* and many another source now attribute this iconic plaint to some unknown boy. But did anyone actually say it? At the time of Fullerton's account, other newspapers reported a courthouse scene similar to that depicted by Hugh Fullerton, but none included the words "Say it ain't so, Joe." Jackson himself always denied that this or anything like it was ever said to him. "I guess the biggest joke of all," he reflected in later years, "was that story that got out about 'Say it ain't so, Joe.' It was supposed to have happened . . . when I came out of the court room. There weren't any words passed between anybody except me and a deputy sheriff. . . . He asked me for a ride and we got in the car together and left. There was a big crowd hanging around in front of the building, but nobody else said anything to me."

Verdict: Joe said "it ain't so" was never said, and he probably was right.

"SCRIBBLE, scribble, scribble." After the second volume of *The History of the Decline and Fall of the Roman Empire* was published in 1787, its author, Edward Gibbon, was said to have presented a copy to the Duke of Gloucester, King George III's brother, to whom he'd already given the first volume. According to a semi-contemporaneous account, this affable nonreader responded, "Another damned thick, square book! Always scribble, scribble, scribble! Eh! Mr. Gibbon?" In a second version another brother of George III, the Duke of Cumberland, while attempting to make conversation at a social event, told the historian, "So, I suppose you are at the old trade again. Scribble, scribble, scribble." Yet a third account, in a literary magazine in 1795, had a similar exchange taking place at Christie's in Pall Mall, with the Duke of Cumberland saying, "I suppose you are at your old trade of basket making, hey, Gibbon, scribble, scribble, scribble, scribble." (Most versions include only three "scribble"s.) George III himself was subsequently given credit for saying, "Scribble, scribble, scribble." In his memoirs Gibbon mentioned no such remark by anyone, though its editor did (in a footnote, citing attributions to both the Duke of Gloucester and the Duke of Cumberland). Whoever may have said it, generations of writers have taken "scribble, scribble, scribble" as a fair approximation of how they spend their time.

Verdict: A comment that may have been made to Edward Gibbon by a member of the British royal family.

"There are no SECOND ACTS in American life." F. Scott Fitzgerald made this observation in working notes for his uncompleted final novel, *The Last Tycoon.* Appropriately enough, these words are among the last ones Fitzgerald recorded. Although his observation is generally taken to mean that Americans—and certainly Fitzgerald himself—burn out young,

...other interpretation is that Americans tend to leap from first-act dilemmas to third-act resolutions, skipping second-act complications.

Verdict: Credit F. Scott Fitzgerald, in notes for *The Last Tycoon.*

"God, grant me the SERENITY to accept the things I cannot change; the courage to change the things I can; and the wisdom to know the difference." In various forms "The Serenity Prayer" is most commonly associated with Alcoholics Anonymous. AA credits theologian Reinhold Niebuhr as its author. According to Niebuhr's daughter Elisabeth Sifton, author of the 2003 book *The Serenity Prayer,* her father composed this prayer at his vacation home in Heath, Massachusetts, during the summer of 1943. That version read: "God give us grace to accept with serenity the things that cannot be changed, courage to change the things that should be changed, and the wisdom to distinguish the one from the other." Because Niebuhr did not believe in copyrighting sacred work, he allowed his entreaty to be reprinted in a prayer book for soldiers during World War II, and by Alcoholics Anonymous after the war. Dale Carnegie included the prayer in his 1948 bestseller *How to Stop Worrying and Start Living,* crediting Reinhold Niebuhr. When questions were raised about its originality, the theologian conceded that versions might have preceded his own, but he thought "The Serenity Prayer" originated with him. Others to whom it has been attributed include St. Francis of Assisi, Adm. Chester Nimitz, and Adm. Thomas C. Hart (presumably because of its inclusion in the soldier's prayer book). A German version that appeared after the war was attributed to an eighteenth-century clergyman named Frederich Oetinger. According to Sifton and biographer Richard Wightman Fox, "Frederich Oetinger" was actually the pseudonym of a writer named Theodor Wilhelm, who translated this poem from a Canadian version he came upon after World War II. Presumably the Canadian version was Niebuhr's. Sifton writes in some detail about Wilhelm's unwarranted claim to have originated the prayer. She has no doubt that it was an original composition by her father. No serious student of the matter disagrees.

Verdict: Credit Reinhold Niebuhr.

"Oh, to be SEVENTY again." Oliver Wendell Holmes, Jr., is supposed to have said this while ogling a comely woman on his ninetieth birthday, in 1931. (Some sources believe Holmes said, "Oh, to be sixty again," and various birthdays are given. *The Magnificent Yankee,* a movie based on the great jurist's life, has him saying, "Oh, to be eighty again.") Other sources credit French Premier Georges Clemenceau with saying the same thing on

his eightieth birthday in 1921. Long before that, another Frenchman, writer-philosopher Bernard de Fontenelle (1657–1757), was said to have remarked, "Ah, if I were only eighty again!" as he struggled late in life to retrieve a lady's fallen fan from the floor. In Germany, Prussian Field Marshal Friedrich von Wrangel (1784–1877) is remembered for having remarked during his nineties, "If only one were eighty!"

Verdict: An old global saw.

GEORGE BERNARD SHAW

When he was governor of Indiana, Evan Bayh gave a speech to an incredulous group of educators in which he quoted George Bernard Shaw as having written:

> *I shall be telling you this with a sigh*
> *Somewhere ages and ages hence:*
> *Two roads diverged in a wood, and I—*
> *I took the one less traveled by,*
> *And that has made all the difference.*

Those lines, of course, owe more to Robert Frost than to George Bernard Shaw.

The acerbic Irish playwright was so quotable that he got, and gets, credit for far more than his share of quotable quotes. This was true even in his lifetime. "I tell you," Shaw once said, "I have been misquoted everywhere, and the inaccuracies are chasing me round the world." Shaw made this statement while vehemently denying that he'd said, "Oh, all Americans are blind, deaf, and dumb anyway" after being introduced to Helen Keller. Shaw thought he'd more likely said, "I wish all Americans were blind, deaf, and dumb." Though well-known for his withering view of Americans ("I have defined the 100 per cent American as a 99 per cent idiot"), it is not likely that Shaw would have ridiculed the deaf and blind Keller, whom he admired. In general Shaw was more caustic than cruel.

As for original Shawiana, a group of "Maxims for Revolutionists" in *Man and Superman* (1903) included **"He who can, does. He who cannot, teaches."** In various forms this maxim was subsequently claimed by, and credited to, a wide range of pretenders.

Another notable line in *Man and Superman* was "The true artist will let his wife starve, his children go barefoot, his mother drudge for his living at seventy, sooner than work at anything but his art."

In his play *The Doctor's Dilemma* (1906), Shaw wrote, **"All PROFESSIONS are conspiracies against the laity."** Years later economist Kenneth Boulding was quoted as saying that trades and professions were likely to organize themselves into "a conspiracy against the public," without mentioning Shaw.

"You see things and you say, 'WHY?' But I dream things that never were; and I say: 'Why not?'" comes from Shaw's 1921 play *Back to Methuselah*. This observation became an unusually familiar quotation after the Kennedy brothers repeated it so often, sometimes citing their source, more often not bothering. By contrast, onetime Australian prime minister Malcolm Fraser freely admitted that his political credo, "Life wasn't meant to be easy," originated in a line from *Back to Methuselah*: **"Life is not meant to be easy, my child; but take courage: it can be delightful."** According to quotographer Nigel Rees, however, in 1912—nine years before *Methuselah* was published—an Anglican bishop had already said, "Life is not easy, nor was it meant to be."

Shaw had little compunction about borrowing material from others. "My plays are full of pillage of this kind," he once admitted. Oscar Wilde was a favorite source. In *Man and Superman* Shaw wrote, **"There are two TRAGEDIES in life. One is to lose your heart's desire. The other is to gain it."** Eleven years earlier Wilde wrote in *Lady Windermere's Fan* (1892), **"In this world there are only two TRAGEDIES. One is not getting what one wants, and the other is getting it."** *Man and Superman* also included the line "Very nice sort of place, Oxford, I should think, for people that like that sort of place." Half a century earlier, Lincoln was credited with saying about a book he'd been given, **"For those who LIKE that sort of thing I should think it just the sort of thing they would like."** (Although this Lincolnism is almost certainly apocryphal, it was circulating as his for decades before Shaw's version appeared.) A line of Shaw's in *John Bull's Other Island* (1904), **"All we ask now is to be let alone,"** may owe a literary debt to Jefferson Davis, who said in his 1861 inaugural address as president of the Confederate States of America, "All we want is to be let alone."

POSSIBLE SHAWISMS:

When a woman proposed that she and Shaw produce a child who would blend her looks with his brains, Shaw's celebrated response was **"But suppose the child inherited your brains and my beauty?"** Usually dancer Isadora Duncan is the target of this rejoinder. Biographer Hesketh Pearson (who knew Shaw personally, and allowed him to rewrite parts of his biography of the playwright) recounted a version involving a Swiss woman who conducted this dialogue by mail.

Alexander Woollcott recounted a story in which, after the opening of one of his plays, the playwright's curtain speech was interrupted by a heckler who shouted, "Shut up, Shaw. Your play is rotten!", prompting Shaw to reply, **"You and I know that, but who are we among so many?"** Various versions of this story are in circulation. Most involve Shaw's 1894 play *Arms and the Man,* and a heckler who said merely, "Boo."

UNLIKELY SHAWISMS:

When Samuel Goldwyn proposed to film Shaw's plays as works of art, the playwright is said to have responded, **"The trouble, Mr. Goldwyn, is that you are only interested in art and I am only interested in money."** After Shaw passed along a newspaper clipping depicting this exchange to editor-author Bennett Cerf, Cerf labeled it "apocryphal" (presumably based on Shaw's counsel). This widely recounted quip may have originated with Goldwyn's busy publicist Howard Dietz.

After visiting William Randolph Hearst's opulent San Simeon ranch in 1933, Shaw supposedly remarked, **"This is the way GOD would have built it if he'd had the money."** The same remark was attributed to many others before and after Shaw's visit to San Simeon. In different contexts that comment had made the rounds for years, available to whoever could get away with claiming it.

In an unlikely episode involving Shaw and Churchill, the playwright sent the parliamentarian two tickets to the opening of a play of his, suggesting that he come with a friend—if he had one. Churchill was said to have responded that he couldn't come on opening night, but would like to come to the second performance—if there was one.

In an even-less-likely exchange, Shaw asked a proper lady sitting next to him at a dinner party whether she'd go to bed with him for ten thousand pounds. After considering his proposition, the lady said she would. When Shaw asked if she'd go to bed with him for one pound, she bridled, asking, "What kind of woman do you think I am?" "We've already established that," Shaw supposedly responded. "Now we're just haggling over the price."

Shaw usually gets unearned credit for **"YOUTH is a wonderful thing. What a crime to waste it on children,"** based primarily on a 1940 *Reader's Digest* attribution without a source. In 1942, *Reader's Digest* attributed **"ENGLAND and America are two countries separated by the same language"** to Shaw. Again it gave no source. The comment subsequently showed up in many quote collections over Shaw's name. Library of Congress researchers could not find this observation in any of the playwright's published work. Its genesis may be Oscar Wilde's earlier line "We have really everything in common with America nowadays, except, of course, language." (See sidebar "Oscar Wilde.")

Shaw is sometimes credited with saying, **"There may be some doubt as to who are the best people to have charge of children, but there can be no doubt that parents are the worst."** That's because in his 1944 book *Everybody's Political What's What*, Shaw quoted poet-businessman William Morris as having said, "The question of who are the best people to take charge of children is a very difficult one: but it is quite certain that the parents are the very worst."

WORDS PUT IN SHAW'S MOUTH:
Like Churchill, Shaw has been credited with saying, "That is an indignity up with which I will not put" when an editor warned him not to end a sentence with a preposition. He's also been mistakenly credited with: **"The world is a COMEDY to those that think, a tragedy to those that feel,"** **"Any man who is not a SOCIALIST at age twenty has no heart. Any man who is still a socialist at age forty has no head,"** **"It is very easy to give up SMOKING. I have done it hundreds of times." "EXPERIENCE is merely the name we give our mistakes," "All TRUTH passes through three stages. First, it is ridiculed. Second, it is violently opposed. Third, it is accepted as being self-evident," "AMERICA has progressed from barbarism to decadence, without the intervening stage of civilization,"** and "Messages are for Western Union." (See sidebar "Show Business.")

"Don't give up the SHIP!" By legend these were the last words of mortally wounded Capt. James Lawrence, as his frigate *Chesapeake* battled its British counterpart *Shannon* off the Massachusetts coast in 1813. According to his attending physician, Captain Lawrence "ordered me to go on deck, and tell the men to fire faster, and not to give up the ship." Three months later, Commodore Oliver Hazard Perry flew on his mainmast a blue battle flag inscribed with the words DON'T GIVE UP THE SHIP, as he defeated British forces on Lake Erie. They became an American rallying cry for the rest of the War of 1812. Thirty-six years earlier, during an engagement with the British in Boston Harbor in 1776, Capt. James Mugford's dying words were said to have been "Don't give up the ship! You will beat them off." As for the subsequent attribution of this slogan to Captain Lawrence, the daughter of *Boston Centinel* editor Benjamin Russell told this anecdote about her father: Before the *Chesapeake* was captured by the British, a sailor made his way from that ship to the *Centinel* office, where he reported Lawrence's fate. Russell asked the sailor what his captain's last words were. The sailor said he didn't know. "Didn't he say, 'Don't give up the ship?'" asked the editor. "Don't know," repeated the sailor. "Oh, he did," said Russell. "I'll make him say it."

Verdict: Probably words put in Lawrence's mouth, and Mugford's too.

"There was a man who cried because he had no SHOES until he met a man who had no feet." After returning from World War II, John Kennedy scribbled in his notebook, "I had no shoes and I murmured until I met a man who had no feet." Kennedy thought this was a Hindu proverb. The genesis of that saying can be found in the classic 1258 work *The Gulistan (The Rose Garden)*, by Persian poet Sa'di. One translation of a *Gulistan* passage reads: "I never complained of the vicissitudes of fortune, nor suffered my face to be overcast at the revolution of the heavens, except once, when my feet were bare, and I had not the means of obtaining shoes. I came to the chief of Kufah in a state of much dejection, and saw there a man who had no feet. I returned thanks to God and acknowledged his mercies, and endured my want of shoes with patience. . . ." A different translation reads: "I had never complained of the vicissitudes of fortune, nor murmured at the ordinances of heaven, excepting on one occasion, that my feet were bare, and I had not wherewithal to shoe them. In this desponding state I entered the metropolitan mosque at Kufah, and there I beheld a man that had no feet. I offered up praise and thanksgiving for God's goodness to myself, and submitted with patience to my want of shoes."

Verdict: Condensed Sa'di.

"SHOOT, if you must, this old gray head, but spare your country's flag."
According to a story popular north of the Mason-Dixon line, early in the
Civil War an old widow named Barbara Frietchie refused Stonewall Jackson's command to lower her Stars and Stripes after his troops occupied
Frederick, Maryland, late in the summer of 1862. Instead she defiantly
waved the American flag from her upstairs window as Jackson's Confederate troops rode by. Widow Frietchie's story inspired "Barbara Frietchie," a
poem by John Greenleaf Whittier that appeared in *Atlantic Monthly.* Its
best-known line was "'Shoot, if you must this old gray head, but spare your
country's flag,' she said." As told to Whittier, Mrs. Frietchie's purported
words were "Fire at this old head, then, boys; it is not more venerable than
your flag!" There was a Frederick resident named Barbara Fritchie (correct
spelling), a frail, bedridden widow of ninety-five who was born in 1766 and
died on December 18, 1862. At least one other Frederick resident—a
Mrs. Mary Quantrell—claimed to have been the actual flag-waver as Jackson's troops rode through town. Most locals put their money on Mrs.
Quantrell. Whittier himself concluded that there was an old woman
named Frietchie in Frederick, that he'd been told she waved a flag out her
attic window, and that if the details of his poem about Barbara Frietchie
weren't accurate, they ought to be.

   Verdict: Poetically licensed verbal melodrama.

"If I have seen farther, it is by standing on the SHOULDERS of giants."
Isaac Newton is generally credited with making this humble observation,
in 1675. Nearly three centuries later, sociologist Robert Merton devoted
an entire book to questioning the attribution. Merton discovered that various versions of a saying about dwarfs seeing farther from the shoulders of
giants had been around for centuries before Newton used his version in a
letter. The portrayal of dwarfs on shoulders was common in medieval
religious art, including some stained-glass windows of the cathedral at
Chartres. The earliest record of this saying that Merton could find was
from the early twelfth century, circa 1126, when Bernard of Chartres was
supposed to have said, "In comparison with the ancients, we stand like
dwarfs on the shoulders of giants." Variations on this theme appeared frequently after that, in a wide range of cultures. Robert Burton gave the saying a boost in 1624 when he included it in *Anatomy of Melancholy,* citing
his contemporary Didacus Stella. In 1891, John Bartlett himself misattributed Burton's version to the Roman poet Lucan (A.D. 39–65), rather than
Luke, as intended by Didacus Stella (with no evidence). This error continued through *Bartlett's* fifteenth edition in 1980, fifteen years after Merton's

book was published. Merton called their mistake "an unfruitful error concocted out of a lazy citation."

Verdict: Credit Bernard of Chartres, probably mouthing common wisdom.

"SHOUTING fire in a crowded theater." This practice is generally thought to define the limits of free speech. In *Schenck v. United States* (1919), Supreme Court Justice Oliver Wendell Holmes, Jr., wrote, "The most stringent protection of free speech would not protect a man falsely shouting fire in a theater and causing panic." Holmes made no reference to the theater being crowded.

Verdict: Credit Oliver Wendell Holmes, Jr., for words somewhat different than the more common version.

SHOW BUSINESS

In show business, the ravenous hunger of scriptwriters for material, columnists for quips, and egos for inflation contributes to an environment in which any good line quickly becomes public property. Although many claim such lines, few have a clear provenance.

"If you have a message, send it by Western Union." This warning about making movies with a "message" could be the single most recycled cliché in the history of moviemaking. It has been variously attributed to Harry Warner, Harry Cohn, Humphrey Bogart, Marlon Brando, Dorothy Parker, George S. Kaufman, Ernest Hemingway, George Bernard Shaw, and, most often, Samuel Goldwyn. Who said it first will probably never be known.

"Never let that bastard back in here—unless we need him." The classic angry mogul's response to a supplicant who's offended him has been put in the mouth of all the usual suspects: Goldwyn, Cohn, Harry and Jack Warner, Louis Mayer, and Adolph Zukor. According to show business chronicler Alva Johnston, George M. Cohan first said this during his days as a Broadway producer. Others say it's simply an old vaudeville gag.

"I don't get ULCERS, I give them." This tough-executive commonplace has been attributed to Goldwyn, Cohn, and RCA founder David Sarnoff (along with sundry business executives, politicians, and coaches).

"I have a foolproof device for judging a picture. If my ass squirms, it's bad; if my ass doesn't squirm, it's good." Producer Harry Cohn was most commonly associated with this gauge of a movie's appeal. When the *New York Times* reported that *60 Minutes* producer Don Hewitt assessed a news report's boredom quotient by whether he "felt an itch in the vicinity of his pants," the CBS executive quickly disabused them.

"It only proves what they always say—give the people what they want to see and they'll come out for it." Comedian Red Skelton's much-repeated comment about Harry Cohn's well-attended 1958 funeral has also been attributed to comedian George Jessel and director Billy Wilder. According to Bert Lahr's son John, his actor father said much the same thing a year earlier, about Louis Mayer's funeral: "If you want a full house, you give the public what it wants." On the same occasion, Sam Goldwyn was credited with saying, "The reason so many people showed up at his funeral was because they wanted to make sure he was dead."

George S. Kaufman was famous for saying about a Broadway producer with whom he was feuding, **"When I die, I want to be cremated and have my ashes thrown in Jed Harris's face."** In time the playwright's vow was adopted by any number of other feuding figures in politics and show business. (Director-producer Norman Krasna, for example, was said to have declared that he wanted to have his ashes thrown in Harry Cohn's face.)

"If you can't write your idea on the back of my calling card, you don't have a clear idea." This sage piece of advice is attributed to Broadway producers David Merrick, George Abbott, and—most often—David Belasco. Others simply call it an unattributed "axiom," or "maxim."

In the early days of television, a young producer told news correspondent Daniel Schorr that the secret of making the transition from print to TV reporting was *sincerity*. **"If you can fake that,"** said the producer, **"you've got it made."** This gag floats around show business (the word "honesty" sometimes substituting for "sincerity"), attributed to a wide range of prominent personalities: Mark Twain, Groucho Marx, George Burns, French dramatist Jean Giradoux, and rocker David Lee Roth. Actress Courteney Cox (*Friends*) is credited with having said, "Honesty is the key to a relationship. If you can fake that, you're in."

"Dying can be a good career move." This cliché of a witticism has been said about Elvis Presley, Glenn Miller, and many another entertainer who attained icon status after a premature death. Author Gore Vidal says he said it too, when rival author Truman Capote died in 1984. In 1969, a year before his own death, guitarist Jimi Hendrix supposedly observed, "Once you are dead, you are made for life."

"A day away from Tallulah is like a month in the country." In the lead sentence of a *New York Times* book review, novelist Wilfrid Sheed mangled this witticism to read "A day with Tallulah Bankhead is equal to a month in the country." As myriad letter writers pointed out, credit for the correct version of this noted quip has been given to Dorothy Parker, Goodman Ace, George S. Kaufman, Alexander Woollcott, Robert Benchley, actress Ilka Chase, and Bankhead's own husband. In her autobiography, Bankhead said publicist Howard Dietz first made this quip about her. Most adjudicators agree.

"I've been around so long I knew _____ before she was a virgin." The blank in this old faithful of a Hollywood quip is usually filled in with "Doris Day." In that form it is sometimes attributed to Groucho Marx, but more often to musician-actor-wit Oscar Levant. When former Oklahoma senator Fred Harris ran for president as an insurgent in 1971, a liberal activist was considered quite witty for observing, "I knew Fred Harris before he was a virgin."

"SHOW me the money!" Because he was a consultant to the movie *Jerry Maguire* and believed its eponymous sports agent hero was modeled after him, agent Drew Rosenhaus took credit for the famous four words Cuba Gooding, Jr., mouthed repeatedly in that movie. "You're looking at the man who invented the phrase 'show me the money,'" Rosenhaus told ABC's Chris Wallace. "I deserve all the credit for it." According to a spokesperson for Cameron Crowe, the movie's screenwriter and director, his movie's protagonist was a composite of many agents, especially Leigh Steinberg. Steinberg, in turn, said that "show me the money" was inspired by a comment his client Tim McDonald made to Crowe. According to Steinberg, when Crowe asked what he was looking for, McDonald, an aspiring National Football League player, said, "The money," signifying respect and recognition, and that upon hearing those words Crowe jotted down the more famous version. Crowe confirmed that *Jerry Maguire*'s most famous line came from his own pen. The director is so credited by the seventeenth

edition of *Bartlett's* (including on its back jacket). The line has a much longer history, however. Early-twentieth-century prizefighters recited this mantra regularly. In 1901, when asked if he would fight Gus Ruhlin for the heavyweight championship, boxer Jim Jeffries responded, "Why, certainly, but I don't propose to fight him for fifty cents. They must show me the money." Five years later, onetime lightweight champion Battling Nelson said, "I'll fight anybody if you show me the money." A year after that, in 1907, when asked if he'd fight Jack Johnson, heavyweight Tommy Burns responded, "Show me the money! Show me the money and I'll fight if it's enough."

Verdict: Longtime jock talk, put on film by Cameron Crowe.

THE SIXTIES

The Age of Aquarius was a golden age for sayings and slogans, most of which originated in that era's various protest movements. Few have a clear provenance.

"Do not fold, spindle, or mutilate." During Berkeley's Free Speech Movement in 1964, one protester pinned a sign on his chest that read "I am a UC student. Please don't bend, fold, spindle or mutilate me." This referred to the punch cards that had been used to process data ever since the 1890 census. (The infamous punch card ballots used in Florida and elsewhere during the 2000 election were a relic of this form of data processing.) A campus as huge as the University of California was utterly dependent on data-crunching cards that featured this warning. Who authored the admonition is obscure. Even the Smithsonian Institution's Steven Lubar, author of a history of punch cards, does not know where it originated.

"There is a time when the operation of the machine becomes so odious, makes you so sick at heart, that you can't take part; you can't even tacitly take part, and you've got to put your bodies upon the gears and upon the wheels, upon the levers, upon all the apparatus, and you've got to make it stop." The most memorable statement of Berkeley protester grievances was made in late 1964 by Free Speech leader Mario Savio, on the steps of the University of California's Sproul Hall.

"You can't TRUST anyone over thirty." At one time or another this young protesters' credo has been attributed to all the most famous movement names (Jerry Rubin, Abbie Hoffman, Mario Savio, etc.), but it is seldom credited to its actual originator: Jack Weinberg of the Free Speech Movement.

"Make love, not war." Erotic folklorist Gershon Legman (1917–1999), said he coined this phrase during a talk at an Ohio university in 1963.

"Suppose they gave a WAR and nobody came?" This peace protest rallying cry has a tangled history dating back at least to a book written in 1936 by Carl Sandburg.

"Do your own thing." According to William Safire, Emerson's 1841 essay "Self-Reliance" included this passage: **"But do your thing, and I shall know you."** In most Emerson collections that line reads, "But do your work, and I shall know you." This is because a creative editor changed the word "thing" to "work" in a 1903 edition of Emerson's essays—a revision that stuck. In *The Canterbury Tales,* "The Clerke's Tale" includes this observation: "Ye been oure lord; dooth with youre owene thyng."

"Keep on truckin'." Popularized by cartoonist R. Crumb in the late 1960s, this phrase appeared in the lyrics of more than one Depression-era song. ("Keep on truckin', Mama, truckin' my blues away.") "Truckin'" was also the name of a dance popular in Harlem at that time. Lexicographer Stuart Berg Flexner thought the term might have originated with itinerants who, as far back as the 1890s, referred to riding a train by holding on to the trucking hardware between its wheels as "trucking it." Another possible source is the terms *trucking up* and *trucking back,* which were used by early cinematographers. The fact that "truckin'" rhymes with a word for sexual intercourse does not detract from its appeal.

"TODAY is the first day of the rest of your life." Despite copious searching, no one has ever found the originator of this sixties commonplace. Nor can anyone determine for a certainty who first said, **"You're either part of the solution or you're part of the PROBLEM."**

"We are the people our parents warned us about." Journalist Nicholas Von Hoffman published a 1968 book about hippies called *We Are the People Our Parents Warned Us Against.* His title recycled a graffiti and poster slogan that was popular in the Age of Aquarius. According to quotographer Nigel Rees this was a common observation between the wars in England, associated with various literary and artistic figures. An early 1990s bumper sticker adapted this saying to read, I'M THE ONE YOUR MAMA WARNED YOU ABOUT.

"Sell the SIZZLE, not the steak." This was the signature slogan of marketing guru Elmer Wheeler. In a bestselling 1938 book, whose first chapter was titled "Don't Sell the Steak—<u>Sell the Sizzle!</u>", Wheeler explained, "What we mean by the 'sizzle' is the biggest selling point in your proposition—the MAIN reasons why your prospects will want to buy. The sizzling of the steak starts the sale more than the cow ever did, though the cow is, of course, very necessary!" Wheeler later wrote books called *The Sizzle Book* (1938) and *Sizzlemanship* (1940).

Verdict: Credit Elmer Wheeler.

"You're only here for a short while so be sure to stop and SMELL the flowers." Worded somewhat differently, this was the motto of famed golfer Walter Hagen. In his 1956 autobiography Hagen wrote, "You're only here for a short visit. Don't hurry. Don't worry. And be sure to smell the flowers along the way."

Verdict: Credit Walter Hagen.

"SMILE when you say that." In a chapter of Owen Wister's 1902 novel *The Virginian* titled "WHEN YOU CALL ME THAT, *SMILE!*", a poker game participant says, "Your bet, you son of a _____." After taking out his pistol, the Virginian responds, "When you call me that, *smile!*" In the 1929 movie version of Wister's book, whose screenplay was written by Howard Estabrook, leading man Gary Cooper says, "You wanna call me that, smile" (after Walter Huston's character says, "When I wanna know anything from you, I'll tell you, you long-legged son-of-a . . ."). In popular usage this catchphrase quickly became "Smile when you say that." Theatrical adaptations of *The Virginian* that were cowritten by Wister launched other enduring sayings, including "This town ain't big enough for both of us," and "You got till sundown to get out."

Verdict: Original version by Owen Wister.

"You can get more done with a SMILE and a gun than with a smile alone." Sometimes attributed to bank robber John Dillinger, in different forms this maxim is most often credited to gangster Al Capone. In the 1987 movie *The Untouchables*, whose screenplay was written by David Mamet, Robert DeNiro, playing Al Capone, says, "I grew up in a tough neighborhood, and we used to say you can get further with a kind word and a gun, than you can with just a kind word." Mark Levell and William J. Helmer include the quotation in *The Quotable Al Capone* (1990), but concede that in its many incarnations, "no source is ever given, and it's just remotely possible

that some low-life yellow journalist, at some time or another, decided that Al Capone, if he didn't say that, could have. Or should have." Capone's rival Edward "Spike" O'Donnell was himself famous for observing, "When arguments fail—use a blackjack." Perhaps variations on this theme floated about in different forms during the Prohibition era, landing on this gangster or that, most frequently Al Capone. Mario Gomes, director of the Al Capone Museum, initially believed Capone probably did say words to that effect. After conferring with gangland historians William J. Helmer and Rick Mattix, however, Gomes concluded, "It's safe to say that it was made up by Mr. Mamet." Mamet, in turn, might have been aware of the early Western *Sandy Burke of the U-Bar-U*. Ads for this 1919 movie proclaimed, "He owned a smile and a gun and he used 'em both."

Verdict: Words put in Al Capone's mouth, most likely by David Mamet.

"A SMOKE-FILLED room." It's taken for granted that this is where Warren Harding's 1920 nomination for president was engineered. That's because, as the Republican convention in Chicago began, Harding's handler Harry Daugherty—his era's Karl Rove—was quoted in the press as saying, "The convention will be dead locked, and after the other candidates have gone their limit, some twelve or fifteen men, worn out and bleary-eyed for lack of sleep, will sit down about two o'clock in the morning around a table in a smoke-filled room in some hotel and decide the nomination. When that time comes, Harding will be selected." Since that seemed to approximate what actually happened, Daugherty's words got the public's attention. To this day "smoke-filled room" signifies political machinations behind closed doors. Although Daugherty's apparent use of that term in 1920 put it on the etymological map, it was already part of political parlance. (Five years before Harding's nomination a news account in the *Chicago Tribune* reported, "Candidates have not been required to talk in smoke filled rooms . . .") When he tried to confirm Daugherty's use of this phrase, journalist-historian Mark Sullivan came a cropper. After interviewing some of those involved, Sullivan finally concluded that what happened was this: While packing his bags in a hotel room, Daugherty was confronted by two reporters requesting an interview. Harding's campaign manager said he didn't have time. One reporter followed him down the hall asking questions anyway. Trying to get a rise out of Daugherty, this reporter speculated that Harding's only chance for the nomination would be one engineered by hot, exhausted delegates in a smoke-filled room at two in the morning. "Make it 2:11," Daugherty snapped. Thus was born his epitaph. Sullivan concluded that Daugherty himself had never said

"smoke-filled room" or anything like it. Those words were put in his mouth.

Verdict: A reporter's words put in Harry Daugherty's mouth.

"It is very easy to give up SMOKING. I've done it hundreds of times." In 1945, *Reader's Digest* attributed this observation to Mark Twain (giving *Coronet* magazine as its source). Their version was: "To cease smoking is the easiest thing I ever did. I ought to know because I've done it a thousand times." This has since become a favorite Twainism, with little agreement on how many times he tried to stop smoking. Unfortunately, that witticism has never been found in Twain's written works or in accounts of his spoken words. In Canada, humorist Stephen Leacock, sometimes called "the Canadian Mark Twain," is credited with saying that it was easy to give up smoking; he'd done it dozens of times.

Verdict: Author unknown; possibly Leacock, probably not Twain.

"Any man who is not a SOCIALIST at age twenty has no heart. Any man who is still a socialist at age forty has no head." Various versions of this comment are attributed most often, and without foundation, to Winston Churchill. In different forms the saying has also been credited to Georges Clemenceau, Aristide Briand, Maurice Maeterlinck, Otto von Bismarck, Benjamin Disraeli, David Lloyd George, George Bernard Shaw, Bertrand Russell, Woodrow Wilson, Wendell Willkie, William Casey, and William F. Buckley. In the mid-nineteenth century, however, French historian and statesman François Guizot (1787–1874) had already said, "Not to be a republican at twenty is proof of want of heart; to be one at thirty is proof of want of head." (*"N'être pas republicain à vingt ans est prevue d'un manqué de coeur; l'être après trente ans est prevue d'un manqué de tête."*)

Verdict: Credit François Guizot.

"I am a SOLDIER so that my son may be a poet." Variations on this theme are common, with various sources given. One version attributed to Thomas Jefferson (but not found in his works) is "I shall be a soldier so that my son may be an engineer and his son an artist." The closest confirmed quotation is contained in a 1780 letter from John Adams to his wife, Abigail: "I must study Politicks and War that my sons may have liberty to study Mathematics and Philosophy. My sons ought to study Mathematicks and Philosophy, Geography, natural History, Naval Architecture, navigation, Commerce and Agriculture, in order to give their Children a

right to study Painting, Poetry, Musick, Architecture, Statuary, Tapestry and Porcelaine" (spelling and punctuation as in original).

Verdict: Condensed John Adams.

"Old SOLDIERS never die, they just fade away." After being fired by Harry Truman, Gen. Douglas MacArthur concluded his 1951 valedictory speech to Congress by saying, "I still remember the refrain of one of the most popular barrack ballads of that day [early in the century], which proclaimed most proudly, that 'Old soldiers never die, they just fade away.'" The song he referred to was a parody of the mid-nineteenth-century hymn "Kind Words Can Never Die," a song soldiers and cadets loved to mock. One version, popular at West Point when MacArthur was a member of the Class of '03, included the lines "Old soldiers never die, / They just fade away." (Other versions can be found on both sides of the Atlantic, including one that appeared in a 1917 London publication called *Tommy's Tunes*.) After citing this ballad, MacArthur closed his speech by saying, "And like the old soldier in that ballad, I now close my military career and just fade away, an old soldier who tried to do his duty as God gave him the sight to see that duty." As William Safire pointed out, MacArthur's departing words brought to mind some from Lincoln's second inaugural address: "with firmness in the right, as God gives us to see the right . . ."

Verdict: MacArthur's most famous line came from a hymn parody.

"SPEAK softly, and carry a big stick." In a speech at the 1901 Minneapolis State Fair, Theodore Roosevelt told his listeners, "A good many of you are probably acquainted with the old proverb 'Speak softly and carry a big stick—you will go far.'" During a subsequent speech in Chicago, Roosevelt called this saying "a homely old adage." In a 1900 letter to a friend, he'd said it was a "West African proverb." Obviously this saying was already familiar when he first repeated it.

Verdict: A saying common enough at the turn of the century that Theodore Roosevelt assumed it was known to many.

"SPEAK truth to power." The modern history of this popular admonition begins with a Quaker pamphlet called *Speak Truth to Power*, published in 1955 by the American Friends Service Committee. According to this pamphlet, which received a fair amount of press attention, its title was a charge to eighteenth-century Quakers. Some believe the saying originated with George Fox (1624–1691), who founded the Religious Society of Friends. Biographer Larry Ingle can find no evidence that Fox ever said or

wrote these words. Ingle is puzzled by the origins of the admonition. He doubts that its origins can be found among eighteenth-century Quakers. Apparently Milton Mayer, a journalist who was on the committee that produced the 1955 pamphlet, suggested its title. Although Mayer thought the phrase was original, a biography of pacifist activist Bayard Rustin by John D'Emilio quoted this passage from a 1942 letter Rustin wrote to his own Friends Meeting: "The primary social function of a religious society is to 'speak the truth to power.'" As Ingle points out, the fact that Rustin put this phrase in quotation marks indicates that he did not consider himself its originator. Who was remains a mystery.

Verdict: Title of a 1955 Quaker pamphlet that adopted a preexisting phrase; original source yet to be determined.

"I don't care what they say about me as long as they SPELL my name right." While studying the history of public relations, Northern Kentucky University Professor of Communication Michael Turney did an extensive survey of this nostrum. Turney found it attributed to Mae West, P. T. Barnum, George M. Cohan, Will Rogers, W. C. Fields, Mark Twain, and Oscar Wilde. (Add Harry Truman to that list, along with fight promoter Chris Dundee, Boston mayor James Michael Curley, and Tammany Hall boss Timothy "Big Tim" Sullivan.) Neither Turney nor any colleague he queried had any idea where this saying originated.

Verdict: Still looking.

"Never trust a man who has only one way to SPELL a word." In the midst of the brouhaha surrounding Dan Quayle's misspelling of "potatoe," the vice president quoted Mark Twain about not trusting any man who could spell a word only one way. Twain scholars couldn't find that comment anywhere in the author's canon. A Quayle aide had found it attributed to Twain in Evan Esar's *Dictionary of Humorous Quotations* (1949)—not exactly a rock-solid source. (Esar gives no sources.) *Yale Dictionary of Quotations* editor Fred Shapiro subsequently found this quip in nineteenth-century joke books. Credit for different forms of the jocular old saw gets passed around, to Thomas Jefferson, Oscar Wilde, and Kansas congressman Jerry "Sockless" Simpson, among others. In his time Andrew Jackson was a popular recipient. Like Quayle, Harding, George W. Bush, et al., Jackson was widely lampooned for his intellectual limitations, with lots of inane remarks getting put in his mouth (e.g., "Elevate them guns a little lower."). He was particularly ridiculed for being a poor speller. Perhaps as a result, Jackson is commonly thought to have said, "It is a damn poor mind that can only think of one way to spell a word." No evidence confirms this.

Verdict: Old gag; not Twain's, probably not Jackson's, either.

JOSEPH STALIN

In his history of the Second World War, Winston Churchill reported a 1935 conversation between Stalin and French Prime Minister Pierre Laval. After they discussed the strength of the French army on the Western Front, and the numbers of its divisions, talk turned to other matters. Laval asked the Soviet leader to extend a hand to Catholics in his country as this would favorably impress the pope. "Oho," was Stalin's response, according to Churchill. **"The pope! How many divisions has he got?"** In his 1969 autobiography, former *New York Times* correspondent C. L. Sulzberger said that Harry Truman told him this exchange took place between Stalin and Churchill himself, at the 1945 Potsdam conference, after the British PM told his Soviet counterpart that the pope would object to his machinations in predominantly Catholic Poland. "That is a true story," Truman told Sulzberger. "I was there." The afternoon after hearing this story, the *Times* man asked former Secretary of State James Byrnes about it. Byrnes said he'd heard the story too, but that it was apocryphal. "It is a good story," he told Sulzberger, "but it is not true. I know it is not true because I was there."

As one of history's most brutal and ruthless tyrants, Joseph Stalin has been credited with more than his share of cynical, callous comments. **"No person, no problem"** is one (alternatively, "No man, no problem," an old Bolshevik saying put in Stalin's mouth). Similarly, **"Death solves all problems."** Another unverified Stalinism is **"Those who vote determine nothing; those who count the vote determine everything." "Sincere diplomacy is no more possible than dry water or iron wood,"** often credited to Stalin, is close to a line that can be found in his published works: "A sincere diplomat is like dry water or wooden iron."

On the other hand, Stalin has been credited with **"HISTORY is written by the victors,"** based on no evidence whatsoever.

In addition:

"You can't make an OMELET without breaking eggs." This

ancient proverb is sometimes said to be Stalin's rationale for making revolution.

"He who is not with us is against us" is also attributed to Stalin. As quotographer Nigel Rees points out, if he ever did say this, the former seminarian might have recalled that in Luke 11:23, Jesus said, "He that is not with me is against me."

In his autobiography, Barry Goldwater wrote that he thought Stalin had said, **"When it comes time to hang the capitalists, they will sell us the rope."** In fact that is a piece of apocrypha more often put in Lenin's mouth

"A single DEATH is a tragedy. A million deaths is a statistic." This cynical observation is most often attributed to Stalin. No source is usually given, however, presumably because none exists.

"I am the STATE!" ("L'état c'est moi!") Louis XIV was said to have made this claim in 1655 to a group of parliamentarians bent on curbing the teenage monarch's power. Contemporary accounts of his struggle with parliament mentioned no such oath. The words are actually those of a former-day Edmund Morris. In an embellished history published a century after Louis was supposed to have made this exclamation, Voltaire portrayed the young king confronting restive subjects in his hunting clothes, riding crop in hand, contemptuously rejecting their demands. Subsequent historians put the words "I am the state!" on the young king's lips. No modern historian gives any credence to this apocryphal oath, or to the confrontation in which it was said to have been made.

Verdict: Apocrypha generated by Voltaire and his successors.

"That's one small STEP for a man, one giant step for mankind." After landing on the moon in 1969, Neil Armstrong uttered the immortal words for which he's best known: "That's one small step for a man, one giant step for mankind." At least that's what Armstrong *meant* to say after taking man's first stroll on the moon. In fact, he forgot the "a." The astronaut's actual words were "That's one small step for man, one giant leap for mankind." This version doesn't make much sense. The National Aeronautics and Space Administration quickly explained that transmission problems clipped the "a" from Armstrong's words. But a close listen to the widely disseminated recording of Armstrong's broadcast makes it clear that there is not enough time between "for" and "man" for an "a" to have been

said. Nor did the astronaut himself ever claim definitely to have said "a" (though he meant to). This posed a dilemma for the press. Should they report Armstrong's actual words or what he meant to say? On the twentieth anniversary of Armstrong's stroll, a computer search of major newspapers found that among fifty citations of his line during the two years preceding, nineteen quoted him as saying "a man" and thirty-one simply "man." The jacket of *One Giant Leap,* Leon Wagener's biography of Neil Armstrong, has him saying, "One small step for man," but in the book itself Armstrong says "one small step for a man . . ." As Wagener points out, although Armstrong considered the thought entirely his own, subsequent research found memos NASA officials wrote before the moon landing that proposed it be treated as "A forward step of all mankind," and noted that simply by landing on the moon, "a giant step will have been taken."

Verdict: Armstrong meant to say "a man," actually said, "man."

ADLAI STEVENSON

An unusually eloquent politician, Adlai Stevenson was and is a primary source of quotations, and misquotations. At the peak of his prestige, the former governor of Illinois and two-time presidential nominee was the beneficiary of many words from other people, and borrowed more than a few himself. Like John Kennedy, Adlai loved to pepper his speeches with quotations, but wasn't always clear about their wording or source. Stevenson once told an interviewer, "I think it was Macaulay who said of some Englishman, Brougham, I believe, **'I wish I was as SURE of anything as he is of everything.'**" In fact, this observation was made *about* Thomas Macaulay by Lord Melbourne.

Shortly before he died in 1965, Stevenson was interviewed by Leon Harris for his book *The Fine Art of Political Wit.* During their conversation Stevenson showed Harris the notebooks he'd kept for more than four decades. In them was a jumble of his own ideas, quotations from others, and political quips that he used in his speeches and writing. The origins of this material often got lost along the way.

A year before he first ran for president, Stevenson said, **"A LIE is an abomination unto the Lord and an ever present help in times of trouble,"** without mentioning that Mark Twain had already said this. While accepting its nomination for president in 1952, Stevenson told the Democratic convention, **"There are no GAINS**

without pains," a thought he borrowed from Poor Richard, who in turn got it from Thomas Fuller and others. During the ensuing campaign Stevenson said of his Republican opponents, **"If the Republicans stop telling LIES about us, we will stop telling the truth about them."** That bit of political wit had been in play for decades before it ended up in Adlai's mouth. When Eleanor Roosevelt died in 1962, he observed that the former First Lady had been someone who would **"rather light CANDLES than curse the darkness,"** failing to note that this was the longtime motto of the Christophers. Adlai's message to friends on his last birthday included the conviction that **"nothing succeeds like excess,"** but not the name of Oscar Wilde, who originated that quip. (See sidebar "Oscar Wilde.") Adlai added, "My dearest friends, forgive me my excesses, and I'll forgive you your successes."

When asked whether the term "brinksmanship" could be credited to him, as it often was, Stevenson told an interviewer, "I cannot claim authorship of brinksmanship. I am not sure whether I read it or heard it or dreamed it up. I am reasonably sure I did not invent it." Another phrase popularized by Stevenson—"quality of life"—was used by novelist J. B. Priestly in 1943. Whether or not it came from Adlai's cortex, the earliest depiction of a vice president as **"a heartbeat away from the presidency"** that William Safire could find was in a 1952 speech by Stevenson in which he warned that vice-presidential candidate Richard Nixon "asks you to place him a heartbeat from the presidency . . ."

Adlai Stevenson more than anyone is credited with **"An EDITOR is one who separates the wheat from the chaff and prints the chaff,"** a witticism that echoed Elbert Hubbard's definition of an editor recorded decades earlier. Another popular Adlaism was **"Flattery is all right, if you don't inhale."** (Other versions substituted "fame," or "success," for "flattery.") Long before Stevenson made that observation, Josh Billings wrote, "Flattery iz like Colone water, tew be smelt ov, not swallowed." Kin Hubbard added, "Flattery won't hurt you if you don't swallow it." (See sidebar "Humorists.") Adlai's version was an improvement.

Adlai Stevenson is still remembered for observing that **"we Americans are suckers for good news."** In a lighter vein, the cerebral politician once said, **"Eggheads of the world unite. You have nothing to lose but your yolks."**

Other celebrated Stevenson quips include:

Man does not live by words alone, in spite of the fact that he sometimes has to eat them.

We say that every American boy has a chance to be president when he grows up—and I've concluded that that's just one of the risks he takes.

A POLITICIAN is someone who approaches every subject with an open mouth.

Well, like all politicians, I really don't care what you call me as long as you call me.

Adlai also made thoughtful observations that still resonate decades later:

Words calculated to catch everyone may catch no one.

My definition of a free society is a society where it is safe to be unpopular.

Technology, while adding daily to our physical ease, throws daily another loop of fine wire around our souls.

Being in office is like being inebriated. If there are any weaknesses in a man's character, it certainly brings them out.

As for familiar quotations, Adlai's principal legacy is the credo of his 1952 campaign: **"Let's talk sense to the American people."**

"I should of STOOD in bed." Joe Jacobs's second-most-familiar quotation (after "We was robbed!") has achieved classic status, despite some confusion about when and why he might have said it. Jacobs was a colorful, rambunctious fight manager beloved by sportswriters for his Runyonesque syntax. *Bartlett's* at first reported that the Jewish fight manager said, "I should of stood in bed" to New York sportswriters after returning from the

1934 World Series in Detroit, where he'd bet on the loser (Chicago). However, Detroit played St. Louis in that year's World Series. In their next edition *Bartlett's* changed the date to 1935. No such remark by Joe Jacobs was
reported by any New York newspaper in the days following the 1935 World
Series between Detroit and Chicago. Other sources think Jacobs said he
should of stood in bed after one of his fighters lost, or fought before a poor
house. Leo Rosten thought this was an understandable Yiddish-based lo-
cution for "Mike" Jacobs to use. The statement has also been attributed to
other sports figures. According to writer John Lardner they're all wrong.
"As it happens," he reported of Jacobs's immortal words, "the great man
coined them two feet from your correspondent's ear. It was the only time
I ever heard a famous quotation in the making." Lardner explained that Joe
Jacobs sat right behind him while watching his first live baseball game on a
frigid first day of the 1935 World Series. When a companion asked what
he thought of the game, Jacobs replied, "I should of stood in bed."
     Verdict: Jacobs said it.

"No man ever stands so straight as when he STOOPS to help a boy." This
was the slogan of Big Brothers of America before it merged with Big Sisters International in 1977. The Big Brothers called their slogan a "saying,"
and thought it might have originated during a public relations campaign on
their behalf after World War I. Like so many orphan sayings this one has
sometimes been called a "Chinese proverb." During the 1930s it appeared
in the American press as an unattributed aphorism. Chicago evangelist
Dwight Moody (1837–1899) is remembered for having said, "He who
kneels the most stands best," suggesting that this general idea was already
in circulation at that time.
     Verdict: Credit an anonymous post–World War I copywriter, possibly
tapping popular theology.

"STRANGER in a strange land." Since his novel *Stranger in a Strange Land*
was published in 1961, this catchphrase has been associated primarily with
Robert Heinlein. Its genesis was Exodus 2:22: "I have been a stranger in a
strange land." Well before that, around 270 B.C., the epigrams of Greek poet
Theocritus included one that paid tribute to the deceased "sage" Eusphenes:
"Nobly have his friends buried him—a stranger in a strange land—and most
dear was he, yea, to the makers of song." Even earlier, according to one translator, Sophocles used the phrase "stranger in a strange land" in two plays:
Oedipus at Colonus (404 B.C.) and *Philoctetes* (409 B.C.).
     Verdict: Ancient catchphrase.

"A mind once STRETCHED by a new idea never returns to its former dimensions." This is widely attributed to Oliver Wendell Holmes, but seldom with a specific source. In Holmes's *The Autocrat of the Breakfast-Table* (1853), the exact quotation is: "Every now and then a man's mind is stretched by a new idea or sensation, and never shrinks back to its former dimensions."

Verdict: Credit Holmes.

"Read over your compositions, and wherever you meet with a passage which you think is particularly fine, STRIKE it out." Although this admonition is routinely ascribed to Samuel Johnson, what Johnson said to James Boswell in 1773 (about a wordy historian named William Robertson) was "I would say to Robertson what an old tutor of a college said to one of his pupils: 'Read over your compositions, and where ever you meet with a passage which you think is particularly fine, strike it out.'" Johnson experts have no idea who that tutor might have been. Twain echoed his advice when he wrote in *Pudd'nhead Wilson*, "As to the adjective: when in doubt, strike it out."

Verdict: Samuel Johnson, conveying someone else's advice.

"From the SUBLIME to the ridiculous there is but a step." ("Du sublime au ridicule il n'y a qu'un pas.") After the Russian debacle of 1812, Napoleon was said to have used these words repeatedly during a conversation with one of his ambassadors. When this ambassador later reported their conversation in a book, the mot was attributed to Bonaparte. In "Age of Reason" (1795), however, Thomas Paine had already written, "One step above the sublime makes the ridiculous, and one step above the ridiculous makes the sublime again." Eight years before that, in 1787, French writer Jean François Marmontel (1723–1799) wrote, "In general, the ridiculous approaches the sublime." ("*En général, le ridicule touche au sublime.*") Obviously, "from the sublime to the ridiculous" was a phrase in common use at that time.

Verdict: A common concept used by Napoleon, Paine, and others.

"He has achieved SUCCESS who has lived well, laughed often, and loved much. . . ." The long depiction of success that begins with these words is routinely misattributed to Emerson (not the least reason being that Ann Landers and Abigail Van Buren did so in their advice columns). Its real author is Bessie Anderson Stanley of Lincoln, Nebraska. In 1905 Mrs. Stanley won the first prize of $250 and publication in *Modern Women*

after submitting her thoughts to a contest that asked entrants to answer the question "What constitutes success?" Her winning entry read, "He has achieved success who has lived well, laughed often and loved much; who has enjoyed the trust of pure women, the respect of intelligent men and the love of little children; who has filled his niche and accomplished his task; who has left the world better than he found it, whether by an improved poppy, a perfect poem, or a rescued soul; who has never lacked appreciation of earth's beauty or failed to express it; who has always looked for the best in others and given them the best he had; whose life was an inspiration; whose memory is a benediction." Mrs. Stanley's son confirmed to quotographer Anthony Shipps that this was the correct version. Other versions have been published. Bessie Stanley's original words sometimes get condensed to "That man is a success who has lived well, laughed often and loved much." In addition to Emerson, Mrs. Stanley's words have been credited to aphorist Elbert Hubbard, clergyman Harry Emerson Fosdick, and author Robert Louis Stevenson.

Verdict: Credit Bessie Stanley.

"The secret of SUCCESS in life is known only by those who have not succeeded." This insight is generally attributed to a frustrated nineteenth-century British writer and academic named John Churton Collins (1848–1908). Collins's son included it in a collection of his father's work as one among many maxims he'd recorded in his notebook. No date is noted (or known, necessarily). This maxim echoes Emily Dickinson's 1859 lines "Success is counted sweetest / By those who ne'er succeed," but it isn't clear that the Englishman would have been familiar with this poem, which was first published in 1891.

Verdict: Credit John Churton Collins for a not-altogether-original thought.

"Never give a SUCKER an even break." In the early twentieth century, writer-raconteur Wilson Mizner popularized and may have coined this phrase. It could have been a saying Mizner picked up during his gambling days in San Francisco and Alaska, then brought with him to New York, where he moved in 1905. Mizner's good friend W. C. Fields later incorporated this credo into an early performance of the 1923 play *Poppy,* then repeated it in his 1936 movie by the same title. It soon became Fields's signature line. But he was the line's publicist, not its author. According to biographer Herbert Goldman "Never give a sucker an even break" was a favorite expression of Fanny Brice's husband, the gangster Nick Arnstein,

who was well acquainted with Fields through his actress wife. Some attribute this saying to P. T. Barnum, with no more evidence than the fact that it "sounds like" him. Since its 1968 edition *Bartlett's* has credited the motto to vaudeville impresario E. F. Albee, apparently because Clifton Fadiman did the same thing in his 1954 compilation *American Treasury.* Fadiman probably got the attribution from a 1953 memoir by vaudevillian Joe Laurie, Jr. Laurie despised Albee and alleged that his motto was "Never give a sucker an even break."

Verdict: An old gambling saw popularized by W. C. Fields via Wilson Mizner.

"There's a SUCKER born every minute." No modern historian takes seriously the routine attribution of this slogan to P. T. Barnum (1810–1891). In his search for the origins of "There's a sucker born every minute," Barnum biographer Arthur H. Saxon discovered an unpublished manuscript by Joseph McCaddon, the brother-in-law of James Bailey (of "Barnum and Bailey") and no friend of Barnum's, that attributed this sentiment to a notorious con man of the early 1880s named Joseph Bessimer. According to McCaddon, Bessimer told a New York police inspector, "There is a sucker born every minute, but none of them die." That was the first time the inspector had heard this expression. Language detective Barry Popik has found three 1883 newspaper articles that refer to "There's a sucker born every minute" as a saying popular among New York City gamblers. In 1890 an Ohio newspaper called this "an old and homely saying."

Verdict: A criminals' commonplace put in P. T. Barnum's mouth.

"I only wish that I could be as SURE of anything as my opponent is of everything." According to his nephew, British Prime Minister Lord Melbourne (William Lamb, 1779–1848) once said about Secretary of War Lord Macaulay (Thomas Babington, 1800–1859), "I wish I was as cocksure of anything as Tom Macaulay is of everything." According to other sources it was another member of parliament, William Windham (1750–1810), who said this about Macaulay. Adlai Stevenson misremembered it as something Macaulay himself had said. Clergyman-author Sydney Smith (1771–1845) has also been credited with the put-down. Later in the nineteenth century Benjamin Disraeli said of William Gladstone, "I only wish that I could be as sure of anything as my opponent is of everything."

Verdict: Credit Lord Melbourne, or William Windham as originator, not Benjamin Disraeli.

"SURVIVAL of the fittest." These four words usually come to mind in tandem with the name Charles Darwin. In fact, it was social philosopher Herbert Spencer who, in his book *Principles of Biology,* condensed Darwin's theory of evolution into this pithy phrase. Darwin endorsed and even admired Spencer's restatement of his theory. As he wrote in *The Origin of Species,* "The expression often used by Mr. Herbert Spencer of the Survival of the Fittest is more accurate, and is sometimes equally convenient."

Verdict: Herbert Spencer's concise summation of Charles Darwin's complex idea.

"Don't SWEAT the small stuff. It's all small stuff." In 1966, Erma Bombeck told readers of her column that "Don't sweat the small stuff" had been her mantra for years. She didn't know where this advice came from, Bombeck admitted, "probably some immortal bard on a rest room wall." Bombeck's advisory later became a favorite of advice columnist Ann Landers, among others. A 1983 *Time* article on how to deal with stress quoted cardiologist Robert S. Eliot as saying, "Rule No. 1 is, don't sweat the small stuff. Rule No. 2 is, it's all small stuff." Eliot subsequently used that motto in two books. Richard Carlson wrote a 1997 bestseller titled *Don't Sweat the Small Stuff . . . and It's All Small Stuff.* Carlson said he took his title from a comment made to him by psychologist Wayne Dyer four years earlier. Nine years before Carlson's book came out, Michael R. Mantell published a book called *Don't Sweat the Small Stuff: P.S. It's All Small Stuff* (1988).

Verdict: Credit Robert S. Eliot for the two-stage version.

"TAXATION without representation is tyranny!" Although firebrand lawyer James Otis is credited with saying this during a 1761 trial in Boston, no such exclamation by Otis was recorded at the time. Some sketchy notes John Adams made during the trial did not include this sentence. It only became part of American lore after an 1823 biography by William Tudor reported that Otis issued this call to arms during the 1761 proceedings. Tudor's biography relied on an 1818 letter by John Adams in which the former president recalled that at this trial fifty-seven years earlier, Otis denounced "the tyranny of taxation without representation." In fact, taxation was not germane to the trial at which Otis spoke (about search warrants called "writs of assistance"). Nonetheless, Tudor wrote of Otis, "From the energy with which he urged this position, that taxation without representation is tyranny, it came to be a common maxim in the mouth of everyone." Modern historians don't take Tudor's claim seriously. They do note that in 1764, in *The*

Rights of the British Colonies Asserted and Proved, Otis wrote, "No parts of his Majesty's dominions can be taxed without their consent." *Bartlett's* records this authentic utterance by Otis in a footnote, but still says "Taxation without representation is tyranny" is attributed to him, giving the date 1763 without further explanation.

Verdict: Revolutionary slogan put in James Otis's mouth.

"Any sufficiently advanced TECHNOLOGY is indistinguishable from magic." This is Arthur C. Clarke's Third Law, so-called. Clarke's "laws" were born after the editor of his works in French began numbering some of the author's assertions. Clarke drew the line at three, noting that this amount was sufficient for both Isaacs: Newton and Asimov. He considered his third law the most interesting. Certainly it is the one most often quoted.

Verdict: Credit Arthur C. Clarke.

"The TEFLON presidency." In the late summer of 1983, Rep. Patricia Schroeder (D-Colo.) prepared eggs for her family's breakfast. As she pulled out a nonstick Teflon frying pan, her mind turned, as it often did, to Ronald Reagan. What was it that kept this bumbler from ever being penalized for his mistakes? Reagan was just like, like—she looked at the pan—like Teflon. Nothing stuck to him. Later that day Representative Schroeder addressed her colleagues on the floor of the House: "Mr. Speaker, after carefully watching Ronald Reagan, he is attempting a great breakthrough in political technology—he has been perfecting the Teflon-coated presidency. . . . Harry Truman had a sign on his desk emblazoned with his motto: 'The buck stops here.' It has obviously been removed and Reagan's desk has been Teflon-coated. . . ." A week later the *New York Times* included Schroeder's first two paragraphs in their "Required Reading" section. Its headline was "The Teflon Presidency." *People* magazine then excerpted the paragraph, which concluded, "Reagan's desk has been Teflon-coated." "Teflon-coated" quickly became a clichéd description of Ronald Reagan's ability to dodge political bullets. In the process, Schroeder's original phrase morphed into many others. In the most popular version she'd called Reagan "the Teflon President." Others preferred "the Teflon candidate." Some thought Reagan had been called "Teflon coated." Vice President George H. W. Bush reported that his boss had been called "the man in the Teflon suit" by "whatshername from Colorado." It did not take long for Pat Schroeder's quip to enter the public domain. Far more people discussed Reagan's "Teflon" quality than knew who'd hung that tag on him.

Verdict: Credit Pat Schroeder.

"TELEVISION is a vast wasteland." In a 1961 speech, Federal Communications Commission chairman Newton Minow said that should one watch television for any length of time, "I can assure you that you will observe a vast wasteland." The word *wasteland* proved to be a powerful hook that embedded this phrase in our memory. As Minow's renown faded, his words were sometimes put in Marshal McLuhan's mouth. Their actual author may have been journalist and speechwriter John Bartlow Martin, who considered television "a vast wasteland of junk." In his memoirs Martin said he put that phrase in Minow's speech. Minow was wise enough to keep "a vast wasteland," but delete "of junk."

Verdict: Minow said it, Martin wrote it.

"TELEVISION is chewing gum for the eyes." Architect Frank Lloyd Wright is often given credit for this depiction of television, as are humorist Fred Allen and author Aldous Huxley. According to quote compiler James Simpson, critic John Mason Brown first compared TV to chewing gum during a 1955 interview with him. He attributed the comment to a friend of his young son. The next year Brown told an interviewer, "So much of television is chewing gum for the eyes," without mentioning his son's friend.

Verdict: Credit a friend of John Mason Brown's son as originator, Brown as messenger.

"It goes with the TERRITORY." In Arthur Miller's 1949 play *Death of a Salesman,* protagonist Willy Loman's friend Charley tells Willy's son Biff, "A salesman has to dream, boy. It comes with the territory." Over time, "goes" replaced "comes" in the most common version of this popular catchphrase. But there's more to the story: In 1648, the Peace of Westphalia established that each German potentate could determine the creed of his subjects. This was codified in the principle *"Cujus est region, illus est religio,"* or "Religion goes with the soil." Was Miller up on his German history?

Verdict: Credit Arthur Miller, with help from Westphalia's peace negotiators.

"The TEST of a civilization . . ." In his 2005 State of the Union address, President George W. Bush said "a society is measured by how it treats the weak and the vulnerable. . . ." Whether Bush knew it or not, this assertion tapped a long rhetorical tradition. In a 1977 speech, Sen. Hubert Humphrey told his audience, "It was once said that the moral test of government is how that government treats those who are in the dawn of life, the children; those who are in the twilight of life, the elderly; and those who are in the

shadows of life—the sick, the needy and the handicapped." This sentence from his speech was frequently noted, and its concept attributed to Humphrey. But—as his opening words implied—this idea was not original to the Minnesota senator, and had many antecedents that take modular form. The crucial tests of a society—or civilization, or government, or country—vary with the speaker or writer. They include: how it treats its sick, needy, handicapped, young, old, unpopular, imprisoned, or dead citizens, or its animals. In *My Several Worlds,* her 1954 autobiography, Pearl Buck wrote, "The test of a civilization is in the way that it cares for its helpless members." Eleven years earlier, in the midst of World War II, Winston Churchill wrote to the home secretary, "Nothing can be more abhorrent to democracy than to imprison a person or keep him in prison because he is unpopular. This is really the test of civilization." In 1910, Churchill had observed in the House of Commons that "The mood and temper of the public in regard to the treatment of crime and criminals is one of the most unfailing tests of the civilization of any country." In his 1870 essay "Civilization," Emerson wrote, "The true test of civilization is, not the census, not the size of cities, not the crops—no, but the kind of man the country turns out." A century earlier, in 1770, Samuel Johnson told James Boswell that "a decent provision for the poor is the true test of a civilization." Similar thoughts have been expressed by or attributed to William Gladstone, Arnold Toynbee, Fyodor Dostoyevsky, Mahatma Gandhi, Harry Truman, Dietrich Bonhoeffer, John Kennedy, Pope John Paul II, Pat Conroy, and many others of lesser renown.

Verdict: A long-standing modular conviction.

"A beautiful THEORY, killed by a nasty, ugly little fact." Paleontologist-author Stephen Jay Gould called this one of the top ten scientific quotations. It was attributed to British scientist Thomas Henry Huxley (1825–1895) by his colleague Francis Galton (1822–1911). Galton said both Huxley and social philosopher Herbert Spencer told him that during a conversation with each other Huxley had made this remark. Their exchange took this form: During a dinner, Spencer told Huxley that he'd written a tragedy. Huxley responded that he knew the plot. Spencer said this was impossible as he'd discussed it with no one. What was it, he asked? "A beautiful theory, killed by a nasty, ugly little fact," said Huxley.

Verdict: Credit Thomas Huxley.

"THERE is no there there." In *Everybody's Autobiography,* Gertrude Stein wrote one of her trademark run-on sentences about revisiting her hometown of Oakland: "She [Gertrude Atherton] took us to see her granddaughter who was teaching in the Dominican convent in San Raphael, we went across the bay on a ferry, that had not changed but Goat Island might just as well not have been there, anyway what was the use of my having come from Oakland it was not natural to have come from there yes write about it if I like or anything if I like but not there, there is no there there."

Verdict: Credit Gertrude Stein.

"There's a THIN man inside every fat man. . . ." A character in George Orwell's 1939 novel *Coming Up for Air* observed that "there's a thin man inside every fat man. . . ." Six years later, in *The Unquiet Grave,* essayist Cyril Connolly wrote, "Imprisoned in every fat man a thin one is wildly signalling to be let out." Today Connolly's livelier version is better remembered than Orwell's original one.

Verdict: Attribute the thought to Orwell, its improvement to Connolly.

"The TIPPING point." In a 1957 *Scientific American* article, sociologist Morton Grodzins used the terms "tip point" and "tipping" to depict the moment when whites begin to move out of a neighborhood where blacks are moving in. Several years later economist Thomas Schelling, a 2005 Nobel laureate, used the term "tipping point" to refer to a wide range of circumstances in which the weight of specific events causes a rapid social shift. Epidemiologists applied the phrase to the point at which widespread outbreaks of disease become epidemics. Those interested in the adoption of technological innovations began to talk of "tipping points" too. By the time Malcolm Gladwell's book *The Tipping Point* (1996) made his title a popular catchphrase, its use was already widespread among physical and social scientists. Early in the twentieth century this phrase had been used to refer to the point at which a car tips over in a sharp turn.

Verdict: Credit Morton Grodzins for the sociological application of this concept, Thomas Schelling for giving it a polish and putting it in play, and Malcolm Gladwell as its primary publicist.

"TODAY is the first day of the rest of your life." The originator of this piece of pseudoprofundity remains a mystery. A cultish drug-rehab group called Synanon claimed that their founder, Charles Dederich, first made this observation in a 1969 speech. That was the year John Denver's song "Today Is the First Day of the Rest of My Life" appeared on an album called *Rhymes and Reasons.* (The composers of its words and lyrics are given by some sources as "p & v garvey," by others as "Mr. and Mrs. Garvey.")

A year before that, it was an unattributed slogan among many miscellaneous observations in Abbie Hoffman's 1968 book *Revolution for the Hell
of It*. That same year columnist Walter Winchell reported that "Today is
the first day of the rest of my life" had been found on the flyleaf of a
teenager's notebook, and a Pennsylvania newspaper credited author Helen
Zelon with advising, "Do something good tomorrow, for tomorrow is the
first day of the rest of your life." Age of Aquarius survivors recall hearing
versions of this slogan, or seeing it posted on walls, as early as the mid-
1960s. Thomas Wolfe has been credited with originating the maxim, as
has Jean-Paul Sartre, in neither case with a specific source.

Verdict: Sixties street wisdom.

"Damn the TORPEDOES—full speed ahead!" As Rear Adm. David Farragut led a U.S. Navy fleet through Mobile Bay during the Civil War, one
of his lead ships hit a mine (then known as a "torpedo") and foundered.
When told that the ship behind it had halted from fear of being torpedoed
itself, Farragut's response was a bit less snappy than the more famous version. According to historians, what he actually said was "Damn the torpedoes! Four bells! Captain Drayton, go ahead." Over time the last two
sentences were converted into "full speed ahead!" or "full steam ahead!"

Verdict: An edited, polished version of Admiral Farragut's actual words.

"When the going gets TOUGH, the tough get going." This slogan has
been attributed to John Kennedy's father, Joseph, Richard Nixon's attorney
general John Mitchell, Notre Dame coach Knute Rockne, and Rockne's
successor, Frank Leahy, who said this about Dwight Eisenhower while
seconding his nomination for president in 1956. Leahy had a sign posted
in his team's locker room: WHEN THE GOING GETS TOUGH, LET THE TOUGH
GET GOING. As nearly any ex-athlete knows, these words have been a locker
room staple for decades, or longer. It is unlikely that their originator will
ever be discovered.

Verdict: An old sports saw.

*"In this world there are only two TRAGEDIES. One is not getting what
one wants, and the other is getting it."* This line from Oscar Wilde's 1892
play *Lady Windermere's Fan* was subsequently put to good use by many another writer. In *Man and Superman* (1903) Shaw wrote, "There are two
tragedies in life. One is to lose your heart's desire. The other is to gain it."
Aphorist Elbert Hubbard later chimed in with "On man's journey through
life he is confronted by two tragedies: One when he wants a thing he can

not get; and the other when he gets a thing and finds he does not want it."
In recent years Irving Kristol has promulgated Kristol's Law: "Being frustrated is disagreeable, but the real disasters in life begin when you get what
you want." This version had another antecedent in Thomas Huxley's 1876
observation that "A man's worst difficulties begin when he is able to do as
he likes." Wilde himself had the last word in *An Ideal Husband* (1899):
". . . when the gods wish to punish us they answer our prayers."

  Verdict: Credit Oscar Wilde for articulating a widespread hunch.

"If this be TREASON, make the most of it!" In late May 1765, a young
lawyer named Patrick Henry rose in Virginia's House of Burgesses to de-
nounce the Stamp Act and defend the colonies' right to tax themselves.
That speech is famous for its dramatic conclusion: "If this be treason,
make the most of it!" This account was reconstructed half a century later
by Henry's biographer, a flowery writer named William Wirt. (Henry spoke
without notes and there were no press accounts of his speech.) To do this,
Wirt—a Henry admirer—consulted the memory of some who were present, including John Tyler and Thomas Jefferson. His reconstruction of
Henry's speech remained the accepted version for more than a century. In
1921, however, a journal kept by a Frenchman who toured America during
the mid-1760s was discovered in a Paris archive. This unnamed tourist,
who may have been a French spy, had witnessed a debate held in Virginia's
House of Burgesses on May 30, 1765. The Frenchman wrote of the debate
(misspellings and all): "Shortly after I Came in one of the members stood
up and said he had read that in former times tarquin and Julus had their
Brutus, Charles had his Cromwell, and he Did not Doubt but soje good
americans would stand up in favour of his Country, but (says he) in a more
moderate manner, and was going to Continue, when the speaker of the
house rose and Said, he, the last that stood up had spoke traison, and was
sorey to see that not one of the members of the house was loyal Enough to
stop him, before he had gone so far, upon which the Same member stood
up again (his name is henery) and said that if he had afronted the speaker,
or the house, he was ready to ask pardon, and he should shew his loyalty to
his majresty King G. the third, at the Expence of the last Drop of his blood,
but what he had said must be attributed to the Interest of his Countrys
Dying liberty which he had at heart, and the heat of passin might have lead
him to have said something more than he intended, but, again, if he said
any thing wrong, he beged the speaker and the houses pardon. some other
Members stood up and backed him, on which that afaire was droped." In
his biography of George Washington, Douglas Southall Freeman concluded

that the Frenchman's version was more "in character" for Henry than the one reconstructed by William Wirt.

Verdict: Patriotic apocrypha.

"The TREE of liberty must be refreshed from time to time with the blood of patriots and tyrants." These words were inscribed on the T-shirt Timothy McVeigh wore the day he bombed the Federal Building in Oklahoma City. This quotation is popular among right-wing zealots, usually, and correctly, attributed to Thomas Jefferson. In a 1787 letter Jefferson wrote those very words. Six years later, in 1793, French revolutionary Bertrand Barère de Vieuzac said in a speech to the National Convention, "The tree of liberty only grows when watered by the blood of tyrants."

Verdict: Credit Jefferson.

"The TRIUMPH of hope over experience." In his chronicle of Samuel Johnson's life, James Boswell said that, in 1770, Dr. Johnson remarked about a man who remarried immediately after the death of a wife to whom he'd been unhappily married, "It was the triumph of hope over experience."

Verdict: Credit Samuel Johnson.

HARRY S. TRUMAN

During the 2004 presidential campaign, Democrats quoted Harry Truman as having said, **"If you run a Republican against a Republican, the Republican will win every time."** Even though this sounds like Truman, no evidence can be found that he ever said it. Nor can researchers at the Harry S. Truman Library confirm another comment Howard Dean sometimes attributed to Truman: that he represented **"the Democratic wing of the Democratic party."**

The thirty-third president of the United States of America was plainspoken, salty, and highly quotable—though not always in the ways we believe. Truman didn't coin **"The BUCK stops here."** That slogan was on a desk sign given him by a friend. He did say, **"If you can't take the HEAT, get out of the kitchen,"** but never claimed authorship. There is no evidence that Truman ever said, **"If you want a friend in Washington, get a DOG,"** an observation commonly, and erroneously, attributed to him.

After Harry Truman died in 1972, he was recalled fondly for having observed of his early days in the Senate: **"For the first six months, you wonder how the hell you ever got here. For the next six months, you wonder how the hell the rest of them ever got here."** When Truman first made that droll observation, he said it was something Illinois senator Ham Lewis told him in the mid-1930s. This actually is an old saw that has made the rounds of Congress for more than a century. An 1899 article in the *Saturday Evening Post* noted, "One of the standing jokes of Congress is that the new Congressman always spends the first week wondering how he got there and the rest of the time wondering how the other members got there."

Truman liked to say that **"A statesman is a politician who's been dead ten or fifteen years."** House Speaker Thomas Reed (1839–1902) peddled this definition long before Truman did, however. According to Reed, a statesman was "a successful politician who is dead."

Truman is among many credited with comments such as **"I don't care what they say about me as long as they SPELL my name right,"** **"It's a RECESSION when your neighbor loses his job; it's a depression when you lose your own,"** and **"It is amazing what you can accomplish if you do not care who gets the CREDIT."** *The Oxford Dictionary of Quotations* credits Truman with "Always be sincere, even if you don't mean it," which is not something the president is known to have said or is likely to have said.

Alluding to his nickname of "Give 'em Hell Harry," Truman said often, in different forms, **"I never did give anybody hell. I just told the truth and they thought it was hell."** (For some reason *The Oxford Dictionary of Quotations* thinks it was "the public," not his opponents, whom Truman supposedly gave hell.)

After the 1948 election, Harry Truman mused in a memo, **"I wonder how far Moses would have gone if he had taken a poll in Egypt? What would JESUS CHRIST have preached if He had taken a poll in the land of Israel? Where would the Reformation have gone if Martin Luther had taken a poll?"** Other politicians subsequently said the much the same thing, usually limited to the Jesus part.

Truman once compared being president to riding a tiger: keep riding or be swallowed (echoing what is said to be an Asian proverb, "Whoever mounts a tiger can never again dismount."). Truman wrote his sister in a letter, "All the president is, is a glorified public relations man who spends his time flattering, kissing and kicking people to get them to do what they are supposed to do anyway." He also observed that "Anybody can be president, and, when he reaches the end of his term, he can go back to being anybody again. It's the job that counts, not the man."

Other memorable comments by Truman include:

There is no indispensable man in a democracy.

Whenever you have an efficient government you have a dictatorship.

Budget figures reveal far more about proposed policy than speeches.

Leadership is the art of getting other people to run with your idea as if it were their own.

It's almost impossible for a man to be president of the United States without learning something.

There is nothing new in the world except the history you do not know.

"Never TRUST the artist. Trust the tale." Although this has been misattributed to Joseph Conrad, it was actually D. H. Lawrence who wrote these lines, in his 1923 book *Studies in Classic American Literature.*

Verdict: Credit D. H. Lawrence.

"You can't TRUST anyone over thirty." Prominent sixties revolutionaries such as Abbie Hoffman, Jerry Rubin, Mario Savio, and Mark Rudd routinely got credit for this credo of youthful protesters. None of them actually said this, at least not originally. The dissident who first publicly advised his peers not to trust anyone over thirty was twenty-four-year-old Jack Weinberg. As protests heated up at the University of California in 1964, Weinberg told a *San Francisco Chronicle* reporter, "We have a saying in the movement that you can't trust anybody over thirty." Weinberg later said those words occurred to him on the spot. Calling them a movement saying was his way of trying to give them more authority.

Verdict: Credit Jack Weinberg.

"All TRUTH passes through three stages. First, it is ridiculed. Second, it is violently opposed. Third, it is accepted as being self-evident." In various

forms this saying is most often attributed to German philosopher Arthur
Schopenhauer (1788–1860). Despite extensive searching—including consultation with two Schopenhauer scholars—computer science professor Jeffrey Shallit of the University of Waterloo in Ontario, Canada, could not find
that remark in any of the German philosopher's writings. Shallit concluded
that Schopenhauer never said it. He did find a related observation in an English translation of the first edition of Schopenhauer's 1818 book, *Die Welt als
Wille und Vorstellung:* "To truth only a brief celebration of victory is allowed
between the two long periods during which it is condemned as paradoxical, or
disparaged as trivial." The livelier "three-stage" version is extremely popular
and often cited. The earliest Schopenhauer attribution Shallit found was in a
1981 *New York Times* interview with children's author Edwin Packard, and in
a book of quotations published that year. Neither gave a source. In a previous
epoch the more common recipient of credit for the "three stages of truth" concept was Swiss-American naturalist Louis Agassiz (1807–1873). In 1866,
Agassiz's friend and colleague Karl Ernst von Baer wrote, "Agassiz says that
when a new doctrine is presented, it must go through three stages. First, people say it isn't true, then that it's against religion, and in the third stage that it
has long been known." (Paleontologist Stephen Jay Gould translated this
from an article in German.) During the post–Civil War period, the three-
stage observation was routinely attributed to Agassiz in a matter-of-fact way
that suggested it was common knowledge he'd said it. In 1867, for example,
The Eclectic Magazine of Foreign Literature ran an article by Henry Sidgwick
in which the Cambridge University professor wrote, "We all remember the
profound epigram of Agassiz, that the world in dealing with a new truth
passes through three stages: It first says that it is not true, then that it is contrary to religion, and finally, that we knew it before." Three years later, in
1870, the *Saturday Evening Post* ran this item: "Mr. Agassiz says that every
great scientific truth goes through three stages. First, people say it conflicts
with the Bible. Next, they say it had been discovered before. Lastly, they say
they always believed it." Shallit found similar quotations about three (or
sometimes four) stages of truth acceptance claimed by or attributed to a wide
range of other prominent figures, including Michel de Montaigne, George
Bernard Shaw, Thomas Huxley, William James, Elbert Hubbard, J. B. S. Hal-
dane, Charles Kettering, and Arthur C. Clarke.

   Verdict: Credit Louis Agassiz, possibly elaborating on an earlier
thought by Arthur Schopenhauer.

**"The best test of TRUTH is the ability to get itself accepted in the
marketplace of ideas."** Most references to the historic dissent of Justice

Oliver Wendell Holmes, Jr., in *Abrams v. United States* (1919) refer to the "marketplace of ideas." He himself did not use that term. What Justice Holmes wrote was this: "But when men have realized that time has upset many fighting faiths, they may come to believe even more than they believe the very foundations of their own conduct that the ultimate good desired is better reached by free trade in ideas—that the best test of truth is the power of the thought to get itself accepted in the competition of the market, and that truth is the only ground upon which their wishes safely can be carried out."

Verdict: Condensed, revised Holmes.

"The opposite of a shallow TRUTH is false. But the opposite of a deep truth is also true." This thought is generally attributed to Danish nuclear physicist Niels Bohr (1885–1962), though seldom with a source. In an essay about his father, Niels, Hans Bohr wrote, "One of the favorite maxims of my father was the distinction between the two sorts of truths, profound truths recognized by the fact that the opposite is also a profound truth, in contrast to trivialities where opposites are obviously absurd." This echoed Oscar Wilde's 1885 observation that "A Truth in art is that whose contradictory is also true." Thomas Mann has been given credit for making a similar observation ("A great truth is a truth whose opposite is also true.") in a 1937 lecture, but that sentence can't be found in published versions of this lecture.

Verdict: Credit Niels Bohr for a less felicitous version than the popular one, with a nod to Oscar Wilde.

"TRUTH is stranger than fiction." This is a crisper version of Lord Byron's words in *Don Juan* (1823): "'Tis strange,—but true; for truth is always strange; / Stranger than fiction: if it could be told." In his 1775 *Speech on the Conciliation of America,* Edmund Burke had observed that "Fiction lags after truth. . . ." The 1858 autobiography of Josiah Henson, on whom Harriet Beecher Stowe's Uncle Tom character was said to have been based, was titled *Truth Stranger Than Fiction.*

Verdict: Basically Byron.

"TRUTH is the first casualty of war." As America entered World War I, California Senator Hiram Johnson (1866–1945) is said to have warned on the floor of the Senate, "The first casualty when war comes is truth." Although this statement is widely attributed to Johnson, it has never been confirmed. Biographer Hal Bochin couldn't verify that the California senator

ever made that assertion. If Johnson did, Bochin thought, it probably was not in a Senate speech (which would be in the *Congressional Record*). In any event, the genesis of this thought is indebted to another Johnson— Samuel—who wrote in *The Idler* in 1758, "Among the calamities of war may be justly numbered the diminution of the love of truth by the falsehoods which interest dictates and credulity encourages." A century earlier, in 1658, one of James Howell's published proverbs was "In too much dispute truth is lost." (This saying was said to have French and English origins.) A long op-ed essay in New York's *Evening Post,* published April 10, 1917, was headlined "The First Casualties in War." That essay's author, a lawyer named Harry Weinberger, identified himself as "born in America, pro-American, and pro-Ally." Nonetheless, warned Weinberger, "The first casualties of war are free speech, free press, and the right to peacefully assemble. . . ." This suggests that the "first casualties of war" concept was not unfamiliar at that time. Nine years later, the author of a 1926 article in *Reformed Church Review* wrote, "Well it is said that 'the first casualty of war is truth, and the second is love.'" In 1928 Arthur Ponsonby published a book called *Falsehood in War-Time,* which incorporated a compilation of quotations on this subject, including "When war is declared, truth is the first casualty," followed by a German analogue: *"Kommt der Krieg ins Land / Gibt Lügen wie Sand."* ("When war enters a country / It produces lies like sand.") Although Ponsonby gave attributions for some of the other quotations, none was given for either the English or German versions of this one. Ten years later, in 1938, *Reader's Digest* credited radio commentator Boake Carter with observing, "In time of war, the first casualty is truth," but gave no citation. Among the quotations John Kennedy scribbled in his notebook after World War II was "In war, truth is the first casualty." Kennedy attributed that thought to the Greek playwright Aeschylus. Others to whom this observation has been attributed include Rudyard Kipling, Winston Churchill, UN Secretary General U Thant, and war correspondent Michael Herr.

    Verdict: Too old and too obvious an idea for specific attribution.

"TURN ON, tune in, drop out." In his 1983 autobiography, Timothy Leary wrote that in mid-1966 Marshall McLuhan advised him to come up with a slogan that would capture the public's imagination. Leary recalled that, after much rumination, six words popped into his head one morning soon afterward, as he was taking a shower. "Dripping wet," wrote Leary, "with a towel around my waist, I walked to the study and wrote down this phrase: 'Turn On, Tune In, Drop Out.'" In fact, from the early 1960s on Leary had

already noodled with variations on this theme. In 1963 he wrote in the *Harvard Review*, "Turn On or Bail Out." Soon after that, in a Philadelphia lecture, Leary spoke of "turning on," then of "tuning in." The proper sequence was not always clear, however, to Timothy Leary or to those recording his words. Sometimes the media reported that turning on came first, sometimes tuning in. At times Dr. Leary himself would exhort listeners to turn on and tune in, and other times to tune in and turn on. More than once he said his slogan was "Drop out, turn on, tune in." In 1966 Leary founded the League for Spiritual Discovery, calling it "a legally incorporated religion dedicated to the ancient sacred sequence of turning on, tuning in, and dropping out." In a mid-1966 lecture at the University of California, Leary finally settled on "turn on, tune in, and drop out" (although the next year he said that the message of the Buddha was "Drop out / Turn on / Tune in."). Whatever its actual origins and form, this catchphrase did its attention-getting job. The producers of Squirt soda pop adapted Leary's mantra for an advertising campaign in which customers were urged to "Turn on to flavor, tune into sparkle, and drop out of the cola rut." Evangelist Billy Graham conducted a European crusade on the theme of "Turn on to Christ, tune in to the Bible, and drop out of sin." How did Timothy Leary feel about this expropriation of his slogan? "I was flattered," he said.

Verdict: Credit Timothy Leary.

MARK TWAIN

Soon after his 1996 reelection, President Bill Clinton advised Americans to recall that "Mark Twain said every dog should have a few fleas—keeps them from worrying so much about being a dog." This observation was actually made by a character in the 1898 novel *David Harum*, written by Edward Noyes Westcott. "'They say a reasonable amount o' fleas is good fer a dog,'" wrote Westcott, "'—keeps him from broodin' over *bein'* a dog, mebbe,' suggested David." (According to turn-of-the-century quotographer William Walsh, this gag had circulated for years before it appeared in *David Harum*.)

Along with Abraham Lincoln, Mark Twain is America's most misquoted figure. Twain was so witty and so prolific that he's hard not to misquote. Even those who know better find it easy to attribute words to him that he never said. In the introduction to his 1991 book *Coming to Terms*, William Safire quoted Twain as saying, **"It AIN'T what**

we don't know that hurts us. It's what we know that ain't so."
Safire then added, "I think that's what he said. It was Twain, wasn't
it?" In a footnote, Safire acknowledged that *The Oxford Dictionary of
Quotations* ascribed a different version of this popular saying to humorist Josh Billings (an accurate ascription). More than a decade
later, in 2004, Safire concluded his *New York Times* column by writing, "As Mark Twain advised, **the problem is not just what we
don't know, but what we do know that AIN'T SO.**"

The urge to attribute witticisms to Mark Twain is nearly irresistible.
Any orphan line with even a hint of drollness comes under the heading
of "sounds like Twain," and is liable to be put in his mouth. Did he say,
**"So I became a newspaperman. I hated to do it, but I couldn't
find honest employment"**? Many think so. Curators of his papers
can't find that one. Nor have they been able to find **"The only way for
a newspaperman to look at a politician is down,"** which has also
been credited to Twain, as well as to H. L. Mencken. Mencken himself,
and others, more reliably attributed this comment to journalist Frank
Simonds (1878–1936). How about **"For every PROBLEM there is always a solution that is simple, obvious, and wrong"**? Sounds like
Twain. A U.S. congressman once quoted him to that effect. In this case
H. L. Mencken is the more likely source of that thought, worded somewhat differently. Library of Congress researchers have never confirmed
Twain's often-quoted reference to **"The finest Congress money can
buy."** The closest words they could find were in a speech Twain wrote
but didn't deliver: "I think I can say, and say with pride, that we have
some legislatures that bring higher prices than any in the world."

Twain buffs Barbara Schmidt and Jim Zwick have exhaustively researched the misattribution to Mark Twain of **"I am not *an* American. I am *the* American."** This misattribution has been made by
filmmaker Ken Burns and by the authors of books about Twain who
reported that he made this observation in his notebook. What they
failed to note was that Twain attributed the comment to his friend
Frank Fuller, just as he attributed to humorist Bill Nye the observation
"WAGNER's music is better than it sounds," a quip commonly
thought to be Twain's own.

"It sometimes seems that Mark Twain is credited with every witty
remark in circulation that cannot be confidently connected with anyone
else," writes R. Kent Rasmussen in the introduction to his well-

researched *The Quotable Mark Twain*. Twain could be the single most misquoted American ever (rivaled only by Abraham Lincoln). He is one of many to whom **"If the only tool you have is a HAMMER everything looks like a nail"** has been misattributed. Twain has also been credited with the orphan quotes **"Never argue with anyone who buys INK by the barrel"** and **"The secret of success is sincerity. If you can fake that, you've got it made."** (See sidebar "Show Business.") But it's not just orphan quotations such as these that land in Twain's lap. Even some that can clearly be attributed to their rightful owner eventually make their way to Mark Twain. CBS reporter Ed Bradley (*60 Minutes*) once credited Twain with Will Rogers's famous line about belonging to no organized party because he was a Democrat. (See sidebar "Will Rogers.") During the 2000 campaign, ABC's Terry Moran remarked, "As Mark Twain said about art, it's **1 percent inspiration, 99 percent perspiration."** That's more plausibly attributed to Thomas Edison, as a saying about genius. Jefferson's observation that advertisements **"contain the only truths to be relied on in a newspaper"** has been attributed to Twain. (See sidebar "Thomas Jefferson.") Twain is one of many credited with Oscar Wilde's witticism **"I can RESIST everything except temptation."** (See sidebar "Oscar Wilde.") Elbert Hubbard's line about editors separating wheat from chaff and printing chaff is sometimes attributed to Twain too (though more often to Adlai Stevenson). A line commonly misattributed to Will Rogers, **"Buy land; they are not making it anymore,"** is also sometimes put in Twain's mouth. (See sidebar "Will Rogers.")

Other quotations commonly misattributed to Twain—all considered in the text—include:

GOLF is a good walk spoiled.

Never trust a man who has only one way to SPELL a word.

Whenever I feel an urge to EXERCISE I lie down until it goes away.

It is better to keep your MOUTH shut and appear stupid than to open it and remove all doubt.

It is very easy to give up SMOKING. I've done it hundreds of times.

> *When I was a BOY of fourteen, my father was so ignorant I could barely stand to have the old man around. But when I got to be twenty-one, I was astonished at how much the old man had learned in seven years.*

The curators of Mark Twain's papers at the University of California/ Berkeley are asked so often about **"The COLDEST winter I ever spent was a summer in San Francisco"** that they've prepared a pamphlet discussing its provenance. Other comments generally attributed to Twain that have a complex heritage include, **"Everybody talks about the WEATHER but nobody does anything about it,"** "There are three kinds of lies: **LIES, damned lies, and statistics,"** and **"The reports of my DEATH are greatly exaggerated."** Press-bashers are fond of quoting Twain's **"Get your facts first, and then you can distort them as much as you please,"** a comment attributed to him by Rudyard Kipling in 1890.

Verified Twainisms include:

Man is the only animal that blushes. Or needs to.

When angry, count four; when very angry, swear.

Courage is resistance to fear, mastery of fear—not absence of fear.

Few things are harder to put up with than the annoyance of a good example.

Always do right. This will gratify some people and astonish the rest.

"*TYPING rather than writing.*" In a 1959 television appearance, Truman Capote said that the output of Beat writers such as Jack Kerouac "isn't writing at all—it's typing." This devastating put-down stuck to Kerouac like chewing gum to the sole of a shoe. In time others took over Capote's verbal brickbat and threw it at their own targets. Gore Vidal, for example, is often quoted as having said about Jacqueline Susann, "She doesn't write, she types."

Verdict: Credit Truman Capote.

"*I don't get ULCERS, I give them.*" Favored by politicians, coaches, movie producers, and sundry hard-charging executives, this wisecrack has long been a common placard slogan. Perhaps it was coined by the same sloganeer who wrote, "The buck stops here." A variation popular among coaches is "I don't have an ulcer, but I'm a carrier."

Verdict: We will probably never know who came up with this one.

"I know you believe you UNDERSTAND what you think I said, but I am not sure you realize that what you heard is not what I meant." In different forms, this popular tongue twister gets attributed to the obfuscator du jour. Many think Richard Nixon said it during the war in Vietnam. Or was it Secretary of State Henry Kissinger? Federal Reserve Board chairman Alan Greenspan subsequently became a popular candidate. Alternatively, semanticist S. I. Hayakawa and linguist Deborah Tannen have also been considered suspects. According to former CBS reporter Marvin Kalb, Vietnam-era State Department spokesman Robert McCloskey actually made this statement to reporters. His words were later posted on the door of the State Department pressroom, Kalb said. Ironically, when Marvin's brother Bernard became the State Department's spokesman, someone (Marvin, perhaps?) gave him a copy of this mouthful to use in case of emergency.

Verdict: Until a better source comes along, credit Robert McCloskey.

"If not US, who? If not now, when?" This pointed question was asked by Ronald Reagan when he was president. Reagan failed to note (and may not even have known) that the Talmud's "Ethics of the Fathers" include these lines uttered by Hillel the Elder: "If I am not for myself who is for me? And when I am for myself what am I? And if not now, when?"

Verdict: Credit Hillel the Elder.

"No man is a hero to his VALET." ("Il n'y a pas de héros pour son valet-de-chambre.") This observation is most often attributed to Madame de Cornuel (Anne-Marie Bigot), a witty Frenchwoman who died in 1694, on the authority of her friend Mademoiselle Aïssé, who repeated it in a 1728 letter. But long before that, in 1595, Montaigne wrote, "Few men are admired by their servants." In the same epoch as Madame de Cornuel's reported observation, French Marshal de Catinat (1637–1712) said, "A man must be indeed a hero to appear such in the eyes of his valet." Around the same time, de Catinat's contemporary Jean de La Bruyère observed, "The nearer we approach great men, the clearer we see that they are men. Rarely do they appear great before their valets." By 1764, Samuel Foote wrote, "It has been said, and I believe with some shadow of truth, that no

man is a hero to his *valet de chambre*"—suggesting how widespread this observation had become by then.

Verdict: A commonplace of French origin.

"The VICE PRESIDENCY isn't worth a pitcher of warm spit." Jack Garner, Franklin Roosevelt's first vice president, actually said that his position "wasn't worth a pitcher of warm piss." *Time* correspondent Hugh Sidey said he passed these words along to his editors in a memo. "Piss" got changed to "spit" in *Time* and other publications, and spit it's been ever since (leading Cactus Jack to observe, "Those pantywaist writers wouldn't print it the way I said it."). As Garner fades in our memory, the "spit" version of this quotation has been misattributed to his fellow Texan, Lyndon Johnson.

Verdict: Credit Jack Garner; don't confuse piss with spit.

"There is no substitute for VICTORY." In 1951 Douglas MacArthur told a joint session of Congress: "In war, indeed, there can be no substitute for victory." A month earlier he'd written to a member of Congress, "There is no substitute for victory." Nearly seven years before that, in an August 1944 letter, Gen. Dwight D. Eisenhower wrote to his wife, Mamie, "In war there is no substitute for victory." It is unlikely that Douglas MacArthur was reading Mamie Eisenhower's mail. What's more likely is that "there is no substitute for victory" was a common saying among military men during the Second World War. It also was the advertising slogan of Victory analgesic ointment at this time. Although he is indelibly associated with this saying, MacArthur was merely its publicist.

Verdict: An old saw publicized by Douglas MacArthur.

"VICTORY has a hundred fathers, but defeat is an orphan." Because John Kennedy made this observation when taking responsibility for the Bay of Pigs fiasco in 1961, we tend to assume the words are his. But JFK himself said, "*There's an old saying* that victory has a hundred fathers and defeat is an orphan." (Emphasis added.) When Arthur Schlesinger, Jr., later asked him about the source of this saying, Kennedy said he didn't know where it came from. A decade earlier, in the 1951 movie *The Desert Fox* (whose screenplay was written by Nunnally Johnson), German Field Marshal Gerd von Rundstedt tells Field Marshal Erwin Rommel, "You must never forget this, my dear fellow: Victory has a hundred fathers. Defeat is an orphan." The 1950 book on which that movie was based, Desmond Young's *Rommel, the Desert Fox,* includes this saying, but from its actual source: the diaries of

Italian foreign minister Count Galeazzo Ciano (1903–1944), which were published after the war. In 1942 Ciano wrote, "As always, victory finds a hundred fathers, but defeat is an orphan." (*"La victoria trova cento padri, e nessuno vuole riconoscere l'insuccesso."*) Other proverbial forms that thought has taken include: "Success has many parents," and "Victory has a hundred memories but defeat has amnesia." According to a Persian proverb, "Winners have large families, but losers are orphans." Obviously—as Kennedy recognized—this observation has a long heritage. Nonetheless, John Kennedy usually gets credit for it, with the number of fathers varying. Respected quotation collections, *Newsweek* magazine, news commentator Jeff Greenfield, and columnist William Safire, to mention just a few, think JFK referred to "one thousand fathers."

Verdict: An old saying popularized by John Kennedy.

VIETNAM

In 1954, Dwight Eisenhower warned that if a single country in Southeast Asia went Communist, many others would follow. He called this "the 'falling domino' principle." As Ike explained: "You have a row of dominoes, you knock over the first one, and what will happen to the last one is that it will go over very quickly." Secretary of State John Foster Dulles relabeled Ike's warning "the Domino Theory." In time it came to be known as **"the domino effect."** (Ike was wrong, but that's another story.)

That phrase is just one of many by-products of the decades of foreign intervention in Southeast Asia, first by the French, then by the Americans. **"LIGHT at the end of the tunnel"** is another—an optimistic scenario projected by John F. Kennedy in 1962 (not Defense Secretary Robert McNamara, Secretary of State Dean Rusk, or Gen. William Westmoreland, as so often is assumed), using a phrase that the French had used long before, while struggling in Vietnam, and the English even earlier.

Lyndon Johnson's attempt to prosecute the war in Vietnam without sacrificing domestic programs was widely called the **"guns and butter"** approach. Although that phrase is generally associated with Johnson, in 1936 Nazi Field Marshal Hermann Goering had already warned, "Guns will make us powerful; butter will only make us fat." The American goal in Vietnam was said to be winning the **"hearts**

and minds" of its people. A reader sent columnist William Safire antecedents from the Bible, a letter John Adams wrote in 1818, and a conversation Teddy Roosevelt had with Dougas MacArthur. Reporters and military officers in Vietnam labeled the "winning hearts and minds" approach "WHAM." This concept became ironic over time, especially after the My Lai Massacre. The Green Berets had their own version: **"Get them by the BALLS, and their hearts and minds will follow."** Air Force General Curtis LeMay had this suggestion for getting the North Vietnamese in line, a suggestion whose final words became notorious: "My solution to the problem would be to tell them frankly that they've got to draw in their horns and stop their aggression, or we're going to **bomb them back into the Stone Age.**"

As controversy about America's role in Vietnam escalated, those on either side of that issue were characterized as **"hawks and doves."** This characterization had a long history. In 1798 Jefferson talked of "war hawks," a phrase that became common for depicting those keen to take the country into combat. Doves, of course, are a longtime symbol of peace. During the 1962 Cuban Missile Crisis, those eager to attack Cuba were termed "hawks," those who counseled restraint, "doves." This division subsequently became commonplace during the war in Vietnam. In subsequent years the term "chicken hawk" was applied to those who rattled sabers of war but avoided military service themselves. During the Vietnam War "chicken hawk" referred to soldiers who were eager for combat but afraid of it, and was the title of a bestselling memoir by helicopter pilot Robert Mason.

One of the most famous quotations to come out of the war in Vietnam was **"We had to DESTROY the village in order to save it."** As reported by war correspondent Peter Arnett, then and now these few words seemed to capture the absurdity of our intervention in Vietnam. The authenticity of this quotation has come into question.

"Kill 'em all—let God sort them out" was a popular gung ho motto among American soldiers in Vietnam. It had a far longer history than they may have realized, dating back in somewhat different form to the Albigensian crusade in the thirteenth century. According to a German monk who was present during the 1209 siege of Beziers in southern France, the abbot of Citeaux, Arnaud-Amaury, was warned that Catholics as well as Protestants were being slaughtered in Beziers. His response was said to be "Kill them all; God will recognize His own."

Richard Nixon was elected president in 1968 partly on the basis of his **"secret plan to end the war."** That wasn't exactly what he said, however. In a 1968 campaign speech Nixon did say he would end the Vietnam War, but couldn't be specific about how he would do so for fear of undercutting President Johnson. In the lead to his report of that speech, a UPI reporter characterized Nixon's approach as a "secret plan." This hook phrase stuck in our memory as if it were Nixon's own. In time it became part of historical conventional wisdom that Richard Nixon once said, "I have a secret plan to end the war." He didn't.

"Eternal VIGILANCE is the price of liberty." This sounds like an axiom of the American Revolution. It is routinely attributed to one or another of its luminaries: Jefferson, Henry, Paine, etc. But the first recorded use of anything like that phrase was in a 1790 speech by Irish statesman John Philpot Curran: "The condition upon which God hath given liberty to man is eternal vigilance." In 1852, during an address before the Massachusetts Antislavery Society, abolitionist Wendell Phillips said, "Eternal vigilance is the price of liberty." Phillips later wrote that he believed this phrase was original to him. No one has proven otherwise.

Verdict: Credit John Philpot Curran for the concept, Wendell Phillips for the most familiar wording.

"It takes a VILLAGE to raise a child." The saying that inspired the title of Hillary Clinton's 1995 book *It Takes a Village* began life as a proverb, apparently in Africa. According to a contemporary South African, a traditional saying in his country is "The whole village raises the child." In *The Prentice-Hall Encyclopedia of World Proverbs,* "The whole village is mother to the motherless" is listed as a Tamil proverb. A 1958 collection of Swahili sayings cites this proverb from Zanzibar (now part of Tanzania): "One hand cannot nurse a child." A missionary to Tanzania used that saying as the basis for an entry in his book *Swahili Proverbs:* "One hand cannot bring up a child. Child upbringing is a communal effort."

Verdict: Global folk wisdom.

"VOTE early and vote often." *Bartlett's* and other quotation collections cite an 1858 speech by South Carolina representative William Porcher Miles in which Miles reported that this admonition was "openly displayed on the election banners in one of our northern cities." Historian James

Morgan suggested that the slogan originated with Martin Van Buren's son John, a prominent New York lawyer in the mid-nineteenth century. Arthur Schlesinger, Jr., thought it characterized the approach of Van Buren's rival, New York political insurgent Mike Walsh. In 1876, Josh Billings wrote, "'Vote early and vote often,' is the politishun's golden rule. Du unto others az yu would be dun by." Chicago and Boston are popular guesses for the birthplace of this slogan, which has been attributed to Chicago gangster Al Capone and Boston mayor James Michael Curley. Trying to pin this catchphrase on anyone in particular is probably a futile exercise.

Verdict: Longtime mock slogan.

"WAGNER'S music is better than it sounds." Although this observation is routinely attributed to Mark Twain, Twain himself attributed the line to popular humorist Bill Nye (1850–1896). Indeed, in 1888, eight years before Nye died, an American magazine reported, "Bill Nye says 'the peculiar characteristic of classical music is that it is really so much better than it sounds.'" The year after Nye's death in 1896, a newspaper filler recalled his observation that "Wagner's music is better than it sounds." A decade later, in 1906, *Lippincott's* magazine reported this exchange between Nye and one Joseph H. Choate about a London concert the humorist had attended: "'I had asked Mr Nye,' said Mr. Choate, 'what was his opinion of Wagner's music. With the most serious expression in the world, Nye replied: 'I must confess that his music is beyond my comprehension; but I always feel sure, when I hear it, that it is really much better than it sounds.'" Yet Nye may have been the purveyor, not the originator, of this famous quip. According to Twain, "The late Bill Nye once said, '*I have been told* that Wagner's music is better than it sounds.'" (Emphasis added.) The phrase "better than it sounds" had appeared in print as early as 1861.

Verdict: Credit Bill Nye, not Mark Twain, for applying to Wagner what was probably an existing catchphrase.

"Everything comes to him who WAITS." An observation by a character in Benjamin Disraeli's 1847 novel *Tancred*, "Everything comes if a man will only wait," echoed one made by François Rabelais three centuries earlier: "Everything comes to him who knows how to wait." (*"Tout vient á poinct qui peult attendre."*) Others have made similar remarks, including Henry Wadsworth Longfellow in 1863: "All things come round to him who will but wait."

Verdict: Rabelais's thought, put in modern play by Disraeli.

"It is well that WAR is so terrible, or we should grow too fond of it."
Robert E. Lee's most memorable remark is said to have been made in
1862 as he watched the savage battle of Fredericksburg. It was first reported in an 1871 biography of Lee by John Esten Cooke, an aide to Confederate General Jeb Stuart. According to the author, Lee said, "It is well
that this is so terrible! We should grow too fond of it!" Thirty-six years later,
the memoir of a Confederate officer added that by legend Lee made this
remark with his hand on the arm of Gen. James Longstreet. Longstreet's
own postwar writing never mentioned this comment. In his four-volume
life of Lee, published in 1934, Douglas Southall Freeman altered its
wording slightly to read, "It is well that war is so terrible—we should grow
too fond of it!" This is the version that most often appears over Lee's name
in standard collections of quotations.

    Verdict: Credit Robert E. Lee, tentatively, for some version of this ob-
servation.

"Suppose they gave a WAR and no one came?" Carl Sandburg's epic
poem *The People, Yes* (1936) included a line that, in a different form, became one of America's best-known antiwar slogans. Sandburg's poem portrayed a little girl who, while watching her first military parade, observes,
"Sometime they'll give a war and nobody will come." This thought didn't attract much attention when it first appeared, nor for many years thereafter.
In 1961 *Scientific American* editor James R. Newman wrote a letter to the
Washington Post in which he misremembered Sandburg's line as "Suppose
they gave a war and no one came?" Writer Charlotte E. Keyes saw Newman's letter and filed it away for future reference. In 1966 Keyes wrote an
article for *McCall's* magazine about her war protester son Gene, using
Newman's misrecollection of Sandburg's line as its title. This title soon
showed up on a bumper sticker that was held up by news anchor David
Brinkley on his NBC newscast. After that the saying caught fire, with little
awareness of its origins. It has been mistattributed to Arlo Guthrie, Allen
Ginsberg, Bertolt Brecht, and others. Some think the saying originated
with Sandburg's colleague Thornton Wilder, but no evidence has been offered to confirm this.

    Verdict: James Newman's adaptation of Carl Sandburg, publicized by
Charlotte Keyes.

"The WAR to end all wars." Although he never used those exact words,
Woodrow Wilson is commonly thought to have called World War I "the war
to end all wars." On the eve of that conflict, H. G. Wells published a book

called *The War That Will End War* (1914). Two decades later, in 1934, Wells wrote, "I launched the phrase 'The War to End War'—and that was not the least of my crimes." Quotographer Nigel Rees says this slogan had already been used to justify previous wars, but gives no specifics.

Verdict: Wells, not Wilson.

"The wrong WAR, in the wrong place, at the wrong time." That is how John Kerry characterized America's Iraqi incursion, during the 2004 presidential campaign. Younger voters in particular may not have realized that Gen. Omar Bradley said basically the same thing about Douglas MacArthur's plan to invade China during the Korean War. While testifying before a Senate committee in 1951, Bradley said, "Frankly, in the opinion of the Joint Chiefs of Staff, this strategy would involve us in the wrong war, at the wrong place, at the wrong time, and with the wrong enemy."

Verdict: Credit Omar Bradley for the original version of this thought.

"WAR is God's way of teaching us geography." The comment "War is God's way of teaching Americans geography," is continually attributed to Ambrose Bierce. Biographer David E. Schultz, who has nearly all of Bierce's writing entered on his computer, cannot find this acerbic remark within that database. Schultz thinks its source more likely is the other person to whom the saying is often attributed: comedian-actor Paul Rodriguez. Rodriguez was quoted in the *Los Angeles Times* as having said at a 1987 Comic Relief event that "War is God's way of teaching us geography."

Verdict: Credit Paul Rodriguez, tentatively.

"WAR is hell." Despite copious searching, no one has ever found William Tecumseh Sherman's most famous three words in any writing or speech by him. Sherman certainly believed war was hell, and apparently said so. A 1914 letter writer to the *New York Times* reported that he'd once had dinner with Sherman and some other men. When asked if his well-known quotation was accurate, Sherman replied that when in the company of men, he'd said often that war is hell. Writing those words down was another matter. During the siege of Atlanta, Sherman wrote that city's mayor, "War is cruelty, and you cannot refine it." During an earlier battle Sherman reportedly said, "War is barbarism." In an 1880 speech at the Ohio State Fair, he told several thousand listeners, "There is many a boy here today who looks on war as all glory, but, boys, it is all hell." This is hardly a unique observation, of course. In fact, in 1860, when Sherman was still headmaster of a military academy in Louisiana, an American magazine

reported, "'War is hell,' said Napoleon I . . ." Napoleon is not actually known to have said this, but the phrase was obviously in circulation on the eve of the Civil War.

Verdict: Sherman probably said, "War is hell," in conversation, but others said it before he did.

"WAR *is nothing more than the continuation of politics by other means."* **("Der Krieg ist nichts anderes als die Fortsetzung der Politik mit anderen Mitteln.")** In his 1832 book *Vom Kriege* (*On War*), Karl von Clausewitz included an observation that is frequently quoted, and misquoted: "War is merely the continuation of policy by other means." Although the exact wording of this comment varies with the translator, all agree that von Clausewitz said war is a "continuation of policy," not "politics."

Verdict: Credit von Clausewitz, saying war is a continuation of policy.

"WAR *is too important to be left to the military."* **("La guerre c'est une chose trop grave pour la confier à des militaires.")** In different forms (the word "serious" is sometimes substituted for "important," "generals" or "soldiers" for "military"), this observation is most often credited to French Premier Georges Clemenceau (1841–1929). British Prime Minister David Lloyd George said that Clemenceau's colleague Aristide Briand (1862–1932) made the comment to him during World War I, but Briand may have been quoting the French diplomat Talleyrand (1754–1838). *Bartlett's* gave the nod to Clemenceau in 1968, Briand in 1980 and 1992, Talleyrand in 2002. *The Oxford Dictionary of Quotations* sticks to Clemenceau, noting the attribution in a 1946 biography, but noting too that Briand and Talleyrand are contenders for credit.

Verdict: A World War I–era French quotation of uncertain origin.

"WARTS *and all."* While running for president in 1988, George H. W. Bush told an audience, "As Abraham Lincoln said, 'Here I stand, warts and all.'" Even though Lincoln had many physical imperfections, no evidence can be found that he made such a self-assessment. More than two centuries before Lincoln's presidency, however, Oliver Cromwell (1599–1658) was renowned for admonishing a portrait painter to "use all your skill to paint my picture truly like me, and not flatter me at all; but remark all these roughnesses, pimples, warts and everything as you see me, otherwise I will never pay a farthing for it." Common usage pared Cromwell's command down to "Paint me as I am—warts and all!" Based on this condensation, the catchphrase "warts and all" became shorthand for candor of all kinds.

Verdict: Condensed Cromwell.

"WASHINGTON is a city of Northern charm and Southern efficiency." In *Portrait of a President,* biographer William Manchester credited this witticism to John F. Kennedy. So did Arthur Schlesinger, Jr., in *A Thousand Days.* To this day it's considered a fine example of JFK's native wit. As the president himself indicated in a 1961 speech, however, the line wasn't his. Kennedy's words were, *"Somebody once said* that Washington was a city of Northern charm and Southern efficiency." (Emphasis added.) "Northern charm" was a catchphrase in use at that time, and the name of a race horse active in 1960.

Verdict: Author unknown; publicized by John Kennedy.

"The battle of WATERLOO was won on the playing fields of Eton." While visiting Eton some years after he defeated Napoleon, the Duke of Wellington (Arthur Wellesley, 1769–1852) is said to have remarked, "The battle of Waterloo was won here" while watching students play cricket. Did the duke actually say this? Pointing out that the phrasing wasn't his, and that his ancestor had little nostalgia for Eton (where he'd spent three unhappy years), the seventh Duke of Wellington offered a reward to anyone who could prove or disprove his authorship of this famous phrase. The winning entry came from Eton's then headmaster, who discovered Wellington's famous observation in a French book about English politics that was published three years after the duke's death in 1852. Based on his own visit to Eton, the Comte de Montalembert wrote, ". . . one understands the Duke of Wellington's *mot* when, revisiting during his declining years the beauteous scenes where he had been educated, remembering the games of this youth, and finding the same precocious vigor in the descendants of his comrades, he said aloud: *'C'est ici qu'a ete gagnee lat bataille de Waterloo.'"* ("It was here that the battle of Waterloo was won.") In 1889, Sir William Fraser translated this passage into English for his compilation *Words on Wellington,* and revised it to read, "The battle of Waterloo was won in the playing fields of Eton."

Verdict: A collaboration between Comte de Montalembert and William Fraser, with possible input from the Duke of Wellington himself.

"Everybody talks about the WEATHER, but nobody does anything about it." This Mark Twain perennial can be found in an unsigned 1897

editorial in the *Hartford Courant*. The *Courant*'s staff at the time included Twain's friend and collaborator Charles Dudley Warner. Twain himself said Warner made the remark, as did *Courant* editor Charles Hopkins Clark. But a closer reading of the editorial in question reveals that its actual wording was: "A well known American writer said once that, while everybody talked about the weather, nobody seemed to do anything about it." Henry McNutty, a retired *Courant* editor, believes this was a little in joke, Warner's tip of the hat to Twain, who continually made quips in conversation that later showed up in print. In a 1923 memoir, journalist Robert Underwood Johnson—who knew Twain—wrote, "Nor have I ever seen in print Mark's saying about the weather, 'We all grumble about the weather, but' (dramatic pause) '—but—but nothing is *done* about it.'"

Verdict: Credit Twain.

"Go WEST, young man, go West." Nineteenth-century New York newspaper editor Horace Greeley regularly advised others to migrate west and settle the country. Despite extensive research by *Yale Dictionary of Quotations* editor Fred Shapiro and an exhaustive study by quotographer Thomas D. Fuller, no one has found this phrase in print under Greeley's byline. An 1850 collection of speeches and writing by Greeley is often given as the source for "Go West, young man" (*Oxford* does) but Fuller could not find this admonition in that book. An 1865 editorial in Greeley's *New York Tribune* has also been given as its source. The closest line Fuller could find in that editorial (addressed to Civil War veterans) was "We earnestly urge upon all such to turn their faces Westward and colonize the public lands." An 1837 article in the *New-Yorker,* then edited by Greeley, included an exhortation to "Fly, scatter through the country—go to the Great West. . . ." Fuller could not find in print any closer analogues to the more popular version of Greeley's advisory. The earliest attribution of the phrase to Greeley that Shapiro found was in an 1872 edition of *Harper's Weekly*. Fuller has concluded that its rhetorical form suggests "Go West, young man" was more likely to have been expressed in one of Greeley's many lectures than in his writing, though not necessarily in a lecture that was recorded or reported. He has no doubt that the editor repeated this advice often. Neither Fuller nor anyone else has been able to verify a widespread account that attributed "Go West, young man" to Indiana newspaper editor John Babson Soulé.

Verdict: Credit Greeley.

MAE WEST

When "Mae West" entered the lexicon as slang for life preservers during World War II, the buxom actress commented, "I've been in *Who's Who* and I know what's what, but it'll be the first time I ever made the dictionary."

Along with Dorothy Parker and Alice Roosevelt Longworth, Mae West was one of the most quotable women of her time. She had less range than either of them, however, dealing primarily in the double entendre. West was listed as the screenwriter of movies that included her most famous quips. Other suggestive one-liners by her were ad-libbed in conversation (or seemed to be anyway). When a television interviewer said she'd heard a lot about her, West responded, "Yeah, but you can't prove a thing." On a *Person to Person* segment considered too hot to broadcast, CBS reporter Charles Collingwood asked West if she had any advice for teenagers. "Yes," replied the lascivious actress. "Grow up."

Mae West popularized the phrase **"tall, dark, and handsome,"** a phrase that had appeared in the American press as early as 1881. What became West's signature line, **"Why don't you COME up and see me sometime?"**, was worded somewhat differently in its original context, her 1933 movie *She Done Him Wrong*. West knew a good line when she heard one, however, and incorporated the popular version in her next movie, *I'm No Angel* (1933 too). This was also the movie in which West said, **"When I'm good, I'm very very good, but when I'm bad, I'm better,"** and **"It's not the men in your life, it's the life in your men."** In her first movie, *Night After Night* (1932), West responded to the comment "My goodness, what beautiful diamonds!" by saying, **"Goodness had nothing to do with it, dearie."** The actress later used this line (minus "dearie") as the title of her autobiography. One of West's most famous lines, addressed to a maid named Beulah in *I'm No Angel,* was **"Peel me a grape."** The 1937 movie *Every Day's a Holiday,* which featured Mae West and credited her as its screenwriter, included the famous line **"Let's get out of these wet CLOTHES and into a dry martini,"** but West did not say and almost certainly didn't write this remark. In that movie she did say, **"Keep a diary and some day it'll keep you."**

One of West's most quoted lines, **"Is that a gun in your pocket,**

or are you just happy to see me?", did not originate in a movie. Different versions of the circumstances in which the actress unleashed this quip float about. Movie maven Leslie Halliwell thought its genesis could be found in a Broadway costume play during which the sword of West's romantic lead got so tangled in his uniform that it stuck out at an embarrassing angle, prompting the actress to comment, "Is that your sword, or are you just pleased to see me?" Others believe the target of the gun version was a male actor, or else a policeman, or a gangster. Late in life West told a reporter that she'd made the comment to a Los Angeles policeman who had been assigned to guard her during a kidnapping scare in the mid-1930s. This buff young cop was part of a group that greeted the actress as she disembarked from a train after being out of town for two weeks. West recalled him saying, "These are from the fellas down at the station" as he handed her a bouquet of flowers. "Then he leant down and kissed me and said, 'And that's from me. It's good to have you back with us, Mae.' And I said, 'Oh yeah, and is that a gun you got in your pocket or are you just glad to see me?'" One suspects it was not the first time West had used this line, or the last. Eventually it resurfaced in the script of her 1977 movie *Sextette*.

Biographers George Eels and Stanley Musgrove credit West with these other quotable quotes:

I used to be Snow White, but I drifted.

I'm no angel, but I've spread my wings a bit.

Too much of a good thing can be wonderful.

It's better to be looked over than overlooked.

Between two evils, I always pick the one I never tried before.

The actress is a minor flypaper figure. West is one among many Depression-era entertainers to whom **"I've been RICH and I've been poor. Rich is better"** has been attributed. The publicity truism **"I don't care what they say about me as long as they SPELL my name right"** has also been credited to Mae West, along with quite a few other celebrities. Perhaps because West's character said, **"I generally avoid temptation, unless I can't RESIST it"** in the 1940 movie *My Little Chickadee,* she is sometimes credited with Oscar Wilde's quip **"I can RESIST everything except temptation."**

"WHERE do we find such men?" This was the stirring climax of President Ronald Reagan's tribute to American soldiers on the fortieth anniversary of D day. In previous speeches Reagan first credited the line to an American admiral in James Michener's novel *The Bridges at Toko-Ri,* then said an actual admiral had spoken these words. Finally, the president took possession of the words (at one point saying it was a question he'd asked his wife Nancy as they passed graves at Normandy). In Michener's novel, while anxiously awaiting the return of American planes to an aircraft carrier during the Korean War, Rear Adm. George Tarrant asks, "Why is America lucky enough to have such men? They leave this tiny ship and fly against the enemy. Then they must seek the ship, lost somewhere on the sea. And when they find it, they have to land upon its pitching deck. Where did we get such men?" During the conclusion of the film based on Michener's book, Frederick March, playing Admiral Tarrant, twice asks, "Where do we get such men?" Without mentioning March, Michener, or Reagan, Rep. J. D. Hayworth (R-Ariz.) asked that very question when ex–National Football League star Pat Tillman was killed while fighting in Afghanistan in 2004.

Verdict: Credit the original version of this thought to James Michener, not Ronald Reagan.

"Tell me what brand of WHISKEY Grant drinks and I'll send a barrel to my other generals." (Wording varies.) Lincoln's alleged response to complaints about Ulysses S. Grant's drinking was one he himself debunked. Among other places it appeared was an 1864 Democratic joke book. Lincoln thought the anecdote was inspired by an earlier one in which George II of England (1683–1760) said of the allegation that Gen. James Wolfe was mad, "If General Wolfe is mad I hope he bites some of my other generals." The president had recounted this anecdote on more than one occasion.

Verdict: Update of an old anecdote, put in Lincoln's mouth.

"The WHOLE nine yards." A wide range of plausible origins has been suggested for this popular catchphrase. Among them are: since fifty-caliber machine gun ammunition belts used by World War II bomber gunners

were nine yards long, those who fired them all were said to have used up "the whole nine yards"; sailors engaged in a ritual of drinking at nine pubs would consume that many "yards" (a type of glass); because nine yards is the amount of fabric a tailor needs to make a first-rate adult's garment, a good-quality garment would be made from "the whole nine yards"; since concrete mixers have a capacity of nine cubic yards, a construction worker who empties one is said to have used "the whole nine yards." Alternatively: Nine cubic yards is the capacity of a rich person's grave, a miner's cart, a garbage truck, or soldier's backpack. Or: Nine yards is the size of an Appalachian burial shroud, a sari worn by Hindu women in ancient India, or the total amount of fabric when all sails are unfurled on a three-masted sailing ship. Nine yards is also said to be the length of hot coals suspects were required to walk in medieval ordeals, and the length of ground an escaping prisoner would have to traverse between inner and outer prison walls—"the whole nine yards." Another possibility arises from the fact that Americans in Vietnam often called Montagnards—an ethnic group said to comprise nine tribes—"Yards" (thus, "all nine Yards"). Few, if any of these explanations have a demonstrated basis in fact. The capacity of cement mixers varies; World War II ammunition was generally measured in weight, or rounds, not belt length; the size of yardarms on sailing ships is not standard, nor is the length of ground between prison walls. We do have an early use of this phrase involving cloth. An 1855 Pennsylvania newspaper portrayed a man who decided to pull the leg of a colleague by having a seamstress make him a shirt using nine yards of cloth, rather than the customary three yards. As the recipient struggled to pull on this billowing garment, his friend exclaimed, "What a silly, stupid woman! . . . she has put the whole nine yards into one shirt!" The year before this vignette appeared, an essayist named "Fanny Fern" (Sara Payson Willis) referred to "nine yards of calico for a dress." In nineteenth-century America "nine yards of calico" became so synonymous with women in general that a traditional square dance tune is called "Swing Nine Yards of Calico." Although this suggests a fabric-based root of "the whole nine yards," that catchphrase only became common after World War II. Military veterans, fliers in particular, recall hearing this phrase from the 1950s on. Its first known appearance in print as slang was in a 1967 book about American pilots in Vietnam, one of whom twice uses the expression "the whole nine yards." (The book's author, Elaine Shepard, herself uses the expression "the full nine yards" once.) By the late 1960s this expression was in common use at the Air Force Academy. In 1969, adjacent to a classified ad for housing suited to "Bachelor Officers," a newspaper published in Fort Walton, Florida—the home of Elgin Air Force Base—advertised a home that "has 'the whole nine yards' in convenience." For now, the best we can say is that "the whole nine yards" may have a textile root but only became a popular catchphrase after World War II, apparently among members of the military, and especially among Vietnam-era Air Force personnel.

Verdict: A postwar catchphrase, popularized by military personnel, with a fabric-based root.

"He who has a WHY to live for can endure almost any how." Since this maxim so succinctly summarizes Victor Frankl's philosophy, it is routinely misattributed to the psychotherapist and Holocaust survivor. This is due in part to the fact that in his preface to Frankl's classic work *Man's Search for Meaning,* Gordon Allport said the founder of "logotherapy" was fond of quoting these words. But, as Allport clearly indicated, their actual author was Friedrich Nietzsche. In *Twilight of the Idols,* Nietzsche wrote, "If we have our own *why* of life, we shall get along with almost any *how.*" ("Man does *not* strive for pleasure"; he added, "only the Englishman does.")

Verdict: Credit Friedrich Nietzsche.

"You see things and you say, 'WHY?' But I dream things that never were; and I say: 'Why not?'" In a 1963 speech John Kennedy correctly attributed these words to George Bernard Shaw. (They're from Shaw's 1921 play *Back to Methuselah.*) Robert Kennedy made them the theme of his 1968 presidential campaign. In his 1982 novel *Shoeless Joe*—which inspired the movie *Field of Dreams*—W. P. Kinsella incorporated a revised version ("Some men see things as they are, and say why, I dream of things that never were, and say why not") over the name "Bobby Kennedy." Ted Kennedy concluded a eulogy for Robert by quoting this favorite saying of his brother, without mentioning Shaw.

Verdict: Credit Shaw.

OSCAR WILDE

Oscar Wilde was the leading aphorist of his era, and of all eras. He snapped off so many clever sayings that inevitably their quality varied widely. Some were little more than wordplay: "Familiarity breeds consent," for example, or "Nothing succeeds like excess." Others combined wit with insight: "We think that we are generous because we credit our neighbors with the possession of those virtues that are likely to be a benefit to us," and "Anybody can sympathize with the sufferings of a friend, but it requires a very fine nature . . . to sympathize with a friend's success."

As would be true of Dorothy Parker in New York a half century later, repeating Oscar Wilde's latest mot was quite fashionable in Victorian London. "Every omnibus-conductor knew his latest jokes," said Wilde's friend Ada Leverson. Some of Wilde's best lines occurred only during conversation. **"One must have a heart of stone to read the death of Little Nell without laughing,"** for example—like many of Wilde's most memorable quips—appears nowhere in his published work. (This one was jotted down by Leverson.)

As did Twain, Churchill, and so many others renowned for spontaneous wit, Wilde kept carefully crafted quips filed in his head, waiting for the proper moment to launch them into conversation. Like a stand-up comedian he continually recycled good lines. Friends noted how often Wilde repeated the same phrases, albeit honed, sharpened, and polished. The best of them moved freely from conversation to essay to fiction to drama. Wilde liked some so well that he used them more than once. **"Nowadays people know the PRICE of everything and the value of nothing,"** for example, appeared in his 1891 novel *The Picture of Dorian Gray*. A year later, in the play *Lady Windermere's Fan*, Wilde defined a cynic as **"A man who knows the PRICE of everything and the value of nothing."** In slightly different form, the thought that **"EXPERIENCE is the name everyone gives to their mistakes"** also appears in both *The Picture of Dorian Gray* and *Lady Windermere's Fan*.

A passage in *A Woman of No Importance* (1893), **"Children begin by loving their parents. After a time they judge them. Rarely, if ever, do they forgive them,"** virtually repeated words Wilde had already written in *The Picture of Dorian Gray*. Wilde also used **"Good Americans, when they die, go to Paris"** in both *Dorian Gray*, and *A Woman of No Importance*. This line was not original to him, however. It had already appeared in Oliver Wendell Holmes's 1853 book *The Autocrat of the Breakfast-Table*, where the quip was attributed to "one of the wittiest of men" (now known to have been Holmes's friend Thomas Gold Appleton). Wilde was hosted by Holmes during his 1882 visit to America and may well have picked up

Appleton's quip at that time. Another line in *Autocrat of the Breakfast-Table,* **"Give us the LUXURIES of life, and we will dispense with the necessaries,"** is often attributed to Wilde in a different form, for no better reason than that it sounds like him.

Aphorisms are a revolving fund. While Wilde did withdraw many sayings from this fund, he deposited far more. **"I can RESIST everything except temptation,"** in *Lady Windermere's Fan,* was later attributed to Mark Twain, W. C. Fields, and Mae West. That play also included **"In this world there are only two TRAGEDIES. One is not getting what one wants, and the other is getting it."** A decade later, in *Man and Superman,* Shaw wrote, **"There are two TRAGEDIES in life. One is to lose your heart's desire. The other is to gain it."** Many another writer subsequently offered his or her own version of this Wildeism.

In her 1972 novel *Murder Being Once Done,* Ruth Rendell wrote, "The tragedy of growing old is not that one is old but that one is young," echoing Wilde's comment in *Dorian Gray* that **"The tragedy of old age is not that one is old, but that one is young."** Rita Mae Brown wrote in *Southern Discomfort* (1982), "A woman who will tell her age will tell anything," apparently not realizing (or not caring) that some readers of that novel might also be familiar with this passage in Wilde's *A Woman of No Importance:* **"One should never trust a woman who tells one her real age. A woman who would tell one that, would tell one anything."**

As an unabashed borrower and involuntary lender of witty remarks, Oscar Wilde was a leading literary cross-pollinator. When asked to discuss the subject of the queen, British television show host David Frost once told an interviewer, "The queen is not a subject," neglecting to note that Wilde had said the same thing decades earlier. Wilde's 1895 play *An Ideal Husband* included the line **"LIFE is never fair,"** perhaps inspiring John Kennedy's **"LIFE is unfair"** comment nearly a century later. In *The Importance of Being Earnest* (1895), Wilde wrote, **"Memory . . . is the diary that we all carry about with us."** In a 1979 issue of *Reader's Digest,* those very words (minus "that") were attributed to aphorist Mary H. Waldrip, who is a kind of an Anglo Elbert Hubbard. **"We have really everything in common with America nowadays, except, of course, language,"** Wilde's articulation of a widespread British sentiment in *The Canterville*

Ghost, 1888), may have inspired similar thoughts attributed to Shaw and others.

Wilde is a primary flypaper figure, with sundry commentaries being attributed to him inaccurately. Though he didn't claim to have invented **"Please do not shoot the PIANIST; he is doing his best,"** these words are often put in Oscar Wilde's mouth (when not being attributed to Twain). In fact, as Wilde reported in *Impressions of America* (1883), he saw this plea on a sign in a Leadville, Colorado, saloon during his 1882 tour of the United States. Other misattributions to Wilde include: **"AMERICA is the only nation in history which miraculously has gone directly from barbarism to degeneration without the usual interval of civilization," "A POLITICIAN is a person who approaches every subject with an open mouth," "Murder your DARLINGS,"** and **"I don't care what they say about me as long as they SPELL my name right."**

Wilde's play scripts were essentially a patchwork quilt of his best remarks, with thin threads of continuity. This simplifies verification of his quotations, at least the ones he recorded in scripts, stories, and essays. Here are just a few verified examples of what in Victorian England were called "Oscariana":

Nowadays most people die of a sort of creeping common sense, and discover, when it is too late, that the only thing one never regrets are one's mistakes.

Nothing that is worth knowing can be taught.

No age borrows the slang of its predecessor.

Men marry because they are tired; women because they are curious. Both are disappointed.

Talk to every woman as if you loved her, and to every man as if he bored you, and at the end of your first season you will have the reputation of possessing the most perfect social tact.

I never travel without my diary. One should always have something sensational to read in the train.

Only dull people are brilliant at breakfast.

It is so easy to convert others. It is so difficult to convert oneself.

The truth is rarely pure and never simple.

I always pass on good advice. It is the only thing to do with it. It is never any use to oneself.

On his deathbed the destitute Wilde said, "I am dying as I lived, beyond my means," but these were not his "last words" as so often gets reported. The same thing is true of "Either the wallpaper goes or I go," also thought by many to be his last words. According to a visitor to his dingy Paris hotel room, long before expiring Wilde said, "My wallpaper and I are fighting a duel to the death. One or the other of us has to go." (See sidebar "Last Words.")

"WINNING isn't everything, it's the only thing." Although this adage is routinely attributed to football coach Vince Lombardi, in a 1953 movie called *Trouble Along the Way,* released when Lombardi was an obscure assistant coach at West Point, the daughter of a football coach played by John Wayne said of him, "Listen, like Steve says, 'Winning isn't everything, it's the only thing!'" That movie's producer-screenwriter, Melville Shavelson, attributed the adage to UCLA football coach Red Sanders. Many of Sanders's colleagues recall hearing him use it as early as the 1930s, when he was coaching high school football in Georgia, and in the late 1940s as he coached Vanderbilt. In 1950, a *Los Angeles Times* columnist wrote of a speech given by UCLA's coach, "Speaking about football victories, Sanders told his group, 'Men, I'll be honest. Winning isn't everything. (Long pause.) Men, it's the only thing!' (Laughter.)" After extensive research, Professor Steve Overman of Jackson State University concluded that this maxim probably originated with Sanders, but that the sardonic coach had meant it as a semi-ironic commentary on the pressure coaches like him felt to win. Credit for the line subsequently got passed around among various coaches (including Joe Kuharich of the Washington Redskins, Sid Gillman of the San Diego Chargers, Michigan's Fielding Yost, Illinois's Bob Zuppke, Maryland's Jim Tatum, Alabama's Paul "Bear" Bryant, and Army's Earl "Red" Blaik) before it landed in Lombardi's lap. According

to biographer David Maraniss, this maxim was one of many that papered Lombardi's locker room walls. A 1962 *Life* profile of Green Bay's coach drew public attention to the "winning is the only thing" exhortation Lombardi repeated often. Six years later, Jerry Kramer's bestselling book *Instant Replay* gave national exposure to Lombardi's favorite saying. Unlike Red Sanders, Vince Lombardi took the winning-is-the-only-thing sentiment quite seriously. So did the many American men who made his vow their mantra. Green Bay's coach may not have originated this saying, but he certainly took possession of it. As Steve Overman concluded, "through his personal style he transformed its import and brought it to center stage in the national dialogue on values. In this sense, the quote belongs to him as much as to Sanders." Late in life Lombardi tried to disavow the win-at-any-price implications of his signature slogan, but by then he'd been quoted too many times (including on camera) as believing that winning was the only thing for his disavowal to attract much attention.

Verdict: Red Sanders's dictum, Vince Lombardi's legacy.

"To be on the WIRE is life. The rest is waiting." In *All That Jazz,* the Bob Fosse–based character played by Roy Scheider says this is his credo. Several years before that 1979 movie, the same thought was attributed to wirewalker Karl Wallenda. Nearly half a century earlier, race driver Rudolf Caracciola was quoted as saying, "To race is to live. All the rest is simply waiting."

Verdict: A daredevil's commonplace.

"Be careful what you WISH for; you may get it." In 1895, a century before Colin Powell listed "Be careful what you choose. You may get it" as the fifth of his thirteen "Rules to Live By," an American children's magazine advised its readers, "You must be careful what you wish for, because if you wish hard enough you are pretty sure to get it. . . ." In *America's Popular Sayings,* Gregory Titelman says this proverb dates back to the mid-nineteenth century. Analogous thoughts are expressed in many different forms ("More tears are shed over answered prayers than unanswered ones," "When the gods wish to punish us they answer our prayers," "Granting our wishes is one of Fate's saddest jokes.").

Verdict: Proverbial wisdom.

"What lies behind us / And what lies before us / Are tiny matters / Compared to what lies WITHIN us." This quotation is especially beloved by coaches, valedictorians, eulogists, and Oprah Winfrey. It usually gets attributed to Ralph Waldo Emerson. No evidence can be found that Emerson said

or wrote these words. Based on no better evidence, some think Oliver Wendell Holmes (Senior or Junior) originated the thought. Others credit Whitman, Thoreau, or Ronald Reagan. A few retreat to "Anonymous."

Verdict: For now "Anonymous" is the only credible attribution.

"A WOMAN needs a man like a fish needs a bicycle." As the most prominent feminist of her time, Gloria Steinem usually gets credit for this quip (which has also been attributed to lawyer Florynce Kennedy and author Gertrude Stein). Steinem herself never claimed the slogan originated with her, and has specifically disowned authorship on more than one occasion. Apparently an Australian educator, journalist, and politician named Irina Dunn coined it in 1970, adapting an aphorism she said she'd read in a philosophy text while studying at Sydney University: "A man needs God like a fish needs a bicycle." Dunn recalled scribbling her version on toilet stall doors at Sydney University and Soren's Wine Bar in the Sydney suburb of Woolloomooloo. The "God" version had long been commonplace among atheists. The feminist variant was used as a line in Bono's 1991 song "Tryin' to Throw Your Arms Around the World," and inspired the 2003 film *Fish Without a Bicycle.*

Verdict: An atheist slogan adapted by Irina Dunn, not Gloria Steinem.

"What does a WOMAN want?" (**"Was will das Weib?"**) This most familiar of Freud quotations cannot be found in his published work. Biographer Ernest Jones said the analyst made this remark to his patient Marie Bonaparte (a descendant of Napoleon). Sure enough, University of California / Davis psychology professor Alan Elms found that famous question scribbled in notes Bonaparte took about a session with Freud. But Elms believes the question may have pertained more to Freud's exasperating relationship with his daughter Anna (who was thirty at the time) than to women in general. If that is so, this comment cannot be used as evidence of Freud's cluelessness about women, as so many take for granted.

Verdict: Freud said words to this effect, but probably not in the way we imagine.

"A WOMAN'S work is never done." So wrote Martha Moore Ballard in her diary on November 26, 1795. Even though this is sometimes attributed to the Maine housewife and midwife, she herself clearly added, "as ye song says . . ." An early seventeenth-century ballad included the line "A woman's work is never done." Thomas Tusser wrote in *The Book of Huswifery* (1580), "Some respite to husbands the weather may send, but

huswives' affairs have never an end." According to *The Prentice-Hall Encyclopedia of World Proverbs,* this saying is of Scottish origin.

Verdict: Too old and too obvious a comment for specific attribution.

"WORK smarter, not harder." This time manager's mantra began to appear in the American press during the early 1960s. In 1962, a Texas newspaper reported that the Home Demonstration Club of Commerce, Texas, hosted a program called "Work Smarter, Not Harder." The next year an article in a Wisconsin newspaper was headlined "Ease Schedule, Work Smarter, Not Harder." That was a key admonition in Alan Lakein's time-management classic *How to Get Control of Your Time and Your Life* (1973). "Above all," Lakein wrote, "this book will show you how to work smarter, not harder. . . ." The phrase "work smarter" dates at least to mid-nineteenth-century America.

Verdict: A postwar advisory of uncertain origin popularized by Alan Lakein.

"WORKERS of the world, unite! You have nothing to lose but your chains." This famous call to revolution is a revision of what Marx and Engels wrote in *The Communist Manifesto:* "The proletarians have nothing to lose but their chains. They have a world to win. Working men of all countries, unite!"

Verdict: Revised Marx and Engels.

"The WORLD must be coming to an end. Children no longer obey their parents, and every man wants to write a book." This passage was allegedly part of a longer lament discovered on an Assyrian stone tablet dated to the 2800 B.C. period. It has been cited in print since at least 1929. No one has given a reliable source for the observation, however, or explained how writers who write on stone tablets could make reference to "books."

Verdict: Apocrypha.

"It's WORSE than a crime, it's a blunder!" ("C'est pire qu'un crime, c'est une faute!") Someone said this after the 1804 execution of military commander Louis de Bourbon-Condé, duc d'Enghien, on the spurious charge that he planned to overthrow Napoleon's government. (The duke was court-martialed at 11 P.M., sentenced to death at 2 A.M., and shot two hours later.) In his memoirs, Napoleon's Minister of Police Joseph Fouché (1759–1820) took credit for the exclamation (*"C'est plus qu'un crime, c'est une faute,"* literally, "It is more than a crime, it is a fault"). In his own mem-

oirs, Napoleon's brother Lucien Bonaparte attributed the comment to French diplomat Charles Maurice de Talleyrand (1754–1838). Yet Talleyrand biographer C. A. Saint-Beuve thought it was politician Antoine Boulay de la Meurthe (1761–1840) who made this remark. In his essay "Experience," Emerson mistakenly attributed the quip to Napoleon himself. *Bartlett's* credited Fouché in its twelfth edition, Boulay thereafter. *The Oxford Dictionary of Quotations* credits Boulay. Quotographer Burton Stevenson thought Fouché's claim was the most direct, therefore the most credible. The truth is that no one knows with any certainty who first said these historic words.

Verdict: If credit must be given, credit Joseph Fouché for a milder version.

"WRITERS are always selling somebody out." Joan Didion concluded the preface to *Slouching Toward Bethlehem* with these much-cited words. Similar thoughts have been attributed to Nora Ephron and Janet Malcolm, among others.

Verdict: Credit Joan Didion.

"Easy WRITING makes hard reading." This observation is typically attributed to Ernest Hemingway. Similar sentiments have been expressed by many a writer (Jonson, Johnson, Byron, etc.). Its closest known antecedent can be found in "Clio's Protest," an 1816 poem by Richard Sheridan that included the lines "You write with *ease* to show your breeding. / But *easy writing's* curst *hard reading*."

Verdict: Credit Sheridan for the thought, and nearly the wording.

"WRITING about music is like dancing about architecture." This much-quoted line has no clear point of origin, but lots of alleged originators. They include rockers Elvis Costello, Frank Zappa, Grace Slick, and David Byrne; jazz musicians Thelonius Monk, Miles Davis, and Charles Mingus; comedians Steve Martin, Martin Mull, and George Carlin; filmmaker Laurie Anderson; author William S. Burroughs; and rock critic Lester Bangs. Alan P. Scott has gathered many such citations in a website devoted to this quotation. According to Scott, it is most often credited to Laurie Anderson because her 1986 video *Home of the Brave* included the line "Talking about music is like dancing about architecture." Anderson herself, who thought about using that line as her video's title, said she got it from Steve Martin. In the 1999 movie *Playing by Heart,* one character says, "Talking about love is like dancing about architecture." (This movie was originally titled *Dancing*

About Architecture.) That version suggests how modularized this popular quotation has become. In addition to "talking about love" or "writing about music," "writing about art" has also been compared to dancing about architecture. Elvis Costello's use of the "writing about music" version, in a 1983 magazine interview, is the oldest one found in print so far, but it's doubtful that the thought originated with him. Some recall hearing it well before Costello's 1983 interview, including a Barry Gilbert who e-mailed Alan Scott that he'd done an improvisational dance about architecture while in college during the late 1970s through 1981.

Verdict: Case wide-open.

"WRITING is easy. You just sit down at the typewriter, open up a vein and bleed it out drop by drop." Sportswriter Red Smith (1905–1982) is frequently quoted to this effect. (Other versions include "There's nothing to writing. All you do is sit down at a typewriter and open a vein"; "Writing is easy. I just open a vein and bleed"; and "Writing a column is easy. You just sit down at your typewriter until little drops of blood appear on your forehead.") Journalist Gene Fowler (1890–1960) is said to have observed that "Writing is easy: all you do is sit staring at a blank sheet of paper until the drops of blood form on your forehead." Variations on this theme have been attributed to novelists Daniel Keyes and Thomas Wolfe, without sources. Whoever said it first, the quotation has a distinguished ancestor in Sydney Smith's comment during the late 1830s about British statesman Charles James Fox (1749–1806): "Fox wrote drop by drop."

Verdict: Credit Red Smith for articulating different versions of a thought common among colleagues, and expressed in a different form by Sydney Smith.

"YOUTH is wasted on the young." George Bernard Shaw usually gets credit for the root of this observation: "Youth is a wonderful thing. What a crime to waste it on children." The earliest known attribution of the quip to Shaw was in a 1939 book called *10,000 Jokes, Toasts, and Stories.* According to that book the playwright made this comment during a dinner conversation. No source was given. In 1940, *Reader's Digest* credited the quotation to Shaw, also without giving a source. It subsequently become a standard part of Shavian lore. The earliest use *Yale Dictionary of Quotations* editor Fred Shapiro could find of "Youth is wasted on the young" was in a 1952 issue of the *Washington Post.* Sammy Cahn's lyrics for the 1960 song "The Second Time Around" noted that "Love, like youth, is wasted on the young."

Verdict: Possibly Shaw; probably not.

BIBLIOGRAPHY

Ackermann, A. S. E. *Popular Fallacies*. London: Old Westminster; Detroit: Gale [1950], 1970.

American Film Institute, "List of the four hundred nominated movie quotes," <http://www.afi.com/Docs/tvevents/pdf/quotes400.pdf> (July 29, 2005).

Anderson, Charles R. *Puzzles and Essays from "The Exchange": Tricky Reference Questions*. New York: Haworth, 2003.

Bailey, Thomas. *Voices of America: The Nation's Story in Slogans, Sayings, and Songs*. New York: The Free Press, 1976.

Baker, Daniel B. *Power Quotes*. Detroit: Visible Ink Press, 1992.

Bartlett, John. *Familiar Quotations*. 9th ed. Boston: Little, Brown, 1891.

_____. *Familiar Quotations*. Edited by Nathan Haskell Dole. 10th ed. Boston: Little, Brown, 1914.

_____. *Familiar Quotations*. Edited by Christopher Morley. 11th ed. Boston: Little, Brown, 1937.

_____. *Familiar Quotations*. Edited by Christopher Morley. 12th ed. Boston: Little, Brown, 1948.

_____. *Familiar Quotations*. 13th ed. Boston: Little, Brown, 1955.

_____. *Familiar Quotations*. Edited by Emily Morison Beck. 14th ed. Boston: Little, Brown, 1968.

_____. *Familiar Quotations*. Edited by Emily Morison Beck. 15th ed. Boston: Little, Brown, 1980.

_____. *Familiar Quotations*. Edited by Justin Kaplan. 16th ed. Boston: Little, Brown, 1992.

_____. *Familiar Quotations*. Edited by Justin Kaplan. 17th ed. Boston: Little, Brown, 2002.

Benham, Sir William Gurney. *Benham's Book of Quotations, Proverbs, and Household Words*. New York: Putnam's [1907] 1949.

_____. *Putnam's Dictionary of Thoughts*. New York: Putnam's, 1930.

Bent, Samuel Arthur. *Familiar Short Sayings of Great Men: With Historical and Explanatory Notes*. [Boston: Houghton Mifflin, 1887]; Detroit: Gale Research, 1968.

Boller, Paul F. *Quotemanship*. Dallas: Southern Methodist University Press, 1967.

Boller, Paul F., and John George. *They Never Said It: A Book of Fake Quotes, Misquotes and Misleading Attributions*. New York: Oxford University Press, 1989.

Bombaugh, Charles C. *Facts and Fancies for the Curious*. Philadelphia: Lippincott, 1905.

Boswell, James. *Boswell's Life of Johnson*. Edited by George Birkbeck Hill. London: Oxford [1791], 1934.

Burnam, Tom. *The Dictionary of Misinformation*. New York: Thomas Y. Crowell, 1975.

_____. *More Misinformation*. New York: Lippincott & Crowell, 1980.

Cerf, Bennett. *Try and Stop Me: A Collection of Anecdotes and Stories, Mostly Humorous*. New York: Simon & Schuster, 1944.

The Columbia Dictionary of Quotations. Edited by Robert Andrews. New York: Columbia, 1996.

Dickson, Paul. *Baseball's Greatest Quotations*. New York: HarperCollins, 1991.

Dirks, Tim, "Greatest Film Misquotes," *The Greatest Films,* <http://www.filmsite.org/moments0.html> (July 30, 2005).

Emerson, Ralph Waldo. *Essays by Ralph Waldo Emerson*. New York: Crowell, 1926.

Evans, Bergen. *Dictionary of Quotations*. [New York: Delacorte, 1968]; New York: Avenel, 1978.

Fadiman, Clifton. *An American Treasury, 1455–1955*. New York: Harper and Brothers, 1955.

Fehrenbacher, Don E., and Virginia Fehrenbacher. *Recollected Words of Abraham Lincoln*. Stanford: Stanford University, 1996.

Frost, Elizabeth. *The Bully Pulpit: Quotations from America's Presidents*. New York: Facts on File, 1988.

Gee, Renie. *Who Said That?* Edited by Graham Donaldson and Mans Ross. London: David & Charles, 1989.

Green, Lee. *Sportswit*. New York: Harper & Row, 1984.

Harnsberger, Caroline Thomas. *Treasury of Presidential Quotations*. Chicago: Follett, 1964.

Harris, Leon A. *The Fine Art of Political Wit*. New York: Dutton, 1964.

Haun, Harry. *The Movie Quote Book*. New York: Lippincott and Crowell, 1980.

Herbert, George. *Outlandish Proverbs*. London: Humphrey, 1640; Ann Arbor, University microfilms.

Herold, J. Christopher, ed. and trans. *The Mind of Napoleon: A Selection from His Written and Spoken Words*. New York: Columbia, 1955.

The Home Book of Quotations, Classical and Modern. 10th ed. Edited by Burton Stevenson. New York: Dodd, Mead, 1964.

Hoyt's New Cyclopedia of Practical Quotations. Edited by Kate Louise Roberts. New York: Funk & Wagnalls, 1922.

Hubbard, Elbert. *A Thousand and One Epigrams*. Englewood Cliffs, N.J.: Prentice-Hall, [1911], 1973.

_____. *Roycroft Dictionary and Book of Epigrams*. East Aurora, N.Y.: Roycrofters, 1923.

Kennedy, Edward M. *Words Jack Loved.* Boston: private printing, 1977.

King, W. Francis H. *Classical and Foreign Quotations: A Polyglot Dictionary of Historical and Literary Quotations, Proverbs and Popular Sayings.* New York: Frederick Ungar, 1958.

Latham, Edward. *Famous Sayings and Their Authors.* [London: Swan Sonnenschein, 1904]; Detroit: Gale, 1970.

Lewis, Alec. *The Quotable Quotations Book.* New York: Thomas Y. Crowell, 1980.

Lipscomb, Andrew A., ed. *The Writings of Thomas Jefferson.* Washington, D.C.: Thomas Jefferson Memorial Association, 1903.

The Macmillan Book of Proverbs, Maxims, and Famous Phrases. Edited by Burton Stevenson. New York: Macmillan, 1948.

The Macmillan Dictionary of Quotations. New York: Macmillan [1987] 1989.

Maggio, Rosalie. *The New Beacon Book of Quotations by Women.* Boston: Beacon Press, 1996.

Magill, Frank N. *Quotations in Context.* New York: Harper & Row, 1965.

Mencken, H. L. *A New Dictionary of Quotations on Historical Principles from Ancient and Modern Sources.* New York: Knopf, 1942.

Mieder, Wolfgang. *The Prentice-Hall Encyclopedia of World Proverbs.* [Englewood Cliffs, N.J.: Prentice-Hall, 1986]; New York: MJF Books, 1986.

Morris, William, and Mary Morris. *Morris Dictionary of Word and Phrase Origins.* New York: Harper & Row, 1988.

Newcomb, Robert H. "The Sources of Benjamin Franklin's Sayings of Poor Richard." Ph.D. diss., University of Maryland, 1957.

Oxford Dictionary of Proverbs. Edited by Jennifer Speake. Oxford: Oxford University Press, 2003.

The Oxford Dictionary of Quotations. 2d ed. London: Oxford University Press [1941] 1955.

The Oxford Dictionary of Quotations. 3rd ed. New York: Oxford University Press [1979] 1980.

The Oxford Dictionary of Quotations. 4th ed. Edited by Angela Partington. New York: Oxford University Press 1992.

The Oxford Dictionary of Quotations. 5th ed. Edited by Elizabeth Knowles. New York: Oxford University Press 1999.

The Oxford Dictionary of Quotations. 6th ed. Edited by Elizabeth Knowles. New York: Oxford University Press 2004.

Partridge, Eric. *A Dictionary of Catch Phrases.* Edited by Paul Beale. [New York: Stein and Day, 1977, 1985]; New York: Dorset Press, 1988.

Pearson, Hesketh. *Common Misquotations.* [London: Hamish Hamilton, 1934]; London: Folcroft, 1973.

Peter, Laurence J. *Peter's Quotations: Ideas for Our Time.* [New York: Morrow, 1977]; New York: Bantam, 1979.

Platt, Suzy. *Respectfully Quoted: A Dictionary of Quotations Requested from the Congressional Research Service.* Washington, D.C.: Library of Congress, 1989.

Random House Dictionary of American Slang. Vol. 1. Edited by J. E. Lighter. New York: Random House, 1994.

Random House Dictionary of American Slang. Vol. 2. Edited by J. E. Lighter. New York: Random House, 1997.

Random House Webster's Quotationary. Edited by Leonard Roy Frank. New York: Random House, 1999.

Rasmussen, R. Kent. *The Quotable Mark Twain.* Chicago: Contemporary, 1997.

The Reader's Digest Treasury of Modern Quotations. New York: Reader's Digest Press, 1975.

Rees, Nigel. *Cassell Companion to Quotations.* London: Cassell [1997] 1999.

Ringo, Miriam. *Nobody Said It Better: 2700 Wise and Witty Quotations About Famous People.* Chicago: Rand McNally, 1980.

Rosten, Leo. *The Power of Positive Nonsense.* New York: McGraw-Hill, 1977.

Safire, William. *William Safire on Language.* New York: Times Books, 1980.

_____. *What's the Good Word?* New York: Times Books, 1982.

_____. *I Stand Corrected.* New York: Times Books, 1984.

_____. *Take My Word for It.* New York: Times Books, 1986.

_____. *You Could Look It Up.* New York: Times Books, 1988.

_____. *Language Maven Strikes Again.* New York: Doubleday, 1990.

_____. *Coming to Terms.* New York: Doubleday, 1991.

_____. *Quoth the Maven.* New York: Random House, 1993.

_____. *Safire's New Political Dictionary.* New York: Random House, 1993.

_____. *In Love with Norma Loquendi.* New York: Random House, 1994.

_____. *Watching My Language.* New York: Random House, 1997.

_____. *Spread the Word.* New York: Times Books/Random House, 1999.

_____. *Let a Simile Be Your Umbrella.* New York: Crown, 2001.

_____. *No Uncertain Terms.* New York: Simon & Schuster, 2003.

_____. *The Right Word in the Right Place at the Right Time.* New York: Simon & Schuster, 2004.

Samuel, Viscount. *A Book of Quotations.* London: Cresset Press, 1947.

Seldes, George. *The Great Quotations.* [New York: Lyle Stuart, 1960]; New York: Pocket Books, 1967.

_____. *The Great Thoughts.* New York: Ballantine, 1985.

Shapiro, Fred R., ed. *Stumpers!: Answers to Hundreds of Questions That Stumped the Experts.* New York: Random House, 1998.

Shipps, Anthony W. *The Quote Sleuth: A Manual for the Tracer of Lost Quotations.* Urbana, Ill.: University of Illinois Press, 1990.

Spinrad, Leonard, and Thelma Spinrad. *Treasury of Great American Sayings.* West Nyack, N.Y.: Parker, 1975.

Stephens, Meic. *A Dictionary of Literary Quotations*. London: Routledge, 1990.

Stimpson, George. *A Book About a Thousand Things*. New York: Harper & Brothers, 1946.

_____. *Information Roundup*. New York: Harper & Brothers, 1948.

Sugar, Bert Randolph. *The Book of Sports Quotes*. New York: Quick Fox, 1979.

Titelman, Gregory. *America's Popular Sayings*. New York: Random House, 2000.

Tripp, Rhoda Thomas. *The International Thesaurus of Quotations*. [New York: Harper & Row, 1970]; New York: Perennial, 1987.

Tuleja, Tad. *Fabulous Fallacies*. New York: Harmony, 1982.

_____. *Quirky Quotations*. New York: Harmony, 1992.

Walsh, William S. *Handy-Book of Literary Curiosities*. Philadelphia: Lippincott, 1892.

Wilde, Oscar. *The Complete Works of Oscar Wilde*. New York: Harper & Row/ Perennial, 1989.

Wilson, Carroll A. *First Appearance in Print of Some Four Hundred Familiar Quotations*. Middletown, Conn.: Wesleyan University, 1935.

Woods, Henry F. *American Sayings: Famous Phrases, Slogans and Aphorisms*. [New York: Duell, Sloan and Pearce, 1945]; New York: Perma Giants, 1950.

SOURCE NOTES

These notes cite my primary sources of information and suggest leads for those who would like to pursue further the origins of specific quotations. In general, I've cited only the most pertinent sources (avoiding, for example, citing repeated illustrations of the same quotations, or misquotations). Where sources are cited from online sites, a link is also listed with which to access that site (if it's still online), as well as the date it was accessed. Page numbers are given for citations in books and periodicals.

Sources that are listed in the bibliography are referred to by last name of author (or first word of title for publications or websites without an author), and date of publication for authors of more than one book. Publications cited frequently are referred to by the following abbreviations:

Bartlett's—*Bartlett's Familiar Quotations,* seventeenth edition (2002) except where indicated.

Home Book—*The Home Book of Quotations, Classical and Modern,* tenth edition (1964).

Hoyt's—*Hoyt's New Cyclopedia of Practical Quotations* (1922).

MDQ—*The Macmillan Dictionary of Quotations* (1987, 1989).

MPMFP—*The Macmillan Book of Proverbs, Maxims, and Famous Phrases* (1948).

ODP—*Oxford Dictionary of Proverbs* (2003).

ODQ—*The Oxford Dictionary of Quotations,* sixth edition (2004) except where indicated.

SNPD—*Safire's New Political Dictionary* (1993).

Newspapers cited frequently are referred to by the following abbreviations:

BG—Boston Globe

CT—Chicago Tribune

DDN—Dayton Daily News

LAT—Los Angeles Times

NYT—New York Times

PI—Philadelphia Inquirer

WSJ—Wall Street Journal

WP—Washington Post

INTRODUCTION

Sources for quotations that are mentioned in the introduction but also appear in the text are cited in notes for those quotations. Citations for quotations discussed in the introduction that do not appear in the text are as follows:

Oxford: "Favourite quotation revealed!" *Ask Oxford,* December 3, 2004, <http://www.askoxford.com/pressroom/archive/favquote/?view=uk> (April 29, 2005).

Kaufman-Parker: Scott Meredith, *George S. Kaufman and His Friends* (Garden City, N.Y.: Doubleday, 1974), 139; Dorothy Parker, *The Portable Dorothy Parker* (New York: Viking, 1944), 321.

Wilde: E. H. Mikhail, *Wilde: Interviews and Recollections* (New York: Harper & Row, 1979), 52.

Mandela-Williamson: "Our Deepest Fear," *Quotations Page Forums,* June 3, 2003, June 24, 2003, <http://www.quotationspage.com/forum/viewtopic.php?t=1144> (August 30, 2005); Marianne Williamson, *A Return to Love* (New York: HarperCollins, 1992), 165.

Caesar: *Atlanta Journal-Constitution,* September 26, 2002; "Snare Drummed," *snopes.com,* October 1, 2002, <http://www.snopes.com/quotes/caesar.htm> (August 30, 2005).

Jefferson: interview with Dan Buck, December 7, 1990; Eyler Coates, *Requests for Information Related to Thomas Jefferson Quotations,* <http://www.geocities .com/Athens/7842/archives/quote022.htm> (August 30, 2005); Martin Gott-lieb *DDN,* June 16, 1995; e-mail from Eleanor Sparagana, University of Virginia, July 8, 2005; David McCullough, *John Adams* (New York Simon & Schuster, 2001), 163; Richard N. Rosenfeld, "The Adams Tyranny," *Harper's,* September 2001, 82.

Cassell—Twain: Rees, 546.

Garner: O. C. Fisher, *Cactus Jack* (Waco, Tex.: Texian, 1982), 106.

Kaplan: Madeleine Blais, "Choice Words," *PI Magazine,* February 2, 1992, 17.

StGeorge: Michael StGeorge, "The Survival of a Fitting Quotation," Edition 1.0, 2005: <http://www.geocities.com/fitquotation/> (July 29, 2005).

Milton—SNPD, xvii.

SOURCES FOR MAIN TEXT AND SIDEBARS

ACADEMIC politics: BG, December 25, 1994; Charles Issawi, *Issawi's Laws of Social Motion* (New York: Hawthorn, 1973), 178; *PS,* Autumn, 1977, 511; Peter, 183; *NYT,* October 18, 1989.

Half the money I spend on ADVERTISING: Martin Mayer, *Madison Avenue, USA* (New York: Harper & Row, 1958; Pocket, 1959) 259; David Ogilvy, *Confessions of an Advertising Man* (London: Longmans Green, 1963; Mayflower-Dell, 1966), 75; *Advertising Age,* June 25, 1990, 24; *Fortune,* December 26, 1994, 26; Rees, 354; William Allen Zulker, *John Wanamaker: King of Merchants* (Wayne, Pa.: Eaglecrest, 1993), 41, 222; Zulker e-mail, June 12, 2005, June 29, 2005.

If you have to ask . . . AFFORD one: Jean Strouse, *New Yorker,* March 29, 1999, 68; Jean Strouse, *Morgan: American Financier* (New York: Random House, 1999), 206.

AFTER us, the deluge: King, 18–9; Latham, 85–6; Home Book, 748; MPMFP, 548–9; Olivier Bernier, *Louis the Beloved: The Life of Louis XV* (Garden City, N.Y.: Doubleday, 1984), ix.

AIN'T I a woman: Carelton Mabee with Susan Mabee Newhouse, *Sojourner Truth: Slave, Prophet, Legend* (New York: New York University Press, 1993), 74–7, 80–1, 257; Nell Irvin Painter, *Sojourner Truth: A Life, a Symbol* (New York: Norton, 1996), 121–31; Nell Irvin Painter, "Representing Truth: Sojourner's Truth Knowing and Becoming Known," in Patricia Bell-Scott and Juanita Johnson Bailey, ed., *Flat-Footed Truths: Telling Black Women's Lives* (New York: Holt, 1998), 99, 107, 117–20, 124; Margaret Washington, ed., *Narrative of Sojourner Truth* (New York: Vintage, 1993), 117–8.

It AIN'T so much: Al Gore, *Earth in the Balance: Ecology and the Human Spirit* (Boston: Houghton Mifflin, 1992), 41; Albert Bigelow Paine, introduction to *Mark Twain's Autobiography,* Vol. 1 (New York: Harper and Brothers, 1924), viii; Mark Twain, *Following the Equator* (Hartford, Conn.: American, 1897), 132; Home Book, 1055; Josh Billings, *The Complete Works of Josh Billings (Henry W. Shaw)* (New York: G. W. Dillingham, 1876), 25, 286; James E. Myers, ed., *America's Phunniest Phellow–Josh Billings: The Delightful, Funny Stories and Sayings of Our Wisest American Humorist* (Springfield, Ill.: Lincoln-Herndon Press, 1986), back cover; Melville D. Landon, *Kings of the Platform and Pulpit* (Columbus, Ohio: Wabash, 1892), 75.

I want to be ALONE: Dirks; Vicki Baum, *Grand Hotel,* Basil Creighton, trans. (Garden City, N.Y.: Doubleday, Doran, 1931), 127; *Life,* January 24, 1955, 113.

AMERICA is great: Platt, 160; Sherwood Eddy, *The Kingdom of God and the American Dream* (New York: Harper and Brothers, 1941), 6; John J. Pitney, "The Tocqueville Fraud," *Weekly Standard,* November 13, 1995; Pitney, "As the Great Tocqueville Never Said," *LAT,* September 15, 1996; Pitney e-mail, February 17, 2005; Rick L. Nutt, *The Whole Gospel for the Whole World: Sherwood Eddy and the American Protestant Mission* (Macon, Ga.: Mercer University Press, 1997); Nutt e-mail, April 11, 2005; *Methodist Review,* November, 1908, 955.

AMERICA is the only nation: Hans Bendix, "Merry Christmas, America!" *Saturday Review of Literature,* December 1, 1945, 9; J. Hampden Jackson, *Clemenceau and the Third Republic* (New York: Macmillan, 1948), 13–9, 252.

We are not AMUSED: Anonymous (Caroline Holland), *The Notebooks of a Spinster Lady 1878–1903* (London: Cassell, 1919), 269; *The Arena,* July, 1902, 12; *People,* June 22, 1987, 35.

An ARMED society: Robert A. Heinlein, *Beyond This Horizon* (New York: Signet, 1948), 147.

An ARMY travels: MPMFP, 94; ODP, 8–9; Herold, 217; Home Book, 1863.

Be ASHAMED to die: Horace Mann, Baccalaureate Address, Antioch College (Yellow Springs, Ohio). Class of 1859, delivered June 29, 1859, in Mary Mann, *Life of Horace Mann* (Boston: Lee and Shepard, 1865), 575.

ASK not what your country: Oliver Wendell Holmes, May 30, 1884, speech before John Sedgwick, Post No. 4, Grand Army of the Republic, Keene, N.H., *Speeches by Oliver Wendell Holmes* (Boston: Little, Brown, 1900), 2–3; Rees, 331; LeBaron Russell Briggs, *Routine and Ideals* (Boston: Houghton Mifflin, 1904), 220–1; *Ohio,* February 1989, 11; *The Ohio Historical Society: Harding Home,* <http://www.ohio history.org/textonly/places/harding/> (August 1, 2005); *Time,* January 28, 1964, 72; Boller, 73; Arthur M. Schlesinger, Jr., *A Thousand Days* (Boston: Houghton Mifflin, 1965), 4; Thurston Clarke, *Ask Not: The Inauguration of John F. Kennedy and the Speech That Changed America* (New York: Holt, 2004), 76–9.

My center is giving way . . . ATTACK: Michael S. Neiberg, *Foch: Supreme Allied Commander in the Great War* (Dulles, Va.: Potomac, 2003), 25; Winston S. Churchill, *The World Crisis* (New York: Scribner's, 1931), 170; Columbia, 80; B. H. Liddell Hart, *Foch: Man of Orléans* (Boston: Little, Brown, 1932), 108.

Never ATTRIBUTE: Robert A. Heinlein, *The Past Through Tomorrow* (New York: Putnam's, 1967, Ace, 1987), 414.

He has no more BACKBONE: New Yorker, January 3, 2005, 77; Harry Thurston Peck, *Twenty Years of the Republic* (New York: Dodd, Mead, 1907), 642; Alben Barkley, *That Reminds Me* (Garden City, N.Y.: Doubleday, 1954), 258–9; Max Lerner, ed., *The Mind and Faith of Justice Holmes* (Boston: Little, Brown, 1943), xxxii; Frost, 93.

If you've got them by the BALLS: Myra MacPherson, "Colson: Power Mechanic" WP, December 5, 1972; Richard Shenkman and Kurt Reiger, *One-Night Stands with American History: Odd, Amusing and Little-Known Incidents* (New York: Morrow 1980; Quill, 1982), 242; Colson letter, March 17, 1992; Morris Udall with Bob Neuman and Randy Udall, *Too Funny to Be President* (New York: Holt, 1988), 167.

I laughed all the way to the BANK: Joseph Laffan Morse, ed., *The Unicorn Book of 1954* (New York: Unicorn, 1955), 306; *Collier's,* September 3, 1954, 76; Bob Thomas, *Liberace: The True Story* (New York: St. Martin's, 1987), 83; Liberace, *Liberace: An Autobiography* (New York: Putnam's, 1973), 41, 101, 165–6.

Don't let the BASTARDS: Safire 1993, 353; Partridge, 162; "Re: Don't let the bastards quote," *Stumpers,* November 23, 1994 <http://listserv.dom.edu/cgi-bin/wa

.exe?A2=ind9411&L=STUMPERS-L&P=R40730>,   <http://listserv.dom.edu/
cgi-bin/wa.exe?A2=ind9411&L=STUMPERS-L&P=R40954> (August 27, 2005);
Mark Israel, "Illegitimis non carborundum," *The alt.usage.english Home Page*,
<http://alt-usage-english.org/excerpts/fxillegi.html> (August 1, 2005).

***BEAM me up*:** Interview with Mike Okuda, Paramount Studios, August 3, 1992;
Dirks; *Sunday Herald* (Glasgow, Scotland), July 24, 2005.

***Your people, sir, is a great BEAST*:** Clinton Rossiter, *Alexander Hamilton and the
Constitution* (New York: Harcourt, Brace and World, 1964), 162; Morris and Mor-
ris, 574; Theophilus Parsons, Jr., *Memoir of Theophilus Parsons* (Boston: Ticknor &
Fields, 1859; New York: Da Capo Press, 1970), 110; William Ander Smith, "Henry
Adams, Alexander Hamilton, and the American People as a 'Great Beast,'" *The
New England Quarterly,* June 1975, 216–30; Henry Adams, *History of the United
States of America During the First Administration of Thomas Jefferson* (New York:
Scribner's, 1891), 85, 109.

***BECAUSE it's there*:** NYT, March 18, 1923; Tom Holzel and Audrey Salkeld, *First
on Everest: The Mystery of Mallory and Irvine* (New York: Holt, 1986), 295–8; Peter
and Leni Gillman, *The Wildest Dream: The Biography of George Mallory* (Seattle,
Wash.: Mountaineers, 2000), 221–2; Rees, 377–8.

***Where's the BEEF?*:** NYT, February 11, 1984; *Philadelphia Daily News,* February
22, 1984; PI, March 10, 1984; *People,* April 2, 1984, 37; Peter Goldman and Tony
Fuller, *The Quest for the Presidency, 1984* (New York: Bantam, 1985), 151–3.

***I don't want to BELONG*:** Arthur Marx, *Life with Groucho* (New York: Simon &
Schuster, 1954), 45; Hector Arce, in Rees, 383; Groucho Marx, *The Groucho Let-
ters* (New York: Simon & Schuster, 1967), 8; Groucho Marx, *Groucho and Me*
(New York: Bernard Geis, 1959; Dell, 1960), 239–40; Pete Delaney, "Delaney
Guest Book," March 12, 1998, <http://www.pce.net/bflogal/guestbook/old.html>
(August 1, 2005).

***Yogi Berra*:** Roy Blount, Jr., "Yogi," *Sports Illustrated,* April 2, 1984, 85–98; Jack
Rosenthal, "As Yogi Says, . . ." *NYT Magazine,* September 15, 1991, 25–6; Harold
Rosenthal letter, February 7, 1993; Yogi Berra with Tom Horton, *Yogi: It Ain't
Over . . .* (New York: McGraw-Hill, 1989); Phil Pepe, *The Wit and Wisdom of Yogi
Berra* (New York: SMP, 1988); Joe Garagiola, *It's Anybody's Ballgame* (Chicago:
Contemporary, 1988); Safire 1991, 205–8; Dickson, 41–5; Yogi Berra, *The Yogi
Book: "I Really Didn't Say Everything I Said"* (New York: Workman, 1998); Yogi
Berra with David Kaplan, *When You Come to a Fork in the Road, Take It!: Inspiration
and Wisdom from One of Baseball's Greatest Heroes* (New York: Hyperion, 2001).
   "Déjà vu": Berra, *Yogi,* 15; Berra, *The Yogi Book*, 30; Safire 1991, 205–6; CT,

February 22, 1966. *"Always go"*: Berra, *Yogi*, 15–6; Berra, *The Yogi Book*, 73; Safire 1991, 205–6; Clarence Day, *Life with Father* (New York: Washington Square, 1935, 1962), 164. *"Nobody ever goes"*: Berra, *The Yogi Book*, 16; Murray Chass, *NYT*, February 13, 1984; Roy Blount, Jr., *Sports Illustrated*, April 2, 1984, 92; Safire 1991, 206; Pepe, *Wit and Wisdom*, 37; Garagiola, *It's Anybody's Ballgame*, 190; John McNulty, *New Yorker*, February 10, 1943, 13. *"It ain't over"*: Blount, *Sports Illustrated*, op. cit., 94. *"Future isn't"*: Jon Talton, *DDN*, November 11, 1990; *NYT Magazine*, September 15, 1991, 25; Paul Dickson, *The Future File* (New York: Rawson, 1977), vii. *"When you come"*: Berra, *The Yogi Book*, 48; Murray Chass, *NYT*, June 24, 1990. *"I'd like to thank"*: Berra, *The Yogi Book*, 10; Garagiola, *It's Anybody's Ballgame*, 191. *"You can observe"*: *NYT*, October 25, 1963; Berra, *Yogi*, 76; Berra, *The Yogi Book*, 95.

The BEST and the brightest: Elizabeth Webber and Mike Feinsilber, *Grand Allusions: A Lively Guide to Those Expressions, Terms and References You Ought to Know but Might Not* (Washington: Farragut, 1990), 39–40; Rees, 277, 288; Wilson, 89; Charles Dickens, *Little Dorrit* (London: Penguin, 1857, 1985), 806; Rudyard Kipling, "The Files," *Rudyard Kipling's Verse* (New York: Doubleday, Doran, 1940), 351; Maxim Gorki, *Through Russia* (London: Dent, 1921, 1951), 107.

The BIGGER they are: ODP 25–6; MPFMP, 749; Maria Leach, ed., *Funk & Wagnalls Standard Dictionary of Folklore, Mythology and Legend* (New York: Harper & Row, 1949, 1972), 57; *Brooklyn Daily Eagle*, August 11, 1900; Albert Payson Terhune, *American Magazine,* June 1926, 19.

A BILLION here: Byron C. Hulsey, *Everett Dirksen and His Presidents* (Lawrence, Kans.: University Press of Kansas), 2, 151, 281, 289; "A billion here, a billion there, . . ." *The Dirksen Center,* <http://www.dirksencenter.org/print_emd_billionhere.htm> (August 1, 2005); Platt, 155; *NYT,* July 5, 1925, January 10, 1938; *LAT,* January 27, 1938; *Saturday Evening Post,* October 9, 1954, 117; *Chicago Daily Tribune,* July 7, 1956.

From BIRTH to age 18: Michael Freedland, *Sophie: The Sophie Tucker Story* (London: Woburn, 1978), 214; Gee, 116; *Bartlett's*, 705; *Berkshire* [Mass.] *Eagle*, July 9, 1948.

When a dog BITES a man: Frank M. O'Brien, *The Story of the Sun* (New York: George H. Doran, 1918), 241; *New York Press*, September 17, 1999; MDQ, 301; Fadiman, 280; *Boston Daily Globe*, November 18, 1921, December 14, 1922; Robert Hendrickson, *The Literary Life and Other Curiosities* (New York: Viking, 1981), 29; Oliver Goldsmith, "An Elegy on the Death of a Mad Dog" (1766), <http://www.engl.virginia.edu/enec981/dictionary/24goldsmithD2.html> (August 1, 2005).

BLOOD and iron: Louis L. Snyder, *The Blood and Iron Chancellor* (Princeton, N.J.: Van Nostrand, 1967), 126–7; Emil Ludwig, Edan and Cedar Paul, trans., *Bismarck: The Story of a Fighter* (Boston: Little, Brown, 1927), 206–7; A. J. P. Taylor, *Bismarck: The Man and the Statesman* (London: Hamish Hamilton, 1955), 56; Werner Richter and Brian Battershaw, trans., *Bismarck* (New York: Putnam's, 1964), 88; Frederic B. M. Hollyday, ed., *Bismarck* (Englewood Cliffs, N.J.: Prentice-Hall, 1970), 16–7; Charlotte Sempell, *Otto von Bismarck* (New York: Twayne, 1972), 68–9; "Bismarck Recommends the Values of Blood and Iron," September 29, 1862, in Houston Peterson, ed., *A Treasury of the World's Great Speeches* (New York: Simon & Schuster, 1965), 527–9; Latham, 197; Burnam 1975, 26; MPMFP, 2449.

BLOOD, sweat, and tears: Martin Gilbert, *Churchill: A Life* (New York: Holt, 1991), 646; Winston S. Churchill, ed., *Never Give In!: The Best of Winston Churchill's Speeches* (New York: Hyperion, 2003), 204–6; Richard Henry Crum, "Blood, Sweat and Tears," *The Classical Journal* 42 (1947) 299–300; Wolfgang Mieder and George B. Bryan, eds. *The Proverbial Winston S. Churchill: An Index to Proverbs in the Works of Sir Winston Churchill* (Westport, Conn.: Greenwood Press, 1995), 62–6; John Donne, "An Anatomy of the World," *The Complete Poetry of John Donne* (New York: New York University Press, 1968), 284; Ernest Hartley Coledridge, ed., *The Works of Lord Byron,* Vol. 5, (New York: Scribner's, 1901), "The Age of Bronze," 571; Milton Bronner, "John Davidson: Poet of Anarchy," *Forum,* September 1910, 305; Lady Tegart, "In the Holy Land," *The Living Age,* May 1939, 250; e-mail from Richard Langworth, July 6, 2005; Winston Spencer Churchill, "Officers and Gentlemen," *Saturday Evening Post,* December 29, 1900, 3; Winston Churchill, *The Unknown War: The Eastern Front* (New York: Scribner's, 1931), 1; Manfred Weidhorn, "Churchill the Phrase Forger," *Quarterly Journal of Speech,* 58 (1972), 169–71, 174; Winston Churchill, "Hope in Spain," February 23, 1939, in Winston S. Churchill, *Step by Step: 1936–1939* (New York: Putnam's, 1939), 294.

A man is known by the BOOKS: June, 1830 entry in Edward Waldo Emerson, ed., *Journals of Ralph Waldo Emerson* (Boston: Houghton Mifflin, 1909), 300; Anderson, 44; William Law, *Christian Perfection, a Contemporary Version* by Marvin D. Hinten (Wheaton, Ill.: Tyndale House, 1986), 75; William Law, *A Practical Treatise upon Christian Perfection* (London: William and John Innys, 1726; London: J. J. Trebeck, 1902), 269–70; Walsh, 180; MPMFP, 386–7; ODP, 55–6.

A man who does not read good BOOKS: *New York Post,* April 6, 1990; *RQ,* summer, 1978, 340; Anderson, 154.

He was BORN on third base: *NYT,* July 20, 1988; *Newsweek,* July 4, 1994, 38; *CT,* December 14, 1986; *Ironwood* (Mich.) *Daily Globe,* September 17, 1935.

When I was a BOY of fourteen: Reader's Digest, September 1937, 22; Platt, xiv, 375; Anderson, 32.

The Pottery Barn rule: You BREAK it: Bob Woodward, *Plan of Attack* (New York: Simon & Schuster, 2004), 150; *WP,* April 28, 2004; *Fresh Air,* National Public Radio, June 3, 2004; *Weekend Edition,* National Public Radio, September 7, 2002; *NYT,* February 12, 2003; William Safire, *NYT Magazine,* October 17, 2004, 24.

Nobody ever went BROKE: Seldes 1985, 283; *CT,* September 19, 1926.

The BUCK stops here: "'The Buck Stops Here' Desk Sign," information sheet, Harry S. Truman Library, Independence, Missouri, February 1977; Robert H. Ferrell, *Truman: A Centenary Remembrance* (New York: Viking, 1984), 138; David McCullough, *Truman* (New York: Simon & Schuster, 1992), 481; Wolfgang Mieder and George B. Bryan, *The Proverbial Harry S. Truman: An Index to Proverbs in the Works of Harry S. Truman* (New York: Peter Lang, 1997), 62–4; Charles Earle Funk, *2107 Curious Word Origins, Sayings and Expressions* (New York: Galahad, 1993), 117–8; *Statesville* (North Carolina) *Daily Record,* June 15, 1946.

We shape our BUILDINGS: Dennis Bardens, *Churchill in Parliament* (Cranbury, N.J.: A. S. Barnes, 1969), 285–6; "A Sense of Crowd and Urgency," October 28, 1943, in Robert Rhodes James, ed., *Winston S. Churchill: His Complete Speeches,* Vol. 7 (New York: Chelsea / Bowker, 1974), 6869; HC Deb 28, October 1943, c403.

The BUSINESS of America: NYT, January 18, 1925; Claude M. Fuess, *Calvin Coolidge: The Man from Vermont* (Hamden, Conn.: Archon Books, 1939, 1965), 358.

The BUTLER did it: Peter Macinnis, "A descant on descants," 2001, <http://members.ozemail.com.au/~macinnis/descants.htm> (August 1, 2005); Cecil Adams, "In whodunits, it's 'the butler did it.' Who did it first?" *The Straight Dope,* September 26, 2003, <http://www.straightdope.com/columns/030926> (August 1, 2005); Anderson, 31; Rees, 24–5; Damon Runyon, "What No Butler?" *Collier's,* August 5, 1933, 7–9, 30.

How can you BUY or sell the sky: Joseph Campbell, with Bill Moyers, *The Power of Myth* (New York: Doubleday, 1988), 34–5; *Weekend Edition,* National Public Radio, June 8, 1991; *Newsweek,* May 4, 1992, 68.

Let them eat CAKE: Jean-Jacques Rousseau, *Confessions,* Book 6, 254; Anderson, 94; Bergen Evans, *The Spoor of Spooks* (New York: Knopf, 1954), 63; Home Book, 1571; MPMFP, 274–5; Alphonse Karr, *Les Guepes* (1843), in Burnam 1975, 139; Tuleja 1982, 150; Louis XVIII, *Relation d'un Voyage a Bruxelles et a Coblentz en*

1791 (Paris, 1823), in ODQ, 512; *The Times* (London, England), April 29, 1959, April 30, 1959.

First they CAME for the communists: Harold Marcuse, "Martin Niemoller's famous quotation: 'First they came for the Communists . . .' " *Niemoller Quotation Page,* November 4, 2004, <http://www.history.ucsb.edu/faculty/marchuse/niem .htm> (December 13, 2004); Ruth Zerner, "Martin Niemoller, Activist As Bystander, the Oft-quoted Reflection," in Marvin Pery and Frederick Schweitzer, ed., *Jewish-Christian Encounters over the Centuries* (New York: Peter Lang, 1994), 327–40; Dennis B. Roddy, *Pittsburgh Post-Gazette,* August 2, 1998; Franklin H. Littell, "First They Came for the Jews," *Christian Ethics Today,* 3 (February 1997), 29.

You CAMPAIGN in poetry: NYT, February 16, 1985; Fred Barnes, "Meet Mario the Moderate," *The New Republic,* April 8, 1985, 18; Jeff Greenfield, ABC News, November 5, 1996, Cable News Network, August 17, 2000; Mark Shields quoting Jim Castelli, *Capital Gang,* Cable News Network, October 28, 2000; *West Wing,* Episode No. 519, NBC TV, April 21, 2004; "Beverley Nichols, Excerpts & Quotes," *Timber Press,* <http://www.timberpress.com/beverleynichols/excerpts.cfm> (August 1, 2005).

It is better to light a CANDLE: William Miller, *Fishbait: The Memoirs of the Congressional Doorkeeper* (Englewood Cliffs, N.J.: Prentice-Hall, 1977), 278–9; Platt, 89; Evans, 87; Morris and Morris, 57–8; Maggio, 450; Home Book, 2299g; Rosten, 111; James Keller, *One Moment Please!* (Garden City, N.Y.: Doubleday, 1950), xii; James Keller, *To Light a Candle: The Autobiography of Fr. James Keller, Founder of the Christophers* (Garden City, N.Y.: Doubleday, 1963), 114; *Frederick* (Maryland) *Post,* July 8, 1940; Evan Esar, *The Humor of Humor* (New York: Bramhall, 1952), 253; Rees, 520; *DDN,* February 27, 2005.

CAN'T we all just get along: NYT, May 2, 1992.

CHANCE favors: Platt, 38; Bartlett's, 533; Peterson, *A Treasury of the World's Great Speeches,* op. cit., 473.

The CHATTERING classes: *Oxford English Dictionary Online,* Draft Addition March 2002; "Who coined the expression 'chattering classes'?" *Guardian Unlimited Notes and Queries,* <http://www.guardian.co.uk/notesandqueries/query/0,5753, -21330,00.html> (August 1, 2005); *The Guardian,* November 25, 1989; *The Chautauquan,* December 1890, 361.

Too much CHECKING on the facts: WSJ, January 31, 1986.

He can't walk and CHEW GUM: *Federal News Service,* January 29, 2004; *New York Daily News,* October 30, 2004; Richard Reeves, *A Ford, Not a Lincoln* (New

York: Harcourt, Brace Jovanovich, 1975), 25; Samuel Shaffer, *On and Off the Floor: Thirty Years as a Correspondent on Capitol Hill* (New York: Newsweek, 1980), 265.

A *CHICKEN in every pot:* Woods, 104–5; Bailey, 376; Safire, SNPD, 117; Seldes 1960, 142; Latham, 125.

CHILDREN learn what they live: "Children Learn What They Live," Dorothy Law Nolte (1954), <http://www.kidscountprogram.org/nolte.html> (August 1, 2005); The Caerwent Community On-line Magazine, Poem of the Month, October 2002, <http://www.caerwentcom.com/poem21.htm> (August 1, 2005); "Children Learn What They Live," Dorothy Law Nolte, <http://www.empowermentresources .com/info2/childrenlearn.html> (August 1, 2005); Anderson, 79–80; *Reader's Digest,* October 1972, 225; Jack Canfield and Mark Victor Hansen, *Chicken Soup for the Soul: 101 Stories to Open the Heart and Rekindle the Spirit* (Deerfield, Fla.: Health Communications, 1993), 84–5; Dorothy Nolte and Rachel Harris, *Children Learn What They Live: Parenting to Inspire Values* (New York: Workman, 1998), <http://www.workman.com/catalog/pagemaker.cgi?0761109196>, (August 24, 2005).

If you bungle raising your CHILDREN: Deane and David Heller, *Jacqueline Kennedy: The Warmly Human Life Story of the Woman All Americans Have Taken to Their Hearts* (Derby, Conn.: Monarch, 1961), 118; Hillary Rodham Clinton, *It Takes a Village* (Simon & Schuster, 1996), 17–8; *Newsweek,* April 8, 1996, 35.

Winston Churchill: "Quotations from Sir Winston Churchill," *The Speech Site,* <http://www.thespeechsite.com/index-eng.htm> (August 31, 2005); "Speeches and Quotes," *The Churchill Centre,* <http://www.winstonchurchill.org/i4a/pages/ index.cfm?pageid=388>, (August 31, 2005); On *Bartlett's:* Winston S. Churchill, *A Roving Commission* (New York: Scribner's, 1930, 1949), 116. *"There, but for":* Richard Langworth e-mail, June 11, 2005; Ringo, 194–5, 279; Rees, 167; *Mankiewicz:* Kael, *The Citizen Kane Book,* op. cit., 33; Bradford: Stimpson 1946, 200. On Attlee: Ringo, 183; Harris, 164; SNPD, 700; Samuel Gallu, *"Give 'em Hell, Harry: Reminiscences* (New York: Viking, 1975), 23; Langworth e-mail, June 11, 2005; Elizabeth Safly e-mail, July 6, 2005. *"And you, madam":* Harris, 173; Langworth e-mail, June 19, 2005; videotape of "It's a Gift," (Universal, 1934), "Memorable Quotes from 'It's a Gift,'" *IMDb* <http://www.imdb.com/title/ tt0025318/quotes>, (May 11, 2005); *"If you were my husband":* Consuelo Vanderbilt Balsan, *The Glitter and the Gold* (New York: Harper and Brothers, 1952), 204–5; Platt, 242; *WP,* April 27, 1971; *Dean:* Cerf, 305; *Smith:* Martin Gilbert, *In Search of Churchill* (New York: Wiley, 1994), 232; Lloyd George: Harris, 131. *"In wartime":* Winston S. Churchill, *Closing the Ring* (Boston: Houghton Mifflin, 1951), 383, 387; Anthony Cave Brown, *Bodyguard of Lies* (New York: Harper & Row, 1975), 389; *The Teheran, Yalta and Potsdam Conferences* (Moscow: Progress

Publishers, 1969), 40. *"The greatest cross"*: Gilbert, *In Search of Churchill,* op. cit., 233; Rees, 167; *"Rum, sodomy"*: Gilbert, ibid., 232. *"Golf is"*: Langworth e-mail, August 6, 2005; *"We shall fight"*: Churchill, *Never Give In!,* op. cit., 218; Manfred Weidhorn, "Churchill the Phrase Forger," *Quarterly Journal of Speech,* 58 (1972) 165; Churchill, *The World Crisis,* op. cit., 803. Winston S. Churchill, *Great Contemporaries* (New York: Putnam's, 1937), 185; Boswell, Vol. 2, 339. *"Today we may say"*: Churchill, *Never Give In!,* op. cit., 305; *"This was their finest hour"*: Churchill, *Never Give In!,* op. cit., 219. *"Never in the field"*: Churchill, *Never Give In!,* op. cit. 237; Mieder and Bryan, *The Proverbial Winston S. Churchill,* op. cit., 74–5; Rees, 164. *"In war, resolution"*: Edward Marsh, *A Number of People: A Book of Reminiscences* (New York: Harper and Brothers, 1939), 152.

Close, but no CIGAR: *Random House Dictionary of American Slang,* Vol. 1, 422; Anderson, 21; Shapiro, 86–7; William Safire, *NYT Magazine,* April 6, 1980, 10.

Sometimes a CIGAR is just a cigar: Alan C. Elms, "Apocryphal Freud: Sigmund Freud's Most Famous 'Quotations' and Their Actual Sources," Jerome A. Winer and James William Anderson, eds., *Sigmund Freud and His Impact on the Modern World: The Annual of Psychoanalysis, Vol.* 29 (Hillsdale, N.J.: Analytic Press, 2001), 83–104. "Frequently Asked Questions," *Freud Museum,* <http://www.freud.org.uk/fmfaq.htm> (July 29, 2005); Peter Gay, *Freud: A Life for Our Time* (New York: Norton, 1988), 169–70; Elisabeth Young-Bruehl, *Anna Freud* (New York: Summit, 1988); "Freud Cigar Quote," *History and Theory of Psychology,* <http://hv.greenspun.com/bboard/q-and-a-fetch-msg.tcl?msg_id=00BGBz> (July 29, 2005); interview with Alan Elms, December 14, 1991; Alan Elms e-mail, May 18, 2000, October 8, 2005; Elms, "Apocryphal Freud," op. cit., 101; Ivan Turgenev, *Fathers and Sons,* George Reavy, trans., (Holicong, Pa.: Wildside, 1862, 2003), 71.

What this country needs is a good five-cent CIGAR: Platt, 44; Thomas R. Marshall, *Recollections of Thomas R. Marshall, Vice-President and Hoosier Philosopher: A Hoosier Salad* (Indianapolis: Bobbs-Merrill, 1925), 245; Charles M. Thomas, *Thomas Riley Marshall: Hoosier Statesman* (Oxford, Ohio: Mississippi Valley, 1939), 173–5, 265; *Saturday Evening Post,* October 16, 1875; Fred C. Kelly, *The Life and Times of Kin Hubbard, Creator of Abe Martin* (New York: Farrar, Straus and Young, 1952), 12.

Civil Rights: *"We Shall Overcome"*: Robert E. Smith, " 'We Shall Overcome': Where the Civil Rights Anthem Came From," *Southern Courier,* January 22, 1966; Miller, *Voice of Deliverance,* op. cit., 188–9; Noah Adams, "Tracing the History of the Song 'We Shall Overcome,' " *All Things Considered,* National Public Radio, January 15, 1999; Mike Hudson, "Song of History, Song of Freedom," *Roanoke Times,* January 14, 2001; Larry Rubin e-mail, April 3, 2005. *"Tell it"*: interview with Robert E. Smith, October 24, 1977; SNPD, 788–9. *"I have a dream"*: Drew D. Hansen, *The Dream: Martin Luther King, Jr., and the Speech That Inspired a Nation*

(New York: Ecco / HarperCollins, 2003), 109–20. *"Black is beautiful"*: Anderson, 101–2. *"Black power"*: *Current Biography 1970*, 66; Powers, *The War at Home*, op. cit., 152–3; Clayborne Carson, *In Struggle: SNCC and the Black Awakening of the 1960s* (Cambridge, Mass.: Harvard, 1981), 209; interview with Steve Schwerner, January 22, 1995; Richard Wright, *Black Power: A Record of Reaction in a Land of Pathos* (New York: Harper & Row, 1954); *NYT*, May 30, 1966 *"I say violence"*: "H. Rap Brown, black militant," *The History Channel*, <http://www.historychannel.com/speeches/archive/speech_397.html> (February 10, 2005); Platt, 355; Jerome C. Weeks letter to *New York Review of Books*, September 23, 1982, 67.

CLOSE your eyes: Partridge, 50–1; Rees, 295; Leonard Lyons, *WP*, May 18, 1943; Nigel Dempster and Peter Evans, *Behind Palace Doors* (London: Orion, 1993), 36.

Let's get out of these wet CLOTHES: Howard Teichmann, *Smart Aleck* (New York: Morrow, 1976), 107; Cerf, 132; Earl Wilson, *Times-Recorder* (Zanesville, Ohio), September 3, 1947; Nathaniel Benchley, *Robert Benchley* (New York: McGraw-Hill, 1955), 146; American Film Institute, No. 217; *LAT*, August 21, 1985; videotape of *Every Day's a Holiday* (Paramount, 1937).

The COLDEST winter: Anderson, 31; *RQ*, winter 1988, 148–9; *Bancroftiana*, November 1981, 10.

Why don't you COME up: Videotape of *She Done Him Wrong* (Paramount, 1933) and of *I'm No Angel* (Paramount, 1933); Dirks; George Eels and Stanley Musgrove, *Mae West: A Biography* (New York: Morrow, 1982), 112; Marybeth Hamilton, *When I'm Bad I'm Better: Mae West, Sex, and American Entertainment* (New York: Harper-Collins, 1995), 131, 267; Jill Watts, *Mae West: An Icon in Black and White* (New York: Oxford, 2001), 109, 157–8, 281, 334; Lemuel Fowler, "He May Be Your Man / But He Comes To See Me Sometimes," © Ted Browne Music Co., 1922; June Sochen, *Mae West: She Who Laughs, Lasts* (Arlington Height Ill.: Harlan Davidson, 1992), 71–2.

The world is a COMEDY: W. S. Lewis and A. Dayle Wallace, eds., *Horace Walpole's Correspondence with the Countess of Upper Ossory* (New Haven, Conn.: Yale, 1965), 315; *The Works of Horatio Walpole, Earl of Oxford*, Vol. 4, (London, 1798), 369.

COMFORT the afflicted: "Inherit the Wind," *Destitute Gulch*, <http://www.destgulch.com/movies/inherit/>, (July 29, 2005); Mencken, 852; Finley Peter Dunne, *Observations by Mr. Dooley* (New York: Harper & Brothers, 1906), 240.

Never COMPLAIN, never explain: Robert Lacey, *Ford: The Men and the Machine* (Boston: Little, Brown, 1986), 590–1; John Morley, *The Life of William Ewart Gladstone* (New York: Macmillan, 1903; St. Clair Shores, Mich.: Scholarly Press, 1972), 123; Harold Nicolson, *The War Years, 1939–1945: Volume II of Diaries and Letters* (New York: Atheneum, 1967), 307; Rees, 210; Partridge, 214.

Nothing CONCENTRATES the mind: Boswell, Vol. 3, 167.

CONSISTENCY is the hobgoblin: Wilson, 113; Emerson, 41.

CONTEMPT prior to investigation: Michael StGeorge, "The Survival of a Fitting Quotation," Edition 1.0, 2005: <http://www.geocities.com/fitquotation/> (July 29, 2005).

As long as I COUNT the votes: Albert Bigelow Paine, *Thomas Nast: His Period and His Pictures* (New York: Chelsea House, 1904, 1980), 164, 197; Leo Hershkowitz, *Tweed's New York: Another Look* (Garden City, N.Y.: Anchor/Doubleday, 1978), xviii; Kenneth D. Ackerman, *Boss Tweed: The Rise and Fall of the Corrupt Pol Who Conceived the Soul of Modern New York* (New York: Carroll & Graf, 2005), 7–8, 371.

My COUNTRY, right or wrong: Alexander Slidell Mackenzie, *Life of Stephen Decatur* (Boston: Charles C. Little and James Brown, 1846), 295; Platt, 70.

One man with COURAGE: Boller and George, 53–4; *NYT,* October 25, 1987; Platt, 172; Kennedy, 6; James Parton, *Life of Andrew Jackson* (New York: Mason Brothers, 1860); *The International Review,* December 1881, 517; Frost, 46; "Veto Message," July 10, 1832 in James D. Richardson, ed., *A Compilation of the Messages and Papers of the Presidents,* Vol. 2 (Washington, D.C.: Bureau of National Literature and Art, 1908), 576–91; ODQ, 458; MDQ, 234; Bailey, 92; Hoyt's, 319; Home Book, 1236; Platt, 217; MPMFP, 1505; Baker, 166.

Two o'clock in the morning COURAGE: Herold, 220; MPMFP, 436; Henry David Thoreau, *Walden* (New York: Norton, 1854, 1966), 80; Paul Theroux, *Mosquito Coast* (Boston: Houghton Mifflin, 1982), 10, 97; Geoffrey C. Ward with Ric Burns and Ken Burns, *The Civil War: An Illustrated History* (New York: Knopf, 1990), 271.

There is no limit . . . gets the CREDIT: *NYT,* April 27, 1989; Safire, 2001, 63–5; MDQ, 510; *The Friend,* March 21, 1903, 284; C. E. Montague, *Disenchantment* (London: Chatto and Windus, 1922), 213.

Organized CRIME is bigger: *NYT,* January 16, 1983; Robert Lacey, *Little Man: Meyer Lansky and the Gangster Life* (Boston: Little, Brown, 1991), 284–5, 315, 423; American Film Institute, No. 151.

When I hear the word CULTURE: Seldes 1985, 214; Rees, 265; *NYT,* April 12, 1981; ODQ, 434; *NYT,* September 17, 1987.

CUT to the chase: Mark Israel, "cut to the chase," *The alt.usage.english Home Page,* <http://alt-usage-english.org/excerpts/fxcuttot.html> (July 30, 2005); Etymologies and Word Origins, <http://www.wordorigins.org/wordorc.htm> (July 30, 2005); J. P. McEvoy, *Hollywood Girl* (New York: Grosset & Dunlap, 1929) 104–6; *Newsweek,* August 13, 1979, 73; *NYT,* November 6, 1981; November 26, 1981; *Toronto Star,* January 31, 1988; *People,* March 7, 1988, 10; *WP,* June 10, 1988; Safire 1991, 293–4.

No matter how CYNICAL: Jane Wagner, *The Search for Signs of Intelligent Life in the Universe* (New York: HarperPerennial, 1987), 26.

If I can't DANCE: Maggio, 450; Alix Kates Shulman, "Dances with Feminists," *Women's Review of Books,* December 1991, 13, Berkeley Digital Library SunSITE, <http://sunsite.berkeley.edu/Goldman/Features/dances_shulman.html> (July 30, 2005).

There's a DANCE: "archy and mehitabel," *donmarquis.com,* <http://www.donmar quis.com/archy/> (June 10, 2005); Don Marquis, *archy and mehitabel* (Garden City, N.Y.: Doubleday; 1927, Dolphin/Doubleday, 1960), 22.

It was a DARK and stormy night: New Yorker, January 12, 2004, 85; Edward Bulwer-Lytton, *Paul Clifford* (Chicago: Belford, Clarke, 1830, 1840, 1848), 1.

Murder your DARLINGS: Sir Arthur Quiller-Couch, *The Art of Writing* (New York: Putnam's, 1916; Capricorn, 1961), 281.

In the long run, we are all DEAD: John Maynard Keynes, *A Tract on Monetary Reform* (London: Macmillan, 1924), 80.

A single DEATH is a tragedy: John LeCarré, *The Spy Who Came in from the Cold* (London: Gollancz, 1963; New York: Dell, 1965), 124; Anne Fremantle, "Unwritten Pages at the End of the Diary," *NYT Book Review,* September 28, 1958; "Bogus Stalin: 'One death a tragedy, million deaths a statistic,'" *American Dialect Society,* May 3, 2004, <http://listserv.linguistlist.org/cgi-bin/wa?A2=ind0405A&L=ADS-L&P =R2815&I=-3> (August 1, 2005); Sue G. Hall, *Bobby Kennedy Off-Guard* (New York: Grosset & Dunlap, 1968), 30.

The reports of my DEATH: interviews with Robert Hirst, December 16, 1991, January 29, 1992; Hirst letter, January 30, 1992; Frank Marshall White, "Mark Twain as a Newspaper Reporter," *Outlook,* December 24, 1910, 966–7; *New York Journal,* June 2, 1897; Twain typescript, April 3, 1906, in Mark Twain papers, The Mark Twain Project, University of California, Berkeley; revision, undated, ibid.; Mark Twain, "Chapters from My Autobiography," *North American Review,* September 21, 1906, 460.

No one on his DEATHBED: Paul Tsongas, *Heading Home* (New York: Knopf, 184), 160; interview with Arnold Zack, October 22, 2003; Harold Kushner, *When*

All You've Ever Wanted Isn't Enough (New York: Summit / Simon & Schuster, 1986), 160–1; Kushner e-mail, April 27, 2005; *Orange County Register* (California), September 9, 1996.

No good DEED: Titelman, 244; Safire, 1999, 80; Brendan Gill, *Here at the New Yorker* (New York: Random House, 1975; Berkeley, 1976), 305, 315.

DEMOCRACY is the worst form of government: Platt, 83; "Parliament Bill," November 11, 1947, in Robert Rhodes James, ed., *Winston S. Churchill: His Complete Speeches*, Vol. 7, op. cit., 7566.

We had to DESTROY the village: Peter Arnett, *Live from the Battlefield* (New York, Simon & Schuster, 1994), 255; *NYT*, February 8, 1968; Peter Braestrup, *Big Story: How the American Press and Television Reported and Interpreted the Crisis of Tet 1968 in Vietnam and Washington* (Boulder, Colo.: Westview Press, 1977), 253–60; B. G. Burkett and Glenna Whitley, *Stolen Valor* (Dallas: Verity Press, 1998), 120–1, 631; Mona Charen, *Useful Idiots: How Liberals Got It Wrong in the Cold War and Still Blame America First* (Washington, D.C.: Regnery, 2003), 33, 267; James Reston, *NYT*, February 7, 1968.

The DEVIL is in the details: Franz Schulze, *Mies van der Rohe: A Critical Biography* (Chicago: University of Chicago, 1985), 281; interview with Franz Schulze, April 21, 1992; Safire, SNPD, 180–1; Safire 1993, 322; Safire 1997, 286–8; E. H. Gombrich, *Aby Warburg: An Intellectual Biography* (London: The Warburg Institute, University of London, 1970), 13–14; Erwin Panofsky, *Meaning in the Visual Arts* (Chicago: University of Chicago, 1955), v; William S. Hecksher, *Rembrandt's Anatomy of Dr. Nicholas Tulp: An Iconological Study* (New York: Washington Square / New York University, 1958), 112; ODP, 71; Sam Hobbs, "God is in the Details," April 2, 2002, FAQ excerpt, *alt.quotations*, <http://groups.google.com/group/alt.quotations/browse_thread/thread/167c7ac92d5bb591/09dfd8605e858e0 2?lnk=st&q=%22devil+is+in+the+details&rnum=1&hl=en#09dfd8605e858e02> (August 1, 2005); "Re: God is in the details," *American Dialect Society*, January 25, 2005, <http://listserv.linguistlist.org/cgi-bin/wa?A2=ind0501D&L=ADS-L&P=R6967&I=0> (August 1, 2005); *The Wordsworth Dictionary of Proverbs*, G. L. Apperson, ed. (Hertfordshire: Wordsworth, 1993), 146; Barbara Wallraff, *Your Own Words* (New York: Counterpoint / Perseus 2004), 174–5; Bartlett's, 851.

The greatest trick the DEVIL: American Film Institute, No. 373; Charles Baudelaire, "The Generous Gambler," in *The Parisian Prowler*, Edward K. Kaplan, trans. (Athens, Ga.: University of Georgia, 1997), 74.

Better to DIE on our feet: *NYT*, June 20, 1941; Seldes 1960, xlviii; Seldes 1985, 25, 199; Dolores Ibarurri, *They Shall Not Pass: The Autobiography of La Pasionaria*

(New York: International, 1966), John Gunther, *Inside Latin America* (New York: Harper & Brothers, 1941), 63; Leigh White, *The Long Balkan Night* (New York: Scribner's, 1944), 390; Frank McLynn, *Villa and Zapata: A History of the Mexican Revolution* (New York: Carroll & Graf, 2001), 90; Mieder, 111; *Friends Intelligencer,* September 29, 1866, 28.

I DISAPPROVE of what you say: John Morley, ed., *The Works of Voltaire,* Vol. 37, (London: E. R. DuMont, 1901), 162; S. G. Tallentyre (Evelyn Beatrice Hall), *The Friends of Voltaire* (London: John Murray, 1906), 199; *Reader's Digest,* June 1934, 50; *NYT Book Review,* September 1, 1935, 19.

A house DIVIDED: Wolfgang Mieder, *"A House Divided": From Biblical Proverb to Lincoln and Beyond* (Burlington, Vt.: Proverbium, 1998), 1, 5, 7–10, 12–3, 16, 18, 20, 22, 24, 60–4.

Those who can, DO: George Bernard Shaw, *Man and Superman* (London: Constable, 1931), 213; Hubbard 1911, 64; Arthur Bloch, *Murphy's Law* (Los Angeles: Price / Stern / Sloan, 1979), 61.

It's not that he DOES it well: TV Guide, November 8, 1986, 19; Boswell, Vol. 1, 462.

If you want a friend in Washington, get a DOG: Elizabeth Safly e-mail, July 5, 2005; Samuel Gallu, *"Give 'em Hell, Harry",* op. cit., 8; *NYT,* March 10, 1989; Editors of *The New Republic, Bushisms* (New York: Workman, 1992), 12.

Any man who hates DOGS: Rosten, 113–7; H. Allen Smith, *Lost in the Horse Latitudes* (Garden City, N.Y.: Doubleday, Doran, 1944), 191–2; *LAT,* March 30, 1986; *Los Angeles Evening Herald and Express,* February 17, 1939; *Time,* February 27, 1939; November 1937, 663.

The better I get to know men . . . loving DOGS: Time, December 8, 1967, 31; MPMFP, 610; ODQ, 653, 796; Rees, 458; *(Searching for) Solid Ground,* Chapter 33, *Words on the Web,* <http://www.wordsontheweb.com/Stories/SFSG/ch33.html> (April 12, 2005).

He marches to a different DRUMMER: Thoreau, *Walden,* op. cit., 215–6; *The Literary World,* August 28, 1880, 292.

There's more old DRUNKARDS: Carl Van Doren, *Benjamin Franklin* (New York: Viking, 1938), 110; MPFMP, 596–7; Willie Nelson, "I Gotta Get Drunk," words and music by Willie Nelson, © 1983, Tree Publishing.

The DUSTBIN of history: Anderson, 24; Rees, 109, 543; Safire 1997, 61–2; Leon Trotsky, *The Russian Revolution,* Max Eastman, trans., F. W. Dupee, ed. (Garden

City, N.Y.: Anchor / Doubleday, 1932, 1959), 446; Keith Gessen, "Exiles on Main Street: Soviet Dissidents in the U.S. of A.," *Feed* magazine, January 2000; "Johnson's Russia List No. 4102," February 12, 2000, <http://www.edi.org/russia/johnson/4102.html> (April 15, 2005); Augustine Birrell, "Carlyle," *Obiter Dicta* (London, 1885), <http://www.gutenberg.org/dirs/etext05/8obit10.txt> (August 29, 2005).

DUTY, then, is the sublimest word: Platt, 93; Charles A. Graves, "The Forged Letter of General Robert E. Lee," paper read before the Virginia State Bar Association, August 1914 (Richmond, Va.: Richmond Press, 1915).

DYING is easy: Time, September 27, 1982, 71, January 30, 1984, 79; *NYT,* November 14, 1982; Clifton Fadiman, ed., *Little, Brown Book of Anecdotes* (Boston: Little, Brown, 1985), 260; Don Widener, *Lemmon: A Biography* (New York: Macmillan, 1975), 184; "Who Said 'Dying Is Easy, Comedy Is Hard'?" *Quotations Page Forums,* August 9, 2005, <http://www.quotationspage.com/forum/viewtopic.php?t=223&sid=a886e3b8710001eaf7fd651e7a47df74> (August 2, 2005).

DYING is no big deal: NYT, January 21, 1982; *Forbes,* September 21, 1998, 296; Mieder, 111; Elias Canetti, *The Human Province* (New York: Seabury Press, 1978), 14; Boswell, Vol. 2, 106–7.

You are what you EAT: Eugene Kamenka, *The Philosophy of Ludwig Feuerbach* (New York: Praeger, 1969), ODP, 87; "Re: 'You Are What You Eat,'" *The Phrase Finder,* January 10, 2002, <http://www.phrases.org.uk/bulletin_board/12/messages/832.html> (December 1, 2004).

An EDITOR is one: Harris, 238; Hubbard 1923, 21; Wilde, 857.

Albert Einstein: As indicated in the text, Alice Calaprice's *The New Quotable Einstein* (Princeton: Princeton University, 2005) is by far the best resource for quotations by Einstein. Most of those cited in this section, and misquotations as well, can be found therein. Citations to Calaprice and other sources are as follows:
"An hour": Jamie Sayen, *Einstein in America* (New York: Crown, 1985), 130; Calaprice, 247. *"Many things":* Seldes 1985, 119. *"God does not":* Max Born, *The Born-Einstein Letters,* Irene Born, trans. (New York: Walker, 1971), 91; Banesh Hoffman, *Albert Einstein, Creator and Rebel* (New York: Viking, 1972), 193; Phillip Frank, *Einstein: His Life and Times,* George Rosen, trans. (New York: Knopf, 1947, 1953), 208, 285; Calaprice, 231, 237. *"Science without religion":* Albert Einstein, *Out of My Later Years* (Secaucus, N.J.: Citadel, 1950, 1956, 1974), 26; Calaprice, 250. *"The unleashed power":* Calaprice 175, 292; Moynihan: "This Week with David Brinkley," ABC-TV, October 20, 1991. *"I do not know":* Alfred Werner interview with Albert Einstein, *Liberal Judaism,* 16 (April–May 1949), 12, in Calaprice,

173. *"I have no special talents"*: Calaprice, 14; *U.S. News & World Report,* December 9, 2002, 63. *"Imagination"*: George Sylvester Viereck, "What Life Means to Einstein," *Saturday Evening Post,* October 26, 1929, 117.

Einstein misattributions: Calaprice, 293–6. Einstein on education: Albert Einstein, *Out of My Later Years* (New York: Philosophical Library, 1950), 36. *"Only twelve people"*: Phillip Frank, *Einstein: His Life and Times,* op. cit., 179; Calaprice, 335–7. *"There is no hitching post"*: Seldes 1985, 119; *NYT,* December 12, 1930. *"If only I had known"*: Gerald Leach, "Einstein's Legacy," *New Statesman,* April 16, 1965; *NYT,* July 2, 1979; Einstein letter to *Reporter,* November 18, 1954, 8; Calaprice, 17. *"Heaven is like"*: Anderson, 55. *"If you are out"*: Albert Einstein, *Relativity: The Special and General Theory,* Robert W. Lawson, trans. (New York: Crown, 1931), vi. *"We use only"*: Calaprice, 290.

Einstein misquotations: Calaprice, 293–6. Interview with Alice Calaprice, June 11, 2005.

ELEMENTARY, my dear Watson: "The Crooked Man," in Sir Arthur Conan Doyle, *The Memoirs of Sherlock Holmes* (London: John Murray, 1893, 1974), 147; *NYT,* October 19, 1929; American Film Institute, No. 2; Daniel Stashower, *Teller of Tales: the Life of Arthur Conan Doyle* (New York: Holt, 1999), 214.

ELEVEN O'CLOCK Sunday morning: Taylor Branch, *Pillar of Fire: America in the King Years* (New York: Simon & Schuster, 1998), 24; Billy Graham, "Why Don't Our Churches Practice the Brotherhood They Preach?" *Reader's Digest,* August 1960, 53; *The Daily Courier* (Connellsville, Pa.), April 28, 1953.

Ralph Waldo Emerson: *"I hate quotations"*: Edward Waldo Emerson and Waldo Emerson Forbes, *Journals of Ralph Waldo Emerson,* Vol. 8 (Boston: Houghton Mifflin, 1912), May 3, 1849, 20. *"Next to"*: "Quotations and Originality," *Letters and Social Aims,* Vol. 8 (Boston: Houghton Mifflin, 1888), 182. *"Wherever Macdonald sits"*: Stimpson 1948, 3–4; "The American Scholar," *Ralph Waldo Emerson: Essays and Journals* (Garden City, N.Y.: International Collectors, 1968), 43. *"When you strike"*: Max Lerner, *The Mind and Faith of Justice Holmes: His Speeches, Essays, Letters and Judicial Opinions* (Boston: Little, Brown, 1943), xxxix; *The Harper Book of American Quotations,* Gordon Carruth and Eugene Ehrlich, eds., (New York: Harper & Row, 1988), 483; ODP, 82. *"The louder he talked"*: "Worship," Ralph Waldo Emerson, *Conduct of Life* in *The Complete Works of Ralph Waldo Emerson,* Vol. 6, 211; Boswell, Vol. 1, 432; James Russell Lowell, *The Biglow Papers* (Boston: Houghton, Mifflin, 1896), 81; *"What you do"*: Emerson, "Social Aims," *Letters and Social Aims,* op. cit., 95. *"Do not go"*: "Emerson on the path," *Stumpers,* January 28, 2000, <http://listserv.dom.edu/cgi-bin/wa.exe?A2=ind0001&L=STUMPERS-L&D=0&m=128001&P=142103> (September 8, 2005), "Emerson Quotation," *Stumpers,* May 20, 2002, <http://listserv.dom.edu/cgi-bin/wa.exe?A2=ind0205&L= STUMPERS-L&D=0&m=160232&P=58421> (September 8, 2005).

We have met the ENEMY and he is us: Walt Kelly, *The Pogo Papers* (New York: Simon & Schuster, 1953), Foreword; Platt, 102; Mrs. Walt Kelly and Bill Crouch, Jr., ed., *The Best of Pogo* (New York: Simon & Schuster, 1982), 156, 163, 224; "We have met the enemy . . . and he is us," *I Go Pogo,* <http://www.igopogo.com/ we_have_met.htm> (March 3, 2005).

We have met the ENEMY and they are ours: Platt, 102; Alexander Slidell MacKenzie, *The Life of Commodore Oliver Hazard Perry* (New York: A. L. Fowle, 1900), 261; Robert B. McAfee, *History of the Late War in the Western Country* (Bowling Green, Ohio: Historical Publications, 1816, 1919), 382; John Benson Lossing, *The Pictorial Field-Book of the War of 1812* (New York: Harper & Brothers, 1868), 530; Logan Esarey, ed., *Messages and Letters of William Henry Harrison,* Vol. 2 1812–1816 (Indianapolis: Indiana Historical Commission, 1922), 539.

ENGLAND and America are two countries separated: Reader's Digest, November 1942, 100; Platt, 105–6; Wilde, 194.

This is the sort of ENGLISH: Paul Brians, "Churchill on Prepositions," *Common Errors in English,* <http://www.wsu.edu/%7Ebrians/errors/churchill.html> (August 3, 2005); Sir Ernest Gowers, *Plain Words: A Guide to the Use of English* (London: His Majesty's Stationery Office, 1948), 73–4; Benjamin G. Zimmer, "A Misattribution No Longer to Be Put Up With," *Language Log,* December 12, 2004, <http:// itre.cis.upenn.edu/~myl/languagelog/archives/001715.html> (August 3, 2005).

Peace, commerce, and honest friendship for all nations, ENTANGLING alliances: Woods, 16; Platt, 121; SNPD, 219; Harnsberger, 90, 200.

The only thing necessary for the triumph of EVIL: "Favourite quotation revealed!" *Ask Oxford,* December 3, 2004, <http://www.askoxford.com/pressroom/ archive/favquote/?view=uk> (April 29, 2005); Martin Porter, "'All that is necessary for the triumph of evil is that good men do nothing' (or words to that effect): A Study of a Web Quotation," January 2002, *Tartarus.Org,* <http://www.tartarus.org/~ martin/essays/burkequote.html> (August 3, 2005); Lee Frank, "9/11/2001: Stumbling into War," *leefrank.com,* September 7, 2002, <http://www.leefrank.com/ 9112001/into_war.html> (August 3, 2005); Harry N. Stull, *WP,* January 22, 1950; *Bartlett's* 1968, 454; *Bartlett's* 1980, ix; Safire 1980, 224–6; Platt, 109; Anderson, 54.

Whenever I feel an urge to EXERCISE: Harry Ashmore, *Unseasonable Truths: The Life of Robert Maynard Hutchins* (Boston: Little, Brown, 1989), 114; J. P. McEvoy, "Garlands for the Living," *American Mercury,* December 1938, 482; "Movies: *Mr. Smith Goes to Washington,*" *WavSource.com,* <http://www.wavsource .com/movies/mr_smith_goes.htm> (May 10, 2005).

EXPERIENCE is the name: Wilde, 56, 663, 418; Rosten, 108–9.

We're EYEBALL to eyeball: Stewart Alsop and Charles Bartlett, "In Time of Crisis," *Saturday Evening Post,* December 8, 1962, 16; SNPD, 231–2; Capt. Jack Jordan, "These Mosquitoes Slap Back," in John F. Loosbrock and Richard M. Skinner, eds., *The Wild Blue: The Story of American Airpower* (New York: Putnam's, 1961), 464; *Random House Dictionary of American Slang,* Vol. 1, 710.

At fifty, everyone has the FACE: George Orwell, *In Front of Your Nose 1945–1950: The Collected Essays, Journalism and Letters of George Orwell,* Vol. 4 (New York: Harcourt, Brace & World, 1968), 515; W. H. Auden and Louis Kronenberger, eds., *The Viking Book of Aphorisms* (New York: Viking, 1962), 391; Albert Camus, *The Fall* (New York: Vintage, 1956), 57; Ward Just, *The American Ambassador* (Boston: Houghton Mifflin, 1987), 52.

FAMOUS for being famous: Daniel Boorstin, *The Image* (New York: Atheneum, 1962), 57; *Washington Times,* June 16, 1996.

The only thing we have to FEAR: Home Book, 655; Bartlett's, 505: Bradford Torrey and Francis H. Allen, *The Journal of Henry D. Thoreau I,* Vols. 1–7 (New York: Dover, 1962), 261; Samuel Rosenman, *Working with Roosevelt* (London: Rupert Hart-Davis, 1952), 93–5; James MacGregor Burns, *Roosevelt: The Lion and the Fox* (New York: Harvest / Harcourt, Brace & World, 1956), 162; SNPD, 509–10; Home Book, 655.

Feminism: "Burn your bra": Judith Hole and Ellen Levine, *Rebirth of Feminism* (New York: Quadrangle, 1971), 123, 136, 229–30; Rick Perlstein, "Correction of Things Past," *Civilization,* December 1998 / January 1999, 27. *"Sisterhood is powerful":* ODQ, 549; Robin Morgan, ed., *Sisterhood Is Powerful* (New York: Random House, 1970), xvi–xvii; Hole and Levine, *Rebirth of Feminism,* op. cit., 118, 179; Colette Price letter to *NYT Book Review,* May 3, 1981, 49. *"If men could get pregnant":* Ms., March 1973, 89; Gloria Steinem, *Outrageous Acts and Everyday Rebellions* (New York: Holt, Rinehart and Winston, 1983), 8.

Good FENCES make good neighbors: Robert Frost, "Mending Wall," *Collected Poems of Robert Frost* (New York: Halcyon, 1939), 47–8; *Dwight's American Magazine, and Family Newspaper,* December 5, 1846, 703; *The Cultivator,* February 1851, 65; *Forester's Boys' and Girls' Magazine, and Fireside Companion,* April 1, 1852, 114; *The New England Farmer,* November 1855, 529; *American Quarterly Church Review, and Ecclesiastical Register,* October 1864, 480; ODP, 132; Wolfgang Mieder, " 'Good Fences Make Good Neighbours': History and Significance of an Ambiguous Proverb," *Folklore* 114 (2003), 155–79.

FIFTEEN minutes of fame: Andy Warhol (Boston: Boston Book and Art, 1968), reprint of catalog, Andy Warhol exhibition at Moderna Museet, Stockholm, February–March 1968; Victor Bockris, *The Life and Death of Andy Warhol* (New York: Bantam, 1989), 147; Cory Meacham, "In the future, everyone will be anonymous for fifteen minutes," *The Anchorage Press,* December 3–9, 1998; Patrick Mondout, "Fifteen Minutes of Fame," *Awesome80s.com,* <http://www.awesome80s.com/ Awesome80s/Culture/Lexicon/15_Minutes.asp> (April 18, 2005); "What's the exact 'fifteen minutes of fame' quote?" *the warhol: Museum Info,* <http://www .warhol.org/museum_info/faq.html> (April 18, 2005); e-mail from Matt Wrbican, assistant archivist, The Warhol Museum, May 3, 2005.

I have not yet begun to FIGHT: Platt, 305; Samuel Eliot Morison, *John Paul Jones: A Sailor's Biography* (Boston: Little, Brown, 1959), 236, 240–2; Benjamin Rush, *The Autobiography of Benjamin Rush* (Princeton: Princeton University Press, 1948), 157.

I propose to FIGHT: John Y. Simon, ed., *The Papers of Ulysses S. Grant,* Vol. 10 (Carbondale, Ill.: Southern Illinois, 1982), 422; E. B. Long, *Personal Memoirs of U. S. Grant* (New York: Da Capo / Plenum, 1885–6, 1982), 419; Bent, 261–2; B. A. Botkin, ed., *A Civil War Treasury of Tales, Legends, and Folklore* (New York: Promontory, 1985), 366–7; John Y. Simon e-mail, October 25, 2004.

Never pick a FIGHT: WSJ, September 28, 1978; *CT,* August 15, 1985; Barbara Semonche e-mail, January 2, 2005; *Overland Monthly and Out West Magazine,* 7; March, 1896; *The Friend,* November 1, 1902, 124.

Don't FIRE until: Bartlett's, 330, 340; Richard Frothingham, *History of the Siege of Boston and of the Battles of Lexington, Concord and Bunker Hill* (Boston: Little, Brown, 1849, 1903), 140; Burnam 1975, 69–70.

If you give a man a FISH: RQ, winter 1978, 184; Tripp, 646; J. J. Servan-Schreiber, *The American Challenge* (New York: Atheneum, 1969), epigraph; *Littell's Living Age,* September 5, 1885, 602.

Only those are FIT to live: Platt, 214; Theodore Roosevelt, *The Great Adventure: Present-Day Studies in American Nationalism* (New York: Scribner's, 1918), 1; Douglas MacArthur, "Veterans of the Rainbow (42d) Infantry Division of World War I," Washington, D.C., July 14, 1935, *Representative Speeches of General of the Army Douglas MacArthur* (Washington, D.C.: U.S. Government Printing Office, 1964), 3.

The FOG of war: Carl von Clausewitz, *On War,* Michael Howard and Peter Paret, ed. and trans. (Princeton: Princeton University, 1976), 101, 140; Safire 2004, 106–8.

FOLLOW the money: LAT, June 15, 1997; *Newsday,* June 16, 1997; Carl Bernstein and Bob Woodward, *All the President's Men* (New York: Simon & Schuster, 1974, Warner 1975), 35; Safire 2003, 111–3; *Lowell* [Mass.] *Sun,* January 6, 1966.

You can FOOL all of the people: Roy P. Basler, ed., *The Collected Works of Abraham Lincoln,* Vol. 3 (New Brunswick, N.J.: Rutgers University, 1953), 81; P. M. Zall, *Lincoln Laughing* (Berkeley: University of California, 1982), 139; Emanuel Hertz, *Lincoln Talks* (New York: Viking, 1939), 138; Fehrenbacher and Fehrenbacher, 277, 315, 335–6, 533, 537, 538; Platt, 119; Alexander K. McClure, *Abe Lincoln's Yarns and Stories* (Chicago: Thompason and Thomas, 1901), 184.

FOOTBALL is a mistake: *Newsweek,* September 6, 1976, 72; *LAT,* January 15, 1978; "The Crier Report," Fox News Network, May 12, 1998; James C. Humes, *The Wit and Wisdom of Winston Churchill* (New York: HarperCollins, 1994), 172; "Miscellaneous Information," *The Churchill Centre,* <http://www.winstonchurchill.org/i4a/pages/index.cfm?pageid=399> (August 4, 2005).

FORM follows function: Louis H. Sullivan, "The Tall Office Building Artistically Considered," *Lippincott's Monthly Magazine,* March, 1896, 408.

Behind every great FORTUNE: Mario Puzo, *The Godfather* (New York: Putnam's, 1969, Signet, 1995), 9; Honoré de Balzac, Katharine Prescott Wormeley, trans., *Père Goriot* (Boston: Roberts Brothers, 1891), 142; H. de Balzac, *Le Père Goriot* (Paris: Galmann-Levy, 1925), 137; Honoré de Balzac, Ellen Marriage, trans., *Old Goriot* (New York: Walter J. Black, 1946), 124; Fred Shapiro, "Behind Every Great Fortune, . . ." *Stumpers,* July 2, 2003 <http://listserv.dom.edu/cgi-bin/wa.exe?A2=ind0307&L=STUMPERS-L&P=R1962> (August 28, 1005); C. Wright Mills, *The Power Elite* (New York: Oxford, 1956), 95.

Benjamin Franklin. Franklin's borrowed proverbs can be found in Robert H. Newcomb, "The Sources of Benjamin Franklin's Sayings of Poor Richard," Ph.D. dissertation, University of Maryland, 1957; Frances M. Barbour, *A Concordance to the Sayings in Franklin's POOR RICHARD* (Detroit: Gale, 1974), and Charles W. Meister, "Franklin as a Proverb Stylist," 24 (May 1952) 157–66. The proportion of Poor Richard's plagiarism is discussed in Newcomb, ibid., 16, interview with Robert Newcomb, December 26, 1991, and Wolfgang Mieder, "'Early to Bed and Early to Rise': From Proverb to Benjamin Franklin and Back," *DeProverbio.com,* Vol. 1, No. 1, 1995, <http://www.deproverbio.com/DPjournal/DP,1,1,95/FRANKLIN.html> (August 11, 2004). Twain: Mark Twain, "The Last Words of Great Men," *Collected Tales, Sketches, Speeches, & Essays 1852–1890* (New York: The Library of America, 1992), 317. *"Our new constitution":* November 13, 1789, letter to Jean-Baptiste Leroy, John Bigelow, ed., *The Complete Works of Benjamin Franklin,* Vol. 10 (New York: Putnam's, 1888), 169–70; MPMFP, 2248, 2282. Thurow: speech to National Press Club, *National Public Radio,* May 28, 1992; *"There never was":* letter to Sir Joseph Banks, July 27, 1783, letter to Josiah Quincy, September 11, 1783, Bigelow, *The Complete Works of Benjamin Franklin,* op. cit., Vol. 8, 320, 354.

There's no such thing as a FREE lunch: Milton Friedman, *There's No Such Thing As a Free Lunch* (LaSalle, Ill.: Open Court, 1975); SNPD, 267–8; Safire 1991,

229; Safire 1999, 69–70; Anderson, 23; John Lardner, *The World of John Lardner* (New York: Simon & Schuster, 1961), 196, 213–4; Robert Heinlein, *The Moon Is a Harsh Mistress* (New York: Putnam's, 1966, Ace, 1987), 129; *NYT,* February 1, 2002; Shapiro, 77; George E. Sokolsky, *Waterloo* [Iowa] *Courier,* October 2, 1949; *Lima* [Ohio] *News,* October 19, 1947.

Those who desire to give up FREEDOM: Leonard W. Labaree, ed., *The Papers of Benjamin Franklin,* Vol. 6 (New Haven: Yale University, 1963), 242; Vol. 21 (New Haven: Yale University, 1978), 498.

FRIENDS are God's apology for relations: Jay McInerney, *The Last of the Savages* (New York: Knopf, 1996), 1; Richard Ingrams, *God's Apology: A Chronicle of Three Friends* (London: Andre Deutsch, 1977; Newton Abbot, Devon: Reader's Union, 1978), title page; Michael Holyroyd, ed., *The Best of Hugh Kingsmill: Selections from His Writings* (London: Victor Gollancz, 1970), 12; Maggio, 450; MDQ, 206; King, 177.

Are we having FUN yet: Bill Griffith, *Zippy Stories* (Berkeley, Calif.: And/Or Press, 1981), cover; Sue Watkins, "Zippy the Pinhead Quote," *Stumpers,* July 11, 2002; <http://listserv.dom.edu/cgi-bin/wa.exe?A2=ind0207&L=STUMPERS-L&P=R10964> (January 25, 2005); "Is He Having Fun Yet?" Interview with Bill Griffith by *Goblin Magazine* (1995) <http://www.zippythepinhead.com/pages/aaishehaving funyet.html> (June 29, 2005).

That was the most FUN: Haun, 300; William Cole and Louis Phillips, eds., *Sex: "The Most Fun You Can Have Without Laughing" . . . and Other Quotations* (New York: St. Martin's, 1990); Mencken, 717; Michael Korda, *Another Life* (New York: Random House, 1999), 171; *People,* December 3, 1990, 8.

Git thar FUSTEST: Ralph Selph Henry, *"First with the Most" Forrest* (Indianapolis: Bobbs-Merrill, 1944); Donn Piatt, *General George H. Thomas: A Critical Biography* (Cincinnati: Robert Clarke, 1893), 599; James Harrison Wilson, *Under the Old Flag* (New York: Appleton, 1912) 184; Basil W. Duke, *Reminiscences of General Basil W. Duke, C.S.A.* (Garden City, N.Y.: Doubleday, Page, 1911), 345–6; Richard Taylor, *Destruction and Reconstruction: Personal Experiences of the Late War* (New York: Longmans, Green, 1955), 244; *Oxford English Dictionary,* second edition, Vol. 9, 1117; *Random House Historical Dictionary of American Slang,* Vol. 2, 593; *NYT,* May 28, 1918.

I have seen the FUTURE: Lincoln Steffens, *The Autobiography of Lincoln Steffens* (New York: Literary Guild, 1931), 799; Bernard Baruch, *The Public Years* (New York: Holt, Rinehart & Winston, 1960), 195; Ella Winter and Granville Hicks, eds., *The Letters of Lincoln Steffens,* Vol. 1 (New York: Harcourt, Brace, 1938) 463;

Justin Kaplan, *Lincoln Steffens: A Biography* (New York: Simon & Schuster, 1974, Touchstone, 1988), 250.

A GAFFE is when a politician: New Republic, May 28, 1984, 6.

There are no GAINS without pains: Newcomb, 292; MPMFP, 924.

She ran the GAMUT of emotions: Alexander Woollcott, *While Rome Burns* (New York: Viking, 1935), 147; Katharine Hepburn, *Me: Stories of My Life* (New York: Knopf / Random House Large Print, 1991), 231; Gary Carey, *Katharine Hepburn* (Thorndike, Maine: Thorndike, 1983), 103.

Mahatma Gandhi: Arjan El Fassed, "Gandhi's First Memo to Thomas Friedman," *Media Monitors Network,* April 11, 2000, <http://www.mediamonitors.net/arjan30.html> (September 6, 2005); Arjan El Fassed, "Spreading Like Wildfire," Letters to the Editor, *Ha'aretz,* April 30, 2001, <http://www.arjanelfassed.mediamonitors.org/let20010430.html> (February 8, 2005). *"The greatness of a nation":* "Quotes," *International Vegetarian Union,* <http://www.ivu.org/history/gandhi/> (May 13, 2005). *"An eye for an eye":* Debi Lee Mandel review, "MGM Studios DVD presents 'Fiddler on the Roof' ": SE (1971), September 17, 2001, <http://digitallyobsessed.com/showreview.php3?ID=1590> (September 6, 2005); "Whole World Blind," *Stumpers,* March 27, 2002, <http://listserv.dom.edu/cgi-bin/wa.exe?A2=ind0203&L=STUMPERS-L&P=R38716> (September 6, 2005); Martin Luther King, Jr., *Stride Toward Freedom: The Montgomery Story* (New York: Harper & Row, 1958), 213; Keith D. Miller, *Voice of Deliverance: The Language of Martin Luther King, Jr. and Its Sources* (New York: Free Press, 1992), 89, 91; John Krampner, "John Briley '51: Epic Screenwriter," *Michigan Today,* March 1993, <http://www.mich.edu/news/MT/93/Mar_and_Oct_93/Mar_93/briley.html> (June 10, 2005). *"I think it would be a good idea":* E. F. Schumacher, *Good Work* (New York: Harper & Row, 1979), 62.; ODQ, 339; Rees, 252; S. R. Tikekar, ed., *Epigrams from Gandhiji* (New Delhi: Government of India, 1971), 19–20; Louis Fischer, *The Life of Mahatma Gandhi* (New York: Harper & Row, 1950, 1983), 280–1; Yogesh Chada, *Gandhi: A Life* (New York: Wiley, 1997), 397. *"Be the change":* The Official Mahatma Gandhi eArchive, <http://web.mahatma.org.in/quotes/quotes.jsp?link=qt> (May 13, 2005); Fred Shapiro, "Re: Gandhi Quote About Change," *Stumpers,* April 22, 2005, <http://listserv.dom.edu/cgi-bin/wa.exe?A2=ind0504&L=STUMPERS-L&P=R22594> (September 6, 2005). *"If someone slaps you":* Meena Nayak e-mail, February 9, 2005. *"A customer":* "Was Gandhi a Marketing Consultant?" *About.com* (Quotations Blog), May 7, 2004, <http://quotations.about.com/b/a/029356.htm> (September 6, 2005).

What's good for GENERAL MOTORS: NYT, January 23, 1953; videotape of *Stagecoach* (United Artists, 1939); Tim Dirks, "*Stagecoach* (1939)," *The Greatest*

Films, <http://www.filmsite.org/stagec.html> (August 5, 2005); William Kittredge and Steven M. Krauzer, *Stories into Film* (New York: Colophon / Harper & Row, 1979), 92–109, 276–7.

GENIUS is 1 percent inspiration: "The Anecdotal Side of Edison," *Ladies' Home Journal,* April 1898, 7; *Scientific American,* December 27, 1902, 463; William Adams Simonds, *Edison: His Life, His Work, His Genius* (Indianapolis: Bobbs-Merrill, 1934), 293; Samuel Insull, *Public Utilities in Modern Life* (Chicago: privately printed, 1924), 192–3; Ronald W. Clark, *Edison: The Man Who Made the Future* (New York: Putnam's, 1977), 89; M. A. Rosanoff, "Edison in His Laboratory," *Harper's Monthly,* September 1932, 406.

GINGER ROGERS did everything: Ann Richards with Peter Knobler, *Straight from the Heart: My Life in Politics and Other Places* (New York: Simon & Schuster, 1989), 24; Deborah Hastings, "Actress, Dancer Ginger Rogers Dead at 83," Associated Press, April 16, 1995; Bob Curran, *Buffalo News,* May 3, 1995; Maggio, 451; Ginger Rogers, *Ginger: My Story* (New York: HarperCollins, 1991), 137; Bob Thaves, *Frank and Ernest,* March 3, 1982, <http://frankandernest.com/cgi/view/display.pl?82-05-03> (September 25, 2004); Bob Thaves e-mail, September 26, 2004.

Win one for the GIPPER: Jerry Brondfield, *Rockne* (New York: Random House, 1976), 97, 219–23; *New York Daily News,* November 12, 1928, in Francis Wallace, *Knute Rockne* (Garden City, N.Y.: Doubleday, 1960), 212–7; *Collier's,* November 22, 1930, 64; American Film Institute, No. 203; *American Rhetoric,* <http://americanrhetoric.com/MovieSpeeches/moviespeechknuterockneallamerican.html> (August 25, 2005).

The GLOBAL village: Philip Marchand, *Marshall McLuhan: The Medium and the Messenger* (New York: Ticknor & Fields, 1989), 75; Wyndham Lewis, *America and Cosmic Man* (Garden City, N.Y.: Doubleday, 1949), 21.

Think GLOBALLY, act locally: Ruth A. Eblen and William R. Eblen, eds. *The Encyclopedia of the Environment* (Boston: Houghton Mifflin, 1994), 703–4; Dubos letter to Lucius Beebe, January 14, 1985, Kay Roberts, "Think Globally, Act Locally," *Stumpers,* February 23, 1998, <http://listserv.dom.edu/cgi-bin/wa.exe?A2=ind9802&L=stumpers-l&O=D&F=&S=&P=170857> (August 6, 2005); *American Scholar,* 46 (Spring, 1977), 152; René Dubos, *The Wooing of Earth* (New York: Scribner's, 1980), 156; René Dubos, *Celebrations of Life* (New York: McGraw-Hill, 1981), 83; *WSJ,* May 17, 1979; *Newsweek,* May 28, 1979, 85. *Future-Trends.com* <http://www.future-trends.com/home_nonflash.html> (August 25, 2005); Frank Feather e-mail, November 2, 2004.

GOD always favors: Voltaire, *The Complete Works of Voltaire,* Vol. 132, Theodore Besterman, ed. (Oxford: The Voltaire Foundation, 1976), 18; Bergen Evans, *The Spoor of Spooks* (New York: Knopf, 1954), 64; Ackermann, 409; ODP, 250; King, 61.

GOD helps those: George Barna, *What Americans Believe* (Ventura, Calif.: Regal, 1991), 80; *News-Gazette* (Champaign-Urbana, Ill.), September 13, 1991; *Authors Guild Bulletin,* Fall 1998, 32; Bartlett's, 61; Newcomb, 294; Hoyt's, 319; MPMFP, 979; ODP, 126.

This is the way GOD would have built: Rees, 582; *People,* February 7, 1977, 32, February 28, 1977, 11; Dan H. Laurence, ed., *Bernard Shaw: Collected Letters, 1926–1950* (New York, Viking, 1988), 332; Walter Wagner, *You Must Remember This* (New York: Putnam's, 1975), 85; MDQ, 585; Howard Teichmann, *George S. Kaufman: An Intimate Portrait* (New York: Atheneum, 1972), 113, 120; Cerf, 27; Fadiman, 903.

We'll win, because GOD'S on our side: Joe Louis with Edna and Art Rust, Jr., *Joe Louis: My Life* (New York: Harcourt Brace Jovanovich, 1978), 174; Chris Mead, *Joe Louis: American* (New York: Scribner's, 1985), 218; Gerald Astor, *And a Credit to His Race* (New York: Saturday Review Press, 1974), 219; Sugar, 47.

Samuel Goldwyn: Alva Johnston, *The Great Goldwyn* (New York: Random House, 1937, Arno, 1978); Arthur Marx, *Goldwyn: A Biography of the Man Behind the Myth* (New York: Norton, 1976); Carol Easton, *The Search for Sam Goldwyn* (New York: Morrow, 1976); A. Scott Berg, *Goldwyn: A Biography* (New York: Knopf, 1989), 396–8; Arthur Mayer, *Merely Colossal* (New York: Simon & Schuster, 1953), 9–15, 170, 249; Norman Zierold, *The Moguls* (New York: Coward-McCann, 1969), 119–29; Wagner, *You Must Remember This,* op. cit., 106–14. <u>Frances Goldwyn</u>: Wagner, ibid., 106–7. <u>Studio screenwriters</u>: Caryl Rollyson, *Lillian Hellman: Her Legend and Her Legacy* (New York: St. Martin's, 1988), Philip French *The Movie Moguls* (Chicago: Regnery, 1969), 46; Marx, *Goldwyn,* op. cit., 9; Ross and Kathryn Petras, *The 776 Stupidest Things Ever Said* (New York: Doubleday, 1993), 36. <u>*Dubious malaprops*</u>: Marx, *Goldwyn,* op. cit., 9–10; Easton, *The Search for Sam Goldwyn,* op. cit., 150; Berg, *Goldwyn,* op. cit., 396–98; Zierold, *The Moguls,* op. cit., 199–20; Hendrickson, *The Literary Life and Other Curiosities,* op. cit., 400–1. Evan Esar, *The Humor of Humor* (New York: Bramhall / Clarkson Potter, 1952), 134; Jonathan Green, *Says Who?* (London: Longman, 1988), 341. <u>*"Include me out"*</u>: *Variety,* February 6, 1974; *New York Post,* April 23, 1976; Marx, *Goldwyn,* op. cit., 9. <u>*"I can answer"*</u>: Zierold, *The Moguls,* op. cit., 127; Berg, *Goldwyn,* op. cit., 396. <u>*"A verbal contract"*</u>: Garson Kanin, *Hollywood* (New York: Viking, 1974), 299; Zierold, ibid., 128. <u>*"I read part"*</u>: Johnston, *The Great Goldwyn,* op. cit., 28. <u>*"Anyone who sees a psychiatrist"*</u>: Kanin, *Hollywood,* op. cit., 299; Marilyn and Hy Gardner, *Glad You Asked That!* (New York: Ace, 1976), 53; *New York Post,* November 22, 1946; *Reader's Digest,* December 1948, 122.

GOLF is a good walk spoiled: George Eberl, *Golf Is a Good Walk Spoiled* (New York: Taylor, 1992); Helen Exley, *Golf: A Good Walk Spoiled* (Watford, England:

Exley Giftbooks, 1995); John Feinstein, *A Good Walk Spoiled* (New York: Little, Brown, 1995); Peter, 476; *Reader's Digest*, December 1948, 122; Rasmussen, xviii; Rees, 546; *Stevens Point* [Wis.] *Daily Journal*, December 19, 1913; e-mail from Sundhil Pflug, Kurt Tucholsky Literaturmuseum, May 20, 2005, citing *Die Welt-bühne*, March 11, 1931, 673.

How can you GOVERN a nation: Ernest Mignon (Constantin Melnick), *Les Mots du Général* (Paris: Artheme Fayard, 1962), 57; *Newsweek*, October 1, 1962; Lewis, x; Tuleja 1992, 56–7; *CT*, December 12, 1991; J. R. Tournoux, *La Tragédie du Général* (Paris: Plon, 1967), 111; Hoyt's, 294; Home Book, 532.

I would rather be GOVERNED by: videotape of October 17, 1965, Buckley ap-pearance, *Meet the Press*, on NBC News, July 11, 2004; William F. Buckley, *Rumbles Left and Right: A Book About Troublesome People and Ideas* (New York: Putnam's, 1963), 134.

GOVERNMENT of the people: Kenelm Foss, *Here Lies Richard Brinsley Sheridan* (New York: Dutton, 1940), 168; Wolfgang Mieder, " 'Government of the People, by the People, for the People': The Making and Meaning of an American Proverb of Democracy," *Proverbium* 20 (2003) 259–308; Wilson, 167; Baker, 29; Spinrad and Spinrad, 118–9; Robert E. Collins, *Theodore Parker: American Transcendentalist* (Metuchen, N.J.: The Scarecrow Press, 1973), 2–3, 43; William Herndon and Jesse W. Weik, *Abraham Lincoln: The True Story of a Great Life*, Vol. 2 (New York: D. Appleton, 1892), 65.

That GOVERNMENT is best: Boller and George, 56; Henry David Thoreau, "Civil Disobedience," *The Portable Thoreau* (New York: Viking, 1947, 1975), 109; *The United States Magazine and Democratic Review*, Vol. 1, No. 1, October 1837, 6.

GRACE under pressure: Ted Koppel, *Primetime Live*, December 26, 1991; John F. Kennedy, *Profiles in Courage* (New York: Harper & Brothers, 1956, Cardinal, 1957), 1; Dorothy Parker, "Profiles: The Artist's Reward," *New Yorker*, November 30, 1929, 31.

I'd walk over my own GRANDMOTHER: John Pierson, *WSJ*, October 15, 1971; Myra MacPherson, *WP*, December 5, 1972; Charles W. Colson, *Born Again* (Old Tappan, N.J.: Revell, 1976), 57; Colson letter, March 17, 1992; Boller and George, 16–7.

The GRAVEYARDS are full: *The Observer* (London, England), May 26, 1999; *NYT*, December 18, 1996; George Will, *DDN*, May 12, 2004; *Denver Post*, Octo-ber 17, 1999; *The Independent* (London, England), December 15, 1990; *Congress Daily (National Journal)*, August 29, 1996; *Chattanooga Free Press*, August 30, 1996; "Paula Zahn Now," Cable News Network, September 27, 2004; *Federal*

News Service, July 28, 1999; *The Herald* (Glasgow, Scotland), April 22, 1999; *Calgary* (Alberta) *Herald,* January 7, 1999; *Federal News Service,* December 15, 1999; *The Pakistan Newswire,* May 26, 2003.

I am the GREATEST: Colman McCarthy, *PI,* September 22, 1998; Green, 64; interview with Thomas Hauser, December 7, 1991; Wilfrid Sheed, *Muhammad Ali* (New York: New American Library, 1976), 70, 72; Lewis, vii.

GREED is good: James B. Stewart, *Den of Thieves* (New York: Simon & Schuster, 1992), 261; Dirks; American Film Institute, No. 376; Movie Speech: *Wall Street* (1987), *American Rhetoric,* http://americanrhetoric.com/MovieSpeeches/moviespeechwallstreet.html> (August 25, 2005).

Never doubt that a small GROUP: The Institute for Intercultural Studies, <http://www.interculturalstudies.org/> (August 8, 2005); "What is the source of the 'Never doubt . . .' quote,'" *The Institute for Intercultural Studies,* <http://www .interculturalstudies.org/faq.html> (August 8, 2005); Stephanie Mills, "Salons and Beyond: Changing the World One Evening at a Time," *Utne Reader,* March/April 1991, 77; Carolyn Warner, *The Last Word: A Treasury of Women's Quotes* (Englewood Cliffs, N.J., Prentice-Hall 1992), 47.

The GUARD dies: King, 159; MPMFP, 2251–2; Hoyt's, 844; SNPD, 519–20; Safire 2004, 250–2; Victor Hugo, *Les Misérables* (New York: Modern Library / Random House, 1862, 1931), 289–91.

Up, GUARDS, and at 'em: Rees, 560; Bent, 564, 618; Hoyt's, 859; Benham 1930, 457b; Walsh, 434; Sir William Fraser, *Words on Wellington* (London: John C. Nimmo, 1889), 96–7.

Better that ten GUILTY persons: Alexander Volokh, "Guilty Men," 146 *University of Pennsylvania Law Review* 173 (1997), <http://www.law.ucla.edu/volokh/guilty.htm> (August 8, 2005); *St. Louis Post-Dispatch,* October 11, 1999; *Dallas Morning News,* August 18, 2004; Platt, xv.

Any good prosecutor . . . HAM sandwich: NYT, February 1, 1985; Sol Wachtler, *After the Madness: A Judge's Own Prison Memoir* (New York: Random House, 1997).

If the only tool you have is a HAMMER: Abraham Kaplan, *The Conduct of Inquiry: Methodology for Behavioral Science* (San Francisco: Chandler, 1964), 28. Frank Bohan, "Maslow quote," *alt.quotations,* <http://groups.google.com/group/alt.quotations/browse_thread/thread/dde28645fefe10bd/ad43091890bc494d?q=like+a+nail&rnum =3&hl=en#ad43091890bc494d> (August 8, 2005); Abraham H. Maslow, *The Psychology of Science* (New York: Harper & Row, 1966), 15–6.

We must all HANG together: P. M. Zall, ed., *Ben Franklin Laughing: Anecdotes from Original Sources by and About Ben Franklin* (Berkeley: University of California, 1980), 153–4; Van Doren, *Benjamin Franklin,* op. cit., 551–2; Freeman Hunt, *American Anecdotes,* Vol. 1 (Boston: Putnam & Hunt, 1830), 97; *The American Joe Miller* (Philadelphia: Carey and Hart, 1839), 181; Jared Sparks, *The Works of Benjamin Franklin* (Boston: Hilliard Gray, 1840), 408; *New-York Mirror,* May 15, 1841, 13; *Water-Cure Journal,* July 1850, 13; *United States Magazine,* August 1856, 185; *Saturday Evening Post,* April 8, 1876, 13; February 24, 1883; *Scribner's Monthly,* November 1880, 167; Francis Von A. Cabeen, "The Society of the Saints of Saint Tammany of Philadelphia," *Pennsylvania Magazine of History and Biography,* 25 (1901) 433.

If you can't take the HEAT: "Remarks at the Wright Memorial Dinner of the Aero Club of Washington," December 17, 1952, *Public Papers of the Presidents of the United States: Harry S. Truman,* 1952–53 (Washington, D.C.: United States Government Printing Office, 1966), 1085–6; *WP,* December 18, 1952; *Time,* April 28, 1952; ODQ, 801; Robert H. Ferrell, *Truman: A Centenary Remembrance,* op. cit., 192; Robert H. Ferrell, *Harry S. Truman: A Life* (Columbia, Mo.: University of Missouri, 1994), 109; David McCullough, *Truman* (New York: Simon & Schuster, 1992), 633.

HELL hath no fury: William Congreve, *The Mourning Bride,* 1697, III:1; Stimpson 1948, 68; ODP, 148; Safire 1997, 46.

The hottest place in HELL: Platt, 230; John F. Kennedy, *The Strategy of Peace* (New York: Harper & Brothers, 1960), 105; Kennedy, 6; Schlesinger, *A Thousand Days,* op. cit., 105; "Churchill Epigrams," <http://c2.com/cgi/wiki?ChurchillEpigrams> (August 8, 2005); Richard Langworth e-mail, June 9, 2005; *Evangelical Magazine and Gospel Advocate,* May 17, 1834, 153; *Friends Intelligencer,* January 15, 1870, 721.

He who HESITATES: Joseph Addison, *Cato,* 1713, IV:1; Pearson, 17.

HIGH SCHOOL is closer: Kurt Vonnegut, Jr., Introduction, John Birmingham, ed., *Our Time Is Now: Notes from the High School Underground* (New York: Praeger, 1970), x.

HISTORY is bunk: CT, May 25, 1916; Alan Nevins and Frank Ernest Hill, *Ford: Expansion and Challenge* (New York: Scribner's, 1957), 138.

HISTORY is written by the victors: John Leo, "The Junking of History," *U.S. News & World Report,* February 28, 1994, 17; "Is this even a quote?" April 28, 2003, *Quotations Page,* <http://www.quotationspage.com/forum/viewtopic.php?t=1021&sid=2460cea15591777211a38038e07a1277> (August 8, 2005); Walter Benjamin, "Theses on the Philosophy of History," 1940, in Walter Benjamin, *Illuminations,* Harry Zohn, trans. (New York: Harcourt, Brace & World, 1955, 1968), 258; Jawaharlal Nehru, *The Discovery of India* (New York: John Day, 1946), 287; *Potter's American Monthly,* April 1879, 314.

HOLD the fort: Home Book, 65; Woods, 153; Evans, 318; Lloyd Lewis, *Sherman: Fighting Prophet* (New York: Harcourt, Brace and Company, 1932), 426; Landon, *King of the Platform and Pulpit,* op. cit., 375–6; Stanley P. Hirshson, *The White Tecumseh: A Biography of General William T. Sherman* (New York: Wiley, 1997), 246; John F. Marszalek, *Sherman: A Soldier's Passion for Order* (New York: Free Press, 1993), 291–2.

All is lost save HONOR: King, 353; MPMFP, 1161.

A man in passion rides a mad HORSE: Newcomb, 77, 313.

There is nothing better . . . than the outside of a HORSE: Publishers Weekly, June 30, 2003; Boller and George, 108; *Time,* December 28, 1987, 52, January 18, 1988, 7; *ABC World News Tonight,* June 11, 2004; *Scribner's Monthly,* October 1872, 751; *Outing, An Illustrated Monthly Magazine of Recreation,* July 1889, 306; *Forest and Stream,* September 1920, 502; Home Book, 929; ODP, 224.

I don't care what you . . . frighten the HORSES: Alan Dent, *Mrs. Patrick Campbell* (London: Museum, 1961, Westport, Conn.: Greenwood 1973), 78; Margot Peters, *Mrs. Pat: The Life of Mrs. Patrick Campbell* (New York: Knopf, 1984), 211; Ted Morgan, *Maugham* (New York: Simon & Schuster, 1980), 78; "Mrs. Patrick Campbell," *Wikiquote,* <http://en.wikiquote.org/wiki/Mrs._Patrick_Campbell> (December 9, 2004).

Humorists: WARD: Melville Landon, *The Complete Works of Artemus Ward (Charles Farrar Browne), With a Biographical Sketch* (New York: Dillingham, 1901); Landon, *Kings of the Platform and Pulpit,* ibid., Fehrenbacher and Fehrenbacher, 121, 417. BILLINGS: Myers, *America's Phunniest Phellow–Josh Billings,* op. cit. Landon, *Kings of the Platform and Pulpit,* op. cit., 75–96; Billings, *The Complete Works of Josh Billings,* op cit.; *"Josh Billings defined:"* Rasmussen, xiv; Paul Fatout, ed., *Mark Twain Speaking* (Iowa City: University of Iowa, 1976), 424. HUBBARD: Kelly, *The Life and Times of Kin Hubbard,* op. cit.; David S. Hawes, ed., *The Best of Kin Hubbard: Abe Martin's Sayings and Wisecracks* (Bloomington: Indiana University, 1984); Rogers on Hubbard: *NYT,* December 27, 1930. DOOLEY: Finley Peter Dunne, *Mr. Dooley on Ivrything and Ivrybody,* Robert Hutchinson, ed. (New York: Dover, 1963), 152–6; Edward J. Bander, *Mr. Dooley and Mr. Dunne: The Literary Life of a Chicago Catholic* (Charlottesville, Va.: Michie, 1981), 52, 63, 109–16, 199–201, Paul Samuelson, "The Case Against Goldwater's

Economics," *NYT Magazine,* October 25, 1964, 28; Paul Samuelson, *Economics,* eleventh edition (New York: McGraw-Hill, 1951, 1980), 126. ALLEN: Neil A. Grauer, "Forgotten Laughter: The Fred Allen Story," *American Heritage,* February 1988, 98–107; Maurice Zolowtow, "Fred Allen: Strictly from Misery (with a rebuttal by Mr. Allen)," in Frank Brookhouser, ed., *Those Were Our Years* (Garden City, N.Y.: Doubleday, 1959), 486–94; *Newsweek,* July 26, 2004, 55; Morris and Morris, 87.

Don't worry about people stealing an IDEA: Robert Slater, *Portraits in Silicon* (Cambridge: MIT, 1987), 88.

There is one thing stronger than . . . an IDEA whose time has come: Seldes 1985, 194; ODQ, 407; Victor Hugo, *History of a Crime* (New York: A. L. Burt, [pref. 1877]), 429.

Immature poets IMITATE: T. S. Eliot, "Philip Massinger," in *The Sacred Wood* (New York: Barnes & Noble, 1920), 125. "Writers Quote," *The Quotations Page,* February 14, 2004, <http://www.quotationspage.com/forum/viewtopic.php?t=1882> (August 9, 2005); Peter Yates, *Twentieth Century Music* (New York: Pantheon, 1967; Minerva / Funk & Wagnalls, 1968) 41.

All the things I like to do are either IMMORAL: Rees, 581; Teichmann, *Smart Aleck,* op. cit., 221; *Reader's Digest,* December 1933, 109; W. C. Fields, "Six of a Kind," (Universal, 1934), *Movie Mirrors Index* <http://www.san.beck.org/mm/1934/SixofaKind.html> (August 9, 2005).

The only good INDIAN: Ward, *The Civil War,* op. cit., 408; Paul Hutton, *Phil Sheridan and His Army* (Lincoln, Nebr.: University of Nebraska, 1985), 180; Edward Sylvester Ellis, *The History of Our Country* (Cincinnati: Jones Brothers, 1900), 1483; Michael V. Sheridan, *Personal Memoirs of Philip Henry Sheridan* (New York: Appleton, 1902), 464–5; *Congressional Globe,* May 28, 1968, 2638; Ellis Paxson Oberholtzer, *A History of the United States Since the Civil War,* Vol. 1 (New York: Macmillan, 1926), 357; Wolfgang Mieder, " 'The Only Good Indian is a Dead Indian': History and Meaning of a Proverbial Stereotype," *The Journal of American Folklore* 106 (1993) 38–60.

No one can make you feel INFERIOR: Bartlett's, 704; Rosalie Maggio e-mails, July 14, 2004, July 24, 2004; John Henderson, "Eleanor Roosevelt Quote About the Future," *Stumpers,* March 30, 2000, <http://listserv.dom.edu/cgi-bin/wa.exe?A2=ind0003&L=STUMPERS-L&P=R60312> (August 8, 2005); Boswell, vol. 5, 274–5.

We do not INHERIT the earth: *RQ,* fall 1990, 26; Celestial Seasonings Chamomile tea, box copy, © 1987; Robert Keller, "Haida Land Claims and South Moresby National Park," *The American Review of Canadian Studies,* 20 (1990) 7;

Roger K. Clendening, "'Forty Acres and a Mule:' In Search of Sherman's Reservation," in Dana Alston, ed., *We Speak for Ourselves: Social Justice, Race and Environment* (Washington, D.C.: The Panos Institute, 1990), 19; David R. Brower with Steve Chapple, *Let the Mountains Talk, Let the Rivers Run: A Call to Those Who Would Save the Earth* (New York: HarperSanFrancisco, 1995, 1996), 1–2.

If you want to know what people are like, share an INHERITANCE with them: DDN, November 21, 1991; *The Oregonian*, April 17, 1996; Johanns Caspar Lavater, *Aphorisms on Man* (1788) (Delmar, N.Y.: Scholars' Facsimiles & Reprints, 1980), 59.

INSANITY consists of doing the same thing: "Albert Einstein Quotes," *Brainy Quote*, <http://www.brainyquote.com/quotes/quotes/a/alberteins133991.html> (August 28, 2005); Rita Mae Brown, *Sudden Death* (New York: Bantam, 1983), 68; "Tools of Recovery: Some Helpful Suggestions [and] Basic Tools to Help You Stay Sober," *ATLCMA*, <http://www.atlanatacma.or/tools.html> (March 17, 2005); Safire 1997, 33; *BG*, April 18, 1998; Clinton Collins, Jr., "Free the Jackson Five!: Won't You Be My Neighbor?" October 2002; *The Rake: Secrets of the City* <http://www.rakemag.com/printable.asp?catID=50&itemID=708&pg=all> (March 21, 2005).

INSANITY is hereditary: Sam Levenson, *You Can Say That Again, Sam!* (New York: Pocket, 1975), 26–7. *Diner's Club*, November 1963, in "Creative Quotations from Sam Levenson," *Creative Quotations*, <http://www.creativequotations.com/one/2009.htm> (July 22, 2004); *New York Post*, July 24, 1998; *Forbes*, June 25, 1979, 128; *People*, November 23, 1981, 139.

The test of a first-rate INTELLIGENCE: F. Scott Fitzgerald, "The Crack-Up," in Edmund Wilson, ed., *The Crack-Up* (New York: Scribner's, 1931, New Directions, 1956), 69; George Orwell, *1984* (New York: Harcourt, Brace, 1949), 215.

May you live in INTERESTING times: Robert F. Kennedy, "Day of Affirmation Address," University of Capetown, Capetown, South Africa, June 6, 1966, <http://www.jfklibrary.org/r060666a.htm> (January 14, 2005); Nikos Kazantzakis, P. A. Brien, trans., *Report to Greco* (New York: Simon & Schuster, 1961, 1965), 449; Stephen E. DeLong, "Sidebar: Get a(n interesting) Life!" <http://hawk.fab2.albany.edu/sidebar/sidebar.htm> (August 10, 2005); George F. Hardy, "On a Dubious Chinese Quote," November 20, 1996, Kevin K. W. Chow, "On a Dubious Chinese Quote," November 11, 1996, *alt.folklore.urban, alt.quotations*, <http://listserv.dom.edu/cgi-bin/wa.exe?A2=ind9805&L=STUMPERS-L&D=0&O=D&P=35228> (August 10, 2005); Dr. Ho Yong, "May You Live in Interesting Times?" *ChinaSprout*, undated, <http://www.chinasprout.com/html/column15.html> (April 28, 2005); Nancy McPhee, *The Book of Insults, Ancient and Modern* (New York: Bell, 1978), 19.

... an IRON CURTAIN has descended: Churchill, *Never Give In!*, op. cit., 413–24; Ignace Feuerlicht, SNPD, 370–2; Franklin R. Rogers, "'Iron Curtain' Again," *American Speech,* 27 (1952) 1401; "A New Look at the Iron Curtain," *American Speech* 30 (1955) 186–9; H. G. Wells, *The Food of the Gods* (New York: Dover, 1904), 789; Emile Hinzelin, *Histoire Illustrée de la Guerre du Droit,* Vol. 2, 407, in Friedrich Henn, "Churchill's 'Iron Curtain,'" *Encounter,* January, 1966, 89; George Crile, *A Mechanistic View of War and Peace* (New York: Macmillan, 1915), 69; *Dial,* April 29, 1915; V. V. Rozanov, S. S. Koteliansky, trans., *Solitaria* (New York: Boni & Liveright, 1918, 1927), 148; Hans Vorst, "Russia As the Germans See Her Now," *Living Age,* January–March, 1918, 21; Ethel Snowden, *Through Bolshevik Russia* (London: Cassell, 1920), 32; P. Mohr, *Information About Eastern Questions,* 1921, in Henn, *Encounter,* ibid., 89; Joseph Goebbels, *Das Reich,* February 23, 1945, in Mieder and Bryan, *The Proverbial Winston S. Churchill,* op. cit., 68; St. Vincent Troubridge, "'Iron Curtain,'" *American Speech* 26 (1951) 49–50; Churchill telegrams in Mieder and Bryan, ibid., 66; Winston S. Churchill, *Triumph and Tragedy* (Boston: Houghton Mifflin, 1953), 573.

Thomas Jefferson: "Thomas Jefferson on Politics & Government: Quotations from the Writings of Thomas Jefferson" *The University of Virginia,* <http:// etext.virginia.edu/jefferson/quotations/> July 6, 2005; *"Every word":* Martin Gottlieb, "What Would Jefferson Say About This?" *DDN,* June 16, 1995. Adair: Douglass Adair, *Fame and the Founding Fathers* (New York: Norton, 1974), 238. *"I tremble":* Thomas Jefferson, *Notes on Virginia* in Lipscomb, Vol. 2, 227. *". . . were it left to me":* letter to Edward Carrington, January 16, 1787, Lipscomb, Vol. 6, 57–8. *"The man who never looks":* letter to John Norvell, June 11, 1807, Lipscomb, Vol. 11, 225; *"I read no newspapers":* letter to Nathaniel Macon, January 12, 1819, Lipscomb, Vol. 15, 179; *"If a due participation":* letter to Elias Shipman and others, a committee of the merchants of New Haven, July 12, 1801, Lipscomb, Vol. 10, 272; Walsh, 366. *"I hold it, that":* letter to James Madison, January 30, 1787, Lipscomb, Vol. 6, 65; *"the mass of mankind":* letter to Roger C. Weightman, June 24, 1826, Lipscomb, Vol. 16, 182; Adair, ibid., 244.

If JESUS Christ had taken a poll: Atlanta Journal, December 14, 1998; Robert H. Ferrell, ed., *Off the Record: The Private Papers of Harry S. Truman* (New York: Harper & Row), 310.

JOHN MARSHALL has made his decision: Marquis James, *Andrew Jackson: Portrait of a President* (Indianapolis: Bobbs-Merrill, 1937), 304–5; Robert V. Remini, *Andrew Jackson and the Course of American Freedom* (New York: Harper & Row, 1981), 276–7; Horace Greeley, *The American Conflict* (Hartford, Conn.: O. D. Case, 1864), Vol. 1, 106.

Samuel Johnson: *"Depend upon it, no man":* Boswell, Vol. 5, 274–5. *"Sir, you know courage":* Boswell, Vol. 2, 339. *"Patriotism is":* Boswell, Vol. 2, 348. "No man *but a blockhead"*: Boswell, Vol. 3, 19. *"I am willing to love all mankind"*: Boswell, Vol. 3, 290. *"He who praises everybody"*: Platt, 273; Boswell, Vol. 3, 225–6. *"The road to hell"*: Boswell, Vol. 2, 360. *"A fishing pole"*: Ackermann, 408–9. *"The true measure"*: St. Louis Post-Dispatch, March 12, 1990; *DDN*, April 1, 1995; *WP*, September 25, 1999; *Investor's Business Daily*, October 17, 2000; *Times-Picayune* (New Orleans). These and other misattributions are discussed on the "Apocrypha" section of the *Samuel Johnson Sound Bite Page* <http://www.samueljohnson.com/apocryph.html> (November 1, 2004).

JOURNALISM is the first draft of history: Martin Walker, United Press International, August 2, 2004; *Maclean's*, November 15, 1993, 24–5; Carol Feisenthal, *Power, Privilege and the Post: The Katharine Graham Story* (New York: Putnam's, 1993, 181–2; Katharine Graham, *Personal History* (New York: Knopf, 1997, Vintage, 1998), 323–4.

A JOURNEY of a thousand miles: Laurence Peter, *Peter's People*, op. cit., 202; Theodore Sorensen, *Kennedy* (New York: Harper & Row, 1965; Bantam, 1966), 831; T. S. Settle, ed., *The Faith of JFK* (New York: Dutton, 1965), 88; Henry Wei, trans., *The Guiding Light of Lao Tzu* (Wheaton, Ill.: Theosophical Publishing House, 1982), 207; "Mistake with Lao Tzu," April 17, 2004, *Quotations Page*, <http://www.quotationspage.com/forum/viewtopic.php?t=1988> (August 10, 2005); James W. Cannon and Warren Dicks, "One hyperbolic once-unctured-torus bundles," *Geometriae Dedicata* 94 (2002) 141–83; "Errata," December 1, 2004, <http:// mat.uab.es/~dicks/Cannon.html> (April 23, 2005).

Don't JUDGE a man: Tripp, 331; Anderson, 20; *RQ*, winter, 1974, 150–1, winter, 1983, 140; Shapiro, 87–8; *QuoteWorld.org*, September 1, 2002, <http://www.quoteworld.org/phpBB/viewtopic.php?t=126> (August 10, 2005); Rabbi Rami M. Shapiro, *Wisdom of the Jewish Sages* (New York: Bell Tower, 1993), 26; Mieder, 245; Harper Lee, *To Kill a Mockingbird* (Philadelphia: Lippincott, 1960), 36.

John F. Kennedy: Schlesinger, *A Thousand Days*, op. cit., 105–6, 689–91; Sorensen, *Kennedy*, op. cit., 69–72; *"I'll hitch my wagon"*: Sorensen, ibid., 71. *"New Frontier"*: SNPD, 391–3; Alf Landon, *America at the Crossroads* (New York: Dodge, 1936), 13; Henry Wallace, *New Frontiers* (New York: Reynal & Hitchcock, 1934). *"For of those"*: Settle, *The Faith of JFK*, op. cit., 44; Morris and Morris, 397. *"He mobilized"*: Clarke, *Ask Not*, op. cit., 68; Rees, 331, 404. *"What we are"*: Settle, *The Faith of JFK*, op. cit., 81. *"Life in politics"*: Sander Vanocur, "Larry King Live," *CNN*, December 6, 2000; "One on One with Paul Costello, *PBS Hawaii*, October 2, 2003. *"French Marshal Lyautey"*: Platt, 341. *"The survivors"*: "Radio and Television Address to the American People on the Nuclear Test Ban Treaty," July 26, 1963, *Public Papers of the Presidents, John F. Kennedy* (Washington, D.C.: Government Printing Office, 1964), 603; *NYT*, July 27, 1963; Platt, 239; Herman Kahn, *On Thermonuclear War* (Princeton: Princeton University,

1961), 20, 40. "*I know that there is a god*": Platt, 173–4; Clarke, *Ask Not,* op. cit., 63–4; *Press-Enterprise* (Riverside, Calif.), July 23, 1998, August 3, 1998; Arthur Schlesinger, Jr., letter to *Time,* August 24, 1998, 8; Boller and George, 90–1. "*A rising tide*": Platt, 313; Titelman, 286. "*I think this is*": Clarke, *Ask Not,* op. cit., 52; "*My views*": Sue G. Hall, ed., *Bobby Kennedy Off-Guard,* op. cit., 60; *Reader's Digest,* June 1934, 50. "*But we also know*": Kennedy, "Day of Affirmation Address," op. cit.

We are all KEYNESIANS now: *Guardian* (London, England), August 30, 1990; *Time,* December 31, 1965, 64–5; Milton Friedman, *Dollars and Deficits: Living with America's Economic Problems* (Englewood Cliffs, N.J.: Prentice-Hall, 1968), 15; Rees, 221–2.

What does not KILL me: Gail Godwin, "A Diarist on Diarists," Joyce Carol Oates, ed., *First Person Singular: Writers on Their Craft* (Princeton, N.J.: Ontario Review Press, 1983), 24; Friedrich Nietzsche, *Twilight of the Idols and the Anti-Christ,* R. J. Hollingdale, trans. (Baltimore: Penguin, 1968), 23.

KINDER, gentler: *NYT,* January 21, 1989; *Port-Folio,* March 17, 1804, 88; *Intellectual Regale: or, Ladies' Tea Tray,* November 19, 1814, 13; Horace Greeley, "The Ideal of a True Life," *The Green Mountain Gem: A Monthly Journal of Literature, Science, and the Arts,* January 1, 1848, 212A; "Mr. Carlyle," *Littell's Living Age,* July 31, 1858, 323; *The Bookman: A Review of Books and Life,* May, 1911, 327; *Newsweek,* October 12, 1992, 8; Harry Crews, *A Childhood* (New York: Harper & Row, 1978), 49; *WSJ,* January 19, 1989; Peggy Noonan, *What I Saw at the Revolution* (New York: Random House, 1990), 312–3.

There, I guess KING GEORGE: Wilson, 45; William M. Fowler, Jr., *The Baron of Beacon Hill: A Biography of John Hancock* (Boston: Houghton Mifflin, 1980), 213; *BG,* January 21, 1962; D. W. Belisle, *History of Independence Hall From the Earliest Period to the Present Time. Embracing Biographies of the Immortal Signers of the Declaration of Independence, with Historical Sketches of the Sacred Relics Preserved in that Sanctuary of American Freedom* (Philadelphia: Arden, 1859), Introduction, <http://www.faculty.fairfield.edu/faculty/hodgson/Courses/city/philadelphia/PHILADEPHIA_ih.html> (August 10, 2005).

A little KNOWLEDGE: Alexander Pope, *An Essay on Criticism,* Alfred S. West, ed. (London: Cambridge University, 1711, 1917), 67.

LAFAYETTE, we are here: John J. Pershing, *My Experience in the World War* (New York: Frederick A. Stokes, 1931), 93; Woods, 163; Morris Rosenblum, "They Never Said It," *American Mercury,* April 1946, 494–5; Bartlett's 1968, 856; Bartlett's, 1980, 693; Burnam 1980, 118.

Ann Landers and Abigail Van Buren: *"I have never heard"*: CT, November 22, 1992. *"If you think"*: DDN, June 25, 1998; "An interview with Sir Claus Moser," <http://www.centreforliteracy:qc.ca/publications/lacmf/Vol15no2/10–16.htm> (June 16, 2005). *"Ginger Rogers"*: CT, December 31, 1989. *"Youth"*: *Evening Tribune* (San Diego), February 15, 1977. *"Practice Random Kindness"*: DDN, May 31, 1997. *"No one can take advantage"*: DDN, May 22, 1994; March 21, 2000; October 7, 2001; *More than once . . . Erma Bombeck*: CT, June 24, 1989; February 24, 1991; April 19, 1991. *"I would rather"*: St. Louis Post-Dispatch, April 19, 1990; Robert Fulghum on *Charlie Rose*, Public Broadcasting System, April 6, 1995; DDN, April 23, 1996; Ann Landers on *Weekend Edition*, National Public Radio, May 4, 1996; *Newsweek*, December 30, 2002–January 6, 2003, 113. *"Lies travel halfway"*: DDN, November 23, 1999; *"The best index"*: DDN, April 1, 1995, June 29, 2002; *"Amateurs built the ark*: CT, November 5, 2001.

Last Words: Mark Twain, "The Last Words of Great Men," *Collected Tales, Sketches, Speeches, & Essays*, op. cit., 315. Roosevelt: Vic Fredericks, *The Wit and Wisdom of the Presidents* (New York: Frederick Fell, 1966), 44. James: interview with Leon Edel, George Plimpton, ed., *Writers at Work*, eighth ser. (New York: Viking, 1988), 60. Stein: Hobhouse, *Everybody Who Was Anybody*, op. cit., 230. Astor: Christopher Sykes, *Nancy: The Life of Lady Astor* (New York: Harper & Row, 1972), 524; Anthony Masters, *Nancy Astor: A Biography* (New York: McGraw-Hill, 1981), 223; John Grigg, *Nancy Astor: A Lady Unashamed* (Boston: Little, Brown, 1980), 184. Brandreth: Gyles Brandreth, *871 Famous Last Words* (New York: Bell / Sterling, 1979, 1982), 5–6. Wilde: Hesketh Pearson, *Lives of the Wits* (London: Heineman, 1962), 246–7; Robert Harborough Sherard, *The Life of Oscar Wilde* (London: T. Werner Laurie, 1906), 421; Robert Harborough Sherard, *The Real Oscar Wilde* (London: T. Werner Laurie, 1917), 330; Jean Paul Raymond (Charles Ricketts), *Oscar Wilde: Recollections* (Bloomsbury: Nonesuch, 1919, 1932), 59; Rupert Hart-Davis, ed., *The Letters of Oscar Wilde* (London: Rupert Hart-Davis, 1962), 848; NYT October 14, 1982; Rees, 571; Richard Ellman, *Oscar Wilde* (New York: Knopf, 1988), 581.

Only when I LAUGH: *Time*, January 7, 1952, 20; Merle Miller, *Plain Speaking* (New York: Berkley, 1974), 372; Partridge, 236.

LEAD, follow, or get out of the way: "TV's Boldest Gambler Bets the Plantation," *Fortune*, January 5, 1987, 104; Christian Williams, *Lead, Follow or Get Out of the Way: The Story of Ted Turner* (New York: Times Books, 1981); Porter Bibb, *It Ain't As Easy As It Looks* (New York: Crown, 1993), 154; Peter, *Peter's People*, op. cit., 8, *Newsweek*, March 2, 1992, 72–3.

When you have a LEMON: Dale Carnegie, *How to Stop Worrying and Start Living* (New York: Simon & Schuster, 1948, Pocket Cardinal, 1953), 145; *Reno Evening*

Gazette, April 25, 1908; *Iowa Recorder,* November 30, 1910; *Indianapolis Star,* June 18, 1911; *Atlanta Constitution,* April 14, 1914; *Reader's Digest,* October 1927, 343; Elmer Wheeler, *Sizzlemanship: Tested Selling Sentences* (New York: Prentice-Hall, 1940), 116; Warren Hinckle, *If You Have a Lemon, Make Lemonade* (New York: Putnam's, 1974, Bantam, 1976), acknowledgments.

Can the LEOPARD change his spots: Pearson, 20; MPMFP, 1673.

LESS is more: Peter Blake, *The Master Builders* (New York: Knopf, 1960), 169; Safire 1991, 264; "Andrea del Sarto" in Robert Browning, *Browning's Poetical Works* (London: Oxford, 1940), 433.

There is LESS in this: NYT, January 4, 1922; Alexander Woollcott, *Shouts and Murmurs* (New York: Century, 1922), 86; Lee Israel, *Miss Tallulah Bankhead* (New York: Putnam's, 1972; Dell, 1973), 63; Tallulah Bankhead, *Tallulah: My Autobiography* (New York: Harper & Brothers, 1952), 82.

Since I did not have time to write you a short LETTER: DDN, May 20, 2005; Bill Clinton, *My Life* (New York: Vintage, 2005), 963; Blaise Pascal, "Provincial Letter Sixteen," December 4, 1656, *Pensées, The Provincial Letters* (New York: Modern Library, 1941), 571.

Give me LIBERTY: Platt, 202; Robert Douthat Meade, *Patrick Henry: Practical Revolutionary* (Philadelphia: Lippincott, 1969), 38–40; William Wirt, *Sketches of the Life and Times of Patrick Henry* (Freeport, N.Y.: Books for Libraries Press, 1817, 1836, 1970), 132–43; Douglas Southall Freeman, *George Washington: A Biography,* Vol. 3 (New York: Scribner's, 1931), 404; Joseph Addison, *Cato,* 1713, II:4.

Where there is LIBERTY: Bartlett's, 340; Platt, 201; Benham 1930, 674a; Home Book, 1104; Mencken, 682; Alfred Owen Aldridge, *Man of Reason: The Life of Thomas Paine* (Philadelphia: Lippincott, 1959), 169.

A LIE can travel: "A Sermon Delivered on Sunday Morning, April 1, 1855, by the Rev. C. H. Spurgeon, at Exeter Hall, Strand [London]," *Spurgeon's Sermons,* Vol. 1, 1855, <http://www.ccel.org/ccel/spurgeon/sermons01.xvi.html> (October 4, 2004); C. H. Spurgeon, *Spurgeon's Gems: Being Brilliant Passages from the Discourses of the Rev. C. H. Spurgeon* (New York: Sheldon & Company, 1858, 1865), 155; *Gettysburg Republican Compiler,* May 29, 1854; *Boston Commercial Gazette,* September 7, 1820, reprinted from *Portland Gazette,* September 5, 1820; Jonathan Swift, *The Examiner,* November 9, 1710, in *The Works of Jonathan Swift,* Vol. 3, Edinburgh, 1778, "Lie can go around the world . . ." *American Dialect Society,* <http://listserv.linguistlist.org/cgi-bin/wa?A2=ind0505B&L=ADS-L&P=R4091&I=-3> (August 10, 2005).

A LIE is an abomination: MDQ, 343; Fatout, *Mark Twain Speaking,* op. cit., 424.

I cannot tell a LIE: Bill Bryson, *Made in America* (New York: Morrow, 1994, Avon, 1996), 61; Paul F. Boller, Jr., *Not So!: Popular Myths About America from Columbus to Clinton* (New York: Oxford, 1995), 29–32; James W. Loewen, *Lies Across America* (New York: New Press, 1995), 362–6.

If they will stop telling LIES: Porter McKeever, *Adlai Stevenson: His Life and Legacy* (New York: Morrow, 1989), 251; John K. Winkler, *William Randolph Hearst: A New Appraisal* (New York: Hastings House, 1955), 150; Platt, 261; Harris, 244.

LIES, damned lies, and statistics: Mark Twain, "Chapters from My Autobiography," *North American Review,* July 5, 1907, 471; *Perry* [Iowa] *Daily Chief,* December 27, 1896; John Bibby, *Quotes, Damned Quotes, and . . .* (Edinburgh: John Bibby, 1983, 1986), 29, 50; *Journal of the Royal Statistical Society* 59 (1896) 87; Mrs. Andrew Crosse, "Old Memories Interviewed," *Living Age,* November 5, 1892, 379; M. Price, "'Some Surgical Sins'—Remarks on a Paper Criticising the Profession," Read before the Philadelphia County Medical Society, December 26, 1894, in *Medical and Surgical Reporter,* January 19, 1895, 87; Leonard Henry Courtney, "To My Fellow-Disciples at Saratoga Springs," *The National Review* (London) 26 (1895) 25, <http://www.york.ac.uk/depts/maths/histstat/lies.htm> (August 11, 2005); *NYT,* January 25, 1896; *WP,* October 20, 1901.

LIFE begins at forty: Walter B. Pitkin, *Life Begins at 40* (New York: Whittlesey, 1932); Rees, 431; MDQ, 325.

LIFE is unfair: "The President's News Conference of March 21, 1962," *Public Papers of the Presidents,* op. cit., 1963, 259; Wilde, 504.

LIFE is what happens: Peter, 305; Barbara Rowes, *The Book of Quotes* (New York: Dutton, 1979), 106; Margaret Millar, *Beyond This Point Are Monsters* (New York: Random House, 1970), 87; *Reader's Digest,* January 1957, 32.

Some say LIFE is the thing: Ruth Rendell, *A Judgement in Stone* (Mattituck, N.Y.: Amereon House, 1977), 74; Maggio, 450; Logan Pearsall Smith, *All Trivia* (New York: Ticknor & Fields, 1934, 1945, 1984), 177.

There is LIGHT at the end of the tunnel: "The President's News Conference of December 12, 1962," *Public Papers of the Presidents,* op.cit., 1962, 870; *Time,* September 28, 1953, 22; Anderson, 22; *Oxford English Dictionary, Supplement,* 1985, 1015; Montagu Norman, "One Step Enough," *Living Age,* December, 1932, 316.

"For those who LIKE that sort of thing: Richard Hanser, "Old Abe v. Incomparable Max," *Lincoln Herald,* 70 (1968) 137–41; George Bernard Shaw, *Man and*

Superman, op. cit., 50; S. N. Behrman, *Portrait of Max* (New York: Random House, 1960), 185–6; Fehrenbacher and Fehrenbacher, 146; *Norfolk County Journal* (Roxbury, Mass.), November 7, 1863, in *Lincoln Herald* 67 (1965) 102.

I never met a man I didn't LIKE: Homer Croy, *Our Will Rogers* (New York: Duell, Sloan and Pearce, 1953), Foreword, 286–8; *Saturday Evening Post,* November 6, 1926, 231; Donald Day, *Will Rogers: A Biography* (New York: David McKay, 1962), 189–90; *BG,* June 16, 1930.

Abraham Lincoln: Boller and George, 77–91; P. M. Zall, *Abe Lincoln Laughing: Humorous Anecdotes from Original Sources by and About Abraham Lincoln* (Berkeley: University of California, 1982), 1–11; Seldes, 1960, 18–22; Albert A. Woldman, "Lincoln Never Said That," *Harper's,* May 1950, 70–4; Fehrenbacher and Fehrenbacher, xliii–liv. Beatty: Matthew Pinsker, "Getting Wrong with Lincoln," <http://hnn.us/articles/760.html> (September 8, 2005); Carl M. Cannon, "The Real Computer Virus," *American Journalism Review,* April 2001, 28–35. *"hurt too much to laugh":* Platt, 80; Fehrenbacher and Fehrenbacher, 319; P. M. Zall, *Abe Lincoln Laughing,* op. cit., 22. *"I remember a good story":* Harris, 94. *"If I ever get a chance":* Fehrenbacher and Fehrenbacher, 198. *"Is this the little woman":* James McPherson, *Battle Cry of Freedom* (New York: Oxford, 1988, Ballantine, 1989), 90; Fehrenbacher and Fehrenbacher, 428. *"A lawyer":* CT, January 27, 1994. *"A statesman":* Newsweek, September 19, 1977, 47. *"I know there is a God":* J. G. Holland, *The Life of Abraham Lincoln* (Springfield, Mass.: Gurdon Bill, 1866), 237; Platt, 173–4; Boller and George, 90–1. *I should think that a man's legs":* Zall, *Abe Lincoln Laughing,* op. cit., 141–2. *"It is more important":* MPMFP, 983; F. B. Carpenter, *The Inner Life of Abraham Lincoln* (New York: Hurd and Houghton, 1868), 182. *"If I were to try to read":* Carpenter, ibid., 258–9; Frank J. Williams, "Lincolniana in 1993," *Journal of the Abraham Lincoln Association,* Vol. 15, No. 2, Summer 1994, <http://jala.press.uiuc.edu/15.2/williams.html> (September 8, 2005). "Last Public Address," April 11, 1865, *The Collected Works of Abraham Lincoln,* vol. 8, Roy P. Basler, ed. (New Brunswick, N.J.: Rutgers, 1953), 401. *"People are about as happy":* Robert S. Eliot, *From Stress to Strength,* op. cit., 170; *Modern Maturity,* January–February 1996, 12; "Re: Lincoln Quote," *Stumpers,* <http://listserv.dom.edu/cgi-bin/wa.exe?A2=ind0404&L=STUMPERS-L&P=R15244> (September 8, 2005).

The LION shall lie down with the lamb: Pearson, 20.

If I'd known I was going to LIVE this long: *Globe and Mail* (Toronto), August 14, 1995; Bartlett's, 700; Rees, 111; "To the Earl of Hertford," December 29, 1763, footnote 1, Charles Duke Yonge, ed., *The Letters of Horace Walpole,* vol. 1, <http://www.gutenberg.org/catalog/world/readfile?fk_files=56135> (August 11, 2005).

LIVE fast, die young: Willard Motley, *Knock on Any Door* (New York: D. Appleton-Century, 1947), 157, 264, 316, 469, 475, 501; *RQ,* spring, 1985, 260.

LIVING well is the best revenge: Calvin Tomkins, *Living Well Is the Best Revenge* (New York: Viking, 1962), 126; Herbert, no. 524.

Mark Hopkins on one end of LOG: Theodore Clarke Smith, *The Life and Letters of James Abram Garfield,* vol. 2 (New Haven: Yale, 1925, New York: Archon, 1968), 812–4; Burton Stevenson, *Famous Single Poems* (Freeport, N.Y.: Books for Libraries, 1935, 1971), 385–90; Carroll A. Wilson, "Familiar 'Small College' Quotations, II: Mark Hopkins and the Log," *Colophon,* spring 1938, 194–208.

Alice Roosevelt Longworth: Howard Teichmann, *Alice: The Life and Times of Alice Roosevelt Longworth* (Englewood Cliffs, N.J.: Prentice-Hall, 1979); Michael Teague, *Mrs. L: Conversations with Alice Roosevelt Longworth* (Garden City, N.Y.: Doubleday, 1981); Carol Feisenthal, *Alice Roosevelt Longworth* (New York: Putnam's, 1988); Betty Boyd Caroli, *The Roosevelt Women* (New York: Basic, 1998); Edward J. Renehan, Jr., *The Lion's Pride: Theodore Roosevelt and His Family in Peace and War* (New York: Oxford, 1998). Race Suicide Club: Teague, *Mrs. L,* op. cit., 82; Renehan, *The Lion's Pride,* op. cit., 46. Throw pillow: Jean Van Den Heuvel, "The Sharpest Wit in Washington," *Saturday Evening Post,* December 4, 1965, 32; *Newsweek,* February 11, 1974, 59; Teichmann, *Alice,* op. cit., 238; Teague, ibid., xi. Willkie: Teichmann, *Alice,* op. cit., 181; Teague, *Mrs. L,* op. cit., xv; June Bingham, "Before the Colors Fade: Alice Roosevelt Longworth," *American Heritage,* February 1969, 43; *NYT,* February 21, 1980. Nicholas Longworth: Feisenthal, *Alice Roosevelt Longworth,* op. cit., 162; Caroli, *The Roosevelt Women,* op. cit., 407. Joseph McCarthy: Teichmann, *Alice,* op. cit., 197; Teague, *Mrs. L,* op. cit., 199; Caroli, *The Roosevelt Women,* op. cit., 391; Bingham, *American Heritage,* op. cit., 43. "Only topless octogenarian": Feisenthal, *Alice Roosevelt Longworth,* op. cit., 250; Caroli, *The Roosevelt Women,* op. cit., 432. "*He wanted to be the bride*": Bingham, *American Heritage,* op. cit., 74; Colin Jarman, ed., *The Guinness Book of Poisonous Quotes* (Chicago: Contemporary Books, 1993), 274. Rebecca West: Teichmann, *Alice,* op. cit., ix. "*He looks like*": SNPD, 436–7; William Safire, *NYT,* March 22, 1980. "*Weaned on a pickle*": Alice Roosevelt Longworth, *Crowded Hours* (New York: Scribner's, 1933; Arno, 1980), 337; Safire, *NYT,* March 22, 1980; Teague, *Mrs. L,* op. cit., 170. Told Teague: Teague, *Mrs. L,* ibid., xiv–xv. "*90 percent mush*": Teichmann, *Alice,* op. cit., 156; Feisenthal, *Alice Roosevelt Longworth,* op. cit., 180; *NYT,* February 21, 1980.

Don't LOOK back: Richard Donovan, "Time Ain't Gonna Mess With Me," *Collier's,* June 13, 1953, 55.

You could LOOK it up: *Saturday Evening Post,* April 5, 1941, 9, 114; Dickson, 427; Safire 1991, 364–6; Burton Bernstein, *Thurber: A Biography* (New York: Dodd, Mead, 1975, Quill / Morrow, 1985), 332.

The LORD prefers common-looking people: Seldes 1960, xiii; Boller, 330–1; Boller and George, 84; James Morgan, *Our President: Brief Biographies of Our Chief Magistrates* (New York: Macmillan, 1924, 1935), 149; John Hay, *Letters of John Hay and Extracts from Diary,* Vol. 1 (Washington, D.C.: private printing, 1908), 142–4; Fehrenbacher and Fehrenbacher, 203, 222, 319, 502.

The LORD works in mysterious ways: William Cowper, "Light Shining out of Darkness," *The Poetical Works of William Cowper,* H. S. Milford, ed. (London: Oxford, 1905, 1934), 455; T. S. Eliot, "The Hippopotamus," in T. S. Eliot, *Selected Poems* (San Diego: Harvest / Harcourt Brace, 1964), 40–1.

Show me a good LOSER: Jerry Brondfield, *Rockne* (New York: Random House, 1976), 102; interview with Jerry Brondfield, June 10, 1977; Richard Nixon, *RN: The Memoirs of Richard Nixon* (New York: Grosset & Dunlap, 1978), 19–20; David Broder, *Morning Call* (Allentown, Pa.), October 27, 1976; Jimmy Carter, *Why Not the Best?* (Nashville, Tenn.: Broadman, 1975), 112; *NYT,* July 15, 1978.

You are a LOST generation: Ernest Hemingway, *The Sun Also Rises* (New York: Scribner's, 1926, 1970), epigraph; James R. Mellow, *A Charmed Circle* (New York: Praeger, 1974), 273–4; Ernest Hemingway, *A Moveable Feast* (New York: Scribner's, 1964), 29–30; Gertrude Stein, *Everybody's Autobiography* (New York: Cooper Square, 1937, 1971), 52–3; *New-York Mirror,* February 22, 1834, 271.

If you LOVE somebody: Anderson, 72; Shapiro, 82–3; Tuleja 1992, 158; Jess Lair, *I Ain't Much Baby—But I'm All I Got* (Greenwich, Conn.: Fawcett Crest, 1969, 1972), 239.

LOVE and work: Erik Erikson, *Childhood and Society* (New York: Norton, 1963), 265; Alan Elms, Alan C. Elms, "Apocryphal Freud: Sigmund Freud's Most Famous 'Quotations' and Their Actual Sources," Winer and Anderson, *Sigmund Freud and His Impact on the Modern World,* op. cit., 83–104; Seldes 1960, 620; Seldes 1985, 348–9; Henri Troyat, Nancy Amphoux, trans., *Tolstoy* (Garden City, N.Y.: Doubleday, 1965, 1967), 158.

LOVE me, love my dog: MPMFP, 602–3; ODP, 189–90; Rees, 87; P. G. Wodehouse, "Love Me, Love My Dog," *Arthur's Classic Novels,* <http://arthursclassicnovels.com/arthurs/wodehouse/lmlmdg10.html> (June 22, 2004).

'Tis better to have LOVED and lost: Lord Tennyson, *In Memoriam* (New York: Mershon, 1850, 1899?), 28; Wilson, 144; MPFMP, 1463.

LUCK is the residue of design: Murray Polner, *Branch Rickey: A Biography* (New York: Atheneum, 1982), epigraph; Harvey Frommer, *Rickey and Robinson* (New

York: Macmillan, 1982), 85; John J. Monteleone, ed., *Branch Rickey's Little Blue Book: Wit and Strategy from Baseball's Last Wise Man* (New York: Mountain Lion / Macmillan, 1995), 11; John C. Chalberg, *Rickey and Robinson: The Preacher, the Player, and America's Game* (Wheeling, Ill.: Harlan Davidson, 2000), 2; Andrew O'Toole, *Branch Rickey in Pittsburgh: Baseball's Trailblazing General Manager for the Pirates, 1950–1955* (Jefferson, N.C.: McFarland, 2000), 6; Branch B. Rickey e-mail, April 27, 2005; *Valley Morning Star* (Harlingen, Tex.), February 16, 1946.

Give me the LUXURIES of life: Oliver Wendell Holmes, *The Autocrat of the Breakfast-Table* (New York: A. L. Burt, 1858, 1900), 121; Fadiman, 741; Walsh, 668; Evans, vi.

MAD, bad: Elizabeth Jenkins, *Lady Caroline Lamb* (Boston: Little, Brown, 1932), 95; *Time,* February 12, 1979, 96, February 16, 1980, 81; Mordechai Richler, *Joshua Then and Now* (New York: Knopf, 1980), 241, 376–7.

Call me MADAM: George Martin, *Madam Secretary: Frances Perkins* (Boston: Houghton Mifflin, 1976), 16–7; Eleanor Roosevelt and Lorena Hickock, *Ladies of Courage* (New York: Putnam's, 1954), 190.

MAKE my day: NYT, March 14, 1985; Bartlett's, 841; *The Christian Journal, and Literary Register,* July 1825, 207; *New-York Mirror,* June 4, 1840, 219.

With MALICE toward none: Bent, 610; MPMFP, 1506.

A MAN in America: John Updike, *The Coup* (New York: Knopf, 1978), 158; *NYT,* June 28, 1984.

A MAN'S got to do: John Steinbeck, *The Grapes of Wrath* (New York: Viking, 1939), 306.

MARRIAGE is a fortress besieged: Qian Zhongshu, Jeanne Kelly and Nakan K. Mao, trans., *Fortress Besieged* (Bloomington: Indiana University, 1947, 1979), xxxi; MPMFP, 1534.

I MARRIED him for better or worse: *Sporting News,* January 3, 2000; Sugar, 116; Lewis, ix; Rees, 578; Partridge, 144.

MARRY in haste: MPMFP, 1538–9; Shakespeare, *Henry VI,* IV:1, 18; ODP, 198–9; William Congreve, *The Old Bachelor,* 1693, V:3.

Down these MEAN streets: Raymond Chandler, "The Simple Art of Murder," *Atlantic Monthly,* December 1944, 59; Arthur Morrison, *Tales of Mean Streets* (London: Methuen, 1894); Martin Birnbaum, *Oscar Wilde: Fragments and Memories* (London: Elkin Matthews, 1920), 32.

The MEDIUM is the message: Marshall McLuhan, *Understanding Media,* op. cit., 7, 9, 13; Marchand, *Marshall McLuhan,* op. cit., 136–7.

The Right Honorable Gentleman is indebted to his MEMORY: King, 249; Latham, 66; Platt, 223; Thomas Moore, *Memoirs of the Life of the Right Honourable Richard Brinsley Sheridan* (New York: Excelsior Catholic, 1825, 1882), 321–2.

Poor MEXICO: "Mexico States Her Position," *Living Age,* September, 1940, 22; Hudson Strode, *Timeless Mexico* (New York: Harcourt, Brace and Company, 1944), 263; Paul Garner, *Porfirio Díaz* (Edinburgh: Longman / Pearson, 2001), 137; McLynn, *Villa and Zapata,* op. cit., 16.

MILLIONS for defense: The *South Carolina Historical and Genealogical Magazine,* Vol. 1, 1901, 100–3, 1978–9; Bombaugh, 131; Spinrad, 103; Platt, 156; *State Papers and Publick Documents of the United States,* Vol. 2 (Boston: T. B. Wait and Sons, 1817), 492; Albert J. Beveridge, *The Life of John Marshall* (Boston: Houghton Mifflin, 1916), 349–50; Joseph Addison, *Cato,* I: 4.

Wilson Mizner: Addison Mizner, *The Many Mizners* (New York: Sears, 1932); Edward Dean Sullivan, *The Fabulous Wilson Mizner* (New York: Heinkle, 1935); Alva Johnston, *The Legendary Mizners* (New York: Farrar, Straus and Young, 1953); John Burke, *Rogue's Progress* (New York: Putnam's, 1975); Jim Tully, "California Playboy," *Esquire,* July 1938, 45, 176–7, 179; Sidney Phillips, "Wilson Mizner," *Diner's Club,* December 1963, 35–7, 60. Irving Berlin: Burke, *Rogue's Progress,* op. cit., 77; Ringo, 275. Mencken: Burke, *Rogue's Progress,* op. cit., viii. Loos: Anita Loos, *A Girl Like I* (New York: Viking, 1966), 21–2; Burke, *Rogue's Progress,* op. cit., 261–2, 281. Mizner remarks: Sullivan, *The Fabulous Wilson Mizner,* op. cit., 53, 266–73; Johnston, *The Legendary Mizners,* op. cit., 66–7; Burke, *Rogue's Progress,* op. cit., x; Tully, *Esquire,* op. cit., 176. On suckers: Sullivan, *The Fabulous Wilson Mizner,* op. cit., 144; Burke, *Rogue's Progress,* op. cit., 124–5; Johnston, *The Legendary Mizners,* op. cit., 208–9; *New Yorker,* January 25, 1947, 19. *"Hello sucker!"*: Sullivan, *The Fabulous Wilson Mizner,* op. cit., 144; Johnston, *The Legendary Mizners,* op. cit., 209; Burke, *Rogue's Progress,* op. cit., 185–6; Glenn Shirley, *Hello Sucker!: The Story of Texas Guinan* (Austin, Tex.: Eakin, 1989), 47. *"Just some mouse"*: Gary Nuhn, *DDN,* October 23, 1991; Steve Gietschier, *Sporting News,* April 20, 1992, 54. *"If you steal"*: Allan Fotheringham, *MacLean's,* June 8, 1983, 56; Burke, *Rogue's Progress,* op. cit., 167; Cerf, 232. *"Living in Hollywood"*: Loos, *A Girl Like I,* op. cit., 21; Fadiman, 240; Johnston, *The Legendary Mizners,* op. cit., 66–7. *"Be nice to people"*: Larry Fields, *Philadelphia Daily News,* May 21, 1979; Fadiman, 995; Partridge, 10–1. *"Life's a tough proposition"*: Hendrickson, *The Literary Life and Other Curiosities,* op. cit., 333. S. J. Perelman, "How I Learned to Wink and Leer," *NYT Magazine,* April 23, 1978, 16. Deathbed remarks: Johnston, *The Legendary Mizners,* op. cit., 304; Burke, *Rogue's Progress,* op. cit., 278; Irvin S. Cobb, *Exit Laughing* (Indianapolis: Bobbs-Merrill, 1941), 500.

Bad MONEY drives out good: Raymond de Roover, *Gresham on Foreign Exchange* (Cambridge, Mass.: Harvard University, 1949), 91–3.

Because that's where the MONEY is: Willie Sutton with Edward Linn, *Where the Money Was* (New York: Viking, 1976), 120; Dickson, *The Official Rules* (New York: Delta, 1978), 173.

MONEY is the mother's milk of politics: NYT, December 14, 2003, December 21, 2003; T. George Harris, "Big Daddy's Big Drive," *Look,* 82; *Time,* December 14, 1962, 20; T. George Harris e-mail, June 24, 2004.

MONEY is the root of all evil: Burnam 1975, 159; Magill, 599–600.

When somebody says, 'This is not about MONEY': Fred C. Kelly, *The Life and Times of Kin Hubbard* (New York: Farrar, Straus and Young, 1952), 165.

You pays your MONEY: Mark Twain, *Huckleberry Finn* (New York: Harper & Row, 1965), 170; ODP, 238; Safire 1991, 359; *Littell's Living Age,* September 18, 1852, 575; Edward J. Bander, *Mr. Dooley and Mr. Dunne,* op. cit., 247; Sigmund Freud, *Wit and Its Relation to the Unconscious* (New York: Moffat, Yard, 1916), 95.

Build a better MOUSETRAP: Emerson and Forbes, *Journals of Ralph Waldo Emerson,* vol. 8, op. cit., 528; Freeman Champney, *Art and Glory: The Story of Elbert Hubbard* (New York: Crown, 1968), 204–6; Kenneth Dirlam and Ernest E. Simmons, *Sinners, This Is East Aurora* (New York: Vantage, 1964), 193–200; *Borrowings: A Collection of Helpful and Beautiful Thoughts* (New York: Dodge, 1889), 52; Burton Stevenson, "The Mouse Trap," *Colophon,* December 1934, pages unnumbered; "More About the Mouse Trap," *Colophon,* summer 1935, 71–85; Home Book, 630–1.

It is better to keep your MOUTH shut: Rasmussen, xviii; "Apocrypha," *The Samuel Johnson Sound Bite Page,* <http://www.samueljohnson.com/apocryph .html> (August 13, 2005); Platt, 134; Woodrow Wilson, "That Quick Comradeship of Letters," address at the Institute of France, Paris, May 10, 1919, in Ray Stannard Baker and William D. Dodd, ed., *War and Peace: Presidential Messages, Addresses and Public Papers (1917–1924) by Woodrow Wilson,* Vol. 1 (New York: Harper & Brothers, 1927), 484.

But it does MOVE: Giuseppe Baretti, *The Italian Library, Containing an Account of the Lives and Works of the Most Valuable Authors of Italy* (London: A. Millar,

1757), 52; Abbé Irailh, *Querelles Littéraires,* Vol. 3 (1761) in *Bartlett's,* 169; MPMFP, 657; Morris Rosenblum, "They Never Said It," *American Mercury,* April 1946, 494; Bent, 241–2; King, 36; Walsh, 252; Ackermann, 409; Colin A. Ronan, *Galileo* (New York: Putnam's, 1974), 220.

Movie Lines: <u>Casablanca</u>: Aljean Harmetz, *Round Up the Usual Suspects: The Making of "Casablanca"* (New York: Hyperion, 1993), 10, 187, 227–8, 230–1, 260, 262; Howard Koch, *Casablanca: Script and Legend* (Woodstock, N.Y.: Overlook, 1973), 17, 87, 95; <u>Bogart</u>: Ezra Goodman, *Bogey: The Good-Bad Guy* (New York: Lyle Stuart, 1965), 31; Burnam 1975, 255; Safire 1994, 31–4; George Bernard Shaw, *Misalliance* (New York: Brentano's, 1914), 28. <u>Cagney</u>: Michael Freedland, *Cagney* (New York: Stein & Day, 1975), 240–1; James Cagney, *Cagney by Cagney* (Garden City, N.Y.: Doubleday, 1976), 74; Doug Warren with James Cagney, *Cagney* (New York: St. Martin's, 1983), 198; *PI* March 15, 1974, March 17, 1974; American Film Institute, No. 44; <u>Grant</u>: Purvis, *TV Guide,* op. cit., 28–9; Hy Gardner, *Evening Bulletin* (Philadelphia), August 24, 1969; *New Yorker,* November 12, 1960, 168. <u>Boyer</u>: Larry Swindell, *Charles Boyer* (Garden City, N.Y.: Doubleday, 1983), 108; Purvis, ibid., 29; *Time,* September 4, 1978, 71; Burnam 1980, 47; <u>Weismuller</u>: *Photoplay,* June 1932, 119; *Burroughs v. Metro-Goldwyn-Mayer,* 683 F.2d 610, (2nd Cir. 1982).

In addition to watching video recordings themselves, classic movie lines can be found on the American Film Institute website, www.afi.com, "List of the Four Hundred Nominated Movie Quotes," www.greatestfilms.org, "Greatest Film or Movie Quotes of All Time," and www.filmsite.org "One Hundred Great Movie Lines We Can't Live Without," (from *Premiere* magazine, August 2000), "Greatest Last Lines and Final Film Quotes," and "Greatest Movie Misquotes," which has the added virtue of including audio clips of some of the lines. Many can also be found in Harry Haun, *The Movie Quote Book* (New York: Lippincott and Crowell, 1980). The Internet Movie Database (www.IMDb.com) has complete information on films referred to. Additional information noted about some of the lines can be found as follows: "<u>You ain't</u>": Rees, 322; Titelman, 376; "You Ain't Heard Nothing Yet" 1919, "The Music of Al Jolson," *Parlor Songs* <http://parlorsongs.com/issues/2002-12/this month/feature.asp> (May 16, 2005). "<u>It ain't</u>": Ronald J. Fields, *W. C. Fields by Himself: His Intended Autobiography* (Englewood Cliffs, N.J.: Prentice-Hall, 1973, Warner, 1974), 94. "<u>We have ways</u>": videotape of *The Lives of a Bengal Lancer* (Paramount, 1935); Safire 1993, 316. "<u>Frankly</u>": Titelman, 235–6; Margaret Mitchell, *Gone with the Wind* (New York: Macmillan, 1936), 1035. "<u>We don't need</u>": Dirks; B. Traven, *The Treasure of the Sierra Madre* (New York: Knopf, 1935, Amereon House, undated), 161. "<u>What a dump</u>": Rees, 197. "<u>This is the West</u>": Kittredge and Krauzer, *Stories into Film,* op. cit., 185–95. "<u>Plastics</u>": *Orlando Sentinel,* August 23, 1992; *The Record* (Bergen, N.J.), February 11, 1997, *WP,* December 7, 2003. "<u>I'm going to make him an offer</u>": Mario Puzo, *The Godfather,* op. cit., 39. "<u>What do we do</u>": *Time,* December 1, 1980, 18; David Olive, *Political Babble* (New York: Wiley, 1992), 50. "<u>I'll have</u>": "AFI's 100 years . . . 100 Movie Quotes," Bravo, September 17, 2005.

MUSIC has charms: William Congreve, *The Mourning Bride,* 1697, I:1.

It's like trying to NAIL Jell-O: "Like nailing jelly to a tree," *The Jargon Lexicon,* <http://www.jargon.net/jargonfile/l/likenailingjellytoatree.html> (August 13, 2005); Safire 1990, 323.

NASTY, brutish, and short: Thomas Hobbes, *Leviathan* (London: Dent, 1651, 1940), 65.

Love your NEIGHBOR: Newcomb, 327; Herbert, No. 141.

NEVER play cards: Bartlett's, 782; ODQ, 71; Nelson Algren, *A Walk on the Wild Side* (New York: Farrar, Straus and Giroux, 1956, Fawcett Crest, 1968), 243; H. E. F. Donahue, *Conversations with Algren* (New York: Hill and Wang, 1964), viii; Bettina Drew, *Nelson Algren: A Life on the Wild Side* (New York: Putnam's, 1989); interview with Bettina Drew, December 4, 1991; interview with Dave Peltz, December 12, 1991.

Be NICE to people: Partridge, 10–1; Johnston, *The Legendary Mizners,* op. cit., 66.

NICE guys finish last: Frank Graham, *New York Journal-American,* July 6, 1946; interview with Red Barber, February 14, 1992; *Baseball Digest,* September 1946, 59–60; Leo Durocher, *Nice Guys Finish Last* (New York: Simon & Schuster, 1975), 14; *NYT,* May 21, 1978.

If NOMINATED: Harper's Weekly, June 24, 1871, 571; William Tecumseh Sherman, *Memoirs of Gen. W. T. Sherman, Written by Himself* (New York: Charles L. Webster, 1891), 466; Lewis, *Sherman,* op. cit., 631; James Merrill, *William Tecumseh Sherman* (New York: Rand McNally, 1971), 401.

NUTS!: Fred MacKenzie, *The Men of Bastogne* (New York: Charter / Grosset & Dunlap, 1968), 163–8; interview with David Maxey, December 13, 1976.

You can't make an OMELET: Boller and George, 120; MPMFP, 671; ODP, 229; *NYT* April 7, 1990; Mieder, 134.

I see ONE-THIRD of a nation ill-housed: Harnsberger, 255; SNPD, 527–9; Rosten, 110–1; H. G. Wells, *In the Days of the Comet* (New York: Airmont, 1906, 1966), 37.

The OPERA ain't over: WP, May 8, 1978, June 11, 1978; Sugar, 37; Anderson, 21; *RQ,* winter 1985, 173; Fabia Rue Smith and Charles Rayford Smith, *Southern Words and Sayings* (Jackson, Miss.: Office Supply Company, 1976), 6; poll of southerners, May 11, 1992, October 1, 1992, December 14, 1992; CBS News, November 7, 2000.

He reminds me of the man . . . because he was an ORPHAN: Fehrenbacher and Fehrenbacher, 286–7; "A Hard Case," in *The Complete Works of Artemus Ward* (New York: G. W. Dillingham, 1901), 115–6.

An OUNCE of prevention: Charles Meister, "Franklin as a Proverb Stylist," *American Literature,* 24 (1952) 164.

PARIS is worth a mass: Latham, 162; King, 257; Ronald S. Love, *Blood and Religion: The Conscience of Henry IV, 1553–1593* (Montreal: McGill-Queen's University, 2001), 305.

Dorothy Parker: John Keats, *You Might As Well Live: The Life and Times of Dorothy Parker* (New York: Simon & Schuster, 1970); Leslie Frewin, *The Late Mrs. Dorothy Parker* (New York: Macmillan, 1986); Marion Meade, *Dorothy Parker: What Fresh Hell Is This?* (New York: Villard, 1988); Hubbard Keavey, *Dallas Morning News,* December 7, 1941; Jim Murray, *LAT,* September 23, 1973. *"Pearls before swine":* Robert E. Drennan, ed., *The Algonquin Wits: Bon Mots, Wise Cracks, Epigrams and Gags* (New York: Citadel, 1968), 113; *DDN,* July 12, 1990; Donald J. Quigley letter to *NYT,* February 4, 1989; Keats, *You Might As Well Live,* op. cit., 48–9; Edwin P. Hoyt, *Alexander Woollcott: The Man Who Came to Dinner* (New York: Abelard-Schuman, 1968), 42. Parker-Woollcott: Woollcott, *While Rome Burns,* op. cit., 142–52; Dorothy Parker, "A Valentine for Mr. Woollcott," Cleveland Amory and Frederic Bradlee, ed., *Vanity Fair: Selections from America's Most Memorable Magazine* (New York: Viking, 1960), 290–1. *"MEN":* Woollcott, *While Rome Burns,* op. cit., 144; Saul Pett, *New York Herald Tribune,* October 13, 1963; Benchley, *Robert Benchley,* op. cit., 145. *"Excuse My Dust":* Woollcott, *While Rome Burns,* op. cit., 146; *Vanity Fair,* June 1925, 51. Parker lines: S. T. Brownlow, ed., *The Sayings of Dorothy Parker* (London: Duckworth, 1992); Dorothy Parker, *The Viking Portable Library: Dorothy Parker* (New York: Viking, 1944). *"Men seldom":* Parker, ibid., 174. *"Brevity":* Meade, *What Fresh Hell Is This?,* op. cit., 35, 417. *"The House Beautiful":* *New Yorker,* March 21, 1931, 36. *"Tonstant Weader":* *New Yorker,* October 20, 1928, 98. *"Razors pain you":* Parker, *The Viking Portable Library,* op. cit., 154. *"If you can read":* Brownlow, *The Sayings of Dorothy Parker,* op. cit., 61.

I expect to PASS through this world: *Friends' Intelligencer,* March 20, 1869, 37, April 2, 1887, 211, February 24, 1894, 122, September 21, 1895, 610; *Advocate of Peace,* January 1872, A2; *Arthur's Illustrated Home Magazine,* November 1875, 677, July 1888, 88; *The Chautauquan,* November 1886, 69; *The Friend,* June 16, 1888, 364; *Current Literature,* July 1894, 17, December 1899, 575, May 1900, 239, August 1903, 255; *Baptist Missionary Magazine,* May 1899, 195; ODQ, 363;

MPMFP, 995–6; Benham 1930, 442b–443a; Bartlett's, 847; Chaucer, "The Tale of Melibee," par. 71, *The Canterbury Tales* (New York: Modern Library, 1929), 210.

This too shall PASS: Platt, 232; *Gospel Messenger and Protestant Episcopal Messenger,* December 1839, 316; *United States Catholic Magazine and Monthly Review,* August 1846, 441; *The Friend,* December 30, 1848, 119, February 17, 1849, 173; *Friends' Review,* January 6, 1849, 255; Edward Fitzgerald, *Polonius: A Collection of Wise Saws and Modern Instances* (London: Alexander Moring, 1852, 1905), 96; Idries Shah, *The Way of the Sufi* (London: Jonathan Cape, 1968), 62, 74; "Sana'i", *Virtual Afghans,* February 25, 2004, <http://www.virtualafghans.com/culture/poetry/sanai> (December 23, 2004).

The PAST is never dead: William Faulkner, *Requiem for a Nun* (New York: Random House, 1951), 92.

Those who cannot remember the PAST: George Santayana, *The Life of Reason or the Phases of Human Progress* (New York: Scribner's, 1905, 1924), 284.

PEACE with honor: André Maurois, *Disraeli: A Picture of the Victorian Age,* Hamish Miles, trans., (New York: D. Appleton, 1928), 334; Benham 1930, 459a; Bent, 47–8; Latham, 50; Walsh, 879–80; Home Book, 1472; Samuel, 144; SNPD, 564–5; *Coriolanus,* III:2; Sir Anthony Weldon, *Characters from 17th Century Histories and Chronicles,* <http://www.blackmask.com/thatway/books168c/charh.htm> (August 13, 2005).

There go the PEOPLE: Platt, 194; Alvin R. Calman, *Ledru-Rollin and the Second French Republic* (New York: Columbia University, 1922), 374.

Eighty PERCENT of success is showing up: William Safire 1993, 170–1; Robert B. Johnson and Richard G. Weingardt, "Leadership: The World Is Run by Those Who Show Up," *Journal of Management in Engineering,* 15 (January–February, 1999), 90–92.

On the whole, I'd rather be in PHILADELPHIA: PI, January 29, 1979; Burnam 1975, 123; *Vanity Fair,* June 1925, 51.

Phony False Forecasts: "Everything": Jeffrey Eber, "'Nothing Left to Invent,'" *Journal of the Patent Office Society* 22 (July 1940) 479–81 Samuel Sass," A Patently False Patent Myth—Still!", *Skeptical Inquirer,* May–June 2003, 43–5, 48; Chris Morgan and David Langford, *The Book of Facts and Fallacies: A Book of Definitive Mistakes and Misguided Predictions* (Exeter, England: Webb & Bower, 1981), 64; Christopher Cerf and Victor Navasky, *The Experts Speak: The Definitive Compendium of Authoritative Misinformation* (New York: Pantheon, 1984, Villard, 1998), 225; Bill Gates, *The Road Ahead* (New York: Viking, 1995), xiii;

"Nothing More to Invent?" *Scientific American,* October 16, 1915, 334. *"I think"*: Cerf and Navasky, *The Experts Speak,* op. cit., 208; Morgan and Langford, *The Book of Facts and Fallacies,* op. cit., 44; Kevin Maney, *The Maverick and His Machine: Thomas Watson, Sr. and the Making of IBM* (New York: Wiley, 2003), 355–6, 463–4; National Academy of Sciences, *Technology and Employment: Innovation and Growth in the U.S. Economy* (Washington, D.C.: National Academies Press, 1987), 25; Paul E. Ceruzzi, *A History of Modern Computing* (Cambridge: MIT, 1998, 2003), 13; Bernard Cohen, *Howard Aiken: Portrait of a Computer Pioneer* (Cambridge: MIT, 2000), 283–93; Lord Bowden, "The Language of Computers," *American Scientist* 58 (1970) 43. *"There is no reason"*: Cerf and Navasky, *The Experts Speak,* op. cit., 231, 383; Paul Freiberger and Michael Swaine, *Fire in the Valley* (New York: McGraw-Hill, 2000), 26–8. *"640k"*: Jon Katz, "Did Gates Really Say 640K Is Enough for Anyone?" *Wired News,* January 16, 1997, <http://www.wired.com/news/print/0,1294,1484,00.html> (September 2, 2005).

Please do not shoot the PIANIST: Oscar Wilde, *Impressions of America* (Sunderland: Keystone Press, 1882, 1906), 31.

One PICTURE is worth: Herbert Adams Gibbons, *John Wanamaker,* vol. 2 (New York: Harper & Brothers, 1926), 19; *NYT,* May 16, 1914; *CT,* October 12, 1914; *Printer's Ink,* December 8, 1921, 96, March 10, 1927, 114; *Oakland Tribune,* December 1, 1924; Wolfgang Mieder, "'A Picture Is Worth a Thousand Words': From Advertising Slogan to American Proverb," *Southern Folklore* 47 (1990) 207–25; "Quotations," *China the Beautiful,* <http://www.chinapage.com/main2.html> (August 26, 2005); Ivan Turgenev, *Fathers and Sons,* Richard Freeborn, trans. (New York: Oxford, 1862, 1999), 97.

You furnish the PICTURES: William Randolph Hearst, Jr., with Jack Casserly, *The Hearsts: Father and Son* (New York: Roberts Rinehart, 1991), 38; John K. Winkler, *William Randolph Hearst: A New Appraisal* (New York: Hastings House, 1955), 95–6; James Creelman, *On the Great Highway* (Boston: Lothrop, 1901), 177–8; Joyce Milton, *The Yellow Kids: Foreign Correspondents in the Heyday of Yellow Journalism* (New York: Harper & Row, 1989), xii–xiii; Pauline Kael, *The Citizen Kane Book* (Boston: Little, Brown, 1971, Bantam, 1974), 94.

If you steal from one person it's PLAGIARISM: Burke, *Rogue's Progress,* op. cit., 127; Johnston, *The Legendary Mizners,* op. cit., 66.

No PLAN survives contact with the enemy: Daniel J. Hughes, ed., Daniel J. Hughes and Harry Bell, trans., *Moltke on the Art of War: Selected Writings* (Novato, Calif.: Presidio, 1993), 92; Baron Von Freytag-Loringhoven, *Generalship in the World War: Comparative Studies,* Vol. 1 (Carlisle, Pa.: U.S. Army War College, 1983), 125–6.

Make no little PLANS: "Speaker Hastert's Remarks to Open the 109th Congress," *U.S. Newswire,* January 4, 2005, <http://releases.usnewswire.com/GetRelease .asp?id=41202> (January 5, 2005); Patrick T. Reardon, "Burnham Quote: Well, It May Be," *CT,* January 1, 1992; Henry H. Saylor, "'Make No Little Plans,' Daniel Burnham Thought It, but Did He Say It?" *Journal of the A.I.A,* 27 (March 1957) 95–9; Thomas S. Hines, *Burnham of Chicago: Architect and Planner* (New York: Oxford, 1974), 401.

Can't anybody here PLAY this game: Robert W. Creamer, *Stengel: His Life and Times* (New York: Simon & Schuster, 1984), 299.

PLAY it again, Sam: Koch, *Casablanca,* op. cit., 87, 95; Harmetz, *Round Up the Usual Suspects,* op. cit., 260; Dirks; Harry Purvis, "Say It Again, Sam," *TV Guide,* December 30, 1978; *Life,* March 21, 1969, 65.

The great PLEASURE in life: Gay Courter, *Flowers in the Blood* (New York: Dutton, 1990), 553; Walter Bagehot, *Literary Studies,* vol. 1, (London: Dent, 1911, 1951), 152.

A POEM is never finished: W. H. Auden, *A Certain World* (New York: Viking, 1970), 423; Paul Valéry, *Oeuvres* (Paris: Gallimard, 1957), 1497 (translation by Rosalie Maggio); Qian Zhongshu, *Fortress Besieged,* op. cit., preface; "Did Picasso Say This?" January 10–2, 1999, *alt.quotations,* <http://groups.google.com/group/ alt.quotations/browse_thread/thread/a3f290b6f0049ce2/19f96583a1f96998 ?q=picasso+%2B+abandoned&rnum=1&h1=en#19f96583a1f96998> (August 15, 2005).

A thousand POINTS of light: Noonan, *What I Saw at the Revolution,* op. cit., 312–3; *NYT,* January 21, 1989; *Newsweek,* October 12, 1992, 6; Linda Sexton, *Points of Light* (Boston: Little, Brown, 1987), epigraph; C. S. Lewis, *The Magician's Nephew* (New York: Macmillan, 1955, Collier, 1970), 99; Thomas Wolfe, *The Web and the Rock* (New York: Harper and Brothers, 1939; Grosset & Dunlap, 1956), 163; *Forest and Stream,* March 1924, 148; *Aldine, The Art Journal of America,* October 1, 1878, 194; *Arthur's Lady's Home Magazine,* May 1872, 291; *Hours at Home,* January, 1866, 229.

Forever POISED between: "Arms Control's Year of Decision: Our Mutual Agenda," The Honorable John D. Holum, Director U.S. Arms Control and Disarmament Agency Remarks to the Council on International Relations (CARI), Buenos Aires, Argentina, March 23, 1995, <http://dosfan.lib.uic.edu/acda/ speeches/holum/arg.htm> (August 15, 2005); *Newsweek,* April 30, 1956, 82; Baker, 144; *NYT,* April 22, 1977; MDQ, 559; *Times* (London, England), January 31, 1991; Rees, 373, 464.

An honest POLITICIAN is one: Bartlett's, 445; SNPD, 756–7; Erwin Stanley Bradley, *Simon Cameron, Lincoln's Secretary of War: A Political Biography* (Philadelphia: University of Pennsylvania, 1966), 420; *NYT,* September 29, 1856; *Lippincott's,* July 1870, 49.

A POLITICIAN is a person who approaches: Paul Steiner, ed., *The Stevenson Wit and Wisdom* (New York: Pyramid, 1965), 82; *Illustrated London News,* October 10, 1908, in *The American Chesterton Society,* <http://www.chesterton.org/qmeister2/17.htm> (April 30, 2005); Rees, 46; Harris, 252.

All POLITICS is local: Tip O'Neill with Gary Hymel, *All Politics Is Local and Other Rules of the Game* (Holbrook, Mass.: Bob Adams, 1994), xii; John A. Farrell, *Tip O'Neill and the Democratic Century* (Boston: Little, Brown, 2001), 65, 689, 697; *Lima* [Ohio] *News,* February 13, 1932; *Reno* [Nev.] *Evening Gazette,* February 16, 1932; *Appleton* [Wis.] *Post-Crescent,* February 17, 1932; *Daily News* (Frederick, Md.), July 1, 1932; *Port Arthur* [Tex.] *News,* July 8, 1932; Edward J. Bander e-mail, February 3, 2005.

Being in POLITICS is like being a football coach: *Appleton Post-Crescent* [Wis.], November 15, 1967; Bill Adler, ed., *The McCarthy Wit* (New York: Fawcett, 1969), 13.

POLITICS ain't beanbag: Finley Peter Dunne, *Mr. Dooley in Peace and War* in Hutchinson, ed., *Mr. Dooley on Ivrything and Ivrybody,* op. cit., 3; Bander, *Mr. Dooley and Mr. Dunne,* op. cit., 169.

POLITICS is the art of the possible: Gee, 300; Rees, 137; Platt, 265; Louis L. Snyder, *The Blood and Iron Chancellor: A Documentary-Biography of Otto von Bismarck* (Princeton, N.J.: D. Van Nostrand, 1967), 6; Latham, 196; King, 68; ODQ, 117.

POLITICS makes strange bedfellows: William Gifford, *The Baviad and Maeviad* (London: J. Wright, 1797), 127; *Workingman's Advocate,* March 10, 1832; Alan Nevins, ed., *The Diary of Philip Hone 1828–1851,* Vol. 1 (New York: Dodd, Mead, 1927), 404; *Weekly Wisconsin Argus* (Madison), October 15, 1851; *National Era,* November 8, 1855, 1786; *The Tempest,* II:2, Magill, 790; Charles Dudley Warner, *My Summer in a Garden* (Boston: James R. Osgood, 1871), 131; Bartlett's 543; ODQ, 629.

POWER corrupts: Dalberg-Acton, John Emerich Edward, *Essays on Freedom and Power* (Boston: Beacon, 1948), 364; *All Things Considered,* National Public Radio, July 8, 1998; "In Reply to Lord Mansfield, in Relation to the Case of John Wilkes," Delivered in the House of Commons, January 9, 1770, The Speeches of Lord Chatham, *Classicpersuasion.org,* <http://classicpersuasion.org/cbo/chatham/chat09.htm> (August 16, 2005).

POWER is the ultimate aphrodisiac: Anne Moir and David Jessel, *Brain Sex: The Real Difference Between Men and Women* (Secaucus, N.J.: Lyle Stuart, 1991), 108; *Chronicle Telegram* (Elyria, Ohio), April 29, 1972; *Daily Times-News* (Burlington, N.C.), June 20, 1972; *San Francisco Sunday Examiner and Chronicle,* August 6, 1772; DuPre Jones, "The Sayings of Secretary Henry," *NYT Magazine,* October 28, 1973.

Freedom of the PRESS: A. J. Liebling, "The Wayward Press: Do You Belong in Journalism?" *New Yorker,* May 14, 1960, 108–9.

Every man has his PRICE: Latham, 14–5; Stimpson 1948, 261–2; MPMFP, 1878; Ackermann, 362; ODP, 94; *Pennsylvania Magazine,* January 1776, 9.

Nowadays people know the PRICE of everything: Wilde, 48, 418; Hubbard 1911, 159; Hubbard 1923, 154; Philip Goodman, *Puck,* July 1918, 40; *CT,* March 7, 1993.

PRIDE goes before a fall: Tripp, 504; ODP, 249; Rees, 96.

PRIVACY is the right to be left alone: Samuel Warren and Louis Brandeis, "The Right to Privacy," *Harvard Law Review,* Vol. 4, No. 5, December 15, 1890. <http://www.lawrence.edu/fast/boardmaw/Privacy_brand_warr2.html> (October 22, 2004).

For every PROBLEM there is always a solution: H. L. Mencken, *A Mencken Chrestomathy* (New York: Knopf, 1949), 443.

You're either part of the solution or . . . PROBLEM: Robert Scheer, introduction to *Eldridge Cleaver: Post-Prison Writings and Speeches* (New York: Random House, 1969), xxxii; *Chronicle Telegram* (Elyria, Ohio), July 6, 1956; *Guthrian* (Guthrie Center, Iowa), January 24, 1961; *Oakland Tribune,* July 6, 1964.

PROFESSIONALS built the Titanic: *Pittsburgh Post-Gazette,* January 7, 1998; *LAT,* December 11, 2002.

All PROFESSIONS are conspiracies: George Bernard Shaw, *The Doctor's Dilemma* (1911) in *Bernard Shaw: Selected Plays* (New York: Dodd, Mead, 1948), 110; Roland Marchand, *Advertising the American Dream* (Berkeley, Calif.: University of California, 1985), 48.

PROMISES are like pie crust: Jonathan Swift, "A Compleat Collection of Genteel and Ingenious Conversation, &c.," in Herbert Davis, ed., *Prose Works, Vol. 4: A Proposal for Correcting the English Tongue, Polite Conversation, Etc.* (Oxford: Basil Blackwell, 1738, 1957), 146; Morris Kominsky, *The Hoaxers* (Boston: Branden Press, 1970), 27–35; Boller and George, 72; *NYT,* January 22, 1983; ODP, 249–50.

PROSPERITY is just around the corner: Lima [Ohio] *Morning News,* August 29, 1909; *Atlanta Constitution,* December 19, 1915; *Mansfield* [Ohio] *News,* April 26, 1919; *Perry* [Iowa] *Daily Chief,* December 24, 1920; *Iowa City Press-Citizen,* January 24, 1921; *Kingsport* [Tenn.] *Times,* November 22, 1921; *Lima News* March 4, 1922; Woodland [Calif.] *Daily Democrat,* May 29, 1922; *Sun-Herald* (Lime Springs, Iowa), October 12, 1922; Woods, 248; *Forum and Century,* February 1932; Gilbert Seldes, *The Years of the Locust (America, 1929–1932)* (Boston: Little, Brown, 1933), 43; Richard Norton Smith, *An Uncommon Man: The Triumph of Herbert Hoover* (New York: Simon & Schuster, 1984), 126; Boller and George, 48; Edward Angly, *Oh Yeah?* (New York: Viking, 1932), 17.

PUBLIC office is a public trust: William C. Hudson, *Random Recollections of an Old Political Reporter* (New York: Cupples & Leon, 1911), 175–83; MPMFP, 1714.

The PUBLIC be damned: Stimpson 1948, 291–2; Woods, 225; Melville E. Stone, *Fifty Years a Journalist* (New York: Greenwood Press, 1921, 1968), 116–8; *NYT,* October 9, 1882, October 13, 1882, August 25, 1918; Elmo Scott Watson, "The Truth About That 'Public Be Damned' Interview," *Nashua* [Iowa] *Reporter,* November 4, 1936; John Steele Gordon, "The Public Be Damned," *American Heritage,* September–October 1989, 18, 20.

A PURITAN is someone: "State of the Union, 1992," George Bush, *Vital Speeches of the Day,* February 15, 1992, 260; *LAT,* August 17, 1992; H. L. Mencken, *A Mencken Chrestomathy,* op. cit., 624.

Practice RANDOM kindness: Adair Lara, *San Francisco Chronicle,* February 19, 1991, May 16, 1991, May 12, 1992, September 17, 1992, April 21, 1994, February 15, 1996, December 23, 1997; Anne Herbert, "Random Kindness and Senseless Acts of Beauty," *Whole Earth Review,* July 1985, 92; "Practice Random Kindness and Senseless Acts of Beauty," *Glamour,* December 1991, 86; Adair Lara, "Conspiracy of Kindness," *Reader's Digest,* May 1992, 109–10; Ann Landers, *DDN,* May 31, 1997; Susan Reed, "Fed up with violence, Chuck Wall calls for an outbreak of random kindness," *People,* December 13, 1993, 101; Jack Smith, *LAT,* April 25, 1994; *San Jose Mercury-News,* June 11, 1994; Anne Herbert and Margaret M. Pavel, *Random Kindness and Senseless Acts of Beauty* (Volcano, Calif. Volcano Press, 1993); William Wordsworth, "Lines Composed a Few Miles Above Tintern Abbey" (1798), Mark Van Doren, ed., *Selected Poetry of William Wordsworth* (New York: Modern Library, 2002), 100; Karen Stone, *Miami Herald,* December 24, 1996.

READ my lips: "Read My Lips," Joe Greene, © 1957, on *Enchantment* (Liberty, 1958); "Read My Lips," Mary Chapin Carpenter, © 1988 on *State of the Heart* (Columbia, 1989); Scott Turow, *Presumed Innocent* (Farrar, Straus & Giroux, 1987, Warner 1988), 117; Safire 1993, 240–3.

REALITY is nothing but: Wagner, *The Search for Signs of Intelligent Life in the Universe,* op. cit., 18.

A RECESSION is when a neighbor loses his job: NYT, October 2, 1986; MDQ, 583–4; James B. Simpson, *Best Quotes of '54, '55, '56.* (New York: Crowell, 1957), 26; *Harlan* [Iowa] *News-Advertiser,* February 9, 1954.

I only REGRET that: Richard E. Mooney, "One Life to Lose in Four Places: The Execution of Nathan Hale," *The New-York Journal of American History* 66 (spring/summer 2005) 43–7; *Morning Call* (Allentown, Pa.), September 26, 1976; George Dudley Seymour, *Captain Nathan Hale, Major John Palsgrave Wyllys, a Digressive History* (New Haven: George Dudley Seymour, 1933), 28; George Dudley Seymour, *Documentary Life of Nathan Hale* (New Haven: George Dudley Seymour, 1941), xxxii, 85–7, 292, 376–82, 402, 409–10, 452–4; Maria Hull Campbell, *Revolutionary Services and Civil Life of General William Hull: Prepared from His Manuscripts, by His Daughter* (New York: Appleton, 1848), 38; Burnam 1975, 104; Judith Ann Schiff, "Old, Yale: Nathan Hale's Many Faces," *Yale,* summer 1988, 16; Joseph Addison, *Cato,* IV:4.

RELIGION is the opium: Safire 1991, 189–90; Karl Marx, *Critique of Hegel's "Philosophy of Right,"* Annette Jolin and Joseph O'Malley, trans. (Cambridge: Cambridge University, 1844, 1970), 131.

No one washes a RENTED CAR: NYT, October 27, 2002, January 22, 2003, August 27, 2003, November 6, 2003; Jill Martyn e-mail, May 3, 2005; James F. Rand e-mail, August 31, 2004.

I can RESIST everything: Wilde, 388.

I shall RETURN: "Memorable Quotations from Public Statements by General MacArthur," *Representative Speeches of General of the Army Douglas MacArthur,* op. cit., vi; William Manchester, *American Caesar* (Boston: Little, Brown, 1978, Dell, 1979), 311–3; Douglas MacArthur, *Reminiscences* (New York: McGraw-Hill, 1964), 145; Michael Schaller, *Douglas MacArthur* (Oxford: Oxford, 1989), 62.

I've been RICH: Leonard Lyons, WP, May 12, 1937; *New York Daily News,* February 10, 1966; interview with Henry McNulty, October 8, 2005; Rees, 544; Rowes, *The Book of Quotes,* op.cit., 21; *The Independent* (London, England), August 9, 1992.

The RICH are different from you and me: "The Rich Boy," in F. Scott Fitzgerald, *Babylon Revisited and Other Stories* (New York: Scribner's, 1960), 152; Ernest Hemingway, "The Snows of Kilimanjaro," *Esquire,* August 1936, 200; Wilson, *The*

Crack-Up, op. cit., 125; Matthew J. Bruccoli, *Some Sort of Epic Grandeur: The Life of F. Scott Fitzgerald* (New York: Harcourt Brace Jovanovich, 1981), 411–3; John Kuehl and Jackson R. Bryer, eds., *Dear Scott / Dear Max* (New York: Scribner's, 1971), 230–2; Ernest Hemingway, *The Snows of Kilimanjaro* (New York: Scribner's, 1927, 1936), 23.

You can never be too RICH: Ralph G. Martin, *The Woman He Loved* (New York: Simon & Schuster, 1973, 1974), 505; Sally Bedell Smith, *In All His Glory: The Life of William S. Paley* (New York: Simon & Schuster, 1990), 326–7, 452, 456–7; Lewis, vii, 23; interview with Truman Capote biographer Gerald Clarke, December 10, 1990.

A RIDDLE wrapped: Melinda Corey and George Ochoa, eds., *The Man in Lincoln's Nose: Funny, Profound, and Quotable Quotes of Screenwriters, Movie Stars, and Moguls* (New York: Fireside / Simon & Schuster, 1990), 121; Churchill, *Never Give In!,* op. cit., 199.

I would rather be RIGHT than president: Glyndon G. Van Deusen, *The Life of Henry Clay* (Boston: Little, Brown, 1937), 318; Robert Seager II, ed., *The Papers of Henry Clay,* Vol. 9 (Lexington, Ky.: University Press of Kentucky, 1988), 283.

The RIGHT stuff: "Major Andre's Letters to Miss Seward," November 1, 1769, *The Pastime: A Literary Paper,* December 22, 1807, 214; Ian Hay, *The Right Stuff* (Boston: Houghton Mifflin, 1908, 1910); Jonathan Daniels, *The Man of Independence* (Philadelphia: Lippincott, 1950), 118.

We was ROBBED: Bartlett's, 747; Peter Heller, *In This Corner . . .* (New York: Simon & Schuster, 1973), 44–5; *NYT,* April 25, 1940; *Daily Mirror,* June 22, 1932; *NYT,* June 22, 1932; *Evening Post,* June 22, 1932; *American,* June 22, 1932.

Will Rogers: Will Rogers, *The Illiterate Digest* (New York: A. L. Burt, 1924); P. J. O'Brien, *Will Rogers: Ambassador of Good Will, Prince of Wit and Wisdom* (Chicago: John C. Winston, 1935); Homer Croy, *Our Will Rogers* (New York: Duell, Sloan and Pearce, 1953); Donald Day, ed., *The Autobiography of Will Rogers* (Boston: Houghton Mifflin, 1949); Donald Day, *Will Rogers: A Biography* (New York: David McKay, 1962); Paula McSpadden Love, ed., *The Will Rogers Book* (Indianapolis: Bobbs-Merrill, 1961); Peter C. Rollins, *Will Rogers: A Bio-Bibliography* (Westport, Conn.: Greenwood, 1984); Reba Collins, ed., *Will Rogers Says. . . . Favorite Quotations Selected by the Will Rogers Memorial Staff* (Oklahoma City: Neighbors and Quaid, 1993); Ben Yagoda, *Will Rogers: A Biography* (New York: Knopf, 1994); Ray Robinson, *American Original: A Life of Will Rogers* (New York: Oxford, 1996). "*My ancestors*": Collins, *Will Rogers Says . . . ,* op. cit., 5; Day, *Will Rogers,* op. cit., 1; Ben Yagoda e-mail, July 15, 2005. "*Enough white blood*": Cleveland Amory, "America's Most Complete Human Document," *Saturday Review,*

August 25, 1962, 14. *"Now . . . everything is funny"*: Rogers, *The Illiterate Digest,* op. cit., 131. *"A fanatic"*: radio broadcast, June 8, 1930 in Collins, *Will Rogers Says . . . ,* op. cit., 78. *"Half our life"*: Collins, *Will Rogers Says . . . ,* op. cit., 4. *"We'll hold the distinction"*: radio broadcast, October 18, 1931 in Collins, *Will Rogers Says . . . ,* op. cit., 26. *"You can't say"*: Day, *The Autobiography of Will Rogers,* op. cit., 218. *"The Income Tax"*: Rogers, *The Illiterate Digest,* op. cit., 71–2. *"But with Congress"*: radio broadcast, May 12, 1935 in Collins, *Will Rogers Says . . . ,* op. cit., 18. *"I tell you folks"*: Rogers, *The Illiterate Digest,* op. cit., 30. *"I am not a member"*: O'Brien, *Will Rogers,* op. cit., 162; Robinson, *American Original,* op. cit. 267; Yagoda e-mail July 15, 2005. *"You know, everybody is ignorant"*: Rogers, *The Illiterate Digest,* op. cit., 64. *"There is nothing"*: Love, *The Will Rogers Book,* op. cit., 67.

When in ROME: ODP, 262; MPMFP, 2005; Mieder, 507.

Theodore Roosevelt: many phrases: Safire 1988, 268; SNPD, xxiii; Gamiel Bradford, *The Quick and the Dead* (Boston: Houghton Mifflin), 31. *"Hat in the ring"*: SNPD, 320. *"Hearts and minds"*: SNPD, 716; MacArthur, *Reminiscences,* op. cit., 33. *"Weasel word"*: Frost, 59; Stewart Chaplin, "The Stained Glass Political Platform," *Century,* June 1900, 305. *"Muckraker"*: SNPD, 469–71; Theodore Roosevelt, "The Man with the Muck-Rake: An address delivered by the President of the United States at the laying of the cornerstone of the Office Building of the House of Representatives, April 14, 1906," *Outlook,* January–April, 1906, 883–7; John Bunyan, *Pilgrim's Progress* (New York: P. F. Collier, 1678, 1909), 205. *"I stand for the square deal"*: Woods, 239; SNPD, 748–9; MPMFP, 498; Mark Twain, *Life on the Mississippi* (New York: Heritage, 1944), 301. *"I wish to preach"*: Ringo 220; Theodore Roosevelt, speech before the Hamilton Club, Chicago, Ill., April 10, 1899, in Charles Hurd, *A Treasury of Great American Speeches* (New York: Hawthorn, 1959), 152. *"It is not the critic"*: "Citizenship in a Republic," Address delivered at the Sorbonne, Paris, April 23, 1910, in *The Works of Theodore Roosevelt, National Edition,* vol. 13, *American Ideals, The Strenuous Life, Realizable Ideals* (New York: Scribner's, 1926), 510. *"A splendid little war"*: letter of John A. Gable, Executive Director, Theodore Roosevelt Association, *NYT,* July 9, 1991. *"In short"*: Theodore Roosevelt, *The Strenuous Life* (New York: Review of Reviews, 1900), 137; *The Works of Theodore Roosevelt,* vol. 13, op. cit., xvii. *"I can do"*: Owen Wister, *Roosevelt: The Story of a Friendship, 1880–1919* (New York: Macmillan, 1930), 87; Teague, *Mrs. L,* op. cit., 84; Renehan, *The Lion's Pride,* op. cit., 47.

A ROSE is a rose: Gertrude Stein, "Sacred Emily," in William Harmon, ed., *The Oxford Book of American Light Verse* (New York: Oxford, 1979), 293; Janet Hobhouse, *Everybody Who Was Anybody: A Biography of Gertrude Stein* (New York: Putnam's, 1975, 1976), 73, 139, 175, 185, 205; Gertrude Stein, *The World Is Round* (New York: William R. Scott, 1939; London: B. T. Batsford, 1939), frontispiece, 75–7; Ernest Hemingway, *The Sun Also Rises* op. cit., 41, 73; Richard Poirier, "Manly Agitations," *New Republic,* June 8, 1998, 29–30.

RUM, Romanism, and rebellion: Woods, 57; MPMFP, 1748; Ellis Paxson Ober-holtzer, *A History of the United States Since the Civil War,* vol. 4 (New York: Macmillan, 1931), 206; Matthew Josephson, *The Politicos* (New York: Harcourt, Brace and World, 1938), 369.

He can RUN: Frost, 29; *New York Herald Tribune,* June 9, 1946; Joe Louis, *My Life Story* (New York: Duell, Sloan and Pearce, 1947), 176; Joe Louis Barrow, Jr., and Barbara Munder, *Joe Louis: 50 Years an American Hero* (New York: McGraw-Hill, 1988), Barney Nagler, *Brown Bomber* (New York: World, 1972), 115.

SATIRE is what closes: Teichmann, *George S. Kaufman,* op. cit., 129; Drennan, ed., *The Algonquin Wits,* op. cit., 81; Jeffrey D. Mason, *Wisecracks: The Farces of George S. Kaufman* (Ann Arbor: UMI Research, 1988), 87; Jeffrey D. Mason e-mail, November 22, 2004; Malcolm Goldstein, *George S. Kaufman: His Life, His Theater* (New York: Oxford, 1979); interviews with Malcolm Goldstein, January 8, 2005, January 30, 2005.

If you like laws and SAUSAGE: "Remarks by Senator Edward M. Kennedy (D-Mass.) to the Brookings Institution," *Federal News Service,* April 5, 2004; Platt, 190; *Decatur* [Ill.] *Republican,* April 29, 1869, May 28, 1874; *Edwardsville* [Ill.] *Intelligencer,* May 4, 1871; *Indiana* [Pa.] *Progress,* May 11, 1871, January 13, 1881; *Hamilton* [Ohio] *Examiner,* June 25, 1874.

SAY it ain't so: *New York Evening World,* September 30, 1920; Oliver Gramling, *AP: The Story of the News* (New York: Farrar and Rinehart, 1940), 292; Bartlett's, 851; *Chicago Herald,* September 29, 1920; *New York Tribune,* September 29, 1920; *New York Evening Post,* September 29, 1920; James T. Farrell, *My Baseball Diary* (New York: A. S. Barnes, 1957), 106; Eliot Asinof, *Eight Men Out: The Black Sox and the 1919 World Series* (New York: Holt, Rinehart and Winston, 1963), 163–4; Donald S. Gropman, *Say It Ain't So, Joe!* (Boston, Little, Brown, 1979), 191–2.

SCRIBBLE, scribble, scribble: Henry Digby Beste, *Personal and Literary Memorials* (London: H. Colburn, 1829), 68; *The Analectic Magazine,* August 1819, 111; *The Tablet,* July 14, 1795, 36; George Birkbeck Hill, *The Memoirs of the Life of Edward Gibbon, with Various Observations and Excursions, by Himself* (London: Methuen, 1900), 127.

There are no SECOND ACTS: F. Scott Fitzgerald, *The Last Tycoon* (New York: Scribner's, 1941, Bantam, 1976), 212; Burnam, 1975, 258–9; *American Heritage,* November 1998, 12.

Oh, God, give us the SERENITY to accept: Anderson, 27–8; Elisabeth Sifton, *The Serenity Prayer: Faith and Politics in Times of Peace and War* (New York: Norton, 2003), 277, 292–5, 301–5, 340–3; Carnegie, *How to Stop Worrying and Start*

Living, op. cit., 85; Richard Wightman Fox, *Reinhold Niebuhr: A Biography* (New York: Pantheon, 1985), 290–1.

Oh, to be SEVENTY again: Jack Smith, *Chicago Sun-Times,* February 14, 1977; Anthony and Sally Sampson, eds., *The Oxford Book of Ages* (Oxford: Oxford, 1985, 1988), 174; Haun, 7; Fadiman, 783; Rees, 174; MDQ, 400.

George Bernard Shaw: <u>Bayh</u>: *The Tennessean* (Nashville), August 9, 1992. *"I have been misquoted everywhere"*: St. John Ervine, *Bernard Shaw: His Life, Work and Friends* (London: Constable, 1956), 532; Michael Holroyd, *Bernard Shaw: Volume III, 1918–1950, The Lure of Fantasy* (New York: Random House, 1991), 308. <u>"Oh, all Americans"</u>: ibid.; Boller and George, 117; Hesketh Pearson, *G.B.S.: A Full-Length Portrait* (New York: Harper & Brothers, 1942), 366; Joseph P. Lash, *Helen and Teacher: The Story of Helen Keller and Anne Sullivan Macy* (New York: Delacorte, 1980), 612–4. *"The true artist"*: Shaw, *Man and Superman,* op. cit., Act 1. *"Life is not meant"*: Shaw, *Back to Methuselah* (London: Constable, 1922), part v, 250; Rees, 245. *"My plays"*: Holroyd, *Bernard Shaw,* Vol. 2, 334. *"All we ask now"*: MPMFP, 54. *"But suppose"*: Copeland, *10,000 Jokes,* op. cit., 560; *NYT,* June 8, 1982, July 23, 1982; *DDN,* July 12, 1990; Pearson, *Lives of the Wits,* op. cit., 265. *"You and I know that"*: Cerf, 121; Teichmann, *Smart Aleck,* op. cit., 229; Pearson, *G.B.S.,* op. cit., 167; Gary Schmidgall, *The Stranger Wilde* (New York: Dutton, 1994), 363. *"The trouble, Mr. Goldwyn"*: Zierold, *The Moguls,* op. cit., 128; *NYT,* September 27, 1936; Cerf, 121; Mayer, *Merely Colossal,* op. cit., 10; Holroyd, *Bernard Shaw,* op. cit., Vol. 3, 307; Bernard F. Dukore, ed., *Not Bloody Likely! And Other Quotations from Bernard Shaw* (New York: Columbia, 1996), xii. <u>Shaw and Churchill</u>: Bill Adler, *The Churchill Wit* (New York: Coward-McCann, 1965), 35. <u>Shaw and proper lady</u>: Anderson, 56; Jerry Adler, *Newsweek,* April 19, 1993, 69; Martin Gottlieb, *DDN,* October 23, 1994. *"There may be some doubt"*: George Bernard Shaw, *Everybody's Political What's What* (New York: Dodd, Mead, 1944), 49, 148.

Don't give up the SHIP!: Platt, 189; Harry L. Coles, *The War of 1812* (Chicago: University of Chicago, 1965), 86; Bombaugh, 388–9; Home Book, 62; John White Chadwick, "Mugford's Victory" in Burton Stevenson, ed., *Poems of American History* (Boston: Houghton Mifflin, 1936), 174–5.

There was a man who cried because he had no SHOES: Schlesinger, *A Thousand Days,* op. cit., 106; Anderson, 48; *RQ,* spring 1984, 268; Platt, 316; Edward Behatsek, trans., W. G. Archer, ed., *The Gulistan or Rose Garden of Sa'di* (New York: Putnam's, 1964, 1965), 158.

SHOOT, if you must: Samuel T. Pickard, *Life and Letters of John Greenleaf Whittier,* Vol. 2 (Boston: Houghton Mifflin, 1894), 454–60; Frank Austen Lewis, "Whittier's Mistake," *The Express,* undated newspaper clipping. "Through

Barbara Fritchie's Home," *Daughters of Union Veterans of the Civil War,* <http://www.rootsweb.com/~orduvcw/home.htm> (May 3, 2005).

If I have seen farther . . . SHOULDERS of giants: Robert K. Merton, *On the Shoulders of Giants: A Shandean Postscript* (New York: Free Press, 1965, Harcourt Brace Jovanovich, 1985), 3–9, 12–3, 32–4, 40–1, 73–9, 177–96, 200–1, 209–11, 218, 245–61, 267–9.

SHOUTING fire in a crowded theater: *Schenck v. United States,* 249 U.S. 47 (1919), 437, <http://caselaw.lp.findlaw.com/cgi-bin/getcase.pl?court+us&vol=249&invol=47> (May 3, 2005).

Show Business: *"If you have a message":* Frank Manciewicz, *NYT,* November 23, 1990. *"Never let that bastard":* Max Wilk, *The Wit and Wisdom of Hollywood* (New York: Atheneum, 1971), 153; Rowes, *The Book of Quotes,* op. cit., 228; Cerf, 38; Alva Johnston, *The Great Goldwyn,* op. cit., 29; Lester Tanzer, *The Kennedy Circle* (Washington, D.C.: Luce, 1961), xv. *"I have a foolproof device":* *Newsweek,* October 27, 1980, 27; French, *The Movie Moguls,* op. cit., 57; *NYT,* April 25, 1989, April 29, 1989. *"It only proves":* Bob Thomas, *King Cohn* (New York: Putnam's, 1967, Bantam, 1968), xvii; French, *The Movie Moguls,* op. cit., 1; John Lahr, *Notes on a Cowardly Lion* (New York: Knopf, 1969, Ballantine, 1970), 210; Ringo, 266, 275. *"When I die":* Teichman, *George S. Kaufman,* op. cit., 256; John Robert Colombo, ed., *Popcorn Paradise: The Wit and Wisdom of Hollywood* (New York; Holt, Rinehart and Winston, 1979), 113. *"If you can't write":* United Technologies advertisement, *WSJ,* February 22, 1979; Tom Logsdon, *LAT,* July 17, 1994. *"If you can fake":* Daniel Schorr, *Christian Science Monitor,* September 5, 2003; "Courteney Cox," *Actressgallery.com,* <http://www.actressgallery.com/cox/> (September 12, 2005). *"Dying can be":* *Newsweek,* April 8, 1991, 45, January 27, 1992, 15; Rees, 290, 551; *Seattle Post-Intelligencer,* June 22, 2000. *"A day away":* *NYT,* March 10, 1983; *NYT Book Review,* October 4, 1992, 3, November 1, 1992, 34, November 8, 1992, 66; Bankhead, *Tallulah,* op. cit., 308. *"I've been around":* Wilk, *The Wit and Wisdom of Hollywood,* op. cit., 51; Oscar Levant, *The Memoirs of an Amnesiac* (New York: Putnam's, 1965), 192; Jules Witcover, *Marathon Man* (New York: Viking, 1977), 146.

SHOW me the money: *Primetime Live,* January 21, 1998; "Ten Questions with Leigh Steinberg," *Sports Hollywood,* <http:www.sportshollywood.com/asksteinberg.html> (May 3, 2005); *LAT,* December 28, 1996; *Houston Chronicle,* May 2, 2002; Bartlett's 842, back jacket; *The National Police,* August 10, 1901, 10; *Reno* [Nev.] *Evening Gazette,* September 7, 1906; *Oakland* [Calif.] *Tribune,* January 6, 1906, August 18, 1907.

The Sixties: *"Do not fold":* Stephen Lubar, " 'Do not fold, spindle or mutilate': A cultural history of the punch card," May 1991, <http://ccat.sas.upenn.edu/slubar/fsm.html> (September 13, 2005). *"There is a time":* Thomas Powers, *The*

War at Home: Vietnam and the American People, 1964–1968 (New York: Grossman, 1973) 33–4, 232. *"Make love"*: R. Z. Sheppard, *Time,* November 10, 1975, 96; Helen Dudar, "G. Legman's Second Thoughts," *Village Voice,* May 1, 1984, 43; Mikita Brottman, *Funny Peculiar: Gershon Legman and the Psychopathology of Humor* (Hillsdale, Ill.: Analytic, 2004), 25. *"Do your own thing"*: Safire 1984, 118–20; Chaucer, *Canterbury Tales,* op. cit., "The Clerkes Tale," 364; Eugene F. Irey, ed., *A Concordance to Five Essays of Ralph Waldo Emerson* (New York: Garland, 1981), 461. *"Keep on truckin'"*: Thomas Marema, "Who Is This Crumb?" *NYT Magazine,* October 1, 1972, 12; David Dodd, "The Annotated Truckin'," <http://arts.ucsc.edu/gdead/agdl/truckin> (September 13, 2005). Stuart Berg Flexner, *Listening to America* (New York: Simon & Schuster, 1982), 312, 382. *"We are the people"*: Nicholas Von Hoffman, *We Are the People Our Parents Warned Us Against* (New York: Quadrangle, 1967), Rees, 315; bumper sticker seen on Interstate 74, western Indiana, December 1, 1991.

Sell the SIZZLE: Elmer Wheeler, *Tested Sentences That Sell* (New York: Prentice-Hall, 1938), 3; Elmer Wheeler, *The Sizzle Book* (New York: Prentice-Hall, 1938); Wheeler, *Sizzlemanship,* op. cit.

You're only here . . . SMELL the flowers: Walter Hagen, *The Walter Hagen Story, by The Haig, Himself* (New York: Simon & Schuster, 1956), 319.

SMILE when you say that: Owen Wister, *The Virginian* (New York: Macmillan, 1902, Grosset & Dunlap, 1940), 29; videotape of *The Virginian,* (Paramount, 1929); Larry Swindell, *The Last Hero: A Biography of Gary Cooper* (Garden City, N.Y.: Doubleday, 1980), 110; American Film Institute; no. 374; Dirks; Safire 1993, 316; Henry Fonda, *Fonda: My Life* (New York: New American Library, 1981, Signet, 1982), 129.

You can get more done with a SMILE: Safire 1997, 119, 294; videotape of *The Untouchables* (Paramount, 1987); Mark Levell and Bill Helmer, *The Quotable Al Capone* (Chicago: Mad Dog Press, 1990), 3, in "Verifying a Capone Quote," December 22–31, 2003, <http://answers.google.com/answers/threadview?id=289592> (August 18, 2005); Harry Hossent, *Gangster Movies* (London: Octopus, 1974), 21; Mario Gomes e-mail, August 18, 2005; *Sandy Burke: Woodland* [Calif.] *Daily Democrat,* May 27, 1919.

A SMOKE-FILLED room: Woods, 100; *Cleveland Plain Dealer,* June 13, 1920; *NYT,* June 13, 1920, *Evening Star* (Washington, D.C.), June 14, 1920; *CT,* February 14, 1915; Mark Sullivan, *Our Times,* Vol. 6 (New York: Scribner's, 1935), 37–8.

It is very easy to give up SMOKING: *Reader's Digest,* December 1945, 26; interview with Robert Hirst of the Mark Twain Project, December 16, 1991, January 29, 1992; Esther Harriott letter to *NYT Magazine,* September 14, 1980, 28.

Any man who is not a SOCIALIST at age twenty: Cerf, 258; Seldes 1985, 157; Benham, 1949, 751; Anderson, 54; *RQ,* summer 1977, 310, winter 1977, 164.

I am a SOLDIER so that my son may be a poet: L. H. Butterfield, Marc Friedlander, and Mary-Jo Kline, eds., *The Book of Abigail and John: Selected Letters of the Adams Family, 1762–1784* (Cambridge, Mass.: Harvard University, 1875), 260.

Old SOLDIERS never die: Representative Speeches of General of the Army Douglas MacArthur, op. cit., 20; MacArthur, *Reminiscences,* op. cit., 405; Home Book, 2298h; ODP, 229; Platt, 324–5; SNPD, 520–1.

SPEAK softly, and carry a big stick: Minneapolis Tribune, September 3, 1901; *Presidential Addresses and State Papers.* I, 265–6, in Albert Bushnell Hart and Herbert Ronald Ferleger, eds., *Theodore Roosevelt Cyclopedia* (Oyster Bay, N.Y.: Theodore Roosevelt Association, 1989), 42; Platt, 123; Henry F. Pringle, *Theodore Roosevelt: A Biography* (New York: Harcourt, Brace, 1931), 214.

SPEAK truth to power: Speak Truth to Power: A Quaker Search for an Alternative to Violence (Philadelphia: American Friends Service Committee, 1955), iv; Larry Ingle, "'Speak Truth to Power': A Thirty Years' Retrospective," *Christian Century,* April 17, 1985, 383–5; H. Larry Ingle, *First Among Friends: George Fox and the Creation of Quakerism* (New York: Oxford, 1994); Larry Ingle e-mail, October 29, 2004; John D'Emilio, *Lost Prophet: The Life and Times of Bayard Rustin* (New York: Free Press, 2003), 48.

I don't care what they . . . SPELL my name right: Michael Turney, "I don't care what the newspapers say about me as long as they spell my name right," *On-Line Readings in Public Relations by Michael Turney,* <http://www.nku.edu/~turney/prclass/readings/3eras1x.html> (April 16, 2005).

Never trust a man who has only one way to SPELL a word: NYT, June 18, 1992; *The Hotline,* June 22, 1992; Evan Esar, *Dictionary of Humorous Quotations* (New York: Horizon, 1949, Paperback Library, 1962), 178; Fred Shapiro, "Quotation Regarding Spelling," *Stumpers,* September 17, 1995, <http://listserv.dom.edu/cgi-bin/wa.exe?A2=ind9509&L=STUMPERS-L&P=R29310> (August 19, 2005); MDQ, 292; *St. Petersburg Times,* February 19, 1990; John William Ward, *Andrew Jackson: Symbol for an Age* (New York: Oxford, 1955), 84–6; Alan Walker Read, "Could Andrew Jackson Spell?" *American Speech* 38 (October, 1963), 188–95.

Joseph Stalin: "The Pope!": Winston S. Churchill, *The Gathering Storm* (Boston: Houghton Mifflin, 1948), 135; *NYT,* September 14, 1948; Platt, 36–7; C. L. Sulzberger, *A Long Row of Candles: Memoirs and Diaries (1934–1954)* (New York: Macmillan, 1969), 365–6. *"No person":* Amy Wilentz, *New Yorker,* April 17, 2000,

35; Simon Sebag Morefiore, *Stalin: The Court of the Red Tsar* (New York: Knopf, 2004), 33. *"Death solves"*: ibid. Kominsky, *The Hoaxers*, op. cit., 500; J. V. Stalin, *Works*, Vol. 2, 1907–1913 (Moscow: Foreign Languages, 1953), 285. *"Those who vote"*: Werner Lange, *Free Press* (Detroit), December 28, 2004. *"Sincere diplomacy"*: J. V. Stalin, *Works*, Vol. 2 (Moscow: Foreign Languages Publishing House, 1953), 285–6. *"He who is"*: Rees, 515. *"When it comes"*: Barry Goldwater, *With No Apologies* (New York: Morrow, 1979), 86; Platt, 51; Safire 1991, 350; Boller and George, 64.

I am the STATE: Bent, 338–42; King, 178–9; Latham, 144; Walsh, 627; Voltaire, *The Age of Louis XIV*, Martyn P. Pollack, trans. (London: Dent, 1751, 1926, 1961), 257–8; Oliver Bernier, *Louis XIV* (New York: Doubleday, 1987), 97.

That's one small STEP for a man: *NYT*, July 21, 1969, July 31, 1969; *WP*, July 20, 1989; Clark DeLeon, *PI*, July 19, 1989, July 26, 1989; William Poundstone, *Big Secrets* (New York: Quill / Morrow, 1983), 183–4; Leon Wagener, *One Giant Leap: Neil Armstrong's Stellar American Journey* (New York: Tom Doherty / Forge, 2004), front jacket flap, 177–8, 192.

Adlai Stevenson: *"Nothing succeeds"*: Grace and David Darling, eds., *Stevenson* (Chicago: Contemporary, 1977), 82. Brinksmanship: SNPD, 85–6; Morris and Morris, 88. *"Quality of life"*: SNPD, 631–2. *"A heartbeat away"*: ibid., 321–2. *"Flattery is all right"*: Ralph L. Woods, *Third Treasury of the Familiar* (New York: Macmillan, 1970), 489; Darling, *Stevenson*, op. cit., 31. *"We Americans are suckers"*: Tripp, 657. *"Eggheads of the world"*: Edward Hanna, Henry Hicks and Ted Koppel, *The Wit and Wisdom of Adlai Stevenson* (New York: Hawthorn, 1965), 7; SNPD, 208–9. *"Man does not live"*: Hanna, *The Wit and Wisdom of Adlai Stevenson*, op. cit., 69. *"We say that every American boy"*: Darling, *Stevenson*, op. cit., 27. *"Well, like all politicians"*: ibid., 27. *"Words calculated to catch"*: Hanna, *The Wit and Wisdom of Adlai Stevenson*, op. cit., 68. *"My definition of a free society"*: ibid., 17. *"Technology, while adding"*: ibid., 77. *"Being in office"*: Darling, *Stevenson*, op. cit., 27. *"Let's talk sense"*: "Governor Adlai Stevenson Agrees to Run for President," July 26, 1952 in Peterson, *A Treasury of the World's Great Speeches*, op. cit., 825.

I should of STOOD in bed: Leo Rosten, *Hooray for Yiddish!* (New York: Simon & Schuster, 1982) 320; Bartlett's 1948, 1001; Bartlett's 1955, 975; Bartlett's 1968, 1037; Bartlett's 1980, 836; Morris and Morris, 524; Jack Smith, *LAT*, November 9, 1989; John Lardner, *Strong Cigars and Lovely Women* (New York: Funk & Wagnalls, 1951), 60.

No man ever stands so straight as when he STOOPS to help a boy: *Reader's Digest*, December 1956, 176; "Quote: No man stands as tall . . ." *Stumpers*, November 10, 1994, <http://listserv.dom.edu/cgi-bin/wa.exe?A2=ind9411&L=STUMPERS-L&P

=R19191> (August 19, 2005); *DDN,* October 22, 1999; *Van Nays* [Calif.] *News,* December 6, 1934; "Quotes—Moody," *Classics Network,* <http://www.literatureclassics.com/browselitquotes.asp?subcategory=O&author=Moody> (August 19, 2005).

STRANGER *in a strange land:* MPMFP, 2224; Andrew Lang, trans., *Theocritus, Bion and Moschus* (Macmillan, 1889, Project Gutenberg EBook No. 4775, 2003), Epigrams, No. 11, <http://www.gutenberg.org/dirs/etext03/thbm10h.htm> (August 19, 2005); *The Tragedies of Sophocles,* Richard C. Jebb, trans. (London: Cambridge University, 1904), 67, 331.

A *mind once* STRETCHED *by a new idea:* Holmes, *The Autocrat of the Breakfast-Table,* op. cit., 265.

Read *over your composition* . . . *is particularly fine,* STRIKE *it out:* Boswell, Vol. 2, 237; Frank Lynch e-mail, October 26, 2004; Mark Twain, *Pudd'nhead Wilson* (New York: Harper & Brothers, 1894, 1922), 83.

From *the* SUBLIME *to the ridiculous:* *National Register,* May 31, 1817, 337; MPMFP, 1987; Thomas Paine, *The Age of Reason* (New York: Putnam's, 1795, 1890), 107; Walsh, 1038; King, 78.

He *has achieved* SUCCESS *who has lived well:* *Chicago Sun-Times,* March 17, 1978; Shipps, 118, 121; Anthony Shipps, *Notes and Queries,* July, 1976, 312; Anderson, 39–40; *Ohio Libraries,* May–June, 1992, 25; Dirk H. Kelder, "Ralph Waldo Emerson: In Search of Success," <http://www.chebucto.ns.ca/Philosophy/Sui-Generis/Emerson/success.htm> (August 19, 2005).

The *secret of* SUCCESS: Rachel Cohen, "The Very Bad Review," *New Yorker,* October 6, 2003, 67; L. C. Collins, *Life and Memoirs of John Churton Collins* (London: John Lane the Bodley Head, 1912), 316; Poem No. 67 in Thomas H. Johnson, ed., *The Complete Poems of Emily Dickinson* (Boston, Little, Brown, 1899, 1960), 35.

Never *give a* SUCKER *an even break:* Jim Tully, *Esquire,* July 1938, 45; Johnston, *The Legendary Mizners,* op. cit., 209; Nicholas Yanni, *W. C. Fields* (New York: Pyramid, 1974), 113; Harold Cary, "The Loneliest Man in the Movies," *Collier's,* November 28, 1925, 28; *New Yorker,* January 25, 1947, 19; Helen Hayes, "Helen Hayes Picks the Ten Most Memorable Stage Performances," *Collier's,* September 22, 1951, 80; Dean Sullivan, *The Fabulous Wilson Mizner* (New York: Henkle, 1935), 290; Simon Louvish, *Man on the Flying Trapeze: The Life and Times of W. C. Fields* (New York: Norton, 1997), 195; Herbert G. Goldman, *Fanny Brice: The Original Funny Girl* (New York: Oxford, 1992), 83; Bartlett's 1968, 842; Bartlett's

2002, 611; Fadiman, 833; Joe Laurie, Jr., *Vaudeville: From the Honky Tonks to the Palace* (New York: Holt, 1953), 342.

There's a SUCKER born every minute: Interview with Robert Pelton, December 17, 19, 1991; Irving Wallace, *The Fabulous Showman: The Life and Times of P. T. Barnum* (New York: New American Library, 1959), 167; A. H. Saxon, *P. T. Barnum: The Legend and the Man* (New York: Columbia University, 1989), 334–7; Barry Popik, "There's a sucker born every minute (NY gambler slang, but not P. T. Barnum)," *The Big Apple,* <http://www.barrypopik.com/article/946> (July 5, 2005); *Atchison* [Kan.] *Globe,* March 28, 1883; *NYT,* December 30, 1883; *Sandusky* [Ohio] *Daily Register,* April 8, 1890.

I only wish that I could be as SURE: Earl Cowper, preface to *Lord Melbourne's Papers,* Lloyd C. Sanders, ed. (London: Longmans, Green, 1889), xii; Home Book, 1229; Harris, 252; Ringo, 200.

SURVIVAL of the fittest: Herbert Spencer, *The Principles of Biology,* vol. 2 (New York: Appleton, 1865, 1898), 444; Charles Darwin, *The Origins of Species* (Chicago: Brittanica, 1859, 1952), 32.

Don't SWEAT the small stuff: *Valley Independent* (Monessen, Penn.), August 16, 1966; *CT,* May 7, 1988, July 10, 1988, September 13, 1988, August 18, 1989; *Time,* June 6, 1983, 48; Robert S. Eliot, M.D., and Dennis L. Breo, *Is It Worth Dying For?* (New York: Bantam, 1984, 1989), 234; Robert S. Eliot, *From Stress to Strength* (New York: Bantam, 1994, 1995), 186; Dr. Richard Carlson, *Don't Sweat the Small Stuff . . . and It's All Small Stuff* (New York: Hyperion, 1997), 3; Michael R. Mantell, *Don't Sweat the Small Stuff: P.S. It's All Small Stuff* (San Luis Obispo, Calif.: Impact, 1988).

TAXATION without representation: Home Book, 2297; Daniel Boorstin, *The Americans: The National Experience* (New York: Random House, 1965), 309; Edward Channing, *A History of the United States* (New York: Macmillan, 1924), 4–5; Samuel Eliot Morison, *Dictionary of American Biography,* Vol. 14 (New York: Scribner's, 1934), 102; Peterson, *A Treasury of the World's Great Speeches,* op. cit., 114–7; James Otis, Esq., *The Rights of the British Colonies, Asserted and Proved* (Boston: Edes and Gill, 1764), 65; Bartlett's, 340.

Any sufficiently advanced TECHNOLOGY: Arthur C. Clarke, *Profiles of the Future* (New York: Holt, Rinehart & Winston, 1984), 36.

The TEFLON presidency: interview with Patricia Schroeder, February 17, 1992; interview with Dan Buck, December 7, 1990; *Congressional Record,* August 2, 1983; *NYT,* August 9, 1983; *People,* August 22, 1983, 88; *Denver Post,* May 5, 1984.

TELEVISION is a vast wasteland: NYT, May 10, 1961; John Bartlow Martin, *It Seems Like Only Yesterday* (New York: Morrow, 1986), 203; James L. Baughman, "Minow's Viewers: Understanding the Response to the 'Vast Wasteland' Address," *Federal Communications Law Journal* 55 (May, 2003) 451, footnote 11.

TELEVISION is chewing gum: Simpson, *Best Quotes of '54, '55, '56*, op. cit., 233; James B. Simpson, *Contemporary Quotations* (New York: Crowell, 1964), 200; James B. Simpson, *Simpson's Contemporary Quotations* (Boston: Houghton Mifflin, 1988), 377; *Syracuse* [N.Y.] *Herald-Journal*, January 21, 1955.

It goes with the TERRITORY: Arthur Miller, *Death of a Salesman* (1949), in *New Voices in the American Theatre* (New York: Modern Library, 1955), 225; King, 53.

The TEST of a civilization: *San Diego Union-Tribune*, February 3, 2005; Anderson, 52–3; *RQ*, winter 1985, 176, spring 1986, 302–3; Platt, 142; Pearl S. Buck, *My Several Worlds: A Personal Record* (New York: John Day, 1954), 337; Platt, 286; Martin Gilbert, *In Search of Churchill* (New York: Wiley, 1984), 269; Ralph Waldo Emerson, "Civilization," *Society and Solitude* (Boston: Fields, Osgood, 1870), 28; Boswell, Vol. 2, 130; "Open Topic," *Quoteland Forum*, May 22, 2001, <http://forum.quoteland.com/1/OpenTopic?a=tpc&s=586192041&f=487195441&m=7341982612&r=2361992612#2361992612> (August 20, 2005).

A beautiful THEORY: Stephen Jay Gould, "Nasty Little Facts," *Natural History*, February, 1985, 14; Frederick S. Dickson, "William Makepeace Thackeray and Henry Fielding," *North American Review*, April 1913, 522; Karl Pearson, *The Life, Letters and Labours of Francis Galton*, Vol. 3a (London: Cambridge University, 1930), 142.

THERE is no there there: Stein, *Everybody's Autobiography*, op. cit., 289.

There's a THIN man inside every fat man: George Orwell, *Coming up for Air* (New York: Harcourt Brace, 1939, 1950), 23; Cyril Connolly, *The Unquiet Grave* (New York: Viking, 1945, 1957), 61.

The TIPPING point: Morton Grodzins, "Metropolitan Segregation," *Scientific American*, October 1957, 34; Gavin McNett, "Idea Epidemics," *Salon.com*, March 17, 2000; William Safire, *NYT Magazine*, July 27, 2003, 15; *Oakland* [Calif.] *Tribune*, June 30, 1910.

TODAY is the first day: Platt, 343; Anderson, 27; *RQ*, summer 1975, 337, winter 1978, 184, winter 1979, 110; "Today Is the First Day of the Rest of My Life," *LyricsFind.com*, <http://www.lyricsfind.com/j/john-denver/unknown-album/today-is-the-first-day-of-the-rest-of-my-life-%28sugacity%29.php> (December 23, 2004); "John Denver Fugacity Lyrics," *123 Lyrics*, <http://www.123lyrics.net/john-denver/fugacity.html> (December 23, 2004); Free (Abbie Hoffman), *Rev-*

olution for the Hell of It (New York: Dial, 1968), 184; Walter Winchell, *Syracuse* [N.Y.] *Herald Journal,* June 11, 1968; *Bucks County* [Pa.] *Courier Times,* July 25, 1968.

Damn the TORPEDOES: A. T. Mahan, *Admiral Farragut* (New York: Greenwood, 1895, 1968), 278; Christopher Martin, *Damn the Torpedoes!* (New York: Abelard-Schuman, 1970), 258.

When the going gets TOUGH: Titelman, 364; ODP, 130; SNPD, 620; *LAT,* August 24, 1956; *Lima* [Ohio] *News,* May 2, 1959.

In this world there are only two TRAGEDIES: Wilde, 417; Shaw, *Man and Superman,* op. cit., 165; Hubbard 1911, 165; Hubbard 1923, 157; George Will, *Newsweek,* November 28, 1977, 132; Platt, 127; Thomas H. Huxley, "Address on University Education," Johns Hopkins University, September 12, 1876, *Essays* (New York: Macmillan, 1929), 283.

If this be TREASON: Brian Tubbs, "If This Be Treason . . . ," August 8, 2000, *Suite101.com,* <http://www.suite101.com/article.cfm/us_founding_era/45545> (September 30, 2004); Meade, *Patrick Henry,* op. cit., 31, 68–9, 166–81; Wirt, *Sketches of the Life and Times of Patrick Henry,* op. cit., 74–85; "Journal of a French Traveler in the Colonies, 1765," *American Historical Review,* 26 (1921), 745; Freeman, *George Washington,* op. cit., 136.

The TREE of liberty: DDN, April 25, 1997; "To Colonel Smith," November 13, 1787, Lipscomb, Vol. 6, 373.

The TRIUMPH of hope over experience: Boswell, Vol. 2, 128.

Harry S. Truman: *"If you run":* Howard Dean, "Talk of the Nation," *National Public Radio,* September 29, 2003; Elizabeth Safly e-mail, July 5, 2005. *"The Democratic wing":* George Will, *DDN,* August 7, 2003. *"For the first six months":* Simpson, *Simpson's Contemporary Quotations,* op. cit., 42; *Current Biography 1974,* 347. *Saturday Evening Post,* November 4, 1899, 356. *"A statesman":* World *Telegram and Sun* (New York), April 12, 1958; "The Hon. Thomas Brackett Reed," *Current Literature,* May 1899, 412. *"Always be sincere":* ODQ, 801. *"I never did":* U.S. Congress, *Memorial Services in the Congress of the United States and Tributes in Eulogy of Harry S. Truman, Late a President of the United States* (Washington, D.C.: United States Government Printing Office, 1973), 27, 178; ODQ, 801. *"I don't know":* Harry S. Truman, *Memoirs,* vol. 1, *Year of Decisions* (Garden City, N.Y., 1955) 19. Presidency like riding a tiger: Harry S. Truman, *Memoirs,* vol. 2, *Years of Trial and Hope* (Garden City, N.Y.: Doubleday, 1956), 1; Kazantzakis, *Report to Greco,* op. cit., 389. *"All the president is":* letter to Mary Truman, November 14, 1947, Margaret Truman, *Harry S. Truman* (New York:

Morrow, 1973), 356. *"Anybody can be president"*: Charles Robbins, *Last of His Kind: An Informal Portrait of Harry S. Truman* (New York: Morrow, 1979), 148. *"There is no indispensable man"*: William Hillman, *Mr. President* (New York: Farrar, Straus and Young, 1952), 13. *"Whenever you have"*: Harry S. Truman, *Truman Speaks* (New York: Columbia, 1960), 51. *"Budget figures reveal"*: Dean Acheson, *Present at the Creation: My Years in the State Department* (London: Hamish Hamilton, 1969), 492. *"Leadership is the art"*: Chuck Henning, ed., *The Wit and Wisdom of Politics* (Golden, Colo.: Fulcrum, 1992), 123. *"It's almost impossible"*: T. S. Settel, ed., *The Quotable Harry S. Truman* (Anderson, S.C.: Droke House; New York: Berkeley, 1975), 134; *"There is nothing new"*: Hillman, *Mr. President*, op. cit., 81.

Never TRUST the artist: Evan Hunter, *NYT Book Review*, March 21, 1982, 11, D. H. Lawrence, *Studies in Classic American Literature* (New York: Viking, 1923), 2.

You can't TRUST anyone over thirty: *San Francisco Chronicle*, November 15, 1964; *WP*, March 23, 1970; *Bill of Rights Journal*, winter 1988, 15; interview with Jack Weinberg, December 5, 1990.

All TRUTH passes through three stages: Jeffrey Shallit, letter, *Skeptic*, vol. 9, no. 3 (2002), 18; Jeffrey Shallit, "Dembski's Curious Incompetence with Quotations," *The Panda's Thumb*, April 3, 2004, <http://www.pandasthumb.org/pt-archives/000102.html> (August 20, 2005); Jeffrey Shalit, "Science, Pseudoscience, and the Three Stages of Truth," unpublished manuscript, March 28, 2005; *NYT*, August 25, 1881; Stephen Jay Gould, *"Absecheulich!* (Atrocious!)" *Natural History*, March 2000, 43; Henry Sidgwick, "The Prophet of Culture," *The Eclectic Magazine of Foreign Literature*, October 1867, 490; *Saturday Evening Post*, July 16, 1870, 3.

The best test of TRUTH: *Abrams v. United States*, 250 U.S. 616, 624 (1919) <http://www.bc.edu/bc_org/avp/cas/comm/free_speech/abrams.html> (June 9, 2004).

The opposite of a shallow TRUTH is false: Hans Bohr, "My Father," S. Rozental, *Niels Bohr* (New York: Interscience / Wiley, 1964, 1967), 328; Oscar Wilde, "The Truth of Masks," Wilde, 1078; Thomas Mann, *Freud, Goethe, Wagner* (New York: Knopf, 1942), 3–48; Thomas Mann, *Essays of Three Decades*, H. T. Lowe-Porter, trans. (New York: Knopf, 1968), 411–28.

TRUTH is stranger than fiction: Wilson, 76; ODP, 316; Pearson, 22; Stimpson 1948, 13.

TRUTH is the first casualty of war: Michael A. Weatherson and Hal Bochin, *Hiram Johnson: A Bio-Bibliography* (Westport, Conn.: Greenwood, 1988); Hal Bochin e-mail, February 12, 2005; Samuel Johnson, *Idler* No. 30, November 11, 1758, in Platt, 360; James Howell, MPMFP, 2388; *Evening Post* (New York), April 10, 1917; *Reformed Church Review,* April, 1926, 158; Arthur Ponsonby, *Falsehood in War-Time* (New York: Dutton, 1928), 11; *Reader's Digest,* January 1938, 39; Schlesinger, *A Thousand Days,* op. cit., 105.

TURN ON, *tune in, drop out:* NYT, June 9, 1996; Timothy Leary, *Flashbacks: An Autobiography* (Los Angeles: Tarcher, 1983), 251–3, 257; Timothy Leary, *The Politics of Ecstasy* (New York: Putnam's, 1968), 13–4, 28, 64, 67, 89–90, 104, 160, 223–5, 236, 254–62, 304–9, 332, 353–8; *Current Biography,* 1970, 246; Leary, *Flashbacks,* ibid., 253.

Mark Twain: "Every dog should have a few fleas": Safire 2001, 88–9; Wilson, 229; Edward Noyes Westcott, *David Harum: A Story of American Life* (New York: Grosset & Dunlap, 1898), 284; William S. Walsh, "The Avatar of the Epigram," *The Bookman,* May 1903, 304. "It ain't what we don't know": Safire 1991, xi; NYT, June 30, 2004. "So I became a newspaperman": Platt, 237. "The only way": Bill Adler, *The Washington Wits* (New York: Macmillan, 1967), 166; Mencken, 939. "The finest Congress": Platt, 57. "I am not an American": Shelley Fisher Fishkin, *Lighting Out for the Territory: Reflections on Mark Twain and American Culture* (New York: Oxford, 1997), 8; Barbara Schmidt, "Frank Fuller, The American, Revisited," www.twain quotes.com, <http://www.twainquotes.com/FullerRevisited.html> (February 11, 2005); Bev Darr, "Scholars clarify a quote attributed to Mark Twain," *Hannibal* (Missouri) *Courier-Post,* November 28, 2001. Rasmussen: Rasmussen, xvi–xvii. Bradley: Mark Crispin Miller, *Boxed In* (Chicago: Northwestern, 1988), 112–3. Moran: ABC News, November 7, 2000. "Get your facts": Robert D. Jerome and Herbert A. Wisbey, Jr., *Mark Twain in Elmira* (Elmira, N.Y.: Mark Twain Society, 1977), 110. "Man is the only animal": Twain, *Following the Equator,* op. cit., 256. "When angry": ibid., 65. "Courage is resistance": ibid., 83. "Few things are harder": ibid. 129. "Always do right": Bernard DeVoto, *Mark Twain in Eruption: Hitherto Unpublished Pages About Men and Events by Mark Twain* (New York: Harper & Brothers, 1922, 1940), frontispiece.

TYPING rather than writing: New Republic, February 9, 1959, 27; Gerald Clarke, *Capote: A Biography* (New York: Simon & Schuster, 1988), 315; Barbara Seaman, *Lovely Me: The Life of Jacqueline Susann* (New York: Morrow, 1987), 391.

I don't get ULCERS: Spinrad and Spinrad, 94.

I know you believe you UNDERSTAND: Bernard and Marvin Kalb, "Of Cannibals, Khrushchev and Kissinger," *TV Guide,* March 31, 1984, 5–6; "Fox Morning News Interview with: Berhard Kalb, Former State Department Spokesman," *Federal News Service,* August 21, 1990.

If not US, who: NYT, October 22, 1981; Safire 1990, 65, 71; R. Trevors Herford, ed., *The Ethics of the Talmud: Sayings of the Fathers* (New York: Schocken, 1945, 1962), 34.

No man is a hero to his VALET: Bent 163–4; Latham, 110; MPMFP, 1137; King, 130; ODP, 220–1.

The VICE PRESIDENCY isn't worth: Time, February 1, 1963, 17; interview with Hugh Sidey, January 3, 1977; O. C. Fisher, *Cactus Jack,* op. cit., 118; Keith Olbermann, *Countdown,* MSNBC, October 17, 2005.

There is no substitute for VICTORY: Platt, 51; "Joint Meeting of the Two Houses of the U.S. Congress," April 19, 1951, *Representative Speeches of General of the Army Douglas MacArthur,* op. cit., 19; Dwight D. Eisenhower, *Letters to Mamie,* John S. D. Eisenhower, ed. (Garden City, N.Y.: Doubleday, 1978), 203; SNPD, 507–8; *Gettysburg* [Pa.] *Times,* May 27, 1943.

VICTORY has a hundred fathers: Schlesinger, *A Thousand Days,* op. cit., 289–90; *BG,* April 17, 2001; SNPD, 841–2; videotape of *The Desert Fox: The Story of Rommel* (Twentieth Century Fox, 1951); Desmond Young, *Rommel, The Desert Fox* (New York: Harper & Row, 1950, Perennial, 1965), 133; September 9, 1942 entry, Count Galeazzo Ciano, *The Ciano Diaries,* Hugh Gibson, ed. (Garden City, N.Y.: Garden City Publishing, 1947), 521; MDQ, 550; *Newsweek,* March 11, 1991, 42; Jeff Greenfield, *NYT Book Review,* May 1, 1977, 15; Safire 1994, 226, 228; Safire 1997, 6–7; Titelman, 348–9; William Safire, *NYT Magazine,* October 15, 2000, 28–9.

Vietnam: "The domino effect": Safire 1986, 161–2; SNPD, 191–2; William C. Effros, ed., *Quotations, Vietnam: 1945–1970* (New York: Random House, 1970), 46–51. *"Guns and butter":* Home Book 2298d; SNPD, 308–9; Robert Stewart, ed., *A Dictionary of Political Quotations* (London: Europa, 1984), 65–6. *"Hearts and minds":* Safire 1986, 142; SNPD 716; MacArthur, *Reminiscences,* op. cit., 33; Thomas Powers, *The War at Home,* op. cit., 225. *"Bomb them back":* General Curtis E. LeMay with MacKinlay Kantor, *Mission with LeMay* (Garden City, N.Y.: Doubleday, 1965), 565. *"Hawks and doves":* SNPD, 852–3; Robert Mason, *Chickenhawk* (New York: Viking, 1983). *"Kill 'em all":* David Lundquist, "Help on quote: Kill them all," *Stumpers,* <http://listserv.dom.edu/cgi-bin/wa.exe?A2=ind9510&L= STUMPERS-L&P=R13049> (September 14, 2005); Jonathan Sumption, *The Albigensian Crusade* (London: Faber and Faber, 1978, 1999), 93; ODQ, 26. *"Secret plan":* Safire 1988, 219–21; Safire, 2004, 321–3; John Chancellor and Walter R. Mears, *The News Business* (New York: Harper & Row, 1983), 30–1; Richard M. Nixon, *RN: The Memoirs of Richard Nixon* (New York: Grosset & Dunlap, 1978), 298.

Eternal VIGILANCE is the price of liberty: Platt, 200; Home Book, 1106; Stimpson 1946, 6.

It takes a VILLAGE to raise a child: Hillary Clinton, *It Takes a Village,* op. cit.; Mieder, 507; Maske Masango to Jane Houston, "Village Quote—Reply," *Stumpers,* <http://listserv.dom.edu/cgi-bin/wa.exe?A2=ind9412&L=STUMPERS-L&P =R41946> (August 22, 2005); S. S. Farsi, *Swahili Sayings from Zanzibar,* vol. 1 (Nairobi: Kenya Literature Bureau, 1958, 1982), 27; Albert Scheven, *Swahili Proverbs* (Washington, D.C.: University Press of America, 1981), 123.

VOTE early and vote often: Bartlett's, 533; Benham 1930, 459a; Home Book, 2278; James Morgan, *Our Presidents* (New York: Macmillan, 1924), 30; Arthur M. Schlesinger, Jr., *The Age of Jackson* (Boston: Little, Brown, 1947), 508; Josh Billings, *The Complete Works of Josh Billings* (New York: G. W. Dillingham, 1876), 253; Tuleja 1992, 68; *Time,* March 5, 1979, 6.

WAGNER'S music is better than it sounds: Rasmussen, xviii; Twain, *Mark Twain's Autobiography,* op. cit., 338; *The Musical Visitor,* December 1888, 319; *Oakland* [Calif.] *Tribune,* February 5, 1897; *Lippincott's,* November 1906, 662; *Saturday Evening Post,* April 13, 1861, 8.

Everything comes to him who WAITS: Earl of Beaconsfield (Benjamin Disraeli), *Tancred, or the New Crusade* (London: Longmans, Green, 1847, 1924), 295; MPMFP, 2440; ODP, 5.

It is well that WAR is so terrible: Manfred Weidhorn, *Robert E. Lee* (New York: Atheneum, 1988), 68; Emory M. Thomas, *Robert E. Lee* (New York: Norton, 1995), 271; John Esten Cooke, *A Life of Gen. Robert E. Lee* (New York: Appleton, 1871), 184; Edward Porter Alexander, *Military Memoirs of a Confederate: A Critical Narrative* (New York: Scribner's, 1907), 302; Gary W. Gallagher, *The Fredericksburg Campaign: Decision on the Rappahannock* (Chapel Hill: University of North Carolina, 1995), xii; Douglas Southall Freeman, *R. E. Lee: A Biography,* vol. 2 (New York: Scribner's), 462.

Suppose they gave a WAR: Carl Sandburg, *The People, Yes* (New York: Harcourt, Brace, 1936), 43; James R. Newman letter, *WP,* September 25, 1961; Charlotte E. Keyes, "Suppose They Gave a War, and No One Came?" *McCall's,* October 1966, 26; Rees, 468; Linda Simon e-mail, February 28, 2005.

The WAR to end all wars: Platt, 365; H. G. Wells, *The War That Will End War* (London: F. & C. Palmer, 1914); H. G. Wells, "How to Bring Peace on Earth," *Liberty,* December 29, 1934, 4–7.

The wrong WAR: William Safire, *NYT Magazine,* September 19, 2004, 24; "Testimony before the Senate Committees on Armed Services and Foreign Relations," May 15, 1951, *Military Situation in the Far East,* hearings, 82d Congress, 1st session, part 2, p. 732 (1951) in *Wikiquote,* <http://en.wikiquote.org/wiki/Omar_Bradley> (October 18, 2004).

WAR is God's way: S. T. Joshi and David E. Schultz, *Ambrose Bierce—An Annotated Bibliography of Primary Sources* (Westport, Conn.: Greenwood, 1999); S. T. Joshi e-mail, March 1, 2005; David E. Schultz e-mail, March 1, 2005; *LAT,* November 16, 1987.

WAR is hell: Hirshson, *The White Tecumseh,* op. cit., 372; *NYT,* September 12, 1914; Sherman, *Memoirs of Gen. W. T. Sherman, Written by Himself,* Vol. 2, op. cit., 126; Basil Liddell Hart, *Sherman: Soldier, Realist, American* (New York: Praeger, 1958), 310; Merrill, *William Tecumseh Sherman,* op. cit., 238, 259, 298, 379–80; Lewis, *Sherman,* op. cit., 635–7; Michael Fellman, *Citizen Sherman* (Lawrence, Kans.: University Press of Kansas, 1995), 306; *Ohio State Journal,* August 12, 1880; *Advocate of Peace,* March–April, 1860, 49.

WAR is nothing more than: Michael Howard, *Clausewitz* (Oxford: Oxford, 1983), 50; Carl von Clausewitz, *On War,* Michael Howard and Peter Paret, ed. and trans., op. cit., 87.

WAR is too important: Jackson, *Clemenceau,* op. cit., 228; George Suarez, *La Vie Orgueilleuse de Clemenceau* (Paris: Editions de France, 1930), 172; Platt, 365; John Bailey, *Letters and Diaries* (London: John Murray, 1935), 176; Samuel, 226; Bartlett's 1968, 786, Bartlett's 1980, 401, Bartlett's 1992, 354, Bartlett's 2002, 369; ODQ, 226.

WARTS and all: Safire 1991, 132–5; Titelman, 351; Rees, 191; *The Galaxy,* May, 1870, 408. *The Friend,* February 10, 1883, 211.

WASHINGTON is a city of Northern: William Manchester, *Portrait of a President* (Boston: Little, Brown, 1967), 200; Schlesinger, *A Thousand Days,* op. cit., 673; "Remarks to the Trustees and Advisory Committee of the National Cultural Center," November 14, 1961, *Public Papers of the Presidents of the United States,* op. cit., 1961, 719; *Press Gazette* (Hillsboro, Ohio), May 20, 1960.

The battle of WATERLOO: Elizabeth Longford, *Wellington: The Years of the Sword* (New York: Harper & Row, 1989), 16–7; Burnam 1980, 12; Rees, 560–1; Seldes 1960, xiv; Ackermann, 501; MPMFP, 2465; Count Charles de Mantalembert, *De L'Avenir Politique de l'Angleterre,* 1856 in Longford, ibid., 16; Fraser, *Words on Wellington,* op. cit., 138.

Everybody talks about the WEATHER: *Hartford Courant,* August 24, 1897, January 5, 1945; interview with Henry McNulty, October 8, 2005; Robert Underwood Johnson, *Remembered Yesterdays* (Boston: Little, Brown, 1923), 322; Platt, 370–1; Rees, 546.

Go WEST, young man: Henry Luther Stoddard, *Horace Greeley: Printer, Editor, Crusader* (New York: Putnam's, 1946), 40; William Harlan Hale, *Horace Greeley: Voice of the People* (New York: Harper & Brothers, 1950), 195–6; Thomas Fuller, "'Go West, young man!'—An Elusive Slogan," *Indiana Magazine of History,* 100 (September 2004) 231–42; Glyndon G. Van Deusen, *Horace Greeley: Nineteenth-Century Crusader* (Philadelphia: University of Pennsylvania, 1953), 173; Jules Archer, *Fighting Journalist: Horace Greeley* (New York: Julian Messner, 1966), 109; Erik S. Lunde, *Horace Greeley* (Boston: Twayne, 1981), 29; interview with Erik Lunde, March 3, 1992; Erik Lunde letter, March 11, 1992.

Mae West: Jon Tuska, *The Films of Mae West* (Secaucus, N.J.: Citadel, 1975); George Eels and Stanley Musgrove, *Mae West: A Biography* (New York: Morrow, 1982); June Sochen, *Mae West: She Who Laughs, Lasts* (Arlington Heights, Ill.: Harlan Davidson, 1992); Marybeth Hamilton, *When I'm Bad, I'm Better: Mae West, Sex, and American Entertainment* (New York: HarperCollins, 1995); Emily Morris Leider, *Becoming Mae West* (New York: Farrar, Straus and Giroux, 1997, DaCapo, 2000); Jill Watts, *Mae West: An Icon in Black and White* (New York: Oxford, 2001). "*I've been in*": Leslie Halliwell, *Halliwell's Filmgoer's Companion* (New York: Scribner's, 1984), 1065. "*Yeah, but you can't*": ibid., 1065. "*Grow up*": Eels and Musgrove, *Mae West,* op. cit., 253; Leider, *Becoming Mae West,* op. cit., 350. "*tall, dark*": Eels and Musgrove, *Mae West,* op. cit., 54; *Freeborn County Standard* (Albert Lea, Minn.) May 19, 1881. "*When I'm good*": videotape of *I'm No Angel* (Paramount, 1933); Eels and Musgrove, *Mae West,* op. cit., 125; Sochen, *Mae West,* op. cit., 77; Hamilton, *When I'm Bad, I'm Better,* op. cit., 191; Tuska, *The Films of Mae West,* op. cit., 90. "*Goodness had*": American Film Institute, No. 250; Tuska, *The Films of Mae West,* op. cit., 62; Eels and Musgrove, *Mae West,* op. cit., 106; Sochen, *Mae West,* op. cit., 63; Hamilton, *When I'm Bad, I'm Better,* op. cit., 176; "*Peel me*": Haun, 240; *Halliwell's Filmgoer's Companion,* op. cit., 1065. "*Keep a diary*": videotape of *Every Day's a Holiday* (Paramount, 1937); Sochen, *Mae West,* op. cit., 90. "*Is that a gun*": Dirks; Halliwell, *Halliwell's Filmgoer's Companion,* op. cit., 1065. Leider, *Becoming Mae West,* op. cit., 289; Watts, *Mae West,* op cit., 219; John Kobal, "Mae West," *Films and Filming,* September 1983, 22. Quotable quotes: Eels and Musgrove, *Mae West,* op. cit., 315.

WHERE do we find such men: Michael Paul Rogin, *Ronald Reagan, the Movie* (Berkeley: University of California, 1987, 1988), 7; Paul D. Erickson, *Reagan Speaks* (New York: New York University, 1985), 38; Ronald Reagan, "Radio Address to the Nation on Armed Forces Day," May 15, 1982, <http://www.reagan.utexas.edu/

resource/speeches/1982/51582a.htm> (February 24, 2002); "Reagan, the Secret Weapon, and D-Day," <http://www.billspricht.net/2004_05_030_archive.html> (February 24, 2005); *New Yorker*, October 29, 1984, 140; *NYT*, September 9, 1985; *LAT*, January 4, 1987; James Michener, *The Bridges at Toko-Ri* (New York: Random House, 1953), 146; videotape of *The Bridges at Toko-Ri* (Paramount, 1954), Valentine Davies, screenwriter; *Arizona Republic*, April 23, 2004.

Tell me what brand of WHISKEY: F. B. Carpenter, *The Inner Life of Abraham Lincoln*, op. cit., 247; David Homer Bates, *Lincoln Stories* (New York: William Edwin Rudge, 1926), 50; Fehrenbacher and Fehrenbacher, 92–3, 28, 349, 147, 444.

The WHOLE nine yards: Safire 1986, 212–4; Safire 1999, 274–5; Safire 2003, 114; John Ruch, *The Other Paper* (Columbus, Ohio), October 14–20, 2000; David Wilton, *Word Myths: Debunking Linguistic Urban Legends* (New York: Oxford, 2004), 34–8; Mark Israel, "the whole nine yards," *alt-usage-english.org*, <http:// alt-usage-english.org/excerpts/fxthewho.html> (August 3, 2005); Michael Quinlon, "The Whole Nine Yards," *World Wide Words*, <http://www.worldwidewords .org/articles/nineyards.htm> (August 26, 2005); Anderson, 20; *The Agitator* (Wellsboro, Pa.), March 29, 1855; Fanny Fern, *Fern Leaves from Fanny's Portfolio*, series two (Auburn and Buffalo, N.Y.: Miller, Orton & Mulligan, 1854), 19; Richard Stratton to Barry Popik, "Re: 'Whole Nine Yards' query on American dialect," *American Dialect Society*, May 13, 2005; <http://listserv.linguistlist.org/ cgi-bin/wa?A2=ind0505b&L=ads-1&D=1&F=&S=&P=18638> (August 10, 2005); Elaine Shepard, *The Doom Pussy* (New York: Trident, 1967), 43, 129, 138; "Air Force Academy Slang," *Current Slang* 2 (spring 1969) 14; *Playground Daily News* (Fort Walton, Fla.), April 28, 1969.

He who has a WHY to live for: Gordon Allport preface to Victor Frankl, *Man's Search for Meaning: An Introduction to Logotherapy* (New York: Pocket, 1939, 1963), xi; Nietzsche, *Twilight of the Idols*, op. cit., 23.

You see things and you say, 'WHY?': "Address Before the Irish Parliament in Dublin, June 28, 1963," *Public Papers of the Presidents of the United States: John F. Kennedy, 1963*, 537; George Bernard Shaw, *Back to Methuselah*, 1922, I:1; *NYT*, June 9, 1968; *Newsweek*, December 28, 1992, 55; W. P. Kinsella, *Shoeless Joe* (Boston: Houghton Mifflin, 1982, Ballantine, 1983), epigraph; Arthur Wortman and Richard Rhodes, eds., *Robert F. Kennedy: Promises to Keep* (Kansas City, Mo.: Hallmark, 1969), 60.

Oscar Wilde: "*Familiarity breeds*": E. H. Mikhail, *Oscar Wilde: Interviews and Recollections* (New York: Harper & Row, 1979), 421. "*Nothing succeeds*": *A Woman of No Importance*, III, Wilde, 464. "*We think that we are generous*": *The Picture of Dorian Gray*, Wilde, 67. "*Anybody can sympathize*": *The Soul of Man Under Socialism*, Wilde, 1101–2. "*Every omnibus-conductor*": Ada Leverson, *Letters to the*

Sphinx from Oscar Wilde (London: Ducksworth, 1930), 29. *"One must have"*: ibid., 42. *"Children begin"*: A Woman of No Importance, II, Wilde, 457. *"Good Americans"*: The Picture of Dorian Gray, Wilde, 43; A Woman of No Importance, I, Wilde, 436; Holmes, *The Autocrat of the Breakfast-Table,* op. cit., 121–2. *"The tragedy of old age"*: The Picture of Dorian Gray, Wilde, 162; Ruth Rendell, *Murder Being Once Done* (Garden City, N.Y.: Crime Club / Doubleday, 1972), 41. *"One should never trust"*: A Woman of No Importance, I, Wilde, 442; Rita Mae Brown, *Southern Discomfort* (New York: Harper & Row, 1982), 1. *"The queen is not"*: John Savage letter to *Playboy,* July 1978, 16. *"Memory . . . is the diary"*: The Importance of Being Earnest, II, Wilde, 340; *Reader's Digest,* November 1979, 157. *"Nowadays most people die"*: The Picture of Dorian Gray, Wilde, 44. *"Nothing that is worth"*: The Critic as Artist, Wilde, 1016. The Picture of Dorian Gray, Wilde, 162. *"No age borrows"*: E. V. Lucas, ed., *A Critic in Pall Mall* (London: Methuen, 1919), 200. *"Men marry"*: A Woman of No Importance, III, Wilde, 460. *"Talk to every woman"*: ibid. *"I never travel"*: The Importance of Being Earnest, III, Wilde, 363. *"Only dull people"*: An Ideal Husband, I, Wilde, 493. *"It is so easy"*: The Critic as Artist, Wilde, 1047. *"The truth is rarely"*: The Importance of Being Earnest, I, Wilde, 326. *"I always pass on"*: An Ideal Husband, II, Wilde, 131.

WINNING isn't everything: "Trouble Along the Way," Warner Brothers, 1953, dialogue transcript, Reel 5-A, page 4; interview with Melville Shavelson, January 11, 1977; interview with Frank Stewart, January 19, 1977; interview with Jack Tobin, January 20, 1977; Joel Sayre, "He Flies on One Wing," *Sports Illustrated,* December 26, 1955, 29; Art Rosenbaum, *LAT,* October 18, 1950; Steven J. Overman, "'Winning Isn't Everything. It's the Only Thing': The Origin, Attributions and Influence of a Famous Football Quote," *Football Studies* 2 (October 1999) 77–99; David Maraniss, *When Pride Still Mattered: A Life of Vince Lombardi* (New York: Simon & Schuster, 1999), 365–70; Marshall Smith, "The Miracle Worker of Green Bay, Wis." *Life,* December 7, 1962, 52; Jerry Kramer, *Instant Replay* (New York: New American Library, 1968, Signet, 1969), 50; Vince Lombardi, *Vince Lombardi on Football* (New York: Van Nostrand Reinhold, 1973, 1981), 4.

To be on the WIRE is life: Videotape of *All That Jazz* (Twentieth Century Fox, 1979), screenplay by Robert Alan Aurthur and Bob Fosse; *PI,* October 27, 1987; *Car and Driver,* November 1985, 127.

Be careful what you WISH for: *DDN,* September 26, 1993; *St. Nicholas,* December 1895, 108; Titelman, 72.

What lies behind us . . . what lies WITHIN us: *DDN,* March 4, 2005; Anderson, 155; Dennis Lien, "Re: Ralph Waldo Emerson—source for one of his quotes," *Stumpers,* February 3, 2000, <http://listserv.dom.edu/cgi-bin/wa.exe?A2=ind000 2&L=STUMPERS-L&P=R5539> (August 23, 2005).

A WOMAN needs a man: Sydney Ladensohn Stern, *Gloria Steinem: Her Passions, Politics, and Mystique* (New York: Birch Lane, 1997), 391–2, 398; *Time,* October 9, 2000, 20; David Sakrison, "A bit of herstory: the definitive word on the origin!", *The Fish and Bicycle Page,* <http://www.geocities.com/SiliconValley/Vista/3255/herstory.htm> (January 4, 2005); Eoin Cameron, "Fish & Bicycle," *ABC Perth,* September 1, 2004, <http://www.abc.net/au/perth/stories/s1189577.htm> (January 4, 2005); Arthur Bloch, *Murphy's Law,* op. cit., 86; Robert Anton Wilson, *Cosmic Trigger: Final Secret of the Illuminati* (Tempe, Ariz.: New Falcon, 1977), 98.

What does a WOMAN want: Ernest Jones, *The Life and Work of Sigmund Freud,* Vol. 2, *Years of Maturity, 1901–1919* (New York: Basic, 1955), Alan C. Elms, "Apocryphal Freud: Sigmund Freud's Most Famous 'Quotations' and Their Actual Sources," Winer and Anderson, *Sigmund Freud and His Impact on the Modern World,* op. cit., 84–9.

A WOMAN'S work is never done: "Browse Martha Ballard's Diary Online," *Martha Ballard's Diary Online,* <http://dohistory.org/diary/indes.html> (January 4, 2005); ODP 338; "Roxburghe Ballads," 1655, Alisa Thomson, "Woman's Work," *Woman's Education Des Femmes* 5 (Spring 1987) 4, <http://www.nald.ca/canorg/cclow/newslet/1987/Sprng_v5/4.htm> (January 4, 2005); Thomas Tusser, "The Preface to the Book of Huswifery," in *Five Hundred Points of Good Husbandry* (London: Lackington, Allen, 1580, 1812), 240; Mieder, 551.

WORK smarter, not harder: *Commerce* [Tex.] *Journal,* May 17, 1962; *Wisconsin Rapids Daily Tribune,* April 5, 1963. Alan Lakein, *How to Get Control of Your Time and Your Life* (New York: Wyden, 1973, Signet, 1974), contents, 17, 159, back cover; *Ladies' Wreath, a Magazine Devoted to Literature, Industry and Religion,* August 1, 1854, 133.

WORKERS of the world: Burnam 1980, 205; Karl Marx and Friedrich Engels, *The Manifesto of the Communist Party* (1848) in *The Essential Left* (London: Unwin, 1961), 47.

The WORLD must be coming to an end: Platt, 91; W. T. Fitch, "Youth," *Overland Monthly and Out West Magazine,* January 1929, 18.

It's WORSE than a crime: King, 388; Latham, 92–3; Benham 1930, 453b, 690a; Home Book, 337; Seldes 1985, 140; Baker, 75; Herold, 277–8; Emerson, 317.

WRITERS are always selling somebody out: Joan Didion, *Slouching Towards Bethlehem* (New York: Farrar, Straus & Giroux, 1968, Delta, 1968), xiv.

Easy WRITING makes hard reading: Morris and Morris, 606; Richard Sheridan, "Clio's Protest," in R. Crompton Rhodes, ed., *The Plays and Poems of Richard Brinsley Sheridan,* Vol. 3 (New York: Russell & Russell, 1962), 117.

WRITING *about music:* Alan P. Scott, "Talking about music is like dancing about architecture," March 5, 2004, <http://home.pacifier.com/~ascott/they/tamildaa .htm> (January 5, 2005); "Re: Debussy," *alt.quotations,* February 19, 1993, <http:// groups.google.com/group/alt.quotations/browse_thread/thread/86f8f418d449edc6/ c4485106c6e7cbbf?q=Re:+Debussy&rnum=1&hl=en#c4485106c6e7cbbf> (August 23, 2005); *New Yorker,* February 1, 1999, 84; Timothy White, "Elvis Costello: A Man of Time Beats the Clock," *Musician,* October 1983, 52.

WRITING *is easy:* Ira Berkow, *Red: A Biography of Red Smith* (New York: Times Books, 1986), 208; Pete Axthelm, *Newsweek,* May 17, 1976, 75; Donald Hall, *NYT Book Review,* July 18, 1982; *Time,* July 16, 1982, 61; James Charlton, *The Writer's Quotation Book* (Wainscott, N.Y.: Pushcart, 1980), 41, 55; Lady Holland, *A Memoir of the Reverend Sydney Smith,* Vol. 1 (London: Longman, Brown, Green and Longmans, 1855), 258.

YOUTH *is wasted on the young:* Lewis Copeland and Faye Copeland, *10,000 Jokes, Toasts and Stories.* (Garden City, N.Y.: Doubleday, 1939, 1965), 555; *Reader's Digest,* April 1940, 84. Fred Shapiro, "Re: Youth quote," *Stumpers,* December 4, 2003, <http://listserv.dom.edu/cgi-bin/wa.exe?A2=ind0312&L=STUMPERS-L&P =R3517> (August 23, 2005); "The Second Time Around," words and music by Sammy Cahn and James Van Heusen, 1960.

ACKNOWLEDGMENTS

For invaluable ongoing help with this project I would like to thank Rosalie Maggio, Gene Keyes, and Sue Weldon. Fred Shapiro, Anthony Shipps, Richard Farson, Leonard Roy Frank, and Jan Miller also gave me helpful consultation and encouragement.

Richard Langworth, Liz Safly, Ben Yagoda, and Alice Calaprice were very helpful in their areas of expertise (Winston Churchill, Harry Truman, Will Rogers, and Albert Einstein).

Librarians at the Olive Kettering Library in Yellow Springs, Ohio—Joe Cali, Amy Killoran, Scott Sanders, and Ritch Kerns—were unusually helpful on this project, as was Connie Collett of the Greene County Public Library, and Barbara P. Semonche of the The Park Library at the University of North Carolina School of Journalism and Mass Communication.

For their help on specific quotations I would like to thank Libby Blackman, Hal Bochin, Bucks Braun, Alexis Dubuis, Alan Elms, Robert Fogarty, Thomas Fuller, Malcolm Goldstein, Mario Gomes, Stephen Goranson, Jane Gordon, T. George Harris, Larry Ingle, Carl Johnson, Lauren Johnston, Landon Jones, S. T. Joshi, David Keyes, Scott Keyes, Harold Kushner, Frank Lynch, Jill Martyn, Jeffrey Mason, Henry McNulty, Meena Nayak, Rick Nutt, Steve Overman, Sundhil Pflug, Bill Phillips, John Pitney, James Rand, Branch Rickey, Doug Reynolds, David Schultz, Steve Schwerner, Jeffrey Shallit, Anthony Shipps, John Simon, Linda Simon, Robert Ellis Smith, Elizabeth Sparagna, Sol Steinmetz, Michael StGeorge, Barbara Wallraff, Mary Tom Watts, Wayne Weber, Matt Wrbican, and William Allen Zulker.

My agent, Michelle Tessler, and editor, Ethan Friedman, did a fine job of shepherding this book to publication. Paul Montazzoli copyedited the manuscript with a deft hand.

Most of all, I would like to thank my wife, Muriel, who gave me an extraordinary amount of help with this project, as she has with so many others.

KEY WORD INDEX

insiders, marriage a fortress besieged, i. want out, 138–9

inspiration, genius 1 percent i., 77, 231

intelligence, nobody went broke underestimating i., 17–8
test of first-rate i., 99

intentions, road to hell paved with good i., 106

interesting, live in i. times, 99–100, 112

invented, everything can be i. has been, 162

investigation, contempt prior to i., 35–6

Iowa, people from I. mistake each other for stars, 95

iron, blood and i., 15

Iron Curtain, I. C. has descended, 28, 100–1

Jane, me Tarzan, you J., 147

Jefferson, possible exception when J. dined alone, 111

Jell-O, nail J. to wall, 153, 184–5

jests, indebted to memory for j., 140

Jesus Christ, if J.C. taken poll, 104, 224

Jews. *See* **communists**

job, recession when neighbor loses j., 177, 224

Joe, say ain't so, J., 188–9

journalism, j. first draft of history, 107

journey, j. of thousand miles, 107, 111

judge, begin loving their parents, after a time j., 249
don't j. until walked in shoes, 107–8

judging, foolproof device for j. picture, 198

Judy, J., J., J., 147

jury, j. indict ham sandwich, 87

just, tremble for country when reflect God j., 102–3

Kansas, not in K. anymore, 149

Keynesians, we are all K., 112

kill, k. 'em all, let God sort, 236
what fails to k. me makes me stronger, 112–3
when strike at king must k., 56

killed, beautiful theory, k. by ugly fact, 219
man k. parents, pleaded for mercy, 127–8, 156–7

killing. *See* **death,** single

kind word. *See* **smile**

kinder, k., gentler, 113

kindness, any k. can show, do now, 57, 76, 158–9
practice random k., 115, 176

king, when strike at k. must kill, 56

King George, guess K.G. able to read, 113–4

kitchen, if can't stand heat, get out of k., 88, 223

knees, better die on feet than live on k., 45

know, ain't things don't k., 3, 93, 94, 229–30

knowing, next best to k. something, 106

knowledge, a little k. dangerous, 114
imagination more important than k., 52

known, if k. live this long, 129–30
man k. by books reads, 16, 55

lady, opera ain't over 'til fat l. sings, 156

Lafayette, L. we are here, 114

laity, all professions conspiracies against l., 174, 192

lamb, lion lie down with l., 129

lame, science without religion l., 51–2

land, buy l. ain't makin' more, 183, 231
how buy sky, l., 19–20
stranger in strange l., 212

landing grounds, fight on l. g., 28

language, duty sublimest word in l., 49
England and America separated by l., 57, 194, 250–1
mobilized English l., 109

lash, rum, sodomy and l., 27

last, nice guys finish l., 154–5

laugh, only when l., 118

laughed, l. all way to bank, 8–9
lived well, l. often, 56–7, 116, 213–4

laughing, most fun without l., 71–2

laws, l. and sausage, shouldn't watch being made, 188

lawyer, l. who represents himself has fool for client, 128

lead, do not go where path may l., 56
l., follow, or get out of way, 118

leader, I follow for I am their l., 76, 161

learn, children l. what live, 24

learned, astonished how much old man l., 17, 232

NAME INDEX

SIDEBAR INDEX